SCO UNIX in a Nutshell

A Desktop Quick Reference for SCO UNIX and Open Desktop

A Desktop Quick Reference

SCO UNIX in a Nutshell

A Desktop Quick Reference for SCO UNIX and Open Desktop

*Ellie Cutler, Daniel Gilly, and
the staff of O Reilly & Associates, Inc.*

O'Reilly & Associates, Inc.

Cambridge · *Köln* · *Paris* · *Sebastopol* · *Tokyo*

SCO UNIX in a Nutshell

Editor: Peter Mui

Production Editor: Ellen Siever

Printing History:

> January 1994: First Edition.

ISBN: 1-56592-037-6

[7/98]

Table of Contents

Part II: User Commands

Part III: Shells

Part IV: Text Editing

Part V: Software Development

Part VI: System and Network Administration

Figures

Introduction

The UNIX operating system originated from AT&T in the early 1970's. The ability of UNIX to run on different hardware from different vendors encouraged developers to modify UNIX and distribute it as their own value-added version of UNIX. SCO UNIX, the version of UNIX developed by the Santa Cruz Operation, Inc., was one of the separate UNIX traditions to evolve as a result.

This quick reference (or "quick ref") describes the SCO UNIX System V Release 3.2, Version 4.0 Operating System and its graphical user interface, the Open Desktop, Release 3.0.

What's in the Quick Ref

This guide presents the major features of SCO UNIX, including:

- Open Desktop

- SCO UNIX user commands

- UNIX Shells

- Text editing

- SCO UNIX programming commands

- SCO UNIX system administration commands

Nowadays, UNIX systems are usually split, or bundled, into various component packages. Some components are included automatically in the system you buy; others are optional—you get them only if you pay extra. Therefore, keep in mind that if your system doesn't include all the SCO UNIX component packages (such as software development and networking) there will be commands in this quick ref that you won't be able to find on your system.

Scope of This Book

The quick ref is divided into six parts:

- Part I, *Open Desktop*. Section 1 describes the Open Desktop, the graphical user interface to SCO UNIX.

- Part II, *User Commands*. Sections 2 and 3 describe the syntax and options of the SCO UNIX user commands, along with tables of commonly-used commands.

- Part III, *Shells*. Sections 4 through 7 describe the syntax and options for the Bourne, Korn, and C shells, and a section on the SCO shell—SCO's menu interface to the command line.

- Part IV, *Text Editing*. Sections 8 through 12 present various editing tools and describe their command sets (alphabetically and by group). Part IV begins with a review of pattern matching, including examples geared toward specific editors.

- Part V, *Software Development*. Sections 13 and 14 describe the syntax and options of the SCO UNIX programming commands, along with tables of commonly-used commands. Coverage includes SCCS, **imake**, and all the program debuggers.

- Part VI, *System and Network Administration*. Sections 15 through 17 describe the syntax and options of the SCO UNIX system administration commands, along with tables of commonly-used commands. **sysadmsh**, SCO's system admistration shell, is also covered.

Audience

This quick reference should be of interest to SCO UNIX users, programmers, and system administrators. The presentation is geared mainly toward people who are familiar with the UNIX system—that is, you know what you want to do, and you even have some idea how to do it. You just need a reminder about the details. For example, if you want to remove the third field from a database, you might think, "*I know I can use the **cut** command, but what are the options?*" In many cases, specific examples are provided to show how a command is used.

This quick reference might also help people who are familiar with some aspects of UNIX but not with others. Many sections include an overview of the particular topic. While this isn't meant to be comprehensive, it's usually sufficient to get you started in unfamiliar territory.

Finally, if you're new to the UNIX operating system, and you're feeling bold, you might appreciate this book as a quick tour of what UNIX has to offer. The overviews in Sections 4, 13, 15, and 20 can point you to the most useful commands, and you'll find brief examples of how to use them, but take note: this book should not be used in place of a good beginner's tutorial on UNIX. This quick ref should be a *supplement*, not a substitute.

For More Information on SCO UNIX

You can communicate electronically to learn more about SCO UNIX and to get help on specific questions and problems.

Usenet Newsgroups

biz.sco.opendesktop   Technical questions and answers and informative postings relating to past, present, and future implementations of the SCO Open Desktop operating environment and its various bundled components.

biz.sco.general   Questions, answers and comments on SCO products in general, and of course resulting discussions.

biz.sco.announce   SCO and SCO Developer product announcements of interest to current and future users of SCO products, and to SCO developers, resellers, and distributors (moderated; followups directed to biz.sco.general).

biz.sco.binaries   SCO custom-installable binary packages of useful third-party "public domain" source code.

biz.sco.sources   Source code ported to work on SCO Xenix, UNIX, or Open Desktop.

biz.sco.wserver   Questions, answers, and discussion on SCO's widget server.

Mailing Lists

Send articles for:	To this address:
biz.sco.general	scogen@xenitec.on.ca
biz.sco.opendesktop	scoodt@xenitec.on.ca
biz.sco.announce	scoannmod@xenitec.on.ca
biz.sco.wserver	scowsr@xenitec.on.ca

CompuServe

On CompuServe, type GO SCOFORUM.

Supplements and Support

SLS (Support Level Supplements) and EFS (Enhanced Feature Support) are SCO's way of fixing bugs and improving performance between releases. Every couple of weeks, SCO posts lists of all SLS's and EFS's. If you're having a problem, look at these lists and see if any of them will help you.

If you have anonymous FTP access, log into **ftp.uu.net** and go to the **sco-archive** directory. There are subdirectories for SLS and EFS. Remember to turn on binary mode before getting any binary files. You can also obtain them via **telnet**. **telnet** to **ftp.uu.net** and log in as **ftp**; supply your username and fully-qualified domain name as the password.

Conventions

The quick ref follows certain typographic conventions, outlined below:

Bold
is used for directories, filenames, commands, programs, and options. All terms shown in bold are typed literally.

Italic
is used to show arguments, options, and variables that should be replaced with user-supplied values. Italic is also used to highlight comments in examples.

`Constant Width`
is used to show the contents of files or the output from commands.

`Constant Bold`
is used in examples and tables to show commands or other text that should be typed literally by the user.

`Constant Italic`
is used in examples and tables to show text; these should be replaced with user-supplied values.

`%`, `$`
are used in some examples as the C shell prompt (`%`) and as the Bourne shell or Korn shell prompt (`$`).

`[ ]`
surround optional elements in a description of syntax. (The brackets themselves should never be typed.) Note that many commands show the argument [*files*]. If a filename is omitted, standard input (i.e., the keyboard) is assumed. End with an end-of-file character.

EOF
indicates the end-of-file character (normally CTRL-D).

`|`
is used in syntax descriptions to separate items for which only one alternative may be chosen at a time.

$\rightarrow$
is used at the bottom of a right-hand page to show that the current entry continues on the next page. The continuation is marked by a $\leftarrow$.

A final word about syntax. In many cases, the space between an option and its argument can be omitted. In other cases, the spacing (or lack of spacing) must be followed strictly. For example, **-w***n* (no intervening space) might be interpreted differently from **-w** *n*. It's important to notice the spacing used in option syntax.

Acknowledgments

The book format and many of the User commands were derived from the original *UNIX in a Nutshell*, by Daniel Gilly.

The cover and interior layout were designed by Edie Freedman. Arthur Saarinen drew the referee figures. Chris Reilley assisted with graphics and screen dumps.

Special thanks to Jim Mohr and Tom Kelly of SCO, who did the lion's share of the technical review and provided invaluable assistance and suggestions. Bob Stockler, who uses SCO UNIX in his retail eyeglass and hearing aid business, lent a fresh perspective to the book—his enthusiasm for both SCO and this Nutshell provided a much-needed lift in the final stages of the project.

Peter Mui and Andy Oram of O'Reilly & Associates donated cheerful editorial guidance.

Lastly, production editor Ellen Siever allowed me the luxury of relaxing knowing this book was in very capable hands. Kismet McDonough, Clairemarie Fisher O'Leary, and Stephen Spainhour provided able assistance with copyediting and production.

We'd Like to Hear From You

We have tested and verified all of the information in this book to the best of our ability, but you may find that features have changed (or even that we have made mistakes!). Please let us know about any errors you find, as well as your suggestions for future editions, by writing:

```
O'Reilly & Associates, Inc.
101 Morris Street
Sebastopol, CA 95472
1-800-998-9938 (in the US or Canada)
1-707-829-0515 (international/local)
1-707-829-0104 (FAX)
```

You can also send us messages electronically. To be put on the mailing list or request a catalog, send email to:

info@oreilly.com

To ask technical questions or comment on the book, send email to:

bookquestions@oreilly.com

Part I

Open Desktop

Part 1 introduces the Open Desktop, SCO's graphical user interface.

The Open Desktop

The Open Desktop is SCO's graphical user interface, providing easy access to all the applications and utilities on your SCO UNIX system. In Open Desktop, files and programs are represented by icons and displayed in windows. Functionality is menu driven. Menu and text manipulation is done with either the mouse or special function keys. The Open Desktop provides you with access to both the SCO UNIX and DOS operating systems underlying the desktop.

Entering and Exiting the Desktop

Figure 1-1 shows the opening window to ODT, the *login box*.

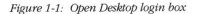

Figure 1-1: Open Desktop login box

The cursor should be in position for you to type in a login name. If it isn't, use the mouse to move the pointer into the login box and click mouse button 1 (usually the left button).

Logging In

Type your login name and press the Enter key. The cursor will move to the Password box. Type your password (it won't be shown) and press the Enter key again. (Note: if the login box is not visible and your screen is blank, try pressing any key to wake up the screen saver. If your screen is still blank, make sure your terminal is turned on. If your screen is not blank, the absence of the login box means that the Desktop has been set up to start differently at your site. See your system administrator for instructions.)

After you finish logging in, you will get the Open Desktop main screen, illustrated in Figure 1-2.

Logging Out

To leave the Open Desktop, click on the word File at the upper lefthand corner of the Desktop, then click on the word Exit in the File menu. A popup box will appear asking you to confirm your logout. Click on OK to proceed to log out.

Navigating the Desktop

When you leave the login box, you will get the Open Desktop main screen, as shown in Figure 1-2. In the main screen, the Accessories icon has been double-clicked, and the Accessories directory is open and is the active window. The icons are described in detail in the following pages.

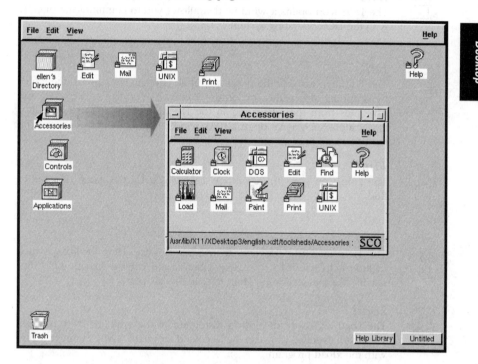

Figure 1-2: The SCO Open Desktop main screen

Accessories Icon

Double-clicking on the Accessories icon opens a window containing icons for basic tools. Some of these tools may already exist as icons in the main Desktop window. If so, they will show up in the Accessories icon as shaded.

The icons found in the Accessories window include:

Calculator

The calculator emulates a TI-30 or HP-10C scientific calculator. The calculator can also be accessed from the UNIX command line with the **xcalc** program.

The Open Desktop   5

Clock

The Clock icon displays an analog or digital clock showing the current time. The clock can also be accessed from the UNIX command line with the **xclock** program.

DOS

The DOS icon opens a window that allows you to communicate directly with the DOS operating system.

Edit

The Edit icon invokes the desktop editor. You can also invoke the editor by dropping a text file icon on the Edit icon. You can create, edit, and save files from the File menu in the Desktop editor. To use an editor application, such as vi, open a UNIX window and invoke the editor from the command line.

Find

The Find icon pops up a window asking you for the name of a file to find.

Help

The Help icon explains how to use the Desktop Help facilities, which include help windows, the Help Library, and context-specific help. For details, see the section on Help later in this chapter.

Load

The Load accessory displays a histogram of the system's load average. The load average can also be accessed from the UNIX command line with the **xload** program.

Mail

The Mail icon accesses the electronic mail program. The mail program can also be accessed from the UNIX command line with the **scomail** program.

Paint

The Paint accessory is used to create and edit graphical images. The Paint accessory can also be accessed from the UNIX command line with the **scopaint** program.

Print

Print a text file by dropping its icon on the Print icon.

UNIX

The UNIX icon opens a window that allows you to communicate directly with the UNIX operating system. The UNIX window can also be accessed from the UNIX command line with the **scoterm** program.

Controls Icon

Double-clicking on the Controls icon presents the Controls window, which houses icons for system controls and for customizing the Open Desktop. The icons are:

Administration

This icon starts **sysadmsh**, the system administration shell, from which you can perform system administration tasks. For more information on **sysadmsh**, see Section 16, *The sysadmsh Shell*.

Color

The Color icon is used to change the color scheme for the Open Desktop. To change colors, select a color scheme from the list of palettes. The color schemes, or palettes, are combination of colors for several items that make up the window, such as background, foreground, active window. To implement the new color scheme, click on OK.

Lock

The Lock icon allows you to freeze your terminal. If you double-click on this icon, the screen goes blank except for a login box in the center. To unlock the screen and resume your session, enter your password in the login box.

Mouse

The Mouse icon is used to configure the mouse. To swap mouse buttons 1 and 3, select "Right Handed" or "Left Handed" from the Mouse window. To set the speed to which the pointer accelerates, drag the acceleration slider. To set the distance (in pixels) the pointer moves before it accelerates, drag the Distance slider.

Preferences

From the Preferences icon, you can modify the appearance of your Desktop. The following menus are available from the Preferences window:

File	Exit from the Preferences window.
Controls	Change Desktop appearance, and icon and cursor types.
Font	Change fonts used in the Desktop.
Pixmap	Change Desktop background patterns.

Session

The Session icon controls the default configuration of the Desktop. Double-clicking on this icon gives you the following choices:

Resume previous session
> Always continue last session where you left off.

Start a new session (my desktop)
> Always start the session with the default Desktop configuration.

Ask each time
> Ask prior to each session which of the above you prefer.

Confirm that I want to log out
> Ask for confirmation before logging out.

Save current configuration
> Save current configuration as the default.

Applications Icon

As with the Accessories icon and the Controls icon, double-clicking on the Applications icon opens the Applications directory (window). Unfortunately, we can't tell you precisely what you'll find in the Applications directory; each system has different applications loaded. However, the same procedure applies to applications as to controls and accessories: double-click on the application's icon to start the program.

Help Icon

Clicking on the Help icon explains how to use the three Open Desktop help facilities: Help menus, the Help Library, and context-specific Help.

Help Menus

There is a Help menu in virtually every screen in the Desktop (see Figure 1-3 for an example). The Help menu contains the following selections:

Menu Item	Action
On Object	Allows you to point to anything with the cursor, click on it, and get help. This selection is not available from the Desktop menu.
On Window	General description of active window
On Keys	List of accelerator keys
Index	**scohelp** table of contents
On Help	How to get help
On Version	Gives version of accessory, control, or application.
Tutorial	Step-by-step instructions

Figure 1-3: Help menu

The Help Library

The Help Library icon is located at the bottom right of the Desktop screen. This library contains all the online books for Open Desktop. To select a book, click on the title. This will bring you to the book's table of contents. Books in the library include:

- Standards Conformance

- Features and Limitations

- Performance and Troubleshooting

- User and Administration Manual Pager

- Desktop Help

Context-specific Help

For information about an icon, drag-and-drop that icon onto the Help icon, as shown in Figure 1-4. For information about something in the window, point to it using the mouse and press the F1 key.

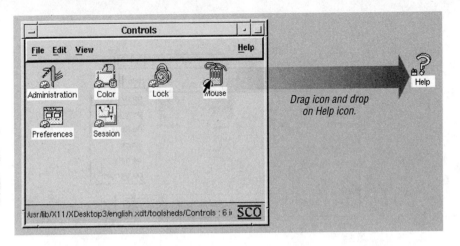

Figure 1-4: Dragging and dropping an icon onto the Help icon

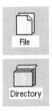

Files and Directories

Files and directories appear in the Desktop as icons on the main screen, as shown in Figure 1-5.

- To view or edit a file, double-click on its icon.

- To delete a file, drop its icon on the Trash icon.

- To view the contents of a directory, double-click on its icon.

Figure 1-5: Deleting a file

Part II

User Commands

Part II describes the commands of interest to users. The first section is an overview, with tables of commonly-used commands. The second section is an alphabetical listing of the SCO UNIX user commands.

Section 2 - *Overview*

Section 3 - *User Commands*

Overview of
User Commands

This section presents an overview of the SCO user commands. Programming and system administration commands are discussed in separate sections.

Common Commands

If you're just beginning to work on a UNIX system, the abundance of commands might prove daunting. To help orient you, the following tables present a sampling of commonly-used user commands. Depending on your configuration, some commands may be unavailable. For example, **ftp** and **telnet** require you to have the SCO networking package installed.

Communication

atdialer, dial	Dial a modem.
biff	Notify of mail arrival.
cu	Connect to UNIX system.
finger	Look up information on users.
ftp	File transfer program
hello	Send message to another user.
mail	Read or send mail.
mesg	Set permissions to write messages.
news	Print current news items.
ping	Indicate whether remote host can be reached.
rlogin	Login to remote UNIX system.
rwall	Write to all users over a network.
talk	Send an interactive message to another user.
telnet	Connect to another system.
uucp	Copy files between systems.
write	Write to other terminals.

Comparisons

cmp	Compare two files.
comm	Compare items in files.
diff	Compare two files.
diff3	Compare three files.
dircmp	Compare directories.
sdiff	Compare two files, side by side.

DOS Commands

doscat	Copy DOS files to standard output.
doscp	Copy files from DOS disk to XENIX filesystem.
dosdir	List DOS files in DOS directory format.
dosformat	Format a DOS disk.
dosls	List DOS files in XENIX ls format.
dosmkdir	Make a directory on DOS disk.
dosrm	Remove files from DOS disk.
dosrmdir	Remove empty directories from DOS disk.

File Management

cat	Join files or display them.
cd	Change directory.
chgrp	Change file group.

chmod	Change access modes on files.
chown	Change file owner.
cp	Copy files.
csplit	Split files at specific locations.
file	Determine a file's type.
head	Show the first few lines of a file.
install	Set up system files.
ln	Create filename aliases.
ls	List files or directories.
mkdir	Create a directory.
more	Display files by screenful.
mv	Move or rename files.
mvdir	Move or rename directories.
pwd	Print your working directory.
rcp	Copy files to/from remote system.
rdist	Copy files to multiple hosts.
rm	Remove files.
rmdir	Remove directories.
split	Split files evenly.
tail	Show the last few lines of a file.
tr	Translate characters.
translate	Translate files from one format to another.
wc	Count lines, words, and characters.

Miscellaneous

banner	Make posters from words.
bc	Precision calculator
cal	Display calendar.
calendar	Check for reminders.
clear	Clear the screen.
graph	Draw a graph.
kill	Terminate a running command.
man	Get information on a command.
nice	Reduce a job's priority.
nohup	Run a job that is not killed by logout.
passwd	Set password.
script	Produce a transcript of your login session.
su	Become a superuser or another user.

NFS and NIS Commands

mount, umount	Mount and unmount filesystems.
on	Execute command remotely.
rusers	Return list of users logged in to local machines.
rwall	Write to all users over a network.

| showmount | Show all remote mounts. |
| yppasswd | Change login password in NIS database. |

Printing

cancel	Cancel a printer request.
lp	Send to the printer.
lpstat	Get printer status.
pr	Format and paginate for printing.

Searching

egrep	Extended version of **grep**.
fgrep	Search files for literal words.
find	Search the system for filenames.
grep	Search files for text patterns.
strings	Search binary files for text patterns.

Storage/Backup

compress	Compress files to free up space.
cpio	Copy archives in or out.
pack	Pack files to free up space.
pcat	Display contents of packed files.
tape	Communicate with a tape drive.
tar	Tape archiver.
uncompress	Expand compressed (.Z) files.
unpack	Expand packed (.z) files.
zcat	Display contents of compressed files.

System Status

crontab	Automate commands.
date	Display or set date.
df	Show free disk space.
dfspace	Report disk space.
du	Show disk usage.
env	Show environment variables.
finger	Point out information about users.
hostname	Print name of current host system.
hwconfig	Show hardware configuration.
mnt	Mount a filesystem.
ps	Show processes.

pstat	Print system facts.
ruptime	Show loads on working systems.
rusers	List who is logged in on remote.
showmount	Show all remote mounts.
shutdown	Revert to single-user mode; shut system down to "power-off" point.
stty	Set or display terminal settings.
umnt	Unmount a filesystem.
uptime	Show system load and performance statistics.
w	Display summaries of system usage.
who	Show who is logged on.
whodo	Display process status.

TCP/IP Commands

biff	Notify of mail arrival.
finger	Look up information on users.
ftp	File transfer program
ping	Indicate whether remote host can be reached.
rcp	Copy files to/from remote system.
rlogin	Login to remote UNIX system.
talk	Send an interactive message to another user.
telnet	Connect to another system.

Text Processing

awk	Pattern-matching language for database files.
cut	Select columns for display.
ex	Line-editor underlying vi.
fmt	Produce roughly uniform line lengths.
fold	Produce exactly uniform line lengths.
join	Merge different columns into a database.
paste	Merge columns or switch order.
sed	Noninteractive text editor.
sort	Sort or merge files.
spell	Report misspelled words.
tr	Translate (redefine) characters.
uniq	Find repeated or unique lines in a file.
vi	Visual text editor.
xargs	Process many arguments in manageable portions.

UUCP Commands

uucp	Copy files between systems.
uudecode	Read uuencoded file and recreate the original file.
uuencode	Convert binary file to a form which can be sent via **mail**.
uuname	List sites that can be accessed using **uucp**.
uupick	Retrieve files sent with uuto.
uuto	Public UNIX-to-UNIX system file copy.

SCO UNIX User Commands

This section presents the user-level SCO UNIX commands (as opposed to the programming-level or system administration-level commands). Each entry is labeled with the command name on the outer edge of the page. The syntax line is followed by a brief description and a list of all available options. Many commands come with examples at the end of the entry. If you need only a quick reminder or suggestion about a command, you can skip directly to the examples.

Typographic conventions for describing command syntax are listed in the Preface. For additional help in locating commands, see the index at the back of this book.

If you can't find a command in this section, it may be listed as a programming-level or administration-level command. See the alphabetical listings in those sections.

at

at *options time* [*date*] [+ *increment*]

Execute commands entered on standard input at a specified *time* and optional *date*. (See also **batch**.) End input with *EOF*. *time* can be formed either as a numeric hour (with optional minutes and modifiers) or as a keyword. *date* can be formed either as a month and date, as a day of the week, or as a special keyword. *increment* is a positive integer followed by a keyword. See below for details.

Options

-l [*job_id*]
Report all jobs that are scheduled for the invoking user or, if *job_id* is specified, report only for those.

-q *letter*
Place job in queue denoted by *letter*, where *letter* is any lowercase letter from a-z. The following letters have special significance:

a   **at** queue
b   **batch** queue
c   **cron** queue

-r [*job_id*]
Remove specified jobs that were previously scheduled. *job_id* is a job identifier returned by **at** or **batch**. To remove a job, you must be a privileged user or the owner of the job. Use **-l** first to see the list of scheduled jobs. See also **atrm**.

Time

hh:mm [*modifiers*]
Hours can have one digit or two (a 24-hour clock is assumed by default); optional minutes can be given as one or two digits; the colon can be omitted if the format is *h*, *hh*, or *hhmm*; e.g., valid times are 5, 5:30, 0530, 19:45. If modifier **am** or **pm** is added, *time* is based on a 12-hour clock. If the keyword **zulu** is added, times correspond to Greenwich Mean Time.

midnight | **noon** | **now**
Use any one of these keywords in place of a numeric time. **now** must be followed by an *increment*.

Date

month num[, *year*]
month is one of the 12 months, spelled out or abbreviated to their first three letters; *num* is the calendar date of the month; *year* is the four-digit year. If the given *month* occurs before the current month, **at** schedules that month next year.

> *day*   One of the seven days of the week, spelled out or abbreviated to its first three letters.

today | tomorrow

> Indicate the current day or the next day. If *date* is omitted, **at** schedules **today** when the specified *time* occurs later than the current time; otherwise, **at** schedules **tomorrow**.

Increment

> Supply a numeric increment if you want to specify an execution time or day *relative* to the current time. The number should precede any of the keywords **minute**, **hour**, **day**, **week**, **month**, or **year** (or their plural forms). The keyword **next** can be used as a synonym of **+ 1**.

Examples

> Note that the first two commands are equivalent:

```
at 1945 pm December 9
at 7:45pm Dec 9
at 3 am Saturday
at now + 5 hours
at noon next day
```

/usr/lib/uucp/atdialer

A generic dial program that reads the commands in the appropriate file in /etc/default. **atdialer** is a binary file and may be linked to any other name (such as *atdialMT* or *atdialUSR*, to dial a Multi-Tech or US Robotics modem, for instance), and that name used in the /usr/lib/uucp/**Devices** file to name the **atdial** program to be used for dialing any particular device.

When called by any of its linked names, **atdialer** looks in etc/default for a similarly named file, which will include setup strings and other information specific to the modem for the call being initiated. Since this file can be edited with any text editor, it expands the range of use of **atdialer** to many other modems. It also will handle all serial port-to-modem speeds from 300 through 38400 bps (baud).

To assist in using **atdialer**, the shell script **make.dialer** (found in /user/lib/uucp) will prompt the user for the entries needed in the text file to be placed in /etc/default for a particular modem, and otherwise set up a new **atdialer** program.

---

awk [*options*] [*program*] [*var=value* ...] [*files*]

Use the pattern-matching *program* to modify the specified *files*. *program* instructions have the general form:

```
pattern { procedure }
```

→

awk
←
	pattern and *procedure* are each optional. When specified on the command line, *program* must be enclosed in single quotes to prevent the shell from interpreting its special symbols. Any variables specified in *program* can be assigned an initial value by using command-line arguments of the form *var=value*. See Section 12 for more information (including examples) on **awk**.
	
	Options
	   -f *file* Use program instructions contained in *file*, instead of specifying *program* on the command line.
	   -F*c* Treat input *file* as fields separated by character *c*. Default input field separator is space or tab.

banner	**banner** *characters* Print *characters* as a poster on the standard output. Each word supplied must contain ten characters or less.
| **basename** | **basename** *pathname* [*suffix*]<br><br>Given a *pathname*, strip the path prefix and leave just the filename, which is printed on standard output. If specified, a filename *suffix* (e.g., .c) is removed also. **basename** is typically invoked via command substitution ( ` ` ) to generate a filename. See also **dirname**.<br><br>*Example*<br>Given the following fragment from a Bourne shell script:<br><br>```
prog_name="`basename $0`"
echo "$prog_name: QUITTING: can't open $ofile"\
     1>&2 ; exit 1
```<br><br>If the script is called **do_it**, then the following message will be printed on standard error:<br><br>```
do_it: QUITTING: can't open output_file
``` |
| **bc** | **bc** [*options*] [*files*]

Interactively perform arbitrary-precision arithmetic or convert numbers from one base to another. Input can be taken from *files* or read from the standard input. To exit, type **quit** or **EOF**.

Options
   -c   Do not invoke **dc**; compile only. (Since **bc** is a preprocessor for **dc**, **bc** normally invokes **dc**.)
   -l   Make available functions from the math library. |

bc is a language (and compiler) whose syntax resembles that of C, but with unlimited-precision arithmetic. **bc** consists of identifiers, keywords, and symbols, which are briefly described below. Examples follow at end.

Identifiers

An identifier is a single character, consisting of the lowercase letters a-z. Identifiers are used as names for variables, arrays, and functions. Within the same program you may name a variable, an array, and a function using the same letter. The following identifiers would not conflict:

x   Variable **x**.

x[*i*]   Element *i* of array **x**. *i* can range from 0 to 2047 and can also be an expression.

x(y,z)   Call function **x** with parameters **y** and **z**.

Input-output keywords

ibase, **obase**, and **scale** store a value. Typing them on a line by themselves displays their current value. More commonly, you would change their values through assignment. The letters A-F are treated as digits whose values are 10-15.

ibase = *n*   Numbers that are input (e.g., typed) are read as base *n* (default is 10).

obase = *n*   Numbers that are displayed are in base *n* (default is 10). Note: Once **ibase** has been changed from 10, use the digit A to restore **ibase** or **obase** to decimal.

scale = *n*   Display computations using *n* decimal places (default is 0, meaning that results are truncated to integers). **scale** is normally used only for base-10 computations.

Statement keywords

A semicolon or a newline separates one statement from another. Curly braces are needed only when grouping multiple statements.

if (*rel-expr*) {*statements*}

        Do one or more *statements* if relational expression *rel-expr* is true; for example:

        `if(x==y) i = i + 1.`

while (*rel-expr*) {*statements*}

        Repeat one or more *statements* while *rel-expr* is true; for example:

        `while(i>0) {p = p*n; q = a/b; i = i-1}`

$\rightarrow$

for (*expr1*; *rel–expr*; *expr2*) {*statements*}

      Similar to **while**; for example, to print the first 10 multiples of 5, you could type:

```
for(i=1; i<=10; i++) i*5
```

break   Terminate a **while** or **for** statement.

Function keywords

define *j*(*k*) {   Begin the definition of function *j* having a single argument *k*. Additional arguments are allowed, separated by commas. Statements follow on successive lines. End with a }.

auto *x*, *y*   Set up *x* and *y* as variables local to a function definition, initialized to 0 and meaningless outside the function. Must appear first.

return(*expr*)   Pass the value of expression *expr* back to the program. Return 0 if (*expr*) is left off. Used in function definitions.

sqrt(*expr*)   Compute the square root of expression *expr*.

length(*expr*) Compute how many digits are in *expr*.

scale(*expr*)   Same, but count only digits to the right of the decimal point.

Math library functions

These are available when **bc** is invoked with **-l**. Library functions set **scale** to 20.

s(*angle*)   Compute the sine of *angle*, a constant or expression in radians.

c(*angle*)   Compute the cosine of *angle*, a constant or expression in radians.

a(*n*)   Compute the arctangent of *n*, returning an angle in radians.

e(*expr*)   Compute **e** to the power of *expr*.

l(*expr*)   Compute the natural log of *expr*.

j(*n*, *x*)   Compute the Bessel function of integer order *n*.

Operators

These consist of operators and other symbols. Operators can be arithmetic, unary, assignment, or relational.

arithmetic	+ − * / % ^
unary	− ++ −−
assignment	=+ =− =* =/ =% =^ =
relational	< <= > >= == !=

Other symbols

/* */	Enclose comments.
( )	Control the evaluation of expressions (change precedence). Can also be used around assignment statements to force the result to print.
{ }	Use to group statements.
[ ]	Indicate array index.
"*text*"	Use as a statement to print *text*.

Examples

Note below that when you type some quantity (a number or expression), it is evaluated and printed, but assignment statements produce no display.

```
ibase = 8       Octal input.
20              Evaluate this octal number.
16              Terminal displays decimal value.
obase = 2       Display output in base 2 instead of base 10.
20              Octal input.
10000           Terminal now displays binary value.
ibase = A       Restore base 10 input.
scale = 3       Truncate results to 3 places.
8/7             Evaluate a division.
1.001001000     Oops! Forgot to reset output base to 10.
obase=10        Input is decimal now, so A isn't needed.
8/7
1.142           Terminal displays result (truncated).
```

The following lines show the use of functions:

```
define p(r,n){  Function p uses two arguments.
   auto v       v is a local variable.
   v = r^n      r raised to the n power.
   return(v)}   Value returned.

scale=5
x=p(2.5,2)      x = 2.5 ^ 2
x               Print value of x.
6.25
length(x)       Number of digits.
3
scale(x)        Number of places right of decimal point.
2
```

bdiff *file1 file2* [*options*]

Compare *file1* with *file2* and report the differing lines. **bdiff** splits the files and then runs **diff**, allowing it to act on files that would normally be too large to handle. **bdiff** reads standard input if one of the files is - . See also **diff**.

$\rightarrow$

bdiff
←
	Options
	
	   n Split each file into *n*-line segments (default is 3500).
	          This option must be listed first.
	
	  -s Suppress error messages from **bdiff** (but not from **diff**).

bfs	**bfs** [*option*] *file* Scan big files. Read a large *file*, using ed-like syntax. This command is more efficient than ed for scanning very large files because the file is not read into a buffer. Files can be up to 1024K bytes. **bfs** can be used to view a large file and identify sections to be divided with **csplit**. Not too useful; holdover from small machines. *Option* - Do not print the file size.
biff	**biff** [*arguments*] TCP/IP command. Notify user of mail arrival and who mail is from. **biff** operates asynchronously. Mail notification works only if your system is running **sendmail** and **lmail**. The command **biff y** enables notification, and the command **biff n** disables notification.
| **cal** | **cal** [[*month*] *year*]<br><br>Print a 12-month calendar (beginning with January) for the given *year* or a one-month calendar of the given *month* and *year*. *month* ranges from 1 to 12. *year* ranges from 1 to 9999. With no arguments, print a calendar for the previous month, current month, and next month.<br><br>*Examples*<br><br>```
cal 12 1994
cal 1994 > year_file
```|
| **calendar** | **calendar** [*option*]<br><br>Read your **calendar** file and display all lines that contain today's or tomorrow's date. The **calendar** file is like a memo board. You create the file and add entries like the following:<br><br>```
5/4     meeting with design group at 2 pm
may 6   pick up anniversary card on way home
```<br><br>When you run **calendar** on May 4, the first line is displayed. **calendar** can be automated by using **crontab** or **at** or by including it in your startup **.profile** or **.cshrc** file. |

Option

      –   Allow a privileged user to invoke **calendar** for all users, searching each user's login directory for a file named **calendar**. Entries that match are sent to a user via mail.

---

cancel [*options*] [*printer*]

Cancel print requests made with **lp**. The request can be specified by its ID, by the *printer* on which it is currently printing, or by the username associated with the request (only privileged users can cancel another user's print requests). Use **lpstat** to determine either the *id* or the *printer* to cancel.

Options

    id   Cancel print request *id.*
    -u *user*   Cancel request associated with *user.*

---

cat [*options*] [*files*]

Read one or more *files* and print them on standard output. Read standard input if no *files* are specified or if – is specified as one of the files; end input with *EOF*. You can use the > operator to combine several files into a new file; use >> to append files to an existing file.

Options

    -e   Print a $ to mark the end of each line. Must be used with -**v**.

    -s   Suppress messages about nonexistent files. (Note: In the BSD version, -**s** squeezes out extra blank lines.)

    -t   Print each tab as ^I and each form feed as ^L. Must be used with -**v**.

    -u   Print output as unbuffered (default is buffered in blocks or screen lines).

    -v   Display control characters and other nonprinting characters.

Examples

```
cat ch1                  Display a file.
cat ch1 ch2 ch3 > all    Combine files.
cat note5 >> notes       Append to a file.
cat > temp1              Create file at terminal; end with EOF.
cat > temp2 << STOP      Create file at terminal; end with STOP.
```

---

cd [*dir*]

Change directory. **cd** is actually a built-in shell command.

| checkmail | **checkmail** [*options*]

Check for mail which has been submitted but not delivered. If invoked with no arguments, the Subject: of each message is given along with a list of addressees who have not yet received the message.

Options

-a	Show all addresses, both delivered and undelivered.
-f	Suppress printing of subject line.
-m	Check all messages in mail queue, not just invoker's.

| chgrp | **chgrp** *newgroup files*

Change the group of one or more *files* to *newgroup*. *newgroup* is either a group ID number or a group name located in **/etc/group**. Only the owner of a file or a privileged user may change its group.

| chmod | **chmod** *mode files*

Change the access *mode* of one or more *files*. Only the owner of a file or a privileged user may change its mode. Create *mode* by concatenating the characters from *who*, *opcode*, and *permission*. *who* is optional (if omitted, default is **a**); choose only one *opcode*.

Who

u	User
g	Group
o	Other
a	All (default)

Opcode

+	Add permission
-	Remove permission
=	Assign permission (and remove permission of the unspecified fields)

Permission

r	Read
w	Write
x	Execute
s	Set user (or group) ID
t	Sticky bit; save text (file) mode or prevent removal of files by nonowners (directory)
u	User's present permission
g	Group's present permission

o	Other's present permission
l	Mandatory locking

Alternatively, specify permissions by a three-digit octal number. The first digit designates owner permission; the second, group permission; and the third, others permission. Permissions are calculated by adding the following octal values:

4	Read
2	Write
1	Execute

Note: A fourth digit may precede this sequence. This digit assigns the following modes:

4	Set user ID on execution
2	Set group ID on execution or set mandatory locking
1	Set sticky bit

Examples

Add execute-by-user permission to *file*:

```
chmod u+x file
```

Either of the following will assign read-write-execute permission by owner (7), read-execute permission by group (5), and execute-only permission by others (1) to *file*:

```
chmod 751 file
chmod u=rwx,g=rx,o=x file
```

Any one of the following will assign read-only permission to *file* for everyone:

```
chmod =r file
chmod 444 file
chmod a-wx,a+r file
```

Set the user ID, assign read-write-execute permission by owner, and assign read-execute permission by group and others:

```
chmod 4755 file
```

---

chown *newowner files*

Change the ownership of one or more *files* to *newowner*. *newowner* is either a user ID number or a login name located in /etc/passwd. Only the current owner of a file, or a privileged user, may change its owner.

---

clear

Clear the terminal display.

cmchk	**cmchk**
	Report hard disk block size.
cmp	**cmp** [*options*] *file1 file2*
	Compare *file1* with *file2*. Use standard input if *file1* is -. See also **comm** and **diff**. The exit codes are as follows:
	0 Files are identical.
	1 Files are different.
	2 Files are inaccessible.
	Options
	-l For each difference, print the byte number in decimal and the differing bytes in octal.
	-s Work silently; print nothing, but return exit codes.
	Example
	Print a message if two files are the same (exit code is 0):
	`cmp -s old new && echo 'no changes'`
col	**col** [*options*]
	A postprocessing filter that handles reverse linefeeds and escape characters, allowing output from tbl (or nroff) to appear in reasonable form on a terminal.
	Options
	-b Ignore backspace characters; helpful when printing man pages.
	-f Process half-line vertical motions, but not reverse line motion. (Normally, half-line input motion is displayed on the next full line.)
	-p Print unknown escape sequences (normally ignored) as regular characters. This option can garble output, so its use is not recommended.
	-x Normally, **col** saves printing time by converting sequences of spaces to tabs. Use -**x** to suppress this conversion.
	Examples
	Run *file* through tbl and nroff, then capture the output on the screen by filtering through **col** and **more**:
	`tbl file	nroff	col	more`
	Save man page output in *file*.**print**, stripping out backspaces (which would otherwise appear as ^H):
	`man file	col -b > file.print`

comm [*options*] *file1 file2*

Compare lines common to the sorted files *file1* and *file2*. Three-column output is produced: lines unique to *file1*, lines unique to *file2*, and lines common to both *files*. comm is similar to **diff** in that both commands compare two files. But comm can also be used like **uniq**; that is, comm selects duplicate or unique lines between *two* sorted files, whereas **uniq** selects duplicate or unique lines within the *same* sorted file.

Options

-        Read the standard input.
-1   Suppress printing of column 1.
-2   Suppress printing of column 2.
-3   Suppress printing of column 3.
-12   Print only lines in column 3 (lines common to *file1* and *file2*).
-13   Print only lines in column 2 (lines unique to *file2*).
-23   Print only lines in column 1 (lines unique to *file1*).

Example

Compare two lists of top-ten movies, and display items that appear in both lists:

```
comm -12 siskel_top10 ebert_top10
```

---

compress [*options*] [*files*]

Reduce the size of one or more *files* using adaptive Lempel-Ziv coding, and move to *file*.**Z**. Restore with **uncompress** or **zcat**.

Options

-b*n*   Limit the number of bits in coding to *n*; *n* is 9-16, and 16 is the default. A lower *n* produces a larger, less densely compressed file.

-c   Write to the standard output (do not change files).

-d   Decompress a compressed file.

-F   Write output file even if compression saves no space.

-f   Compress unconditionally; i.e., do not prompt before overwriting files. Also, compress even if compression does not decrease the size (i.e., if there is no saving of space).

-H   Compress a file by approximately 20 percent more using the LZH algorithm.

-P *fd* Read list of filenames from pipe associated with the file descriptor *fd*.

-q   Generate no output except error messages, if any.

-v   Print the resulting percentage of reduction for *files*.

copy	**copy** [*options*] ... *source* ... *dest*

Copy contents of one directory to another directory. *source* may be an existing file, directory, or special file. *dest* must be a file or directory name different from *source*. If the files and directories do not exist at the destination, they are created with the same modes and flags as the source. If the destination files do exist, the owner and mode are not changed.

Options

-a	Ask user before attempting a copy. When used with -v, override verbose option so messages regarding copy action are not displayed.
-ad	Ask user whether -r flag applies when a directory is discovered. If answer does not begin with **y**, directory is ignored.
-l	Use links whenever possible; otherwise a copy is made.
-m	Set modification time and access time to that of source. If not set, modification time is set to time of copy.
-n	For files only. Destination file must be new, otherwise destination file is not changed.
-o	Set owner and group to those of source. If not set, owner is user who invoked program.
-r	Recursively examine directories as encountered. If not set, any directories found are ignored.
-v	Print messages revealing what the program is doing. If used with -a, message is not displayed.

Example

Verbosely copy all files in current directory to **/tmp/food**:

```
copy -v . /tmp/food
```

cp	**cp** [*options*] *file1 file2* **cp** [*options*] *files directory*

Copy *file1* to *file2*, or copy one or more *files* to the same names under *directory*. If the destination is an existing file, the file is overwritten; if the destination is an existing directory, the file is copied into the directory (the directory is *not* overwritten). If one of the inputs is a directory, use the -r option.

Example

Copy two files to their parent directory (keep the same names):

```
cp outline memo ..
```

cpio	**cpio** *flags* [*options*]

Copy file archives in from or out to tape or disk, or to another location on the local machine. Each of the three flags -i, -o, or -p accepts different options.

cpio -i [*options*] [*patterns*]

Copy in (extract) files whose names match selected *patterns.* Each pattern can include filename metacharacters from the Bourne shell. (Patterns should be quoted or escaped so they are interpreted by **cpio**, not by the shell.) If no pattern is used, all files are copied in. During extraction, existing files are not overwritten by older versions in the archive (unless **-u** is specified).

cpio -o [*options*]

Copy out a list of files whose names are given on the standard input.

cpio -p [*options*] *directory*

Copy files to another directory on the same system. Destination pathnames are interpreted relative to the named *directory.*

Comparison of valid options

Options available to the **-i**, **-o**, and **-p** flags are shown respectively in the first, second, and third row below. (The **-** is omitted for clarity.)

```
i: 6 A b B c C d   f H I k K m M   r R s S t u v V
o: a A   B c C       H       L M O           v V
p: a         d             1Lm       R       u v V
```

Options

-a Reset access times of input files.

-A Suppress absolute pathnames.

-b Swap bytes and half-words. Words are 4 bytes.

-B Block input or output using 5120 bytes per record (default is 512 bytes per record).

-c Read or write header information as ASCII characters; useful when source and destination machines are of differing types.

-C *n* Like **B**, but block size can be any positive integer *n*.

-d Create directories as needed.

-E *file* Extract filenames listed in *file* from the archives.

-f Reverse the sense of copying; copy all files *except* those that match *patterns.*

-I *file* Read *file* as an input archive.

-k Skip corrupted file headers and I/O errors.

-K*volumesize*

Specify *volumesize* as size of media volume.

-l Link files instead of copying.

-L Follow symbolic links.

-m Retain previous file modification time.

cpio ←	**-M** *msg* Print *msg* when switching media. Use variable *%d* in the message as a numeric ID for the next medium. **-M** is valid only with **-I** or **-O**.
	-O *file* Direct the output to *file*.
	-r Rename files interactively.
	-R *ID* Reassign file ownership and group information to the user's login *ID* (privileged users only).
	-s Swap bytes.
	-S Swap half-words.
	-t Print a table of contents of the input (create no files). When used with the **-v** option, resembles output of **ls -l**.
	-u Unconditional copy; old files can overwrite new ones.
	-v Print a list of filenames.
	-V Print a dot for each file read or written (this shows **cpio** at work without cluttering the screen).
	-6 Process a UNIX 6th Edition archive format file.

Examples

Generate a list of old files using **find**; use list as input to **cpio**:

```
find . -name "*.old" -print | cpio -ocBv\
    > /dev/rst8
```

Restore from a tape drive all files whose name contains **save** (subdirectories are created if needed):

```
cpio -icdv "save" < /dev/rst8
```

To move a directory tree:

```
find . -depth -print | cpio -padm /mydir
```

crontab	**crontab** [*file*] **crontab** *flags* [*user*]

Run **crontab** on your current crontab file, or specify a crontab *file* to add to the crontab directory. A privileged user can run **crontab** for another user by supplying a *user* after any of the flags. A crontab file is a list of commands, one per line, that will execute automatically at a given time. Numbers are supplied before each command to specify the execution time. The numbers appear in five fields, as follows:

Minute	0-59
Hour	0-23
Day of month	1-31
Month	1-12
Day of week	0-6, with 0 = Sunday

Use a comma between multiple values, a hyphen to indicate a range, and an asterisk to indicate all possible values. For example, assuming the crontab entries below:

```
59 3 * * 5      find / -print | backup_program
 0 0 1,15 * *   echo "Timesheets due" | mail user
```

The first command backs up the system files every Friday at 3:59 a.m., and the second command mails a reminder on the first and 15th of each month.

Flags

-l   List the user's file in the crontab directory.

-r   Delete the user's file in the crontab directory.

---

crypt [*password*] < *file* > *encryptedfile*

Encrypt a *file* to prevent unauthorized access. *password* is either a string of characters you choose or the flag -**k**, which assigns the value of environment variable CRYPTKEY as the password. The same *password* is used to encrypt a file or to decrypt an encrypted file. If no password is given, **crypt** prompts for one. **crypt** is available only in the United States (due to export restrictions).

---

csh [*options*] [*arguments*]

Command interpreter that uses syntax resembling C. **csh** (the C shell) executes commands from a terminal or a file. See Section 5 for information on the C shell, including command-line options.

---

csplit [*options*] *file arguments*

Separate *file* into sections and place sections in files named **xx00** through **xx**n (n < 100), breaking *file* at each pattern specified in *arguments*. See also **split**.

Options

-f *file*   Name new files *file*00 through *file*n (default is **xx00** through **xx**n).

-k   Keep newly created files, even when an error occurs (which would normally remove these files). This is useful when you need to specify an arbitrarily large repeat argument, {n}, and you don't want an out of range error to cause removal of the new files.

-s   Suppress all character counts.

Arguments

Any one or a combination of the following expressions. Arguments containing blanks or other special characters should be surrounded by single quotes.

→

csplit ←	*/expr/*	Create file from the current line up to the line containing the regular expression *expr*. This argument takes an optional suffix of the form +*n* or -*n*, where *n* is the number of lines below or above *expr*.
	%*expr*%	Same as */expr/* except no file is created for lines previous to line containing *expr*.
	num	Create file from current line up to line number *num*.
	{*n*}	Repeat argument *n* times. May follow any of the above arguments. Files will split at instances of *expr* or in blocks of *num* lines.

Examples

Create up to 20 chapter files from the file **novel**:

```
csplit -k -f chap. novel '%CHAPTER%' '{20}'
```

Create up to 100 address files (**xx00** through **xx99**), each four lines long, from a database named **address_list**:

```
csplit -k address_list 4 {99}
```

---

ct

ct [*options*] *telno*

Spawn a **getty** to a remote terminal by dialing the telephone number of a modem attached to that terminal. The set of legal characters for *telno* is 0-9, – (delays), = (secondary dial tones), *, and #. **ct** will try each ACU line in **/usr/lib/uucp/Devices** until it finds an available line with appropriate attributes or runs out of entries. For successful connections, **ct** writes a log file, **/usr/adm/ctlog**, containing: login name of invoking user, speed of connection, date and time of connection, length of connection, and telephone number dialed.

Options

-h   Prevent hangup—wait for termination of specified **ct** process before returning control to user's terminal.

-s*speed*
    Set data rate. *speed* is expressed in baud; default rate is 1200.

-v   Send running narrative to standard error output stream.

-w*n*   Set maximum number of minutes **ct** is to wait for a free line before giving up.

-x*n*   For debugging—produce detailed output of program execution on stderr. *n* is a single digit.

---

cu

cu [*options*] [*destination*]

Call up another UNIX/XENIX system or a terminal via a direct line or a modem. A non-UNIX system can also be called.

Options

-e	Send even-parity data to remote system.
-h	Emulate local **echo** and support calls to other systems expecting terminals to use half-duplex mode.
-l*line*	Communicate on *line* device (e.g., **/dev/tty001**). *dir* can be used to talk directly to a modem on that line instead of talking to another system via that modem.
-n	Prompt user for a telephone number.
-o	Use odd parity (opposite of -e).
-oe	7-bits, ignores parity.
-s*n*	Set transmission rate to *n* (e.g., 1200, 2400, 9600 bps). Default is **Any**.
-t	Dial an ASCII terminal that has auto answer set.
-x*n*	Print diagnostics. The debugging level *n* is a single digit from 0-9 (9 is most useful).

Destination

telno	Connect to the modem at telephone number *telno*.
system	Call the *system* known to **uucp** (run **uuname** to list valid system names).

cu runs as two processes: transmit and receive. Transmit reads from standard input and passes lines to the remote system; receive reads data from the remote system and passes lines to standard output. Lines that begin with a tilde (~) are treated as commands and are not passed.

Transmit options

~.	Terminate the conversation.
~!	Escape to an interactive shell on the local system.
~!*cmd*...	
	Run command on local system (via **sh -c**).
~$*cmd*...	
	Run command locally; send output to remote system.
~+*cmd*...	
	Run *cmd* on local system but take standard input from remote system.
~%cd	Change directory on the local system.
~%take *file* [*target*]	
	Copy *file* from remote system to *target* on the local system. If *target* is omitted, *file* is used in both places.
~%put *file* [*target*]	
	Copy *file* from the local system to *target* on the remote system. If *target* is omitted, *file* is used in both places.
~ ~ ...	
	Use two tildes when you want to pass a line that begins with a tilde. This lets you issue commands to more than one system in a **cu** chain. For example, use ~~.

to terminate the conversation on a second system **cu**'d
to from the first.

~%b   Send a BREAK sequence to remote system.

~%d   Turn debug mode on or off.

~t   Print termio structure for local terminal.

~l   Print termio structure for communication line.

~%nostop
          Toggle between XON/XOFF input control protocol and
          no input control.

Examples

Connect to terminal line **/dev/ttya** at 1200 baud:

```
cu -s1200 -l/dev/ttya
```

Connect to modem with phone number 555-9876:

```
cu 5559876
```

Connect to system named **usenix**:

```
cu usenix
```

---

cut *options* [*files*]

Cut out selected columns or fields from one or more *files*. Option
-c or -f must be specified. *list* is a sequence of integers. Use a
comma between separate values and a hyphen to specify a range
(e.g., 1-10,15,20 or 50-). See also **paste**, **join**, and **newform**.

Options

-c *list* Cut the column positions identified in *list*.

-d *c*   Use with -f to specify field delimiter as character *c*
           (default is tab); special characters (e.g., a space) must
           be quoted.

-f *list* Cut the fields identified in *list*.

-s   Use with -f to suppress lines without delimiters.

Examples

Extract usernames and real names from **/etc/passwd**:

```
cut -d: -f1,5 /etc/passwd
```

Find out who is logged on, but list only login names:

```
who | cut -d" " -f1
```

Cut characters in the fourth column of *file*, and paste them back
as the first column in the same file:

```
cut -c4 file | paste - file
```

date [+*format*]

Print the current date and time, specifying an optional display *format*. *format* can consist of literal text strings (blanks must be quoted) as well as field descriptors, whose values will appear as described below (the listing shows some logical groupings).

Format

%n	Insert a newline.
%t	Insert a tab.
%m	Month of year (01-12).
%d	Day of month (01-31).
%y	Last two digits of year (00-99).
%D	Date in %m/%d/%y format.
%b	Abbreviated month name.
%Y	Four-digit year (e.g., 1996).
%h	Same as %b.
%B	Full month name.
%H	Hour in 24-hour format (00-23).
%M	Minutes (00-59).
%S	Seconds (00-59).
%T	Time in %H:%M:%S format.
%I	Hour in 12-hour format (01-12).
%p	String to indicate a.m. or p.m. (default is AM or PM).
%r	Time in %I:%M:%S %p format.
%a	Abbreviated weekday.
%A	Full weekday.
%w	Day of week (Sunday = 0).
%U	Week number in year (00-53); start week on Sunday.
%W	Week number in year (00-53); start week on Monday.
%j	Julian day of year (001-366).
%Z	Time zone name.
%x	Country-specific date format.
%X	Country-specific time format.
%c	Country-specific date and time format (default is %a %b %e %T %Z %Y; e.g., Mon Feb 1 14:30:59 EST 1993).

Strings for setting date

A privileged user can set the date by supplying a numeric *string*. *string* consists of time, day, and year concatenated in one of three ways: *time* or [*day*]*time* or [*day*]*time*[*year*]. Note: You don't type the brackets.

time   A two-digit hour and two-digit minute (*HHMM*); *HH* uses 24-hour format.

date

←

day   A two-digit month and two-digit day of month (*mmdd*); default is current day and month.

year   The year specified as either the full four digits or just the last two digits; default is current year.

Examples

Set the date to July 1 (0701), 4 a.m. (0400), 1995 (95):

```
date 0701040095
```

The command:

```
date +"Hello%t Date is %D %n%t Time is %T"
```

produces a formatted date as follows:

```
Hello        Date is 05/09/93
             Time is 17:53:39
```

---

dc

dc [*file*]

An interactive desk calculator program that performs arbitrary-precision integer arithmetic (input may be taken from a *file*). Normally you don't run **dc** directly, since it's invoked by **bc** (see **bc**). **dc** provides a variety of one-character commands and operators that perform arithmetic; **dc** works like a Reverse Polish calculator; therefore, operators and commands follow the numbers they affect. Operators include + − / * % ^ (as in C); some simple commands include:

p   Print current result.

q   Quit **dc**.

c   Clear all values on the stack.

v   Take square root.

i   Change input base; similar to **bc**'s **ibase**.

o   Change output base; similar to **bc**'s **obase**.

k   Set scale factor (number of digits after decimal); similar to **bc**'s **scale**.

!   Remainder of line is a UNIX command.

Examples

```
3 2 ^ p    Evaluate 3 squared, then print result.
9
8 * p      Current value (9) times 8, then print result.
72
47 - p     Subtract 47 from 72, then print result.
25
v p        Square root of 25, then print result.
5
2 o p      Display current result in base 2.
101
```

Note: Spaces are not needed except between numbers.

dd [*option=value*]

Make a copy of an input file (**if=**) using the specified options and send the results to the output file (or standard output if **of** is not specified). Any number of options can be supplied, although **if** and **of** are the most common and are usually specified first. Because **dd** can handle arbitrary block sizes, it is useful when converting between raw physical devices.

Options

bs=*n*	Set input and output block size to *n* bytes; this option supersedes **ibs** and **obs**.
cbs=*n*	Set the size of the conversion buffer (logical record length) to *n* bytes. Use only if the conversion *flag* is **ascii**, **ebcdic**, **ibm**, **block**, or **unblock**.
conv=*flags*	

Convert the input according to one or more (comma-separated) *flags* listed below. The first five *flags* are mutually exclusive.

ascii	EBCDIC to ASCII.
ebcdic	ASCII to EBCDIC.
ibm	ASCII to EBCDIC with IBM conventions.
block	Variable-length records (i.e., those terminated by a newline) to fixed-length records.
unblock	Fixed-length records to variable-length.
lcase	Uppercase to lowercase.
ucase	Lowercase to uppercase.
noerror	Continue processing when errors occur (up to five in a row).
swab	Swap all pairs of bytes.
sync	Pad input blocks to **ibs**.

count=*n*	Copy only *n* input blocks.
files=*n*	Copy *n* input files (e.g., from magnetic tape), then quit.
ibs=*n*	Set input block size to *n* bytes (default is 512).
if=*file*	Read input from *file* (default is standard input).
obs=*n*	Set output block size to *n* bytes (default is 512).
of=*file*	Write output to *file* (default is standard output).
iseek=*n*	Seek *n* blocks from start of input file (like **skip** but more efficient for disk file input).
oseek=*n*	Seek *n* blocks from start of output file.
seek=*n*	Same as **oseek** (retained for compatibility).
skip=*n*	Skip *n* input blocks.

You can multiply size values (*n*) by a factor of 1024, 512, or 2 by appending the letter **k**, **b**, or **w**, respectively. You can use the letter **x** as a multiplication operator between two numbers.

→

dd
←
	Examples
	Convert an input file to all lowercase:
	
	    `dd if=caps_file of=small_file conv=lcase`
	
	Retrieve variable-length data; write it as fixed-length to *out*:
	
	    data_retrieval_cmd
		dd of=out conv=sync,block

df	**df** [*options*] [*name*]
	
	Report the number of free disk blocks and inodes available on all mounted file systems or on the given *name*. (Unmounted file systems are checked with **-F**.) *name* can be a device name (e.g., **/dev/hd***), the directory name of a mounting point (e.g., **/usr**), a directory name, or a remote resource name (e.g., an NFS resource).
	
	Options
	
	  -f Report free blocks but not free inodes.
	  -i Report percent of inodes used, as well as number of inodes used and free.
	  -t Report total allocated space as well as free space.
	  -v Report percent of blocks used, as well as number of blocks used and free.

dfspace	**/etc/dfspace** [*filesystem . . .*] Report disk space. **dfspace** is a shell script interface to the **df** command. With no arguments, **dfspace** reports the disk space used, percentage of disk space used, and total disk space available for each mounted filesystem. Disk space is reported in megabytes. *filesystem* will provide disk space for that particular filesystem.
dial	**/usr/lib/uucp/dial***X ttyname telno speed* **/usr/lib/uucp/dial***X* **-h** [**-c**] *ttyname speed* **/usr/lib/uucp/uuchat** *ttyname speed chat-script* Dial a modem. **dial***X* dials a modem attached to *ttyname*. *X* is a dialer name, such as "HA1200." uucico invokes **dial** with a *ttyname*, *telno* (telephone number), and *speed*. **dial** attempts to dial the phone number on the specified line at the given speed. When using **dialHA12** or **dialHA24**, *speed* can be a range of baud rates. The range is specified with the form: *lowrate–highrate*, where *lowrate* is the minimum acceptable connection baud rate and *highrate* is the maximum. The **dial** program to be used on a particular line is specified in the fifth field of the entry for that line in **/usr/lib/uucp/Devices**. If there is no **dial** program of that name, then **uucico**, **ct**, and **cu** use a built-in dialer, together with the chat-script of that name, in **/usr/lib/uucp/Dialers**.

Options

−c   Tell dialer to wait for a connection and adjust the line rate to match before returning.

−h   Hang up the modem.

Dialer programs

Several dialer programs are provided. Source for these is provided in their respective .c files.

Binary File	Modem
dialHA12	Hayes Smartmodem 1200 or compatible
dialHA24	Hayes Smartmodem 2400 or compatible
dialHA96V	Hayes Smartmodem 9600 or compatible
dialMUL	Multitech Multimodem 224 EH
dialVA3450	Racal Badic 3451 modem
dialVA96	Racal Badic 9600 modem
dialTBIT	Telebit Trailblazer Modem

Return codes

dial returns the status of the attempt through the following dial return codes:

bit 0x80 = 1

Connection attempt failed.

bits 0x0f = n

If bit 0x80 is a 1, the following bits are the dialer error code n:

0	General or unknown error code
1	Line being used
2	A signal has aborted the dialer
3	Dialer arguments are invalid
4	Phone number is invalid
5	Baud rate is invalid or dialer could not connect at requested baud rate
6	Can't open the line
7	ioctl error on the line
8	Timeout waiting for connection
9	No dial tone detected.
10	Unused
11	Unused
12	Unused
13	Phone is busy.
14	No carrier is detected.
15	Remote system did not answer.

Error codes 12-15 indicate that the problem is at the remote end.

diff	**diff** [*options*] [*diroptions*] *file1 file2*

Compare two text files. **diff** reports lines that differ between *file1* and *file2*. Output consists of lines of context from each file, with *file1* text flagged by a < symbol and *file2* text by a > symbol. Context lines are preceded by the ed command (**a, c,** or **d**) that would be used to convert *file1* to *file2*. If one of the files is -, standard input is read. If one of the files is a directory, **diff** locates the filename in that directory corresponding to the other argument (e.g., **diff my_dir/junk junk**). If both arguments are directories, **diff** reports lines that differ between all pairs of files having equivalent names (e.g., **olddir/program** and **newdir/program**); in addition, **diff** lists filenames unique to one directory, as well as subdirectories common to both. See also **sdiff** and **cmp.**

Options

-b Ignore repeating blanks and end-of-line blanks; treat successive blanks as one.

-e Produce a script of commands (**a, c, d**) to recreate *file2* from *file1* using the ed editor.

-f Produce a script to recreate *file1* from *file2*; the script is in the opposite order, so it isn't useful to ed.

-h Do a half-hearted comparison; complex differences (e.g., long stretches of many changes) may not show up; -e and -f are disabled.

diff3	**diff3** [*options*] *file1 file2 file3*

Compare three files and report the differences with the following codes:

==== All three files differ.

====1 *file1* is different.

====2 *file2* is different.

====3 *file3* is different.

Options

-e Create an ed script to incorporate into *file1* all differences between *file2* and *file3*.

-x Create an ed script to incorporate into *file1* all differences between all three files.

-3 Create an ed script to incorporate into *file1* differences between *file1* and *file3*.

dircmp	**dircmp** [*options*] *dir1 dir2*

Compare the contents of *dir1* and *dir2*. See also **diff** and **cmp.**

Options

    -d   Execute **diff** on the files which differ.

    -s   Don't report files that are identical.

    -w*n*   Change the output line length to *n* (default is 72).

---

dirname *pathname*

Print *pathname* excluding last level. Useful for stripping the actual filename from a pathname. See also **basename**.

---

disable *tty*...
disable [*options*] *printers*

Turn off terminals and printers, respectively. For terminals, manipulate the **/etc/conf/cf.d/init.base** file and signal **init** to disallow logins on a particular terminal. For printers, stop print requests from being sent to *printer*.

Options

    -c   Cancel any requests currently printing.

    -r[*reason*]

           Associate a *reason* with disabling the printer. *reason* applies to all printers listed up to next **-r** option. It is reported by **lpstat**.

    -W   Disable *printers* when print requests currently printing have finished.

Examples

    A printer named *linepr* is disabled because of a paper jam:

```
disable -r"paper jam" linepr
```

---

diskcmp [*options*]

Compare the contents of one floppy disk with the contents of a second floppy disk, using the **cmp** utility.

Options

    -48ds9

           For low density 48tpi (360K) floppies. This is the default setting.

    -96ds9

           For medium density 96tpi (720K) floppies.

    -96ds15

           For high density 96tpi (1.2M) floppies

    -135ds9

           For low density 135tpi (720K) 3.5 inch floppies.

    -135ds18

           For high density 135tpi (1.44M) 3.5 inch floppies.

→

diskcmp ←	-d	Computer has dual floppy drives.
	-s	Use the **sum** command to compare contents of source and target floppies; give error message if two do not match.

---

diskcp

diskcp [*options*]

Make a copy of a source floppy disk onto a target floppy disk. On machines with one floppy drive, **diskcp** temporarily transfers the image to the hard disk until a target floppy is inserted into the floppy drive.

Options

- 48ds9
  For low density 48tpi (360K) floppies (default).
- 96ds9
  For medium density 96tpi (720K) floppies.
- 96ds15
  For high density 96tpi (1.2M) floppies
- 135ds9
  For low density 135tpi (720K) 3.5 inch floppies.
- 135ds18
  For high density 135tpi (1.44M) 3.5 inch floppies.
- -d   Computer has dual floppy drives.
- -f   Format target floppy disk before image is copied.
- -r   Use second floppy drive as source drive.
- -s   Use the **sum** command to compare contents of source and target floppies; give error message if two do not match.
- -u   Print usage message.

---

doscat

doscat [*options*] *files* . . .

Display a DOS file—copy one or more DOS files to standard output.

Options

- -c   Halt execution if file on mounted filesystem is encountered.
- -m   Copy files with newline conversions.
- -r   Copy files without newline conversions.

---

doscp

doscp [*options*] *file1 file2*
doscp [*options*] *file* . . . *directory*

Copy files between a DOS disk and a UNIX System filesystem.

Options

-c   Halt execution if file on mounted filesystem is encountered.

-m   Copy files with newline conversions.

-r   Copy files without newline conversions.

---

dosdir [*option*] *directory* ...

List DOS files in the standard DOS-style directory format.

Option

-c   Halt execution if file on mounted filesystem is encountered.

---

dosformat [*options*] *drive*

Create DOS-formatted diskette. Drive may be specified in either DOS drive convention, using default file **/etc/default/msdos**, or using the UNIX System special filename. **dosformat** cannot be used to format a hard disk.

Options

-c   Halt execution immediately if a file on a mounted filesystem is encountered.

-f   Suppress interactive feature.

-q   Suppress information normally displayed.

-v   Prompt user for volume label (maximum size 11 characters) after diskette has been formatted.

---

dosls [*option*] *directory* ...

List DOS directories and files in a UNIX System format.

Option

-c   Halt execution if file on mounted filesystem is encountered.

---

dosmkdir [*option*] *directory* ...

Create a directory on a DOS disk.

Option

-c   Halt execution if file on mounted filesystem is encountered.

---

dosrm	**dosrm** [*option*] *file* ... Remove files from a DOS disk. ***Option*** -c Halt execution if file on mounted filesystem is encountered.
dosrmdir	**dosrmdir** [*option*] *directory* ... Delete a directory from a DOS disk. ***Option*** -c Halt execution if file on mounted filesystem is encountered.
dtox	**dtox** *filename* > *output.file* Convert a file from MS-DOS format to UNIX format. **dtox** strips both the end-of-line carriage returns and the end-of-file CTRL-z from MS-DOS files.
dtype	**dtype** [*option*] *device* ... Determine type of a disk, print pertinent information on standard output, then exit with corresponding code (see below). When more than one *device* is given, exit code corresponds to last argument. **dtype** only works reliably for floppy diskettes. Based on the file /etc/magic. ***Option*** -s Suppress information printing to standard output.

Miscellaneous disk types

Exit code	Message (optional)
60	error (specified)
61	empty or unrecognized data

Storage disk types

Exit code	Message (optional)
70	backup format, volume n
71	tar format [, extent e of n]
72	cpio format
73	cpio character (-c) format

XENIX or UNIX disk types

Version or type	Exit code	Message (optional)
System III	120	XENIX 2.x filesystem [needs cleaning]
System V	130	XENIX 3.x or later filesystem [needs cleaning]
	140	UNIX 1K filesystem [needs cleaning]

MS-DOS Disk Types

Version or type	Exit code	Message (optional)
1.x	80	DOS 1.x, 8 sec/track, single-sided
	81	DOS 1.x, 8 sec/track, dual-sided
2.x	90	MS-DOS 8 sec/track, 40 tracks/side, single-sided, 5.25 inch
	91	MS-DOS 8 sec/track, 40 tracks/side, dual-sided, 5.25 inch
	92	MS-DOS 9 sec/track, 40 tracks/side, single-sided, 5.25 inch
	93	MS-DOS 9 sec/track, 40 tracks/side, dual-sided, 5.25 inch
	94	MS-DOS fixed disk
data	100	MS-DOS data disk, n sec/track, single-sided
	101	MS-DOS data disk, n sec/track, dual-sided
	102	MS-DOS data disk, 9 sec/track, single-sided
	103	MS-DOS data disk, 9 sec/track, dual-sided
3.x	110	MS-DOS 9 (3.5 inch) or 15 (5.25 inch) sec/track, 80 tracks/side, dual-sided
	111	MS-DOS 18 sec/track, 80 tracks/side, dual-sided, 3.5 inch
	112	MS-DOS 8 sec/track, 80 tracks/side, single-sided, 3.5 inch or 5.25 inch
	112	MS-DOS 8 sec/track, 80 tracks/side, dual-sided, 3.5 inch or 5.25 inch

du [*options*] [*directories*]

Print disk usage; i.e., the number of 512-byte blocks used by each named directory and its subdirectories (default is current directory).

→

du ←	**Options** -a Print usage for all files, not just subdirectories. -f Display usage of files in current filesystem only. -r Print cannot open message if a file or directory is inaccessible. -s Print only the grand total for each named directory. -u Ignore files that have more than one link.

---

du
←

Options

-a   Print usage for all files, not just subdirectories.

-f   Display usage of files in current filesystem only.

-r   Print cannot open message if a file or directory is inaccessible.

-s   Print only the grand total for each named directory.

-u   Ignore files that have more than one link.

---

echo

echo [-n] [*string*]

This is the **/bin/echo** command. **echo** also exists as a command built into the C shell and Bourne shell.

Examples

```
echo "testing printer" | lp
echo "TITLE\nTITLE" > file ; cat doc1 doc2 >> file
echo "Warning: ringing bell \07"
```

---

ed

ed [*options*] [*file*]

The standard text editor. If the named *file* does not exist, **ed** creates it; otherwise, the existing *file* is opened for editing. As a line editor, **ed** is generally no longer used because **vi** and **ex** have superseded it. Some utilities, such as **diff**, continue to make use of **ed**.

Options

-C   Same as -**x**, but assume *file* began in encrypted form.

-p *string*
   Set *string* as the prompt for commands (default is *). The **P** command turns the prompt display on and off.

-s   Suppress character counts, diagnostics, and the ! prompt for shell commands.

-x   Supply a key to encrypt or decrypt *file* using **crypt**.

---

edit

edit [*options*] [*file*]

A line-oriented text editor that runs a simplified version of **ex** for novice users. The **set** variables **report**, **showmode**, **novice**, and **magic** are preset to report editing changes, to display edit modes (when in :**vi** mode), and to require literal search patterns (no metacharacters allowed), respectively.

Options

-C   Same as -**x**, but assume files are already encrypted.

-r   Recover file after a system crash or editor crash.

-x   Encrypt file when it is written.

egrep [options] [regexp] [files]

Search one or more *files* for lines that match a regular expression *regexp*. **egrep** doesn't support the metacharacters \(, \), \n, \<, \>, \{, or \}, but does support the other expressions, as well as the extended set +, ?, |, and ( ). Remember to enclose these characters in quotes. Regular expressions are described in Section 8, *Pattern Matching*. Exit status is 0 if any lines match, 1 if not, and 2 for errors. See also **grep** and **fgrep**. **egrep** typically runs faster than those commands.

Options

-b	Precede each line with its block number.
-c	Print only a count of matched lines.
-e *regexp*	Use this if *regexp* begins with -.
-f *file*	Take expression from *file*.
-h	List matched lines but not filenames (inverse of -l).
-i	Ignore uppercase and lowercase distinctions.
-l	List filenames but not matched lines.
-n	Print lines and their line numbers.
-v	Print all lines that *don't* match *regexp*.

Examples

Search for occurrences of *Victor* or *Victoria* in *file*:

```
egrep 'Victor(ia)*' file
egrep '(Victor|Victoria)' file
```

Find and print strings such as *old.doc1* or *new.doc2* in *files*, and include their line numbers:

```
egrep -n '(old|new)\.doc?' files
```

enable *tty* | *printers*

Turn on (enable) terminals and line printers. For terminals, **enable** allows logins on a particular terminal (*tty*). For line printers, **enable** allows *printers* to process print requests taken by **lp**.

Example

To enable terminal *tty01*:

```
enable tty01
```

env [option] [variable=value ...] [command]

Display the current environment or, if environment *variables* are specified, set them to a new *value* and display the modified environment. If *command* is specified, execute it under the modified environment.

→

env ←	**Option** - Ignore current environment entirely.

---

ex

ex [*options*] *files*

A line-oriented text editor; a superset of ed and the root of vi. See Section 9, *The Vi Editor*, and Section 10, *The Ex Editor*, for more information.

Options

-c*command*
> Begin edit session by executing the given ex *command* (usually a search pattern or line address). If *command* contains spaces or special characters, enclose it in single quotes to protect it from the shell. For example, *command* could be ':set list' (show tabs and newlines) or /*word* (search for *word*) or '$' (show last line). (Note: -c*command* was formerly +*command*.)

-L   List filenames that were saved due to an editor or system crash.

-r *file*   Recover and edit *file* after an editor or system crash.

-R   Edit in read-only mode to prevent accidental changing of files.

-s   Suppress status messages (e.g., errors, prompts); useful when running an ex script. (-s was formerly the - option.)

-t *tag*   Edit the file containing *tag* and position the editor at its definition (see **ctags** for more information).

-v   Invoke vi. Running vi directly is simpler.

-x   Supply a key to encrypt or decrypt *file* using **crypt**.

-C   Same as -x but assume that *file* began in encrypted form.

Examples

Either of the following examples will apply the ex commands in exscript to text file **doc**:

```
ex -s doc < exscript
cat exscript | ex -s doc
```

---

expr

expr *arg1 operator arg2* [*operator arg3* ...]

Evaluate arguments as expressions and print the result. Strings can also be compared and searched. Arguments and operators must be separated by spaces. In most cases, an argument is an integer, typed literally or represented by a shell variable. There are three types of operators: arithmetic, relational, and logical. Exit status for **expr** is 0 (expression is nonzero and nonnull), 1 (expression is 0 or null), or 2 (expression is invalid).

Use these to produce mathematical expressions whose results are printed.

+ Add *arg2* to *arg1*.
– Subtract *arg2* from *arg1*.
* Multiply the arguments.
/ Divide *arg1* by *arg2*.
% Take the remainder when *arg1* is divided by *arg2*.

Addition and subtraction are evaluated last, unless they are grouped inside parentheses. The symbols *, (, and) have meaning to the shell, so they must be escaped (preceded by a backslash or enclosed in single quotes).

Relational operators

Use these to compare two arguments. Arguments can also be words, in which case comparisons are defined by the locale. If the comparison statement is true, the result is 1; if false, the result is 0. Symbols > and < must be escaped.

=, ==
       Are the arguments equal?
!= Are the arguments different?
>   Is *arg1* greater than *arg2*?
>= Is *arg1* greater than or equal to *arg2*?
<   Is *arg1* less than *arg2*?
<= Is *arg1* less than or equal to *arg2*?

Logical operators

Use these to compare two arguments. Depending on the values, the result can be *arg1* (or some portion of it), *arg2*, or 0. Symbols | and & must be escaped.

| Logical OR; if *arg1* has a non-zero (and non-null) value, the result is *arg1*; otherwise, the result is *arg2*.
& Logical AND; if both *arg1* and *arg2* have a non-zero (and non-null) value, the result is *arg1*; otherwise, the result is 0.
: Sort of like **grep**; *arg2* is a pattern to search for in *arg1*. *arg2* must be a regular expression in this case. If part of the *arg2* pattern is enclosed in \(\), the result is the portion of *arg1* that matches; otherwise, the result is simply the number of characters that match. By default, a pattern match always applies to the beginning of the first argument (the search string implicitly begins with a ^). To match other parts of the string, start the search string with .*.

→

expr
←

Examples

Division happens first; result is 10:

```
expr 5 + 10 / 2
```

Addition happens first; result is 7 (truncated from 7.5):

```
expr \( 5 + 10 \) / 2
```

Add 1 to variable **i**; this is how variables are incremented in shell scripts:

```
i=`expr $i + 1`
```

Print 1 (true) if variable **a** is the string "hello":

```
expr $a = hello
```

Print 1 (true) if **b** plus 5 equals 10 or more:

```
expr $b + 5 \>= 10
```

In the examples below, variable **p** is the string "version.100". This command prints the number of characters in **p**:

```
expr $p : '.*'          Result is 11
```

Match all characters and print them:

```
expr $p : '\(.*\)'          Result is "version.100"
```

Print the number of lowercase letters at the beginning of **p**:

```
expr $p : '[a-z]*'          Result is 7
```

Match the lowercase letters at the beginning of **p**:

```
expr $p : '\([a-z]*\)'    Result is "version"
```

Truncate **$x** if it contains five or more characters; if not, just print **$x**. (Logical OR uses the second argument when the first one is 0 or null; i.e., when the match fails.)

```
expr $x : '\(.....\)' \| $x
```

In a shell script, rename files to their first five letters:

```
mv $x `expr $x : '\(.....\)' \| $x`
```

(To avoid overwriting files with similar names, use **mv -i**.)

---

factor

factor [*num*]

Produce the prime factors of *num* or wait for input, and factor the resulting number.

false

A null command that returns an unsuccessful (nonzero) exit status. Normally used in Bourne shell scripts. See also **true**.

---

fgrep [*options*] [*pattern*] [*files*]

Search one or more *files* for lines that match a literal, text-string *pattern*. Because **fgrep** does not support regular expressions, it is faster than **grep** (hence **fgrep**, for fast **grep**). Exit status is 0 if any lines match, 1 if not, and 2 for errors. See also **egrep** and **grep**.

Options

-b   Precede each line with its block number.
-c   Print only a count of matched lines.
-e *pat* Use this if pattern *pat* begins with - .
-f*file* Take a list of patterns from *file*.
-h   Print matched lines but not filenames (inverse of -l).
-i   Ignore uppercase and lowercase distinctions.
-l   List filenames but not matched lines.
-n   Print lines and their line numbers.
-v   Print all lines that *don't* match *pattern*.
-x   Print lines only if *pattern* matches the entire line.

Examples

Print lines in *file* that don't contain any spaces:

```
fgrep -v ' ' file
```

Print lines in *file* that contain the words in **spell_list**:

```
fgrep -f spell_list file
```

---

file [*options*] *files*

Classify the named *files* according to the type of data they contain. **file** checks the magic file (usually **/etc/magic**) to identify some file types.

Options

-c   Check the format of the magic file (*files* argument is invalid with -c).
-f *list* Run **file** on the filenames in *list*.
-L   Follow symbolic links. By default, symbolic links are not followed.
-m *file*
      Use *file* as the magic file instead of **/etc/magic**.

$\rightarrow$

file

←

Many file types are understood. Output lists each filename, followed by a brief classification such as:

```
ascii text
c program text
c-shell commands
data
empty
iAPX 386 executable
directory
[nt]roff, tbl, or eqn input text
shell commands
symbolic link to ../usr/etc/arp
```

Example

List all files that are deemed to be troff/nroff input:

```
file * | grep roff
```

find

find *pathname(s) condition(s)*

An extremely useful command for finding particular groups of files (numerous examples follow this description). **find** descends the directory tree beginning at each *pathname* and locates files that meet the specified *conditions*. At least one *pathname* and one *condition* must be specified. The most useful conditions include **-print** (which must be explicitly given to display any output), **-name** and **-type** (for general use), **-exec** and **-size** (for advanced users), and **-mtime** and **-user** (for administrators).

Conditions may be grouped by enclosing them in \(\) (escaped parentheses), negated with ! (use \! in the C shell), given as alternatives by separating them with **-o**, or repeated (adding restrictions to the match; usually only for **-name**, **-type**, **-perm**).

Conditions

-atime +*n* | -*n* | *n*
  Find files that were last accessed more than *n* (+*n*), less than *n* (-*n*), or exactly *n* days ago. Note that **find** will change the access time of directories supplied as *pathnames*.

-cpio *dev* Take matching files and write them on device *dev*, using **cpio**.

-ctime +*n* | -*n* | *n*
  Find files that were changed more than *n* (+*n*), less than *n* (-*n*), or exactly *n* days ago. Change refers to modification, permission or ownership changes, etc.; therefore, **-ctime** is more inclusive than **-atime** or **-mtime**.

-depth Descend the directory tree, skipping directories and working on actual files first (and *then* the parent directories). Useful when files reside in unwritable directories (e.g., when using **find** with **cpio**).

-**exec** *command* { } \;

> Run the UNIX *command* on each file matched by **find**, (provided *command* executes successfully on that file; i.e., returns a 0 exit status). When *command* runs, the argument { } substitutes the current file. Follow the entire sequence with an escaped semicolon (\;).

-**follow** Follow symbolic links and track the directories visited (don't use this with -**type l**).

-**group** *gname*

> Find files belonging to group *gname*. *gname* can be a group name or a group ID number.

-**inum** *n* Find files whose inode number is *n*.

-**links** *n* Find files having *n* links.

-**local** Find files that physically reside on the local system.

-**mount** Search for files that reside only on the same filesystem as *pathname*. (Use -**xdev** on BSD systems.)

-**mtime** +*n* | -*n* | *n*

> Find files that were last modified more than *n* (+*n*), less than *n* (-*n*), or exactly *n* days ago.

-**name** *pattern*

> Find files whose names match *pattern*. Filename metacharacters may be used, but should be escaped or quoted.

-**newer** *file*

> Find files that have been modified more recently than *file*; similar to -**mtime**.

-**ok** *command* { } \;

> Same as -**exec**, but prompts user to respond with **y** before *command* is executed.

-**perm** *nnn*

> Find files whose permission flags (e.g., **rwx**) match octal number *nnn* exactly (e.g., 664 matches -**rw-rw-r--**). Use a minus sign to make a "wildcard" match of any specified bit (e.g., -**perm -600** matches -**rw-******, where * can be any mode).

-**print** Print the matching files and directories, using their full pathnames.

-**size** *n*[**c**]

> Find files containing *n* blocks, or if **c** is specified, *n* characters long.

-**type** *c* Find files whose type is *c*. *c* can be **b** (block special file), **c** (character special file), **d** (directory), **p** (fifo or named pipe), **l** (symbolic link), or **f** (plain file).

$\rightarrow$

find
←

-user *user*
          Find files belonging to a *user* name or ID.

Examples

List all files (and subdirectories) in your home directory:

```
find $HOME -print
```

List all files named **chapter1** in the **/work** directory:

```
find /work -name chapter1 -print
```

List all files beginning with *memo* owned by *ann*:

```
find /work /usr -name 'memo*' -user ann -print
```

Search the filesystem (begin at root) for manpage directories:

```
find / -type d -name 'man*' -print
```

Search the current directory, look for filenames that *don't* begin with a capital letter, and send them to the printer:

```
find . \! -name '[A-Z]*' -exec lp {} \;
```

Find and compress files whose names *don't* end with .Z:

```
compress `find . \! -name '*.Z' -print`
```

Remove all empty files on the system (prompting first):

```
find / -size 0 -ok rm {} \;
```

Search the system for files that were modified within the last two days (good candidates for backing up):

```
find / -mtime -2 -print
```

Recursively **grep** for a pattern down a directory tree:

```
find /book -print | xargs grep '[Nn]utshell'
```

---

finger

finger [*options*] *users*

Display data about one or more *users*, including information listed in the files **.plan** and **.project** in each *user*'s home directory. You can specify each *user* either as a login name (exact match) or as a first or last name (display information on all matching names). Networked environments recognize arguments of the form *user@host* and *@host*.

Options

  -b   Omit user's home directory and shell from display.

  -f   Used with **-s** to omit heading that normally displays in short format.

-i	Show "idle" format, a terse format (like -s).	**finger**
-l	Force long format (default).	
-p	Omit .**plan** file from display.	
-q	Show "quick" format, the tersest of all (requires an exact match of username).	
-s	Show short format.	
-w	Used with -s to omit user's full name that normally displays in short format.	

format [*options*] *device* [*-i interleave*]

format

Format floppy disks for use on a UNIX system. **format** can be used either interactively or from the command line. *device* is the device to be formatted. The default device is specified in /**etc/default/format**. **format** does not format floppies for use under DOS.

Options

-f   Suppress interactive feature—run **format** from the command line. Regardless of whether you run **format** interactively, track and head information is displayed.

-i *interleave*
     Specify the interleave factor. Place this option after the *device* argument.

-n   Do not verify the diskette (overrides verify entry in /**etc/default/format**).

-q   Quiet option. Suppress track and head output information normally displayed. To produce no output at all, combine with -f option.

-v   Format verification.

ftp [*options*] [*hostname*]

ftp

TCP/IP command. Transfer files to and from remote network site *hostname*. **ftp** prompts the user for a command. The commands are listed below, following the options.

Options

-d   Enable debugging.

-g   Disable filename globbing.

-i   Turn off interactive prompting.

-n   No auto-login upon initial connection.

-v   Verbose on. Show all responses from remote server.

-t   Enable packet tracing.

Commands

![*command* [*args*]]
     Invoke an interactive shell on the local machine. If arguments are given, the first is taken as a command to

→

execute directly, with the rest of the arguments as that command's arguments.

$ macro-name [args]

Execute the macro *macro-name* that was defined with the **macdef** command. Arguments are passed to the macro unglobbed.

account [passwd]

Supply a supplemental password that will be required by a remote system for access to resources once a login has been successfully completed. If no argument is given, the user will be prompted for an account password in a non-echoing mode.

append local-file [remote-file]

Append a local file to a file on the remote machine. If *remote-file* is not given, the local filename is used after being altered by any **ntrans** or **nmap** setting. File transfer uses the current settings for *type, format, mode,* and *structure.*

ascii   Set the file transfer type to network ASCII (default).

bell   Sound a bell after each file transfer command is completed.

binary   Set file transfer type to support binary image transfer.

bye   Terminate FTP session and exit **ftp.**

case   Toggle remote computer filename case mapping during **mget.**

cd remote-directory

Change working directory on remote machine to *remote-directory.*

cdup   Change working directory of remote machine to its parent directory.

chmod [mode] [remote-file]

Change file permissions of *remote file.*

close   Terminate FTP session and return to command interpreter.

cr   Toggle carriage return stripping during ASCII-type file retrieval.

delete remote-file

Delete file *remote-file* on remote machine.

debug [debug-value]

Toggle debugging mode. If *debug-value* is specified, it is used to set the debugging level.

dir [remote-directory] [local-file]

Print a listing of the directory contents in the directory *remote-directory,* and, optionally, place the output in *local-file.* If no directory is specified, the current working directory on the remote machine is used. If no local file is specified, output comes to the terminal.

disconnect

Synonym for **close**.

form *format*

Set the file transfer form to *format*. Default format is *file*.

get remote-file [*local-file*]

Retrieve the *remote-file* and store it on the local machine. If the local filename is not specified, it is given the same name it has on the remote machine, subject to alteration by the current **case**, **ntrans**, and **nmap** settings.

glob   Toggle filename expansion for **mdelete**, **mget**, and **mput**. If globbing is turned off, the filename arguments are taken literally and not expanded.

hash   Toggle hash-sign (#) printing for each data block transferred.

help [*command*]

Print help information for *command*. With no argument, **ftp** prints a list of the known commands.

idle   Get/set idle timer on remote machine.

image   Synonymous to **binary**.

lcd [*directory*]

Change working directory on local machine. If *directory* is not specified, user's home directory is used.

ls [*remote-directory*] [*local-file*]

Print abbreviated listing of contents of directory on remote machine. If *remote-directory* is not specified, current working directory is used.

macdef *macro-name*

Define a macro. Subsequent lines are stored as the macro *macro-name*; a null line terminates macro input mode.

mdelete *remote-files*

Delete the *remote-files* on the remote machine.

mdir *remote-files local-file*

Like **dir**, except multiple remote files may be specified.

mget *remote-files*

Expand the remote-files on the remote machine and do a **get** for each filename thus produced.

mkdir *directory-name*

Make a directory on the remote machine.

mls *remote-files local-file*

Like **nlist**, except multiple remote files may be specified, and the local file must be specified.

mode [*mode-name*]

Set file transfer mode to *mode-name*. Default mode is stream mode.

$\rightarrow$

modtime [*file-name*]
> Show last modification time of the file on the remote machine.

mput [*local-files*]
> Expand wildcards in the list of local files given as arguments and do a **put** for each file in the resulting list.

newer *remote-file* [*local-file*]
> Get file if remote file is newer than local file.

nlist [*remote-directory*] [*local-file*]
> Print list of files of a directory on the remote machine. If *remote-directory* is unspecified, the current working directory is used.

nmap [*inpattern outpattern*]
> Set or unset the filename mapping mechanism. The mapping follows the pattern set by *inpattern*, a template for incoming filenames, and *outpattern*, which determines the resulting mapped filename. If no arguments are specified, the filename mapping mechanism is unset.

ntrans [*inchars* [*outchars*]]
> Set or unset the filename character translation mechanism. Characters in a filename matching a character in *inchars* are replaced with the corresponding character in *outchars*. If no arguments are specified, the filename mapping mechanism is unset. If arguments are specified:
>
> - Characters in remote filenames are translated during **mput** and **put** commands issued without a specified remote target filename.
>
> - Characters in local filenames are translated during **mget** and **get** commands issued without a specified local target filename.

open *host* [*port*]
> Establish a connection to the specified *host* FTP server. An optional *port* number may be supplied, in which case **ftp** will attempt to contact an FTP server at that port.

prompt
> Toggle interactive prompting.

proxy *ftp-command*
> Execute an FTP command on a secondary control connection.

put *local-file* [*remote-file*]
> Store a local file on the remote machine. If *remote-file* is left unspecified, the local filename is used after processing according to any **ntrans** or **nmap** settings in naming

the remote file. File transfer uses the current settings for *type*, *file*, *structure*, and *transfer mode*.

pwd   Print name of the current working directory on the remote machine.

quit   Synonym for bye.

quote *arg1 arg2 . . .*
       Send the arguments specified, verbatim, to the remote FTP server.

recv *remote–file* [*local–file*]
       Synonym for get.

reget   Retrieve a file restarting at the end of the local-file.

restart   Restart the transfer of a file from a particular byte-count.

rhelp [*command–name*]
       Request help from the remote FTP server. If *command-name* is specified, it is supplied to the server as well.

rstatus [*file–name*]
       Show status of remote-machine, or, if *file-name* specified, *file-name* on remote machine.

rename [*from*] [*to*]
       Rename file *from* on remote machine to *to*.

reset   Clear reply queue.

rmdir [*directory–name*]
       Delete a directory on the remote machine.

runique
       Toggle storing of files on the local system with unique filenames.

send *local–file* [*remote–file*]
       Synonym for put.

sendport
       Toggle the use of PORT commands.

size *file–name*
       Return size of *file-name* on remote machine.

status   Show current status of ftp.

site [*command*]
       Get/set site-specific information from/on remote machine.

struct [*struct–name*]
       Set the file transfer structure to *struct-name*. By default, stream structure is used.

sunique
       Toggle storing of files on remote machine under unique file names.

system   Show type of operating system running on remote machine.

tenex   Set file transfer type to that needed to talk to TENEX machines.

→

ftp ←	**trace** Toggle packet tracing.
	type [*type-name*] Set file transfer **type** to *type-name*. If no type is specified, the current type is printed. The default type is network ASCII.
	umask [*mask*] Set user file-creation mode mask on the remote site. If mask is omitted, the current value of the mask is printed.
	user *user-name* [*password*] [*account*] Identify yourself to the remote FTP server. **ftp** will prompt the user for the password, if not specified and the server requires it, and the account field.
	verbose Toggle verbose mode.
	? [*command*] Synonym for help.
getopt	**set -- `getopt** *optstring* **$*`** Parse command options. *optstring* is a string of recognized option letters. The special option -- is used to delimit the end of the options. The shell arguments ($1 $2 ...) are reset so that each option is preceded by a dash and is in its own shell argument. This command has been superseded, but is included for backwards compatibility; **getopts** should be used instead.
getoptcvt	**/usr/lib/getoptcvt** [*option*] *file* Convert shell scripts to use **getopts** instead of **getopt**. **getoptcvt** reads the shell script in *file*, converts it to use **getopts**, and writes the results to standard output. ***Option*** -b The results of running **/usr/lib/getoptcvt** will be portable to earlier UNIX releases.
getopts	**getopts** *string name* [*arg*] Same as built-in Bourne and Korn shell commands **getopts**.
graph	**graph** [*options*] Draw a graph. **graph** takes pairs of numbers from the standard input as abscissas and ordinates of a graph. Successive points are connected by straight lines. The graph is encoded on the standard output for display by the **tplot** filters. If the coordinates of a point are followed by a non-numeric string, that string is printed as a label beginning on the point. Labels may be surrounded with

quotes, in which case they may be empty or contain blanks and numbers; labels never contain newlines.

Options

-a   Supply abscissas automatically.

-b   Break (disconnect) the graph after each label in the input.

-c   Character string given by next argument is default label for each point.

-g   Next argument is grid style: 0 no grid, 1 frame with ticks, 2 full grid (default).

-l   Next argument is label for graph.

-m   Next argument is mode (style) of connecting lines: 0 disconnected, 1 connected (default).

-s   Save screen, do not erase before plotting.

-x [l]   If l is present, x axis is logarithmic. Next one (or two) arguments are lower (and upper) x limits. Third argument, if present, is grid spacing on x axis.

-y [l]   Similar to above for y.

-h   Next argument is fraction of space for height.

-w   Next argument is fraction of space for width.

-r   Next argument is fraction of space to move right before plotting.

-u   Next argument is fraction of space to move up before plotting.

-t   Transpose horizontal and vertical axes.

---

greek [*option*]

Select terminal filter. **greek** is a filter that reinterprets the extended character set, as well as the reverse and half-line motions, of a 128-character TELETYPE Model 37 terminal for certain other terminals. With no argument, **greek** attempts to use the environment variable **$TERM**.

Option

-T*terminal*

     Currently, the following terminals are recognized:

300	DASI 300
300-12	DASI 300 in 12-pitch
300s	DASI 300s
300s-12	DASI 300s in 12-pitch
450	DASI 450
450-12	DASI 450 in 12-pitch
1620	Diablo 1620 (alias DASI 450)
1620-12	Diablo 1620 (alias DASI 450) in 12-pitch
2621	Hewlett-Packard 2621, 2640, and 2645
2640	Hewlett-Packard 2621, 2640, and 2645
2645	Hewlett-Packard 2621, 2640, and 2645

$\rightarrow$

greek		
←	4014	Tektronix 4014
	hp	Hewlett-Packard 2621, 2640, and 2645
	tek	Tektronix 4014

grep

grep [*options*] *regexp* [*files*]

Search one or more *files* for lines that match a regular expression *regexp*. Regular expressions are described in Section 8, *Pattern Matching*. Exit status is 0 if any lines match, 1 if not, and 2 for errors. See also **egrep** and **fgrep**.

Options

-b   Precede each line with its block number.

-c   Print only a count of matched lines.

-h   Print matched lines but not filenames (inverse of -l).

-i   Ignore uppercase and lowercase distinctions.

-l   List filenames but not matched lines.

-n   Print lines and their line numbers.

-s   Suppress error messages for nonexistent or unreadable files.

-v   Print all lines that *don't* match *regexp*.

-y   Non-standard XENIX option. Turn on matching of letters of either case in the input so that case is insignificant.

Examples

List the number of users who use the C shell:

```
grep -c /bin/csh /etc/passwd
```

List header files that have at least one #include directive:

```
grep -l '^#include' /usr/include/*
```

List files that don't contain *pattern*:

```
grep -c pattern files | grep :0
```

hd

hd [*-format*] [*options*] [*file*]

Display files in hexadecimal, octal, decimal, and character formats. Default is with the following flags set: **-abx -A**. This says that addresses (file offsets) and bytes are printed in hexadecimal and that characters are also printed. If no *file* argument is given, the standard input is read.

Options

-s *offset*

Specify beginning offset in file where printing is to begin. If no *file* is given, or if a seek fails because input is a pipe, *offset* bytes are read from the input and

discarded. Otherwise, a seek error will terminate processing of currrent file.

offset may be decimal, hexadecimal (preceded by 0x),
or octal (preceded by 0). It is optionally followed by
one of the following multipliers: **w**, for words (2 bytes);
l, for long words (4 bytes); **b**, for half kilobytes (512
bytes); or **k**, for kilobytes (1024 bytes).

-n *count*

Specify number of bytes to process. *count* is in same
format as *offset*, above.

Format Flags

If no output format is given, but a base specifier is present, the
output format is set to -**acbwl**. If no base specifier is given, but
an output format is present, the base specifier is set to -**xdo**. If
neither is present, the format flag is set to -**abx** -**A**.

acbwlA

Output format specifiers for addresses, characters,
bytes, words, longs, and ASCII, respectively. Only one
base specifier will be used for addresses. The address
will appear on the first line of output that begins each
new offset in the input.

xdo Output base specifiers for hexadecimal, decimal, and
octal.

t   Print a text file, each line preceded by the address in
the file.

---

head [- *n*] [*files*]

Print the first few lines of one or more *files*. Use *–n* to print the
first *n* lines (default is 10).

Examples

Display the first 20 lines of **phone_list**:

```
head -20 phone_list
```

Display the first ten phone numbers having a 202 area code:

```
grep '(202)' phone_list | head
```

---

hello *user* [*tty*]

Send messages from one user to another. When first called, **hello**
displays the following message:

```
Message from sender's-system! sender's-name sender's-tty
```

→

hello ←	Recipient may write back at this point. Communication continues until interrupted (DEL or CTRL-C on most terminals). When interrupted, **hello** prints: (end of message) on the other terminal, and exits.
hostname	**hostname** [*option*] [*nameofhost*] TCP/IP command. Set or print name of current host system. Superuser can set the hostname with *nameofhost* argument. **Option** -s Trim domain information from the printed name.

hp	**hp** [*options*]
	
	Handle special functions of Hewlett-Packard 2640 series of terminals. Primary purpose is producing accurate representations of most **nroff** output. Typical usage is in conjunction with text processing software, for instance:
	
	    nroff -h *files* ... **| hp**
	
	Exit codes are 0 for normal termination, 2 for all errors.
	
	Options
	    -e Maximal use made of added display modes: overstruck characters presented in underlined mode; superscripts shown in half-bright mode; subscripts shown in half-bright, underlined mode. If -e is omitted, **hp** assumes your terminal lacks display enhancements feature.
	    -m Request minimization of output by changing newlines to CTRL-Ms.

hwconfig	**/etc/hwconfig** [*options*] ...
	
	Return configuration information contained in **/usr/adm/hwconfig/** or in file specified on command line with -f *filename* option. Using combinations of the remaining options, the user can view as much information as needed from the configuraton file. The display format is as follows:
	
	    magic_char device_name base+finish vec dma rest
	
	where:
	    magic_char
	        is the character "%".
	    device_name
	        is the name of the device driver.

base+finish
are the starting and finishing addresses of the driver working space.

vec   is the interrupt vector number in decimal.

dma is the DMA channel number.

rest is a possibly empty list of *parameter=value* pairs. *hwconfig* returns 0 for success, 1 for conflicts detected, 2 for invalid arguments. It is runnable only by *root*.

Options

-c   Check for device conflicts.

-f *filename*
Use *file* as input file instead of default **/usr/adm/hwconfig**.

-h   Use long format of device configuration content, with headers.

-l   Use long format of device configuration content.

-n   Always print out device name.

param Show all values of *param* throughout configuration file. Current valid system parameters are: **name, base, offset, vec, dma, unit, type, nports, hds, cyls, secs, drvr**.

param=val
Show only information from line where *param* equals the value *val*.

-q   Check quietly for device conflicts; display nothing. When used with -c, display conflicts only.

-n, -l, and -h are in increasing overriding power. That is, if -n and -l are both specified, -l will be used. *param* on its own indicates a query for its corresponding values(s), whereas *param=value* indicates a matching *<token,val>* pair in the input file. -l is used by default if there are no queries and no explicit option.

i286emul [*arg* ...] *prog286*

Emulate UNIX 80286—allow programs from UNIX SVR2 or R3 on the Intel 80286 to run on UNIX SVR3 on the Intel 80386. The UNIX system recognizes an attempt to **exec** a 286 program, and automatically **exec**'s the 286 emulator with the 286 program name as an additional argument. Following are some of the differences between a program running on a 286 and a 286 program using **i286emul** on a 386:

- A 286 program under **i286emul** always has 64K in the stack segment if it is a large-model process, or 64K in the data segment if it is a small-model process.

- System calls and signal handling use more space on the stack under **i286emul** than on a 286.

→

i286emul	• Attempts to unlink or write on the 286 program will fail on the 286 with **ETXTBSY**, but will not fail under **i286emul**.
←	• The 286 program must be readable for the emulator to read it.

ismpx

ismpx [*option*]

Test whether standard input is running under **layers**. (Command name comes from "Is the multiplexor running?") Output is either **yes** (exit status 0) or **no** (exit status 1). Useful for shell scripts that send programs to a windowing terminal or depend on screen size.

Option

 -s   Suppress output and return exit status only.

Example shell script

```
if ismpx -s
then jwin
fi
```

join

join [*options*] *file1 file2*

Join two relations specified by the lines of *file1* and *file2*. (Read standard input if *file1* is -.) The output contains the common field and the remainder of each line from *file1* and *file2*. In the options below, *n* can be 1 or 2, referring to *file1* or *file2*.

Options

 -a *n*   List unpairable lines in file *n* (or both if *n* is omitted).

 -e *s*   Replace any empty output field with the string *s*.

 -j *nm* Join on the *m*th field of file *n* (or both files if *n* is omitted).

 -o *n.m* Each output line contains fields specified by file number *n* and field number *m*. The common field is suppressed unless requested.

 -t *c*   Use character *c* as field separator for input and output.

Examples

Assuming the following input files:

```
% cat score
olga    81      91
rene    82      92
zack    83      93
% cat grade
olga    B       A
rene    B       A
```

List scores followed by grades, including unmatched lines:

```
% join -a score grade
olga 81 91 B A
rene 82 92 B A
zack 83 93
```

Pair each score with its grade:

```
% join -o 1.1 1.2 2.2 1.3 2.3 score grade
olga 81 B 91 A
rene 82 B 92 A
```

kill [*option*] *IDs*

Send a signal to terminate one or more process *IDs*. You must own the process or be a privileged user. This command is similar to the **kill** command that is built into the Bourne, Korn, and C shells. A minus sign before an *ID* specifies a process group ID. (The built-in version doesn't allow process group IDs, but it does allow job IDs.)

Option

    -*signal*   The signal number (from **ps -f**) or name (from **kill -l**). With a signal number of 9, the kill is absolute.

ksh [*options*] [*arguments*]

Korn shell command interpreter. See Section 5, *The Bourne Shell and Korn Shell*, for more information, including command-line options.

last [*options*] [*username*]

Indicate last logins of users and teletypes. **last** checks the *wtmp* file, which records all logins and logouts, for information about users, tty lines or any group of users and lines. Options specify a username and/or tty. With no options, **last** displays a record of all logins and logouts, in reverse chronological order.

Options

    -**h**   No header.

    -**n** *limit*
             Limit report to *n* lines.

    -**t** *tty*   Specifies tty.

    -**w** *wtmpfile*
             Use *wtmpfile* instead of **/etc/wtmp**. This file must have same format as **/etc/wtmp**.

layers [*options*] [*layers_program*]

A layer multiplexor for windowing terminals. **layers** manages asynchronous windows on a windowing terminal. *layers_program* is a

→

layers
←
	file containing a firmware patch that **layers** downloads to the terminal (before layers are created or startup *commands* are executed).
	
	Options
	
	    -d Print sizes of the text, data, and bss portions of a downloaded firmware patch on standard error.
	
	    -f *file* Initialize **layers** with a configuration given by *file*. Each line of *file* is a layer to be created and has the format *x1 y1 x2 y2 commands*, specifying the origin, the opposite corner, and start-up commands. E.g.:
	
	             `10 10 800 240 date; who; exec $SHELL`
	
	    -m *size* Set data part of **xt** packets to maximum *size* (32-252).
	
	    -p Print downloading protocol statistics and a trace of a downloaded firmware patch on standard error.
	
	    -s Report protocol statistics on standard error after exiting **layers**.
	
	    -t Turn on **xt** driver packet tracing and produce a trace dump on standard error after exiting **layers**.

line	**line** Read the next line from standard input and write it to standard output. Exit status is 1 upon *EOF*. Typically used in shell scripts to read from the terminal. *Example* Print the first two lines of output from **who**: `who	(line ; line)`

ln	**ln** [*options*] *sourcename targetname*
	ln [*options*] *sourcenames targetdirectory*
	
	Create pseudonyms (links) for files, allowing them to be accessed by different names. In the first form, link *sourcename* to *targetname*, where *targetname* is usually a new filename. If *targetname* is an existing file, it is overwritten; if *targetname* is an existing directory, a link named *sourcename* is created in that directory. In the second form, create links in *targetdirectory*, each link having the same name as the file specified.
	
	Options
	
	    -f Force the link to occur (don't prompt for overwrite permission).
	
	    -s Create a symbolic link. This lets you link across file systems and also see the name of the link when you run **ls** -l (otherwise there's no way to know the name that a file is linked to).

lock [*options*]

Lock a user's terminal. Request password from user, request again for verification, then lock terminal until password is reentered. **lock** uses the **/etc/default/lock** file, which has two entries:

> DEFLOGOUT = *number*
> MAXLOGOUT = *number*

DEFLOGOUT specifies the default time, in minutes, that a terminal will remain locked before the user is logged out. It can be overridden by *–number*. **MAXLOGOUT** is the maximum number of minutes the user is permitted to lock a terminal. If **DEFLOGOUT** and *–number* are not specified, **MAXLOGOUT** is used.

Options

- number
> Set time limit for **lock** to *number* of minutes instead of system default.

-v   Specifies verbose operation.

lp [*options*] [*files*]

Send *files* to the printer. To send standard input, specify - as one of the *files*.

Options

-c
> Copy *files* to print spooler. If changes are made to *file* while it is still queued for printing, the printout is unaffected (the default behavior).

-d *dest*   Send output to destination printer named *dest*.

-f *form–name* [-d any]
> Print request on preprinted form *form-name*. With -d **any**, request is printed on any printer that has the requested form mounted and can handle all other needs of the print request.

-H *special–handling*
> Print according to the value of *special-handling*: **hold** (notify before printing), **resume** (resume a held request), **immediate** (print next; privileged users only).

-L   Send print job to printer attached to terminal.

-m   Send mail after files are printed.

-n *number*   Specify the *number* of copies to print.

-o *options*   Set one or more printer-specific *options*. Standard options include:

> **nobanner**
> > Omit banner page (separator) from request.
>
> **nofilebreak**
> > Suppress formfeeds between files.

→

cpi=*scaled-decimal-number*
> Print request for "characters per inch" with character pitch set to *scaled-decimal-number* characters per inch. Pitch can also be **pica**, **elite**, or **compressed**.

lpi=*scaled-decimal-number*
> Prints this request for "lines-per-inch" with the line pitch set to *scaled-decimal-number* lines per inch. Cannot be used with -f option.

length=*scaled-decimal-number*
> Print output of request with pages *scaled-decimal-number* lines long; e.g., 11i (inches), 66 (lines).

width=*scaled-decimal-number*
> Print output of request with page-width set to *scaled-decimal-number* columns wide; e.g., 8.5i (inches) 72 (columns).

stty=*stty-option-list*
> Specify a quoted *stty-option-list* of **stty** options.

-P *page–list*
> Print only the page numbers specified in *page-list*.

-q *n*   Print request with priority level *n* (39 = lowest).

-R   Remove file after printing it.

-s   Suppress messages.

-S *name*   Use the named print wheel or character set for printing.

-t *title*   Use *title* on the printout's banner page.

-T *content–type*
> Print request on a printer that can support specified *content-type*.

-w   Write a terminal message after *files* are printed (same as -m if user isn't logged on). Confirm the printing with a message on the user's terminal.

-y *mode*   Print according to locally-defined *modes*.

Examples

Send mail after printing five copies of **report**:

```
lp -n 5 -m report
```

Format and print **thesis**; print **title** too:

```
nroff -ms thesis | lp - title
```

---

lpr

lpr [*files*]

Send *files* to the printer. **lpr** is a link to **lp**. The names may be used interchangeably.

---

lprint [*option*] [*files*]

Send a *file* to a printer attached to a user's terminal. **lprint** uses the file /etc/termcap.

Option

   –   Print from standard input instead of *file*.

lpstat [*options*]
rlpstat *local_printer_name*

Print the **lp** print queue status. **rlpstat** prints information about the status of remote **lp** print service. With options that take a *list* argument, omitting the list produces all information for that option. *list* can be separated by commas or, if enclosed in double quotes, by spaces.

Options

–a [*list*]	Show whether the *list* of printer or class names is accepting requests.
–c [*list*]	Show information about printer classes named in *list*.
–d	Show the default printer destination.
–D	Use after –p to show a brief printer description.
–f [*list*]	Verify that the *list* of forms is known to **lp**.
–l	Use after –f to describe available forms, after –p to show printer configurations, or after –S to describe printers appropriate for the specified character set or print wheel.
–o [*list*]	Show the status of output requests. *list* contains printer names, class names, or request IDs.
–p [*list*]	Show the status of printers named in *list*.
–r	Show whether the print scheduler is on or off.
–s	Summarize the print status (shows almost everything).
–S [*list*]	Verify that the *list* of character sets or print wheels is known to **lp**.
–t	Show all status information (reports everything).
–u [*list*]	Show request status for users on *list*. *list* can be:

user	*user* on local machine.
all	All users on local machine.
host!*user*	*user* on machine *host*.
host!**all**	All users on *host*.
all! *user*	*user* not on local machine.
all!**all**	All users not on local machine.

–v [*list*]	Show device associated with each printer named in *list*.

ls

ls [*options*] [*directories*]

List contents of directories. If no *directories* are given, list the files in the current directory. With one or more *names*, list files contained in a directory *name* or that match a file *name*. *names* can include filename metacharacters. The options let you display a variety of information in different formats. The most useful options include -F, -R, -l, and -s. Some options don't make sense together; e.g., -u and -c.

Related commands

l	List files with full (long) information.
lc	List files in columns.
lf	List files indicating directories, executables, and symbolic links.
lr	List files, recursively listing any subdirectories encountered.
lx	List files in columns, but sorted across the page rather than down the page.

Options

-1	Print one entry per line of output.
-A	List all files, including the normally hidden . files. Does not include . and ..
-a	List all files, including the normally hidden . files.
-b	Show nonprinting characters in octal.
-c	List files by creation/modification time.
-C	List files in columns (the default format).
-d	List only the directory name, not its contents.
-f	Interpret each *name* as a directory.
-F	Flag filenames by appending / to directories, * to executable files, and @ to symbolic links.
-g	Like -l, but omit owner name (show group).
-i	List the inode for each file.
-l	Long format listing (includes permissions, owner, size, modification time, etc.).
-L	List the file or directory referenced by a symbolic link rather than the link itself.
-m	Merge the list into a comma-separated series of names.
-n	Like -l, but use GID and UID numbers instead of owner and group names.
-o	Like -l, but omit group name (show owner).
-p	Mark directories by appending / to them.
-q	Show nonprinting characters as ?.
-r	List files in reverse order (by name or by time).
-R	Recursively list subdirectories as well as current directory.

-s	Print size of the files in blocks.
-t	Sort files according to modification time (newest first).
-u	Sort files according to the file access time.
-x	List files in rows going across the screen.

Examples

List all files in the current directory and their sizes; use multiple columns and mark special files:

```
ls -asCF
```

List the status of directories **/bin** and **/etc**:

```
ls -ld /bin /etc
```

List C source files in the current directory, the oldest first:

```
ls -rt *.c
```

Count the files in the current directory:

```
ls | wc -l
```

machid
machid: i286, iAPX286, i386, i486

Get truth value dependent on processor type.

Syntax

i286	Return true value if machine is a 286.
iAPX286	
	Return true value if machine is a 286.
i386	Return true value if machine is a 386 or fully compatible.
i486	Return true value if machine is a 486 or fully compatible.

Although SCO UNIX does not support these other machines, the commands **vax**, **mc68k**, **pdp11**, **u370**, **u3b**, **u3b15**, **u3b2**, and **u3b5** are all available and work in a similar manner. They will all return a false value.

mail [*options*] [*users*]

Read mail or send mail to other *users*. Type **?** for a summary of commands. The **mail** utility allows you to compose, send receive, forward, and reply to mail. **mail** has two main modes: compose mode, where you create a message, and command mode, where you manage your mail.

→

This section presents **mail** commands, options, and files, grouped in tables. To get you started, here are two of the most basic commands:

To read your mail, type:

    mail

To write a message to *user*, type:

    mail *user*

Compose mode commands

Command	Description
~!	Execute a shell escape from compose mode.
~?	List compose mode escapes.
~b	Add or change the *Bcc:* header.
~c	Add or change the *Cc:* header.
~d	Read in the *dead.letter* file.
~h	Add or change all the headers.
~m/~M	Read a message (indented/non-indented) into current message.
~q	Abort current message composition.
~r	Append file to current message.
~s	Add or change `Subject:` header.
~t	Add names to `To:` list.

Command mode commands

Command	Description
!	Execute a shell command.
alias (a)	Create alias lists.
delete (d)	Delete message.
dp	Delete current message and display next one.
edit (e)	Edit message.
exit (x)	Exit mail without updating folder.
file (fi)	Switch folders.
folder (fold)	Access messages saved in a file.
forward (f,F)	Forward message (indented/non-indented).
headers (h)	List message headers at current prompt.
headers (h+)	Move forward one window of headers.
headers (h-)	Move back one window of headers.
hold (ho)	Hold messages in system mailbox.
lpr (l)	Send message to lineprinter.
mail (m)	Read mail.
mail *user*(m)	Compose message to *user*.
preserve (pr)	Preserve messages in system mailbox.
print (p)	Display non-deleted messages.
quit (q)	Exit mail and update folder.
reply (r)	Send mail to author only.

Command	Description
Reply (R)	Send mail to all on distribution list.
save (s)	Save message to folder.
set (se)	Set **mail** options.
shell (sh)	Enter a new shell.
undelete (u)	Restore deleted message.
unset (uns)	Unset **mail** options.
visual (v)	Edit message with $VISUAL.
write (w)	Write message to file.

Related commands

The following are user commands that relate to e-mail:

Command	Description
cnvtmbox	Convert old-style mailboxes to MMDF format.
mail	Send message or enter **mail** utility.
rcvalert	Mail receipt notification.
rcvfile	Insert message into named file.
rcvprint	Print message automatically.
rcvtrip	Send automatic response to message.
rsend	Redistribute mail.

mail options

These options are used inside of the .mailrc file.

Option	Description
askcc	Prompt for carbon copy recipients.
asksub	Prompt for `Subject:` line.
chron	Display messages in chronological order, most recent last.
folder	Define directory to hold mail folders.
hold	Keep message in system mailbox upon quitting.
mchron	Display messages in chronological order, most recent first.
prompt	Set prompt to a different string.
screen	Set screen size.

Special files

File	Description
calendar	Contains reminders that the operating system mails to you.
.maildelivery	Mail delivery configuration file.
.mailrc	Mail configuration file.
triplog	Keeps track of your automatic response recipients.
tripnote	Contains automatic message.

man

/usr/bin/man [*options*] [*section*] [*title*]

Display information from the on-line reference manuals. **man** locates and prints the named*title* from the designated reference *section*.

Options

-a   Show all pages matching *title*.

-b   Leave blank lines in output.

-c   Invoke **col**.

-d*dir* Specify directory *dir* to be added to the search path for entries.

-p*pager*
      Select paging program *pager* to display the entry.

-T*term*
      Format the entry and pass the given *term* value to the processing program, then print it on the standard output.

-t*proc* If an unprocessed manual page is available, pass it to *proc* for formatting. *proc* can be any command script in **/usr/man/bin** or an absolute filename of a text processing program elsewhere on the system.

-w   Print pathnames of entries on standard output.

Section names

Some of the more commonly-used manual sections are:

ADM   System administration

C   Commands

M   Miscellaneous

F   File formats

HW   Hardware dependent

S   Subroutines and libraries

CP   Programming commands

DOS   DOS subroutines and libraries

LOCAL Local utilities for your system

---

mcart

mcart *command* [*device*]

Magnetic tape maintenance program. **mcart** sends commands to, and receives status from, the Irwin tape driver. The Irwin driver has a special default file, **/etc/default/mcconfig**, containing special driver options. If a device name is specified on the command line, it overrides the default device. In addition, the Irwin driver uses a daemon startup program, **/etc/mcdaemon**, to provide background ECC encode/decode. **mcart** is automatically invoked by **tape** when options specific to the Irwin driver are used. For more information, see the **tape** command.

Commands

format Format the tape cartridge. If no argument is given, the entire tape will be formatted.

drive Display information about the Irwin driver and the tape drive. Following is an example display:

```
Special file: /dev/rctmini
Driver version: 1.0.6a
Drive type: 285XL
Drive firmware: A0
Controller tyep: SYSFDC
Unit select (0-3): 3
```

info Display Irwin cartridge information:

```
Cartridge state: Formatted
Cartridge format: 145
Write protect slider position: RECORD
```

capacity

Cartridge capacity in 512-byte blocks.

kapacity

Cartridge capacity in 1024-byte blocks. **capacity** and **kapacity** give the total usable data storage capacity of a formatted tape cartridge.

---

mesg [*options*]

Change the ability of other users to send **write** messages to your terminal. With no options, display the permission status.

Options

n Forbid **write** messages.

y Allow **write** messages (the default).

---

mkdir [*options*] *directories*

Create one or more *directories*. You must have write permission in the parent directory in order to create a directory. See also **rmdir**.

Options

-e For historical compatibility; toggles use of EUID and EGID instead of RUID and RGID.

-m *mode* Set the access *mode* for new directories.

-p Create intervening parent directories if they don't exist.

$\rightarrow$

mkdir
←
	Examples
	Create a read-only directory named **personal**:
	
	    `mkdir -m 444 personal`
	
	The following sequence:
	
	    `mkdir work; cd work`
	    `mkdir junk; cd junk`
	    `mkdir questions; cd ../..`
	
	could be accomplished by typing this:
	
	    `mkdir -p work/junk/questions`

mkfifo	**mkfifo** *path* . . . Make a FIFO special file—a first-in first-out pipe named by *path*. The new FIFO has the permissions 666. **mkfifo** returns exit code 0 if all FIFO special files were created successfully; otherwise, it prints a diagnostic and returns non-zero.

mknod	**/etc/mknod** *name* [*options*] *major minor*
	/etc/mknod *name* [*options*]
	
	Build special files. **mknod** creates a directory entry and corresponding inode for a special file. *name* specifies name of the entry; *major* specifies major device type; *minor* specifies minor device, which may be either decimal or octal. Except for the -**p** option, only superusers can use this command.
	
	Options
	
	  -b Indicates special file is block-type (disks, tape). For use in first form of **mknod** syntax only.
	
	  -c Indicates special file is character-type. For use in first form of **mknod** syntax only.
	
	  -p Create named pipes.
	
	  -s Create semaphores.
	
	  -m Create shared data (memory).

more	**more** [*options*] [*files*] Display the named *files* on a terminal, one screenful at a time. After each screen is displayed, press RETURN to display the next line or press the spacebar to display the next screenful. Press **h** for help with additional commands, **q** to quit, **/** to search, or **:n** to go to the next file. **more** can also be invoked using the name **page**. *Options* -c Page through the file by clearing each window instead of scrolling. This is sometimes faster.

-d	Display the prompt Hit space to continue, Del to abort.
-f	Count logical rather than screen lines. Useful when long lines wrap past the width of the screen.
-l	Ignore formfeed (CTRL-L) characters. Cause carriage return to be of the form CTRL-M.
-r	Force display of control characters, in the form ^x.
-s	Squeeze; display multiple blank lines as one.
-u	Suppress underline characters and backspace (CTRL-H).
-v	Display non-interpreted control characters as ^C, where C is the corresponding printable ASCII character.
-w	Wait for a user keystroke before exiting.
-n	Use n lines for each window (default is a full screen).
+num	Begin displaying at line number num.
+/pattern	Begin displaying two lines before pattern.

Examples

Page through *file* in "clear" mode, and display prompts:

```
more -cd file
```

Format **doc** to the screen, removing underlines:

```
nroff doc | more -u
```

View the man page for the **grep** command; begin near the word "BUGS" and compress extra white space:

```
man grep | more +/BUGS -s
```

/etc/mount [*options*] [*special*] [*resource*] [*directory*]
/etc/umount [*special*] [*resource*] [*directory*]

NFS/NIS command. Mount and unmount filesystems. **mount** announces to the system that *special*, a block special device, or *resource*, a remote resource, is available to users from the mount point *directory*. *directory* must exist already; it becomes the name of the root of the newly mounted *special* or *resource*. When invoked with arguments, **mount** adds an entry to the table of mounted devices, **/etc/mnttab**. If invoked with no arguments, **mount** prints the entire mount table. If **mount** is invoked with any of the partial argument lists *special*, *resource*, or *directory*, it will search **/etc/default/filesys** to fill in the missing arguments.

umount removes the entry to the table of mounted devices. It announces to the system that the previously mounted *special* or *resource* is to be made unavailable. If invoked with *special* or *directory*, **umount** will search **/etc/default/filesys** to fill in the missing

$\rightarrow$

mount ←	arguments. **umount** fails if *special* or *resource* are either not mounted or busy.

Options

- **-c** Remote reads and writes should not be cached in the local buffer pool.

- **-f**[*fstyp*]

  Indicates that *fstyp* is the filesystem to be mounted. If this argument is omitted, it defaults to the root *fstyp*. If *fstyp* is NFS, then any NFS options may be added after the *fstyp*, separated by commas. Available NFS options are:

bg	Background this mount.
noac	Don't cache attributes. Note: Use of this option will drastically cut performance on the filesystem being mounted.
nosuid	Ignore **setuid** and **setgid** bits during exec.
port=n	Set server IP port number to n.
retrans=n	Set number of NFS retransmissions to n. Default is 5.
rsize=n	Set read buffer size to n bytes.
soft	Return error if server does not respond.
timeo=n	Set initial NFS timeout to n tenths of a second. Default is 300 seconds.
wsize=n	Set write buffer size to n bytes.

- **-r** Indicates the *special* or *resource* is to be mounted read-only.

- **-v** Verbose—display a message indicating each filesystem being mounted.

---

mpstat

mpstat [*options*]

Display multiprocessor CPU load status. **mpstat** displays system processor activity information on the screen, in the form of a Multiprocessor Activity window, for each of the processors installed on your system. **mpstat** only comes with an MPX system; it is not part of the standard operating system.

Options

- **-b** Use current screen colors.

- **-c** *CPU*

  Lock **mpstat** on processor number *CPU*. Cannot be used with **-x** option.

- **-h** Hide statistics of locked CPU.

- **-o** Run Options window.

- **-V** Display Corollary **mpstat** version number.

- **-x** Allow **mpstat** to free run on any CPU (default). Cannot be used with **-c** option.

CPU Activity Display Window

The CPU Activity Display Window displays CPU activity. The percentage of kernel code running, the percentage of user code running, and the percentage of CPU idle time are indicated as follows:

- Dark shaded block or : specifies one unit (5%) of kernel code.

- Light shaded block or # specifies one unit (5%) of user code.

- The amount of space within the CPU Activity Display Window indicates the percentage of CPU idle time (one space equals 5%).

---

mscreen [*options*]

Serial multiscreens utility. **mscreen** allows a serial terminal to have multiple login screens similar to the **multiscreen** console. It is designed to be invoked from the **.profile** or **.login** files. There must be an entry for the terminal type in **/etc/mscreencap**.

Options

-n *number*
> Select number of serial multiscreens desired up to the maximum defined for the terminal type.

-s
> Silent mode—suppress startup messages and screen switch messages on dumb terminals.

-t
> Disable transparent tty checking.

---

mv [*option*] *sources target*

Move or rename files and directories. **mv** works as follows:

Source	Target	Result
File	*name*	Rename file as *name*.
File	Existing file	Overwrite existing file with source file.
Directory	*name*	Rename directory as *name*.
Directory	Existing directory	Move directory to be a sub-directory of existing directory.
One or more files	Existing directory	Move files to directory.

Option

-f
> Force the move, even if *target* file exists; suppress messages about restricted access modes.

---

nawk	**nawk** [*options*] [*'program'*] [*files*] [*variable=value*] In SCO UNIX, nawk is linked to awk. See Section 12, *The Awk Scripting Language*, for more details and command-line options.

newform	**newform** [*options*] *files*
	
	Format *files* according to the options specified. Options can appear more than once and can be interspersed between *files* (except for -s, which must appear first).
	
	Options
	
	-a[*n*] Append *n* characters to the end of each line or, if *n* isn't specified, append characters until each line has the length specified by -l.
	
	-b[*n*] Delete *n* characters from beginning of each line or, if *n* isn't specified, delete characters until each line has the length specified by -l.
	
	-c*m* Change prefix/append character to **k** (default is a space).
	
	-e[*n*] Same as -b, but delete from the end. -c must precede -a or -p.
	
	-f Display *tabspec* format used by last -o option.
	
	-i'*tabspec*'
	    Expand tabs to spaces using *tabspec* conversion (default is eight spaces); *tabspec* is one of the options listed under **tabs**.
	
	-l[*n*] Use line length *n* (default is 72). If -l is not specified, default line length is 80. -l usually precedes other options that modify line length (-b, -e, -c, -a, or -p).
	
	-o'*tabspec*'
	    Turn spaces into tabs using *tabspec* conversion.
	
	-p[*n*] Same as -a, but pad beginning of line.
	
	-s Strip leading characters from each line (up to and including first tab); the first seven characters are moved to the end of the line (without the tab). All lines must contain at least one tab.
	
	Example
	Remove sequence numbers from a COBOL program:
	
	`newform -11 -b7 file`

news	**news** [*options*] [*item_files*] Consult the news directory for information on current events. With no arguments, **news** prints all current *item_files*. Items usually reside in **/usr/news**. This is *not* an interface for USENET news.

Options

-a	Print all news items, whether current or not.
-n	Print names of news items, but not their contents.
-s	Report the number of current news items.

---

nl [*option*] *command* [*arguments*]

Execute a *command* and *arguments* with lower priority (i.e., be "nice" to other users).

Option

-*n*	Run *command* with a niceness of *n* (1-19); default is 10. Higher *n* means lower priority. A privileged user can raise priority by specifying a negative *n* (e.g., −5).

---

nl [*options*] [*file*]

Add line numbers to a file. Numbering resets to 1 at the start of each page. A page is composed of header, body, and footer sections. The start of each page section is signaled by input lines containing nothing but section delimiters:

```
header    \:\:\:
body      \:\:
footer    \:
```

Empty sections are valid. Different line-numbering options are available within each section. The default scheme is no numbering for headers and footers.

Options

-b*type*	Number lines according to *type*. Values are:
	a — All lines.
	n — No lines.
	t — Text lines only (the default).
	p"*exp*" — Lines containing *exp* only.
-f*type*	Like -b but number footer (default *type* is n).
-h*type*	Like -b but number header (default *type* is n).
-i*n*	Increment each line number by *n* (default is 1).
-l*n*	Count *n* consecutive blank lines as one line.
-n*format*	Set line number *format*. Values are:
	ln — Left justify, omit leading zeros.
	rn — Right justify, omit leading zeros (default).
	rz — Right justify.
-p	Do not reset numbering at start of pages.
-s*c*	Separate text from line number with character(s) *c* (default is a tab).

→

---

nl
←

-v*n*	Number each page starting at *n* (default is 1).
-w*n*	Use *n* columns to show line number (default is 6).

Examples

List the current directory, numbering files as 1), 2), etc.:

```
ls | nl -w3 -s') '
```

Number C source code and save it:

```
nl prog.c > print_prog
```

Number only lines that begin with #include:

```
nl -bp"^#include" prog.c
```

---

nohup

nohup *command* [*arguments*]

Continue to execute the named *command* and optional command *arguments* after you log out (make command immune to hangups; i.e., no hangup). In the C shell, **nohup** is built in. In the Bourne shell, **nohup** allows output redirection; output goes to **nohup.out** by default.

---

on

on [*options*] *host command* [*argument*] . . .

NFS/NIS command. Execute a command remotely. All environment variables are passed, and the current working directory is preserved. User must have an account on the remote machine.

Options

-i	Interactive mode—use remote echoing and special character processing.
-n	No input. When remote program reads from standard input, it gets end-of-file instead of standard input of **on**.
-d	Debug mode. Print out messages as work is being done.

---

pack

pack [*option*] *files*

Compact each *file* and place the result in *file*.z. The original file is replaced. To restore packed *files* to their original form, see **pcat** and **unpack**.

Option

| - | Print number of times each byte is used, relative frequency, and byte code. |

---

page

page [*options*] [*files*]

Same as **more**.

passwd [*options*] [*user*]

Create or change a password associated with a *user* name. Only the owner or a privileged user may change a password. Owners need not specify their *user* name.

Option

- **-s**   Display password information:
  1. *user* name.
  2. Password status (**NP** for no password, **PS** for password, **LK** for locked).
  3. The last time the password was changed (in *mm/dd/yy* format).
  4. Number of days that must pass before *user* can rechange the password.
  5. Number of days before the password expires.
  6. Number of days prior to expiration that *user* is warned of impending expiration.

Options (privileged users only)

- **-a**   Use with **-s** to display password information for all users. *user* should not be supplied.
- **-d**   Delete password; *user* is no longer prompted for one.
- **-f**   Force expiration of *user*'s password; *user* must change password at next login.
- **-l**   Lock *user*'s password; mutually exclusive with **-d**.
- **-n**   Set item 4 of *user*'s password information. Usually used with **-x**.
- **-r** *retries*

  Up to *retries* attempts may be made to choose a new password for *user*.
- **-u**   Remove locks applied to *user*.
- **-w**   Set item 6 for *user*.
- **-x**   Set item 5 for *user*. Use –1 to disable password aging, 0 to force expiration like **-f**.

---

paste [*options*] *files*

Merge corresponding lines of one or more *files* into vertical columns, separated by a tab. See also **cut**, **join**, **newform**, and **pr**.

Options

- **-**   Replace a filename with the standard input.
- **-d'***char***'**   Separate columns with *char* instead of a tab. *char* can be any regular character or the following escape sequences:

\n	Newline
\t	Tab
\\	Backslash
\0	Empty string

---

paste
←
	Note: You can separate columns with different characters by supplying more than one *char*.
	
	  -s Merge subsequent lines from one file.
	
	Examples
	
	Create a three-column *file* from files *x, y,* and *z:*
	
	    paste *x y z* > file
	
	List users in two columns:
	
	    who
		paste - -
		
		Merge each pair of lines into one line:
		
		    paste -s -d"\t\n" list

---

pcat	**pcat** *files* Display (as with **cat**) one or more packed *files*. See also **pack** and **unpack**.

---

pcpio	**pcpio -o** [*options*] **pcpio -i** [*options*] [*pattern* ...] **pcpio -p** [*options*] *directory* Copy file archives in and out—produce and read files which conform to the **cpio Archive/Interchange File Format** specified in *IEEE STD. 1003.1-1988.* **pcpio** exits with one of the following values: 0 if all input files were copied, 2 if errors were encountered in copying or accessing files or directories. **pcpio -i** (copy in) utility extracts files from the standard input, assumed to be the product of a previous **pcpio -o** (copy out). Only files with names matching *pattern* are selected. Default for *patterns* is selecting all files. **pcpio -p** (pass) utility reads the standard input to obtain a list of pathnames of files that are conditionally created and copied into the destination *directory* based on options described below. The following restrictions apply to **pcpio**: • Pathnames are restricted to 256 characters. • Appropriate privileges are required to copy special files. • Blocks are reported in 512-byte quantities. **Options** -a Reset access times of input files after they've been copied. Can only be used with **pcpio -o** or **pcpio -i**.

-B	Input/output to be blocked 5120 bytes to the record. Can only be used with **pcpio -o** or **pcpio -i** for data directed to or from character special files.
-c	Write header information in ASCII characters for portability. Can only be used with **pcpio -o** or **pcpio -i**.
-d	Creates directories as needed. Can only be used with **pcpio -o** or **pcpio -p**.
-f	Copy in all files except those in *patterns*. Can only be used with **pcpio -i**.
-L	Follow symbolic links.
-l	Whenever possible, link files rather than copy them. Can only be used with **pcpio -p**.
-m	Retain previous modification times. Can only be used with **pcpio -i** or **pcpio -p**.
-r	Rename files interactively. Should only be used with **pcpio -i** or **pcpio -p**.
-t	Print a table of contents of the input. Can only be used with **pcpio -i**.
-u	Copy files unconditionally. Can only be used with **pcpio -i** or **pcpio -p**.
-v	Verbose. With **pcpio -i**, this option cause names of affected files to be printed. With **-t**, it provides a detailed listing.

pg [*options*] [*files*]

Display the named *files* on a terminal, one page at a time. After each screen is displayed, you are prompted to display the next page by pressing the RETURN key. Press **h** for help with additional commands; press **q** to quit. See also **more** and **page**.

Options

-c	Clear screen (same as **-c** of **more**).
-e	Do not pause at the end of a file.
-f	Do not split long lines.
-n	Issue a **pg** command without waiting for a carriage return (**more** works this way).
-p*str*	Use string *str* for the command prompt. The special variable %d displays the page number.
-s	Display messages in standout mode (reverse video).
-*n*	Use *n* lines for each window (default is a full screen).
+*num*	Begin displaying at line number *num*.
+/*pat*	Begin displaying at first line containing pattern *pat*.

$\rightarrow$

Example

```
pg -p 'Page %d :' file
```

ping

ping [*options*] *host*

TCP/IP command. Indicate whether a remote host can be reached. **ping** sends ICMP ECHO_REQUEST packets to network hosts. ECHO_REQUEST datagrams (pings) have an IP and ICMP header, followed by a *structtimeval* and an arbitrary number of pad bytes used to fill out the packet. **ping** is intended for use in network testing, measurement, and management. Because of the load it can impose on the network, it is unwise to use **ping** during normal operations or from automated scripts.

Options

-c *count*
> Stop after sending (and receiving) *count* ECHO_RESPONSE packets.

-d
> Set SO_DEBUG option on socket being used.

-f
> Flood ping—output packets as fast as they come back, or 100 times per second, whichever is more. This can be very hard on a network and should be used with caution.

-i *wait*
> Wait *wait* seconds between sending each packet. Default is to wait one second between each packet. This option is incompatible with the -f option.

-l *preload*
> Send *preload* number of packets as fast as possible before falling into normal mode of behavior.

-n
> Numeric output only. No attempt will be made to look up symbolic names for host addresses.

-p *pattern*
> Specify up to 16 pad bytes to fill out packet sent. This is useful for diagnosing data-dependent problems in a network. For example, -p ff will cause the sent packet to be filled with all ones.

-q
> Quiet output—nothing is displayed except the summary lines at startup time and when finished.

-R
> Set the IP record route option, which will store the route of the packet inside the IP header. The contents of the record route will only be printed if the -v option is given and will only be set on return packets if the target host preserves the record route option across echos, or the -l option is given.

-r
> Bypass the normal routing tables and send directly to a host on an attached network.

-s *packetsize*
>Specify number of data bytes to be sent. Default is 56, which translates into 64 ICMP data bytes when combined with the eight bytes of ICMP header data.

-v
>Verbose—list ICMP packets received other than ECHO_RESPONSE.

ps [*options*]

Report on active processes. In options, *list* arguments should either be separated by commas or put in double quotes. In comparing the amount of output produced, note that -e > -d > -a and -l > -f.

Options

-a
>List all processes except group leaders and processes not associated with a terminal.

-d
>List all processes except session leaders.

-e
>List all processes.

-f
>Produce a full listing.

-g*list*
>List data only for specified *list* of group leader ID numbers (i.e., processes with same ID and group ID).

-l
>Produce a long listing.

-n*list*
>Use the alternate *list* of names (default is **/unix**).

-p*list*
>List data only for process IDs in *list*.

-t*list*
>List data only for terminals in *list* (e.g., **tty1**).

-u*list*
>List data only for usernames in *list*.

pstat [*options*] [*file*]

Print system facts. **pstat** interprets the contents of certain system tables, searching for the tables in either *file*, if given, or in **/dev/mem** and **/dev/kmem**. Without options, **pstat** prints information for all three tables: inode table, process table, and file table.

Options

-a
>Describe all process slots rather than just active ones. Must be used with -**p**.

-f
>Print the open file table with the following headings:
>
>| | |
>|---|---|
>| LOC | Core location of this table entry |
>| FLAGS | Miscellaneous stream state variables |
>| CNT | Number of processes that know this open file |
>| INO | Location of inode table entry for this file |
>| OFFS | File offset, see **lseek**. |

-i
>Print inode table with the following headings:
>
>| | |
>|---|---|
>| LOC | Core location of this table entry |
>| FLAGS | Miscellaneous state variables |

$\rightarrow$

CNT	Number of open file-table entries for this inode
DEVICE	Major and minor device number of filesystem in which this inode resides.
INO	I-number within device
FS	Filesystem type. 1 indicates UNIX.
MODE	Mode bits
NLK	Number of links to this inode
UID	User ID of owner
SIZE/DEV	Number of bytes in an ordinary file, or major and minor device of special file

-n *namelist*
> Use file *namelist* as an alternate namelist in place of /unix.

-p
> Print process table for active processes with the following headings:

LOC	Core location of this table entry
S	Run state
F	Miscellaneous state variables, ORed together
PRI	Scheduling priority, see **nice**
SIG	Signals received (signals 1-16 coded in bits 0-15).
UID	Real user ID
TIM	Time resident in seconds; times over 127 coded as 127.
CPU	Weighted integral of CPU time, for the scheduler
NI	Nice level, see **nice**.
PGRP	Process number of root of process group
PID	Process ID number
PPID	Process ID number of parent process
ADDR 1, ADDR 2	
	If in core, the physical page frame numbers of the u-area of the process. If swapped out, the position in the swap area is measured in multiples of 1024 bytes.
WCHAN	Wait channel number of a waiting process
LINK	Link pointer in list of runnable processes
INODP	Pointer to location of shared inode
CLKT	Countdown for **alarm**, measured in seconds

-s *swapfile*
> Use *swapfile* as the swapfile, in place of /dev/swap.

-u *ubase1 ubase2*
> Print information about a user process. *ubase1* and *ubase2* are the physical page frame numbers of the u-area of the process. They may be obtained by using the long listing (-1 option) of **ps**. If *ubase1* and *ubase2* do not correspond to a valid u-page, **pstat** exits with an error.

-U *ubase1 ubase2*
     Same as -**u**, but gets u-area from the swap device.

---

ptar [*options* [*modifiers*]] *device block* [*filename* ...]

Process tape archives. **ptar** reads and writes archive files which conform to the **Archive/Interchange File Format** specified in *IEEE Std. 1003.1-1988*. If no *filename* is given, the entire contents of the archive are extracted.

Options

-c   Create new archive; writing begins at beginning of archive instead of after last file.

-r   Write named file to end of archive.

-t   List names of all files in archive.

-u   Add named files to archive if they are not already there or have been modified since last written into archive. This implies the -**r** option.

-x   Extract named files from archive. If a named file matches a directory whose contents had been written onto the archive, that directory is recursively extracted.

Modifiers to options

-b   Use next argument on command line as blocking factor for tape records. Default is 1; maximum is 20. This option should only be used with raw magnetic tape archives.

-f   Use next argument on command line as name of archive instead of using default, which is usually a tape drive. If - is specified as filename, write to standard output or read from standard input. Thus, **ptar** can be used as head or tail of a pipeline.

-L   Follow symbolic links.

-l   Report if all links to files being archived cannot be resolved. If -**l** is not specified, no error messages are written to standard output. This modifier is only valid with the -**c**, -**r**, and -**u** options.

-m   Do not restore modification times. Modification time of file will be time of extraction. This modifier is invalid with the -**t** option.

-o   Cause extracted files to take on user and group identifier of user running the program rather than those on the archive. This modifier is invalid with the -**x** option.

-v   Operate verbosely—print name of each file processed, preceded by option letter. With -**t** option, -**v** gives more information about archive entries than just the name.

$\rightarrow$

ptar ←	-w Print action to be taken, followed by name of file, then wait for user confirmation. If word beginning with **y** is given, action is performed; any other input means "no." This modifier is invalid with the -t option.

purge

purge [*options*] [*files*] . . .

Overwrite specified *files*, either those specified on the command line or those listed in a policy file maintained by the system administrator. *files* are regular, directory, or special files. Some block special files and character special files can be overwritten, as can disks, floppies, and magnetic tapes. The console, ttys, printers, and other "infinite output" devices cannot be purged with this command.

Options

-f   Do not warn about files which are not present or are inaccessible.

-m *num*
    Overwrite each file *num* times.

-o   Overwrite other (non-system and non-user) files and filesystems. This purges all entries in the policy file which are not of type **system** or **user**. This flag has no -t equivalent.

-r   Recursively purge directories. Without this option, no action is taken upon directories.

-s   Overwrite files and devices designated as "system" in the policy file.

-t *type* Overwrite files identified in policy file as being part of group *type*.

-u   Overwrite files and devices designated as "user" in the policy file.

-v   Verbose operation—list name of each file as it is overwritten.

-z   Write binary zeroes to system memory, including memory buffers of intelligent devices. This will close down the system immediately and should only be done from single-user mode, or when no users are logged on. Only the superuser may use this option.

pwd

pwd

Print the full pathname of the current working directory. Note: The built-in versions **pwd** (Bourne and Korn shells) and **dirs** (C shell) are faster, so you might want to define the following C-shell alias:

```
alias pwd dirs -l
```

random [*option*] [*scale*]

Generate a random number on standard output and return the number as an exit value. By default, the number is either 0 or 1. If *scale* is given a value between 1 and 255, the range of the random value is from 0 to *scale*. If *scale* is greater than 255, an error message is printed. If error occurs, **random** returns an exit value of 0.

Option

-s   Silent—random number returned as an exit value but not printed on standard output.

rcp [*options*] *file1 file2*
rcp [*options*] *file* ... *directory*

TCP/IP command. Copy files between two machines. Each *file* or *directory* is either a remote filename of the form *rhost:path*, or a local filename.

Options

-p   Preserve modification times and modes of the source files.

-r   If any of the source files are directories, **rcp** copies each subtree rooted at that name.

/usr/bin/rcvalert [*size*]

Mail receipt notification. **rcvalert** displays a line of mail header information on the screen when a letter is received. *size* specifies the size of the message. **rcvalert** is invoked by MMDF and is run by inserting a pipe entry to it in the .**maildelivery** file in your home directory.

Example

The following entry in the .**maildelivery** file invokes **rcvalert**:

```
*    -    pipe   R    rcvalert    $(size)
```

/usr/bin/rcvfile *directory* [*options*]

Insert message into named file. **rcvfile** examines the Subject: field of a mail message and stores the message in a file if the Subject: line contains the **rcvfile** keyword as the first word in the line. The destination filename is created by concatenating the **directory** value, a slash (/), and the filename given in the subject

→

rcvfile
←
	field after the **rcvfile** keyword. **rcvfile** is invoked by MMDF and is run by inserting a pipe entry to it in the .**maildelivery** file in your home directory.
	
	Options
	   -l*logfile*
	        Set the *logfile* where a record of **rcvfile** activity is made.
	   -m Create any missing directories in pathname of file to be created.
	
	Examples
	   A typical entry in .**maildelivery** is:
	
	       `subject  rcvfile  pipe  A  rcvfile`
	
	   or
	
	       `Addr  user=file  pipe  A  rcvfile`

rcvprint	**/usr/bin/rcvprint**
	
	Print message automatically. **rcvprint** pipes the body of the message into a program that prints the message on a line printer. **rcvfile** tries a variety of different programs until it finds one that will execute, waits to see how the program coped, then reports back to the local channel. **rcvalert** is invoked by MMDF, and is run by inserting a pipe entry to it in the .**maildelivery** file in your home directory.
	
	Example
	   A typical entry in .**maildelivery** is:
	
	       `subject  printer  pipe  A  rcvprint`

rcvtrip	**/usr/bin/rcvtrip** [*option*] [*addresss*]
	
	Notify mail sender that recipient is away. **rcvtrip** is invoked by MMDF. To use **rcvtrip**, put the following line in your .**maildelivery** file:
	
	       `*  -  pipe  R  rcvtrip  $(sender)`
	
	You can also place a custom reply message in a file named *tripnote*. You should create an empty file *triplog* (see below).
	
	Option
	   -d Extensive output is generated for debugging purposes.
	
	Files
	   $HOME/*tripnote*
	        Contains a reply message to be sent to those sending you mail.

SCO UNIX in a Nutshell

$HOME/_triplog_

    Contains a list of who sent a message, subject of message, when it arrived, and if a response was sent.

$HOME/_logfile_

    If it exists, becomes the output file for logging diagnostic information.

$HOME/_.alter_egos_

    Optional file composed of _user@domain_ lines for all addresses to be considered "you". This is needed if you have multiple hosts forwarding their mail to you.

$HOME/.maildelivery

    Mail delivery specification file.

Example

To enable use of **rcvtrip**, put the following line in your **.maildelivery** file:

```
*    -    pipe  A   rcvtrip  $(sender)
```

---

rdist [_options_] [_name..._]
rdist [options]

TCP/IP command. Remote file distribution client program. **rdist** maintains identical copies of files over multiple hosts. It reads commands from a _distfile_ to direct the updating of files and/or directories. _distfile_ is specified either with the -**f** option, the -**c** option, or with -, in which case standard input is used.

Options

    -b   Perform a binary comparison and update files if they differ.

    -c _name_ [_login@_] _host_[:_dest_]

        Interpret ([_login@_]_host_[:_dest_]) as a small _distfile_.

    -d _var=value_

        Define _var_ to have _value_. This option defines or overrides variable definitions in the _distfile_.

    -f _distfile_

        Use specified _distfile_.

    -h   Follow symbolic links.

    -i   Ignore unresolved links.

    -m _host_

        Limit which machines are to be updated.

    -n   Print commands without executing them.

    -q   Quiet mode—suppress files printing to standard output.

    -R   Remove extraneous files.

    -v   Verify that files are up-to-date on all hosts.

    -w   Whole mode—whole filename is appended to the destination directory name.

$\rightarrow$

rdist ←	-y Younger mode—do not update files that are younger than the master copy.

---

remote

remote [*options*] *machine command* [*arguments*]

Execute commands on a remote system. **remote** is a limited networking facility that permits execution of UNIX commands across serial lines. A command line consisting of *command* and any blank-separated *arguments* is executed on the remote *machine*. A machine's name is located in the file **/etc/systemid**.

Options

    -        Use standard input for *command* on the remote *machine*. Standard input comes from the local host and not from the remote *machine*.

    -f *file*   Use specified *file* as standard input for *command* on the remote *machine*. *file* exists on the local host and not on the remote *machine*.

    -m   Mail user to report completion of *command*. By default, mail reports only errors.

    -u *user*
           Any mail goes to named *user* on *machine*.

Example

The following command executes an **ls** command on the directory **/tmp** of the machine *machine1*:

```
remote machine1 ls /tmp
```

---

resend

resend [*options*] *addresses*

Redistribute mail using the Resent- notation. **resend** takes as input a standard mail message, adding the various Resent- components to it, then handing it over to **submit**. The usual method of operation is to pipe a message into **resend** and supply the addresses to resend the message to on the command line.

Options

    -r   Error returns for this message not required.

    -w   Enables you to follow delivery attempt. **submit** and its children will print out what they are doing.

    --*subargs*
           Any argument starting with -- is passed directly to **submit** after losing the --.

    -t *addresses*
           Breaks up block of *addresses* onto several Resent-To: lines. Put this option after the *addresses* argument on the command line.

-c *addresses*
> Builds up a list of `Resent-Cc:` addresses. Put this option after the *addresses* argument on the command line.

rksh [*arguments*]

Restricted version of **ksh** (the Korn shell), used in secure environments. **rksh** prevents you from changing out of the directory or from redirecting output.

rlogin *rhost* [*options*]

TCP/IP command—remote login. **rlogin** connects the terminal on the current local host system to the remote host system *rhost*. The remote terminal type is the same as your local terminal type. The terminal or window size is also copied to the remote system if the server supports it.

Options

-8   Allow an eight-bit input data path at all times.
-L   Allow **rlogin** session to be run without any output post-processing.
-e*c*   Specify escape character *c*.
-l *username*
> Specify a different *username* for the remote login. Default is the same as your local username.

rm [*options*] *files*

Delete one or more *files*. To remove a file, you must have write permission in the directory that contains the file, but you need not have permission on the file itself. If you do not have write permission on the file, you will be prompted (**y** or **n**) to override.

Options

-f   Remove write-protected files without prompting.
-i   Prompt for **y** (remove the file) or **n** (do not remove the file).
-r   If *file* is a directory, remove the entire directory and all its contents, including subdirectories. Be forewarned: use of this option can be dangerous.
--   Mark the end of options (**rm** still accepts -, the old form). Use this when you need to supply a filename beginning with -.

/usr/bin/rmb

Filter to reduce blank lines in a file. Any series of blank lines greater than two will be reduced down to two lines.

rmdir	**rmdir** [*options*] *directories*
	Delete the named *directories* (the name itself, not the contents). *directories* are deleted from the parent directory and must be empty (if not, **rm -r** can be used instead). See also **mkdir**.
	Options
	-p Remove *directories* and any intervening parent directories that become empty as a result; useful for removing subdirectory trees.
	-s Suppress standard error messages caused by -p.
rsh	**rsh**
	Restricted version of **sh** (the Bourne shell) that is intended to be used where security is important. **rsh** prevents you from changing out of the directory or from redirecting output. For more information, see Section 5, *The Bourne Shell and Korn Shell*.
ruptime	**ruptime** [*options*]
	TCP/IP command—show host status of local machines. These status lines are formed from packets broadcast by each host on the network once a minute. Machines for which no status report has been received for five minutes are shown as being down.
	Options
	-l Sort listing by load average.
	-t Sort listing by uptime.
	-r Reverse sort order.
	-u Sort listing by number of users.
rusers	**rusers** [*options*] [*host*...]
	NFS/NIS command—list who is logged in on remote machines (RPC version). **rusers** produces output similar to the **who** command. When *host* arguments are given, **rusers** will only query the list of specified hosts. A remote host will only respond if it is running the **rusersd** daemon. Broadcasting does not work through gateways (this is a bug).
	Options
	-a Give a report for a machine even if no users are logged on.
	-h Sort alphabetically by hostname.
	-i Sort by idle time.
	-l Give a longer listing in the style of **who**.
	-u Sort by number of users.

rwall [options] hostname

NFS/NIS command—write to all users over a network. **rwall** reads a message from standard input until end-of-file. It then sends this message, preceded by the line Broadcast Message . . . , to all users logged in on *hostname*.

Options

-n *netgroup*
> Send to specified network groups defined in *netgroup* instead of *hostname*.

-h *hostname*
> Send to specified *hostname*. This option is used when both a *hostname* and a *netgroup* are specified.

rwho [option]

TCP/IP command—list users logged in on local networks. **rwho** produces output similar to **who**. Without options, only users who have typed in the last hour are listed. For each user listed, **rwho** displays the username, hostname, and the date and time the user logged in.

Option

-a   List all users on active nodes.

sddate [name lev date]

Print and set backup dates. With no argument, print contents of backup date file **/etc/ddate**.

Arguments

date   Time in the following form:

> *mmddhhmm[yy]*

> where the first *mm* is a two-digit month in the range of 01-12, *dd* is a two-digit day of the month from 01-31, *hh* is a two-digit military hour from 00-23, and the final *mm* is a two-digit minute from 00-59. An optional two-digit year, *yy*, is presumed to be an offset from the year 1900, that is, 19*yy*.

lev   Backup level number

name   Last component of device pathname.

sdiff	**sdiff** [*options*] *file1 file2*

Produce a side-by-side comparison of *file1* with *file2*. Output is:

text *text*	Identical lines
text <	Line exists only in *file1*.
> *text*	Line exists only in *file2*.
text | *text*	Lines are different.

Options

-1	Print only left column if lines are identical.
-o *outfile*	Send identical lines of *file1* and *file2* to *outfile*, print line differences and edit *outfile* by entering, when prompted, the following commands:

	e	Edit an empty file.
	e b	Edit both left and right columns.
	e l	Edit left column.
	e r	Edit right column.
	l	Append left column to outfile.
	q	Exit the editor.
	r	Append right column to outfile.
	s	Silent mode; do not print identical lines.
	v	Turn off silent mode.

-s	Do not print identical lines.
-w*n*	Set line length to *n* (default is usually 130).

Example

Show differences using 80 columns and ignore identical lines:

```
sdiff -s -w80 list.1 list.2
```

sed	**sed** [*options*] [*files*]

Stream editor—edit one or more *files* without user interaction. See Section 11, *The Sed Editor*, for more information on **sed**.

Options

-e '*instruction*'	
	Apply the editing *instruction* to the files.
-f *script*	Apply the set of instructions from the editing *script*.
-n	Suppress default output.

setcolor	**setcolor** [*options*] [*argument*] **setcolour**

Set screen color and other screen attributes. Both foreground and background colors can be set independently in a range of 16 colors. With no arguments, **setcolor** produces a usage message displaying all available colors, then resets the screen to its previous state.

Options and arguments

-b   Set background to specified color.

-c *first last*

Set first and last scan lines of cursor.

color [*color*]

Set foreground to the first color. Set background to second color if a second color choice is specified.

-g *color* [*color*]

Set foreground graphics characters to first color, background to second color.

-k   Switch on keyclick option.

-n [*color* [*color*]]

Reset screen to default settings and switch off -k option. If no arguments given, screen is set to white characters on black background, otherwise set to specified *colors*.

-o   Set color of screen border. This only works on CGA adaptors.

-p *pitch duration*

Set pitch and duration of bell. Pitch is period in microseconds, and duration is measured in fifths of a second. When using this option, a CTRL-g (bell) must be echoed to the screen for the command to work. For example:

```
setcolor -p 2500 2
echo ^G
```

-r *color* [*color*]

Set foreground reverse video characters to the first color, background to the second color.

---

setkey *keynum string*

Assign function keys—assign the given ASCII *string* to be the output of the computer function key given by *keynum*. The function keys are defined in the string-mapping table, an array of 512 bytes (typedef strmap_t) where null terminated strings can be put to redefine the function keys. *string* can contain control characters. This command only works on the console.

Examples

The command:

```
setkey 1 date
```

→

setkey ←	assigns the string `date` as the output of function key 1. The command:
	setkey 2 "pwd ; lc\n"
	assigns the command sequence `pwd ; lc` to function key 2.
sh	**sh** [*options*] [*arguments*]
	The standard command interpreter (or Bourne shell) that executes commands from a terminal or a file. See Section 5, *The Bourne Shell and Korn Shell*, for more information on the Bourne shell, including command-line options.
shl	**shl**
	Control more than one shell (layer) from a single terminal. From the **shl** prompt level, you can issue the commands listed below (abbreviating them to any unique prefix if desired). The *name* text string should not exceed eight characters. See also **layers**.

    block *name* [*name2* ...]
        Block the output for each layer *name* (same as **stty loblk**), when not current layer.

    create [*name*]
        Create the layer *name* (no more than seven total).

    delete *name* [*name2* ...]
        Delete the layer *name*.

    help or **?**   Provide **shl** command syntax.

    layers [-1] [*name* ...]
        Print information about layers. -1 provides a **ps**-like display.

    name   Make layer *name* be the current level.

    quit   Exit **shl** and kill all the layers.

    resume [*name*]
        Return to latest layer or to layer *name*.

    toggle   Flip back to the previous layer.

    unblock *name* [*name2* ...]
        Do not block output for each layer *name* (same as **stty -loblk**).

showmount	**/usr/bin/showmount** [*options*] [*host*]
	NFS/NIS command—show all remote mounts; list all the clients that have remotely mounted a filesystem from *host*. This information is maintained by the **mountd** server on *host*, and is saved across crashes in the file **/etc/rmtab**. The default value for *host* is the value returned by **hostname**.

Options

-a   Print all remote mounts in the format:

        hostname:directory

        Where *hostname* is the name of the client, and *directory* is the root of the filesystem that has been mounted.

-d   List directories that have been remotely mounted by clients.

-e   Print the list of exported filesystems.

---

sleep *seconds*

Wait a specified number of *seconds* before executing another command.

---

sort [*options*] [*files*]

Sort the lines of the named *files*. See also **uniq**, **comm**, **join**.

Options

-b   Ignore leading spaces and tabs.

-c   Check whether *files* are already sorted, and if so, produce no output.

-d   Sort in dictionary order.

-f   "Fold"; ignore uppercase/lowercase differences.

-i   Ignore nonprinting characters (those outside ASCII range 040-176).

-m   Merge sorted input files.

-M   Compare first three characters as months, ignoring any leading white spaces.

-n   Sort in arithmetic order.

-o*file*   Put output in *file*.

-r   Reverse the order of the sort.

-T *tempdir*

        Directory pathname to be used for temporary files.

-t*c*   Separate fields with *c* (default is any white space).

-u   Identical lines in input file appear only one (*u*nique) time in output.

-y*kmem*   Adjust the amount of memory (in kilobytes) **sort** uses. If *kmem* is not specified, allocate the maximum memory.

-z*recsz*   Provide *recsz* bytes for any one line in the file. This prevents abnormal termination of **sort** in some cases.

+*n* [-*m*]   Skip *n* fields before sorting, and sort up to field position *m*. If *m* is missing, sort to end of line. Positions take the form *a*.*b*, which means character *b* of field *a*. If .*b* is missing, sort at the first character of the field.

$\rightarrow$

---

sort ←	*Examples* List files by decreasing number of lines: `wc -l *	sort -r`  Alphabetize a list of words, remove duplicates, and print the frequency of each word:      `sort -fd wordlist	uniq -c`  Sort the password file numerically by the third field (user ID):      `sort +2n -t: /etc/passwd`

spell

spell [*options*] [*files*]
/usr/lib/spell/hashmake
/usr/lib/spellin *n*
/usr/lib/spell/hashcheck *spelling_list*

Compare the words of one or more named *files* with the system dictionary and report all misspelled words. **hashmake** generates hash codes for a list of words. **spellin** writes a spelling list from hash codes. **hashcheck** recreates the hashed codes in a hashed spelling list.

Options

-b   Check for British spelling.

-i   Ignore all included files.

-l   Follow *all* included files.

-v   Print all words not literally in the spelling list and indicate plausible derivations from the words in the spelling list.

-x   Show every possible word stem.

+*wordlist*
    Use the sorted *wordlist* file as a local dictionary to add to the system dictionary; words in *wordlist* are not treated as misspelled.

Example

Run **spell** once:

    `spell file1 file2 > jargon`

After editing the **jargon** file, use it as a list of special terms. The second run of **spell** produces genuine misspellings:

    `spell +jargon file[12] > typos`

spline

spline [*options*] ...

Interpolate smooth curve. **spline** takes pairs of numbers from the standard input as abscissas and ordinates of a function. It produces a similar set, which is approximately equally spaced and includes the input set, on the standard output. The cubic spline output has two continuous derivatives and enough points to look smooth when plotted.

Options

-a *n*   Supply abscissas automatically; spacing is given by the next argument or assumed to be 1 if next argument is not a number.

-k *n*   The constant **n** used in the boundary value computation is set by the next argument. By default, $n = 0$.

-n *n*   Space output points so that approximately n intervals occur between the lower and upper x limits. By default, $n = 100$.

-p   Make output periodic—match derivatives at ends. First and last input values should normally agree.

-x *l* [*u*]

Next 1 (or 2) arguments are lower (and upper) x limits. Normally these limits are calculated from the data. Automatic abscissas start at lower limit (default 0).

---

split [*option*] [*infile*] [*outfile*]

Split *infile* into several files of equal length. *infile* remains unchanged, and the results are written to *outfile***aa**, *outfile***ab**, etc. (default is **xaa**, **xab**, etc.). If *infile* is - (or missing), standard input is read. See also **csplit**.

Option

- *n*   Split *infile* into files, each *n* lines long (default is 1000).

Examples

Break *bigfile* into 1000-line segments:

```
split bigfile
```

Join four files, then split them into ten-line files named **new.aa**, **new.ab**, etc. Note that without the –, **new.** would be treated as a nonexistent input file:

```
cat list[1-4] | split -10 - new.
```

---

strings [*options*] *files*

Search object or binary *files* for sequences of four or more printable characters that end with a newline or null. See also **od**.

Options

-       Search entire *file*, not just the initialized data portion of object files.

$\rightarrow$

strings ←	-o Display the string's offset position before the string. -*number* Minimum string length is *number* (default is 4).

stty

stty [*options*] [*modes*]

Set terminal I/O options for the current standard input device. Without options, **stty** reports the terminal settings, where a ^ indicates the CONTROL key and ^` indicates a null value. Most modes can be switched using an optional – (shown in brackets). The corresponding description is also shown in brackets. Privileged users can set or read settings from another device using the syntax:

```
stty [options] [modes] < device
```

Options

-a	Report all option settings.
-g	Report current settings in hex.

Control modes

0	Hang up phone.
n	Set terminal baud rate to *n* (e.g., 2400).
[-]clocal	[Enable]disable modem control.
[-]cread	[Disable]enable the receiver.
cs*n*	Select character size (5-8).
[-]cstopb	[One]two stop bits per character.
[-]ctsflow	Enable CTS protocol for a modem or non-modem line.
[-]hup	[Do not]hang up connection on last close.
[-]hupcl	Same as previous.
ispeed *n*	Set terminal input baud rate to *n*.
ospeed *n*	Set terminal output baud rate to *n*.
[-]ortsfl	[Disable]enable unidirectional (enables bidirectional) flow control if ctsflow and rtsflow are both set.
[-]parenb	[Disable]enable parity generation and detection.
[-]parodd	Use [even]odd parity.
[-]rtsflow	Enable RTS signaling for a modem or non-modem line.

Flow control modes

The following table shows the flow control modes available by combining the ortsfl, ctsflow, and rtsflow flags:

Flag settings			*Flow control mode*
ortsfl	rtsflow	ctsflow	Enable unidirectional flow control.
ortsfl	rtsflow	-ctsflow	Assert RTS when ready to send.
ortsfl	-rtsflow	ctsflow	No effect.
ortsfl	-rtsflow	-ctsflow	Enable bidirectional flow control.

-ortsfl rtsflow ctsflow	Enable bidirectional flow control.
-ortsfl rtsflow -ctsflow	No effect.
-ortsfl -rtsflow ctsflow	Stop transmission when CTS drops.
-ortsfl -rtsflow -ctsflow	Disable hardware flow control.

Input modes

[-]brkint	[Do not]signal INTR on break.
[-]cs2scancode	
	Put console keyboard into codeset 2/(AT) mode and interpret transmitted codes accordingly.
[-]icrnl	[Do not]map CR to NL on input.
[-]ignbrk	[Do not]ignore break on input.
[-]igncr	[Do not]ignore CR on input.
[-]ignpar	[Do not]ignore parity errors.
[-]inlcr	[Do not]map NL to CR on input.
[-]inpck	[Disable]enable input parity checking.
[-]isscancode	
	Expect terminal device to not send/send PC scancodes. Do not use on console.
[-]istrip	[Do not]strip input characters to seven bits.
[-]iuclc	[Do not]map uppercase to lowercase on input.
[-]ixany	Allow [XON]any character to restart output.
[-]ixoff	[Do not]send START/STOP characters when queue is nearly empty/full.
[-]ixon	[Disable]enable START/STOP output control.
[-]parmrk	[Do not]mark parity errors.
[-]xscancode	[Do not]translate PC scancodes to characters on input. Do not use on console.

Output modes

bs$n$	Select style of delay for backspaces (0 or 1).
cr$n$	Select style of delay for carriage returns (0-3).
ff$n$	Select style of delay for formfeeds (0 or 1).
nl$n$	Select style of delay for linefeeds (0 or 1).
[-]ocrnl	[Do not]map CR to NL on output.
[-]ofdel	Set fill character to [NULL]DEL.
[-]ofill	Delay output with [timing]fill characters.
[-]olcuc	[Do not]map lowercase to uppercase on output.
[-]onlcr	[Do not]map NL to CR-NL on output.
[-]onlret	On the terminal, NL performs [does not perform] the CR function.
[-]onocr	Does not [does] output CRs at column zero.
[-]opost	[Do not]postprocess output.
tab$n$	Select style of delay for horizontal tabs (0-3).
vt$n$	Select style of delay for vertical tabs (0 or 1).

→

stty
←

Local modes

[-]echo	[Do not]echo every character typed.
[-]echoe	[Do not]echo ERASE character as BS-space-BS string.
[-]echok	[Do not]echo NL after KILL character.
[-]echonl	[Do not]echo NL.
[-]icanon	[Disable]enable canonical input (ERASE and KILL processing).
[-]iexten	[Disable]enable extended functions for input data.
[-]isig	[Disable]enable checking of characters against INTR, and QUIT.
[-]lfkc	Same as **echok**; obsolete.
[-]noflsh	[Enable]disable flush after INTR or QUIT.
[-]tostop	[Do not]send SIGTTOU when background processes write to the terminal.
[-]xcase	[Do not]change case on local output.

Control assignments

ctrl–char c	Set control character to *c*. *ctrl–char* is: **eof, eol, erase, intr, kill, quit, start, stop, susp, swtch**.
min, time *n*	Set min or time to *n*.
line *i*	Set line discipline to *i* (1-126).

Combination modes

cooked	Same as –**raw**.
[-]evenp	Same as [–]**parenb** and **cs[8]7**.
ek	Reset ERASE and KILL characters to CTRL-h and CTRL-u.
[-]lcase	[Un]set **xcase**, **iuclc**, and **olcuc**.
[-]LCASE	Same as [-]**lcase**.
[-]nl	[Un]set **icrnl** and **onlcr**. –**nl** also unsets **inlcr**, **igncr**, **ocrnl**, and **onlret**.
[-]oddp	Same as [-]**parenb**, [-]**parodd**, and **cs7[8]**.
[-]parity	Same as [-]**parenb** and **cs[8]7**.
[-]raw	[Disable]enable raw input and output (no ERASE, KILL, INTR, QUIT, EOT, SWITCH, or output post-processing).
sane	Reset all modes to reasonable values.
[-]tabs	[Expand to spaces]preserve output tabs.
term	Set all modes suitable for terminal type *term* (**tty33, tty37, vt05, tn300, ti700, or tek**).

su

su [*option*] [*user*] [*shell_args*]

Create a shell with the effective user ID of another *user*. If no *user* is specified, create a shell for a privileged user (that is, become a

superuser). Enter *EOF* to terminate. You can run the shell with
particular options by passing them as *shell_args* (e.g., if the shell
runs **sh**, you can specify -**c** *command* to execute *command* via **sh**,
or -**r** to create a restricted shell).

Option

    -         Go through the entire login sequence (i.e., change to
              user's environment).

---

sum [*options*] *file*

Calculate and print a checksum and the number of (512-byte)
blocks for *file*. Useful for verifying data transmission.

Options

    -1   Print a long (32-bit) checksum. Default is to print 16-bit
           checksum.

    -r   Use an alternate checksum algorithm;

---

swconfig [*options*]

Produce a list of software modifications to the system. **swconfig**
displays modifications to the system software since its initialization,
telling the user what sets have been installed or removed from the
system, as well as what release and what parts of the packages
were installed at that time.

Options

    -a   List all information contained in **/usr/lib/custom/history**,
           but sorted by date. -**a** groups products installed at the
           same time, but displays entries in reverse chronological
           order.

    -p   Display package information in addition to default
           information. A list of all packages in a set is stored and
           their installed status tracked by the sequence of infor-
           mation in **/usr/lib/custom/history**.

---

tabs [*tabspec*] [*options*]

Set terminal tab stops according to *tabspec*. The default *tabspec*, –8,
gives the standard UNIX tab settings. Specify *tabspec* as a predefined set of tab stops for particular languages, for example: **a** (IBM
assembler), **c** (COBOL), **f** (FORTRAN), **p** (PL/1), **s** (SNOBOL), and **u**
(UNIVAC). *tabspec* can also be a repeated number, arbitrary numbers, or called from a file.

Tabspec

    -*n*   Repeat tab every *n* columns (e.g., $1+n$, $1+2*n$, etc.).
    n1,n2,...
           Arbitrary ascending values. If *n* is preceded by +, it is
           added (i.e., tab is relative to previous position).

→

---

tabs	-a	1, 10, 16, 36, 72
←	-a2	1, 10, 16, 40, 72
	-c	1, 8, 12, 16, 20, 55
	-c2	1, 6, 10, 14, 49
	-c3	1, 6, 10, 14, 18, 22, 26, 30, 34, 38, 42, 46, 50, 54, 58, 62, 67
	-f	1, 7, 11, 15, 19, 23
	-p	1, 5, 9, 13, 17, 21, 25, 29, 33, 37, 41, 45, 49, 53, 57, 61
	-s	1, 10, 55
	-u	1, 12, 20, 44
	--*file*	Read first line of *file* for tabs.

Options

+m*n*   Set left margin to *n* (default is 10).

-T*type*   Set terminal *type* (default is TERM).

---

tail

tail [*options*] [*file*]

Print the last ten lines of the named *file* on standard output. Use only one of -f or -r.

Options

-f   Don't quit at the end of file; "follow" file as it grows. End with a CTRL-C.

-*n*[*k*]   Begin printing at *n*th item from end of file. *k* specifies the item to count: **l** (lines, the default), **b** (blocks), or **c** (characters).

-*k*   Same as previous, but use the default count of 10.

+*n*[*k*]   Like -*n*, but start at *n*th item from beginning of file.

+*k*   Like -*k*, but count from beginning of file.

Examples

Show the last 20 lines containing instances of .Ah:

```
grep '.Ah' file | tail -20
```

Show the last ten characters of variable **name**:

```
echo "$name" | tail -c
```

Print the last two blocks of **bigfile**:

```
tail -2b bigfile
```

---

talk

talk *person* [*ttyname*]

TCP/IP command—talk to another user. *person* is either the login name of someone on your own machine, or *user@host* on another host. To talk to a user who is logged in more than once, use *ttyname* to indicate the appropriate terminal name. Once

---

communication has been established, the two parties may type simultaneously, with their output appearing in separate windows. To redraw the screen, type CTRL-L. To exit, type your interrupt character; **talk** then moves the cursor to the bottom of the screen and restores the terminal.

tape [options] command [device]

Magnetic tape maintenance program. **tape** sends commands to, and receives status from, the tape subsystem. It can communicate with QIC-02 cartridge tape drives, SCSI tape drives, and QIC-40, QIC-80 and Irwin mini-cartridge tape drives. **mcart** is automatically invoked by **tape** when options specific to the Irwin driver are used. **tape** reads /etc/default/tape for the default device name for sending commands and receiving status. If *device* is specified on the command line, it overrides the default device.

Options

Specify the type of device with the following device type flags:

-8   QIC-80 mini-cartridge tape

-a *arg* Pass an argument, *arg*, to *command*. -a can also be used with the **format** command (QIC-40, QIC-80 and Irwin tape drives) and the **setblk** command (SCSI drives).

-c   QIC-02 cartridge tape

-f   QIC-40 mini-cartridge tape

-i   Irwin mini-cartridge tape

-s   SCSI tape (including HP DAT)

Commands

The following commands can be used with the various tape drivers supported under UNIX. The letters following each description indicate which of the following drivers support each command:

A   All drivers
C   QIC-02 cartridge tape driver
F   QIC-40, QIC-80 mini-tape drivers
I   Irwin mini-cartridge tape driver
S   SCSI tape driver

amount
          Report amount of data in current or last transfer. (C,S,F)

erase Erase and retension the tape cartridge. (C,S,F)

load   Load tape cartridge. (S)

reset Reset tape controller and tape drive. (C,S,F)

reten Retension tape cartridge. Use periodically to remedy slack tape problems. (A)

→

rewind Rewind to beinning of tape. (A)

status Following is an example of status output:

```
status: status message
soft errors: n
underruns: m
```

status Current status of the drive.

soft errors
> Number of recoverable errors occurring during last tape operation. A recoverable error is one correctable by the drive or controller.

underruns
> Number of times tape drive had to stop and restart due to tape buffer underflows.

partition
> Partition an HP DAT tape into logical partitions 1 and 2. Size of partition 2 is specified on the command line; size of partition 1 is remainder of tape. (HP DAT only.)

unload Unload tape cartridge. (S)

format Format tape cartridge. If argument is provided with -a flag, number of tracks specified by argument will be formatted. If no argument is given, entire tape is formatted. (F,I)

getbb Print list of bad tape blocks detected during last tape operation. (F)

map Print map of bad blocks on tape. Format is as follows:

```
track n: ------------X------...
```

> Each - represents a good block on the track; an X represents a block marked as bad. (F)

putbb Read list of bad tape blocks from the standard input and add them to bad block table on the tape. (F)

rfm Wind tape forward to next file mark. (C,S)

rsm Position tape forward to the next setmark. (HP DAT only.)

wfm Write file mark at current tape position. (C,S)

wsm Write setmark at current tape position. (HP DAT only.)

eod Position tape to EOD. (HP DAT only.)

setblk Set tape block size to specified byte size. (S)

Irwin-specific commands

The following commands are all specific to Irwin drives:

drive Display information about the Irwin driver and the tape drive. Following is an example display:

```
Special file: /dev/rctmini
Driver version: 1.0.6a
Drive type: 285XL
Drive firmware: A0
```

```
Controller type: SYSFDC
Unit select (0-3): 3
```

Special file

Name of the special file used to access the driver

Driver version

Version of driver linked with the kernel

Drive type

Equivalent tape drive model number as determined by MC driver

Drive firmware

Firmware part number and revision level

Controller type

Mnemonic for floppy controller to which tape drive attached

Unit select (0-3) type

Controller's unit select, in range 0 through 3. Unit selects the drive.

info   Display Irwin cartridge information.

```
Cartridge state: Formatted
Cartridge format: 145
Write protect slider position: RECORD
```

Cartridge state

Current state of cartridge's format

Cartridge format

Format on cartridge's tape

Write protect slider position

RECORD or **PROTECT**

capacity

Cartridge capacity in 512-byte blocks.

kapacity

Cartridge capacity in 1024-byte blocks. **capacity** and **kapacity** give the total usable data storage capacity of a formatted tape cartridge.

---

tar [*options*] [*files*]

Copy *files* to or restore *files* from an archive medium. If any *files* are directories, **tar** acts on the entire subtree. Options need not be preceded by -. Note that options are supplied as one group, with any arguments placed afterward in corresponding order.

Function options (choose one)

c   Create a new archive.

r   Append *files* to the end of an existing archive.

t   Print the names of *files* if they are stored on the archive (if *files* not specified, print names of all files).

$\rightarrow$

tar	u	Add files if not an archive or if modified.
←	x	Extract *files* from an archive (if *files* not specified, extract all files).

Options

A	Suppress absolute filenames.
b *n*	Use blocking factor *n* (default is 1; maximum is 20).
e	Prevent files from being split across volumes.
f *arch*	Store files in or extract files from archive *arch*.
F *file*	Take succeeding arguments from *file*.
l	Print error messages about links that can't be found.
L	Follow symbolic links.
k *size*	Size of archive volume in kilobytes. Minimum value is 250.
m	Do not restore file modification times; update them to the time of extraction.
n	Archive device is not a magnetic tape.
p	Keep ownership of extracted files same as that of original permissions.
q	Exit immediately after each file has been extracted.
T	Truncates files greater than 14 characters on extraction.
v	Verbose.
w	Wait for user confirmation (**y**).
n	Select device *n*, where *n* is 0,...,9999. The default is found in **/etc/default/tar**.

Examples

Create an archive of **/bin** and **/usr/bin** (**c**), show the command working (**v**), and store on the tape in **/dev/rmt0**:

```
tar cvf /dev/rmt0 /bin /usr/bin
```

List the tape's contents in a format like **ls** **-l**:

```
tar tvf /dev/rmt0
```

Extract the **/bin** directory:

```
tar xvf /dev/rmt0 /bin
```

Create an archive of the current directory and store it in a file **backup.tar** on the system.

```
tar cvf - `find . -print` > backup.tar
```

(The − tells **tar** to store the directory on standard output, which is then redirected.)

---

tee	**tee** [*options*] [*files*]

Duplicate the standard input; send one copy to standard output and another copy to *files*.

Options

-a   Append output to *files* rather than overwriting them.

-i   Ignore all interrupts.

-u   Causes output to be unbuffered.

Examples

Display a **who** listing on the screen and store it in two files:

```
who | tee userlist ttylist
```

Display misspelled words and add them to existing **typos**:

```
spell ch02 | tee -a typos
```

---

telnet [*options*] [*host* [*port*]]   telnet

Access remote systems. **telnet** is the user interface that communicates with another host using the **TELNET** protocol. If telnet is invoked without *host*, it enters command mode, indicated by its prompt, `telnet>`, and accepts and executes the commands listed below. If invoked with arguments, **telnet** performs an **open** command (see below) with those arguments. *host* indicates the host's official name. *port* indicates a port number (default **TELNET** port).

Options

-8   Use an eight-bit data path.

-a   Automatic login into the remote system.

-d   Toggle socket level debugging.

-e [*escape_char*]

     Set initial **TELNET** escape character to *escape_char*. If *escape_char* omitted, there will be no pre-defined escape character.

-E   Stop any character from being recognized as an escape character.

-L   Use an eight-bit data path on output.

-l *user*

     When connecting to remote system, and if remote system understands **ENVIRON**, send *user* to the remote system as the value for variable **USER**.

-n *tracefile*

     Open *tracefile* for recording the trace information.

-r   Use a user interface similar to **rlogin**. In this mode, the escape character is set to the tilde character (~), unless modified by -e.

Commands

CTRL-Z

     Suspend **telnet**.

→

! [*command*]

> Execute a single command in a subshell on the local system. If *command* is omitted, an interactive subshell will be invoked.

? [*command*]

> Get help. With no arguments, print a help summary. If a command is specified, print the help information for just that command.

check   Verify current settings for current special characters.

close   Close a **TELNET** session and return to command mode.

display *argument* . . .

> Display all, or some, of the **set** and **toggle** values.

export   Switch to local defaults for the special characters.

import   Switch to remote defaults for the special characters.

mode [*type*]

> Depending on state of **TELNET** session, *type* is one of several options:
>
> ?   Print out help information for the **mode** command.
>
> character   Disable **TELNET LINEMODE** option, or, if remote side does not understand option, enter "character at a time" mode.
>
> edit/-edit   Attempt to enable/disable the **EDIT** mode of the **TELNET LINEMODE** option.
>
> isig/-isig   Attempt to enable/disable the **TRAPSIG** mode of the **LINEMODE** option.
>
> line   Enable **TELNET LINEMODE** option, or, if remote side does not understand option, attempt to enter "old line by line" mode.
>
> softtabs/-softtabs
>
>   Attempt to enable/disable the **SOFT_TAB** mode of the **LINEMODE** option.

open *host* [*user*] [[-] *port*] [-a] [-1 *user*]

> Open a connection to the named *host*. If no *port* number is specified, attempt to contact a **TELNET** server at the default port.

quit   Close any open **TELNET** session and exit telnet.

status   Show current status of **telnet**. This includes the peer one is connected to as well as the current mode.

send *arguments*

> Send one or more special character sequences to the remote host. Following are the arguments which may be specified:
>
> ?   Print out help information for **send** command.
>
> abort   Send **TELNET ABORT** sequence.
>
> ao   Send **TELNET AO** sequence, which should cause the remote system to flush all output

from the remote system to the user's terminal.

ayt Send **TELNET AYT** (are you there) sequence.

brk Send **TELNET BRK** (Break) sequence.

ec Send **TELNET EC** (Erase Character) sequence, which causes the remote system to erase the last character entered.

el Send **TELNET EL** (Erase Line) sequence, which causes the remote system to erase the last character entered.

eof Send **TELNET EOF** (End Of File) sequence.

eor Send **TELNET EOR** (End Of Record) sequence.

escape Send current **TELNET** escape character (initially [ ).

ga Send **TELNET GA** (Go Ahead) sequence.

getstatus If the remote side supports the **TELNET STATUS** command, **getstatus** sends the subnegotiation request that the server send its current option status.

ip Send **TELNET IP** (Interrupt Process) sequence, which causes the remote system to abort the currently running process.

nop Send **TELNET NOP** (No OPeration) sequence.

susp Send **TELNET SUSP** (SUSPend process) sequence.

synch Send **TELNET SYNCH** sequence, which causes the remote system to discard all previously typed (but not read) input.

? Display legal **set** and **unset** commands.

set *argument value*

unset *argument value*

Set any one of a number of telnet variables to a specific value or to "TRUE". The special value "off" turns off the function associated with the variable. **unset** disables any of the specified functions. The values of variables may be interrogated with the aid of the **display** command. The variables which may be specified are:

ayt If **TELNET** is in **localchars** mode, this character is taken to be the alternate AYT character.

echo This is the value (initially [) which, when in line-by-line mode, toggles between doing local echoing of entered characters and suppressing echoing of entered characters.

eof If **telnet** is operating in **LINEMODE** or in the old line-by-line mode, entering this charac-

→

ter as the first character on a line will cause the character to be sent the remote system.

erase   If **telnet** is in **localchars** mode and operating in the character-at-a-time mode, then when this character is entered, a **TELNET EC** sequence will be sent to the remote system.

escape   This is the **TELNET** escape character (initially [), which causes entry into the **TELNET** command mode when connected to a remote system.

flushoutput

If **telnet** is in **localchars** mode and the **flushoutput** character is entered, a **TELNET AO** sequence is sent to the remote host.

forw1   If **TELNET** is in **localchars** mode, this character is taken to be the alternate end-of-line character.

forw2   If **TELNET** is in **localchars** mode, this character is taken to be the alternate end-of-line character.

interrupt If **TELNET AO** is in **localchars** mode and the **interrupt** character is entered, a **TELNET IP** sequence is sent to the remote host.

kill   If **TELNET IP** is in **localchars** mode and operating in the "character-at-a-time" mode, then when this character is entered, a **TELNET EL** sequence is sent to the remote system.

lnext   If **TELNET EL** is in **LINEMODE** or in the old "line-by-line" mode, then this character is taken to be the terminal's **lnext** character.

quit   If **TELNET EL** is in **localchars** mode and the **quit** character is entered, a **TELNET BRK** sequence is sent to the remote host.

reprint   If **TELNET BRK** is in **LINEMODE** or in the old "line-by-line" mode, this character is taken to be the terminal's **reprint** character.

start   If the **TELNET TOGGLE-FLOW-CONTROL** option has been enabled, this character is taken to be the terminal's **start** character.

stop   If the **TELNET TOGGLE-FLOW-CONTROL** option has been enabled, this character is taken to be the terminal's **stop** character.

susp   If **TELNET** is in **localchars** mode, or if the **LINEMODE** is enabled and the **suspend** character is entered, a **TELNET SUSP** sequence is sent to the remote host.

tracefile File to which output generated by **netdata** is written.

worderase   If TELNET BRK is in LINEMODE or in the old "line-by-line" mode, this character is taken to be the terminal's **worderase** character.

slc [*state*]

Set state of special characters when **TELNET LINEMODE** option has been enabled.

environ [*arguments* [...]]

Manipulate variables that may be sent through the **TELNET ENVIRON** option. Valid arguments for **environ** are:

define *variable value*

Define *variable* to have a value of *value*.

undefine *variable*

Remove *variable* from the list of environment variables.

export *variable*

Mark *variable* to be exported to the remote side.

inexport *variable*

Mark *variable* to not be exported unless explicitly requested by the remote side.

send *variable*

Send environment variable.

toggle *arguments* [...]

Toggle various flags that control how **TELNET** responds to events. The flags may be set explicitly to TRUE or FALSE using the **set** and **unset** commands listed above. The valid arguments are:

?   Display legal **toggle** commands.

autoflush   If **autoflush** and **localchars** are both TRUE, then when the **ao** or **quit** characters are recognized, **TELNET** will refuse to display any data on the user's terminal until the remote system acknowledges it has processed those **TELNET** sequences.

autosynch   If **autosynch** and **localchars** are both TRUE, then when the **intr** or **quit** character is entered, the resulting **TELNET** sequence sent will be followed by the **TELNET SYNCH** sequence. Initial value for this **toggle** is false.

binary   Enable or disable the **TELNET BINARY** option on both the input and output.

inbinary   Enable or disable the **TELNET BINARY** option on the input.

outbinary   Enable or disable the **TELNET BINARY** option on the output.

crlf	If this **toggle** value is true, carriage returns will be sent as CR-LF. If false, carriage returns will be sent as CR-NUL. Initial value for **toggle** is false.
crmod	Toggle carriage return mode. Initial value for **toggle** is false.
debug	Toggle socket level debugging mode. Initial value for **toggle** is false.
localchars	If true, **flush**, **interrupt**, **quit**, **erase**, and **kill** characters are recognized locally, then transformed into appropriate **TELNET** control sequences. Initial value for **toggle** is true.
netdata	Toggle display of all network data. Initial value for **toggle** is false.
options	Toggle display of some internal **telnet** protocol processing pertaining to **TELNET** options. Initial value for **toggle** is false.
prettydump	When **netdata toggle** is enabled, and if **prettydump** is enabled, the output from the **netdata** command is reorganized into a more user friendly format; spaces are put between each character in the output, and an asterisk will precede any **TELNET** escape sequence.
skiprc	Toggle does not process ~/.telnetrc file. Initial value for **toggle** is false.
termdata	Toggle printing of hexadecimal terminal data. Initial value for **toggle** is false.

---

test

test *expression*
          or
[*expression*]

Evaluate an *expression* and, if its value is true, return a zero exit status; otherwise, return a nonzero exit status. In shell scripts, you can use the alternate form [*expression*]. This command is generally used with conditional constructs in shell programs.

---

tic

tic [*options*] *file*

Terminfo compiler. **tic** translates a *terminfo* file from the source format into the compiled format, placing the results in the directory **/usr/lib/terminfo**. If the **TERMINFO** environment variable is set, the compiled results are placed there instead of **/usr/lib/terminfo**. *file* contains one or more *terminfo* descriptions in source format. Each description in the file describes the capabilities of a particular terminal. When a **use=entry=name** field is discovered in a terminal entry being compiled, **tic** reads in the binary from **/usr/lib/terminfo** to complete the entry. The compiled format is necessary for use with the library routines described in **curses**. For more information, see the Nutshell Handbook *termcap & terminfo*.

Options

-c   Only check *file* for errors. Errors in **use=** links are not detected.

-v [*n*]   Verbose—output to standard error. Optional integer *n* is a number from 1 to 10, inclusive, indicating desired detail level of information. Default is 1.

---

time *command* [*arguments*]

time

Execute a *command* and print the total elapsed time, execution time, process execution time, and system time of the process (all in seconds).

---

touch [*options*] [*date*] *files*

touch

For one or more *files*, update the access time and modification time (and dates) to the current time and date, or update to the optional *date*. *date* is a date and time in the format *mmddhhmm*[*yy*]. **touch** is useful in forcing other commands to handle files a certain way; e.g., the operation of **make**, and sometimes **find**, relies on a file's access and modification time.

Options

-a   Update only the access time.

-c   Do not create nonexistent files.

-m   Update only the modification time.

---

tput [*options*] *capname* [*arguments*]

tput

Print the value of the terminal capability *capname* (and its associated numeric or string *arguments*) from the **terminfo** database. *capname* is a **terminfo** capability such as **clear** or **col**. (See the Nutshell Handbook *termcap & terminfo*.) The last four options are mutually exclusive and are not used when specifying a *capname*. Exit statuses are: 0 when a Boolean *capname* is set to true or when a string *capname* is defined; 1 when a Boolean is false or when a string is undefined; 2 for usage errors; 3 for unknown terminal *type*; 4 for unknown *capname*.

Options

-T*type*   Print the capabilities of terminal *type* (default is the terminal in use).

-S   Read *capname* from standard input (this allows **tput** to evaluate more than one *capname*).

init   Print initialization strings and expand tabs.

$\rightarrow$

SCO UNIX
User Commands

tput	reset	Print reset strings if present; act like **init** if not.
←	longname	Print the terminal's long name.

Examples

Show the number of columns for the **xterm** window:

```
tput -Txterm cols
```

Define shell variable **restart** to reset terminal characteristics:

```
restart=`tput reset`
```

---

tr

tr [*options*] [*string1* [*string2*]]

Translate characters—copy standard input to standard output, performing substitution of characters from *string1* to *string2* or deletion of characters in *string1*.

Options

- **-c** Complement characters in *string1* with respect to ASCII 001-377.
- **-d** Delete characters in *string1* from output.
- **-s** Squeeze out repeated output characters in *string2*.

Examples

Change uppercase to lowercase in a file:

```
cat file | tr '[A-Z]' '[a-z]'
```

Turn spaces into newlines (ASCII code 012):

```
tr ' ' '\012' < file
```

Strip blank lines from **file** and save in **new.file** (or use \011 to change successive tabs into one tab):

```
cat file | tr -s "" "\012" > new.file
```

Delete colons from **file**; save result in **new.file**:

```
tr -d : < file > new.file
```

---

translate

translate [*options*] [*infile*] [*outfile*]

Translate files from one format to another. **translate** uses standard input and standard output unless otherwise specified with *infile* and *outfile*. To convert character and file formats (especially tapes), use the **dd** command.

Options

In the options below, *format* is assumed to be a file in the directory **/usr/lib/translate**, if a full pathname is not provided.

- **-ae** Translate from ASCII to EBCDIC.

-af *format*
>Translate from ASCII format to a user-defined format.

-bm
>Translate from binary/object code to mailable ASCII **uuencode** format.

-ea
>Translate from EBCDIC to ASCII.

-ef *format*
>Translate from EBCDIC format to a user-defined format.

-fa *format*
>Translate from user-defined format to ASCII format.

-fe *format*
>Translate from a user-defined format to EBCDIC format.

-mb
>Translate from mailable ASCII **uuencode** format to original binary.

---

true

A null command that returns a successful (zero) exit status. See also **false**.

---

tset [*options*] [*type*]

Set terminal modes. Without arguments, the terminal is reinitialized according to the TERM environment variable. **tset** is typically used in startup scripts (**.profile** or **.login**). *type* is the terminal type; if preceded by a ?, **tset** prompts the user to enter a different type, if needed. Press RETURN to use the default value, *type*. See also **reset**.

Options

-
>Print terminal name on standard output; useful for passing this value to TERM.

-e*c*
>Set erase character to *c*; default is CTRL-H (backspace).

-h
>Search **/etc/ttytype** for information (overlook TERM environment variable).

-I
>Do not output terminal initialization setting.

-k *c*
>Set line-kill character to *c* (default is CTRL-U).

-m[*port*[*baudrate*]:*tty*]
>Declare terminal specifications. *port* is the port type (usually **dialup** or **plugboard**). *tty* is the terminal type; it can be preceded by ? as above. *baudrate* checks the port speed and can be preceded by any of these characters:
>
>>**>** Port must be greater than *baudrate*.
>>
>>**<** Port must be less than *baudrate*.
>>
>>**@** Port must transmit at *baudrate*.
>>
>>**!** Negate a subsequent >, <, or @ character.

-Q
>Do not print **Erase set to** and **Kill set to** messages.

→

tset
←
	-r Report the terminal type.
	   -s Output **setenv** commands (for **csh**), or **export** and assignment commands (for **sh** or **ksh**).
	   -S Output only strings to be placed in the environment variables, without shell commands printed for -s.

Examples

   Set terminal type to **gt42**:

```
tset gt42
```

---

tsort	**tsort** [*file*] Perform a topological sort on *file*. Typically used to reorganize an archive library for more efficient handling by **ar** or **ld**.

Example

   Find the ordering relationship of all object files, and sort them for access by **ld**:

```
lorder *.o | tsort
```

---

tty	**tty** [*option*] Print the device name of your terminal. This is useful for shell scripts and often for commands that need device information.

Option

   -s   Return only the codes: 0 (a terminal), 1 (not a terminal), 2 (invalid options used).

---

umask	**umask** [*value*] Print the current value of the file creation mode mask, or set it to *value*, a three-digit octal code specifying the read-write-execute permissions to be turned off. **umask** is available as a built-in command in the Bourne and C shells.

Examples

   Turn off write permission for others:

       `umask 002`   *Produces file permission* -rw-rw-r--

   Turn off all permissions for group and others:

       `umask 077`   *Produces file permission* -rw-------

   Note that you can omit leading zeroes.

---

umnt	**usr/bin/umnt** *directory* Unmount selected filesystems.

---

umount *argument*

NFS/NIS command—unmount filesystems. For details, see the **mount** command.

---

uname [*options*]

Print the current UNIX system name.

Options

-A   Print activation state information.

-a   Report hardware name, node name, operating system release, and system name.

-m   The hardware name

-n   The node name (the default)

-r   The operating system release

-s   The system name

-S *system_name*
     Change the system name and node name by specifying a *system_name*. Must be superuser to use this option.

-v   The operating system version

-X   Print all the above information, plus OEM number, kernel ID, bus type, serial number, processor, license, origin number and number of CPUs.

---

uncompress [*option*] [*files*]

Restore the original file compressed by **compress**. The .Z extension is implied, so it can be omitted when specifying *files*.

Option

-c   Same as **zcat** (write to standard output without changing *files*).

-F   Force overwrite of existing file.

-f   Overwrite previous output file.

-P *fd*   Read list of filenames from pipe associated with file descriptor *fd*.

-q   Generate error messages only (if any).

-v   Print name and what replaces it.

---

uniq [*options*] [*file1* [*file2*]]

Remove duplicate adjacent lines from sorted *file1*, sending one copy of each line to *file2* (or to standard output). Often used as a filter. Specify only one of -c, -d, or -u. See also **comm** and **sort**.

$\rightarrow$

uniq
←

Options

-c   Print each line once, counting instances of each.

-d   Print duplicate lines once, but no unique lines.

-u   Print only unique lines (no copy of duplicate entries is kept).

-*n*   Ignore first *n* fields of a line. Fields are separated by spaces or by tabs.

+*n*   Ignore first *n* characters of a field.

Examples

Send one copy of each line from list to output file list.new:

```
uniq list list.new
```

Show which names appear more than once:

```
sort names | uniq -d
```

Show which lines appear exactly three times:

```
sort names | uniq -c | grep "^ *3 "
```

---

units

units

Interactive command to convert units to their equivalents in other scales. The file **/usr/lib/unittab** gives a complete list of the units.

---

unpack

unpack *files*

Expand one or more *files*, created with **pack**, to their original form. See **pcat** and **pack**.

---

uptime

uptime

Print the current time, amount of time logged in, number of users logged in, and the system load averages. This output is also produced by the first line of the **w** command.

---

usemouse

usemouse [*options*] *parameters*

Map mouse input to keystrokes. **usemouse** merges data from a mouse into the input stream of a tty. The data is translated to arrow keys or any other arbitrary ASCII strings. Using no arguments sets the mouse for use with the default map **/etc/default/usemouse** (see below). Alternate map files can be found in the **/user/lib/mouse** directory. To terminate **usemouse**, exit the shell with CTRL-d.

Options

-b   Supress bell for duration of mouse usage.

-c *cmd*

Run *cmd* with **usemouse**. *cmd* defaults to the shell specified in the **SHELL** environment variable. If **SHELL** is unspecified, **/bin/sh** is used. When *cmd* terminates, **usemouse** terminates as well.

-f *conffile*

Select alternate configuration file, *conffile*. *conffile* should use the format of **/etc/default/usemouse**.

-h *horiz_sens*

Horizontal sensitivity. Horizontal mouse movements smaller than this threshold are ignored. The sensitivity defaults to 5 units. Minimum value is 1 unit, maximum is 100 units. The lower the value, the more sensitive your mouse is to motion.

-t *type*   Select a predefined configuration file. **type** can be any file in **/usr/lib/mouse**. These files are identical in format to **/etc/default/usemouse**.

-v *vert_sens*

Vertical sensitivity. Vertical mouse movements smaller than this threshold are ignored. The sensitivity defaults to 5 units. Minimum value is 1 unit, maximum is 100 units. The lower the value, the more sensitive your mouse is to motion.

Parameters

These are *name=value* pairs indicating what ASCII string to insert into the tty input stream when the given event is received. Valid parameters include:

rbu=*string*	String to generate on right button up
rbd=*string*	String to generate on right button down
mbu=*string*	String to generate on middle button up
mbd=*string*	String to generate on middle button down
lbu=*string*	String to generate on left button up
lbd=*string*	String to generate on left button down
rt=*string*	String to generate on mouse right
lt=*string*	String to generate on mouse left
up=*string*	String to generate on mouse up
dn=*string*	String to generate on mouse down
ul=*string*	String to generate on mouse up-left
ur=*string*	String to generate on mouse up-right
dr=*string*	String to generate on mouse down-right
dl=*string*	String to generate on mouse down-left
hsens=*num*	Sensitivity to horizontal motion

| vsens=*num* | Sensitivity to vertical motion |
| bells=*yes/no* | Whether to remove CTRL-G characters |

Default map file (etc/default/usemouse)

Mouse	Keystroke
Left button	vi top of file (1G) command
Middle button	vi delete character (x) command
Right button	vi bottom of file (G) command
Up	Up arrow key
Down	Down arrow key
Left	Left arrow key
Right	Right arrow key
Up and left	Not defined
Up and right	Not defined
Down and left	Not defined
Down and right	Not defined
Bells	Not defined

Examples

To set up the mouse for use with vi, type:

```
usemouse -t vi
```

This will not start vi. To start up the mouse for use with vi, type:

```
usemouse -t vi -c vi
```

This invokes the vi map along with the command; the mouse disengages when you quit out of vi.

uucp [*options*] [*source*!]*file* [*destination*!]*file*

Copy a file (or group of files) from the source to the destination. The *source* and *destination* can be remote systems. The destination file can be a directory.

Options

-c	Do not copy files to the spool directory (the default).
-C	Copy files to the spool directory for transfer.
-d	Make directories for the copy when they don't exist (the default).
-f	Do not make directories when they don't exist.
-g*x*	Set grade (priority) of job. *x* is typically a single letter or digit, where a and 1 give the highest transfer priority. Use **uuglist** to show values for *x*.
-j	Print the **uucp** job number.
-m	When copy is complete, send mail to person who issued **uucp** command.

-n*user* When copy is complete, send mail to *user* on the
　　　　remote system.

-r　　　Queue job, but don't start transfer program (**uucico**).

-s*file*　Send transfer status to *file* (a full pathname); overrides
　　　　-m.

-x*n*　　Debug at level *n* (0-9); higher numbers give more out-
　　　　put.

Example

This shell script sends a compressed file to system **orca**:

```
compress $1
uucp -C -n$2 -m $1.Z orca\!/usr/spool/uucppublic
uncompress $1
```

With -**C**, the transfer is made on a copy in the spool directory.
(Normally, **uucp** gets the file from its original location, so you
can't rename it or uncompress it until the call goes through.)
The script also notifies sender and recipient when the transfer
finishes.

---

uudecode [*file*]

UUCP command—read a uuencoded file and recreate the original
file with the same mode and name (see **uuencode**).

---

uuencode [*source_file*] [*remote_file*]

UUCP command—convert a binary *file* to a form which can be sent
to *usr* via **mail**. The encoding uses only printing ASCII characters
and includes the mode and *name* of the file. When *file* is recon-
verted via **uudecode** on the remote system, output will be sent to
name. (Therefore, when saving the encoded mail message to a file
on the remote system, *don't* store it in a file called *name* or you'll
overwrite it!) Note that **uuencode** can take standard input, so a
single argument will be taken as the name to be given to the file
when it is decoded.

---

uuname [*options*]

UUCP command—list UUCP sites that can be accessed using **uucp**.

Options

-c　　Return name of systems known to **cu**.

-l　　Display local system name.

---

uupick [*option*]

UUCP command—retrieve files sent by **uuto**. To do this, enter the
uupick command with no arguments. **uupick** searches the public

→

uupick ←	directory for any files sent to you, then prompts you to retrieve them. *Option* -s *system* Search **/usr/spool/uucppublic** only for files sent from *system*.

uuto	**uuto**
	
	UUCP command—copy files to the public directory of a UUCP site to which your system is connected. The public directory on most XENIX and UNIX systems is **/usr/spool/uucppublic**. Files sent with **uuto** are placed in the directory **/usr/spool/uucppublic/receive**/*username/source_computer*, where *username* is the login of the user to whom you are sending files and *source_computer* is the sitename of your system.
	
	Option
	
	    -m Send mail to the sender when the copy is complete.
	    -p Copy the source file into the spool directory before transmission.

vedit	**vedit** [*options*] [*files*] Same as running vi, but with the **showmode** and **novice** flags set, the **report** flag set to 1, and **magic** turned off (metacharacters have no special meaning). Intended for beginners.
vi	**vi** [*options*] [*files*] A screen-oriented text editor based on ex. For more information on vi, see Section 9, *The Vi Editor*.

vidi	**vidi** [*options*] *font*
	vidi *mode*
	
	Set font or video mode, respectively, for a video device. With no arguments, **vidi** lists all valid video mode and font commands.
	
	Font options
	
	    Available fonts include font8x8, font8x14, and font 8x16.
	    font Load *font* from */usr/lib/vidi/font*.
	    -d Write *font*.
	    -f *fontfile* Set file for *font*.
	
	Mode options
	
	    mono Move current screen to monochrome adapter.
	    cga Move current screen to Color Graphics adapter.
	    ega Move current screen to Enhanced Graphics adapter.

vga	Move current screen to Video Graphics adapter.
internal	Activate internal monitor on Compaq portable with plasma screen.
external	Activate external monitor on Compaq portable with plasma screen.

Text and graphics modes

The following tables list the available text and graphics modes:

Text Mode	Cols	Rows	Font
c40x25	40	25	8x8
e40x25	40	25	8x14
v40x25	40	25	8x16
m80x25	80	25	8x14
c80x25	80	25	8x8
em80x25	80	25	8x14
e80x25	80	25	8x14
vm80x25	80	25	8x16
v80x25	80	25	8x16
e80x43	80	43	8x14

Graphics Mode	Pixel Resolution	Colors	Adapter
mode5	320x200	4	CGA (EGA VGA)
mode6	640x200	2	CGA (EGA VGA)
modeD	320x200	16	EGA (VGA)
modeE	640x200	16	EGA (VGA)
modeF	640x350	2 (mono)	EGA (VGA)
mode10	640x350	16	EGA (VGA)
mode11	640x480	2	VGA
mode12	640x480	16	VGA
mode13	320x200	256	VGA

---

view [*options*] [*files*]

Same as **vi -R**.

---

vmstat [*options*] [*interval* [*count*]]

Report paging and system statistics. The default report gives a summary of the number of processes in various states, paging activity, system activity, and cpu cycle consumption. If *interval* is given, the number of events that have occurred in the last *interval* seconds is shown. *count* is number of times to display information. If no *interval* or *count* are specified, the totals since system bootup are displayed.

$\rightarrow$

vmstat	*Options*	
←	-f	Report number of **forks** done.

-n *namelist*
Use *namelist* file as alternate symbol table instead of
/unix.

-l *lines*
For default display, repeat header every *lines* reports
(default is 20).

-s   Verbose listing of paging and trap activity.

Default report

Fields in the default report are:

procs   Number of processes
- r   In the run queue
- b   Blocked waiting for resources
- w   Swapped out

These values always reflect the current situation, even if
totals since boot are being displayed.

paging   Report on performance of demand paging system:
- frs   Free swap space
- dmd   Demand zero and demand fill pages
- sw   Pages on swap
- cch   Pages in cache
- fil   Pages on file
- pft   Protection faults
- frp   Pages freed
- pos   Processes swapped out successfully
- pif   Processes swapped out unsuccessfully
- rso   Regions swapped out
- rsi   Regions swapped in

system   Report on general system activity. Unless totals since
boot are being shown, these figures are averaged over
the last *interval* seconds:
- sy   Number of system calls
- cs   Number of context switches

cpu   Percentage of cpu cycles spent in various operating
modes:
- us   User
- su   System
- id   Idle

---

w   **w** [*options*] [*users*]

Print summaries of system usage, currently logged-in users, and
what they are doing. **w** is essentially a combination of **uptime**,
who, and **ps** -a. Display output for one user by specifying *user*.

Options

-h   Suppress headings and **uptime** information.

-l   Display in long format (the default).

-q   Do a quick format with limited information.

-n *namelist*

Use alternate *namelist* instead of **/unix**.

-s *swapdev*

Use *swapdev* in place of **dev/swap**. Useful when examining core files.

-t   Only print header (equivalent to **uptime**).

-u *utmpfile*

Use *utmpfile* instead of **/etc/utmp**.

-w   Output both heading line and summary of users.

---

wait

Wait for all background processes to complete, and report their termination status. Used in shell scripts.

---

wc [*options*] [*files*]

Print a character, word, and line count for *files*. If no *files* are given, read standard input. See other examples under **ls** and **sort**.

Options

-c   Print character count only.

-l   Print line count only.

-w   Print word count only.

Examples

Count the number of users logged in:

```
who | wc -l
```

Count the words in three essay files:

```
wc -w essay.[123]
```

Count lines in variable $**file** (don't display filename):

```
wc -l < $file
```

---

who [*options*] [*file*]
who am i

Display information about the current status of the system. With no options, list the names of users currently logged in to the system. An optional system *file* (default is **/etc/utmp**) can be supplied to give additional information.

$\rightarrow$

who	*Options*	
←	-A	Display UNIX accounting information.
	-a	Use all options.
	-b	Report information about the last reboot.
	-d	Report expired processes.
	-f	Suppress pseudo-ttys except for remote logins.
	-H	Print headings.
	-l	Report inactive terminal lines.
	-n*x*	Display *x* users per line (works only with -q).
	-p	Report previously spawned processes.
	-q	"Quick." Display only the usernames and total number of users.
	-r	Report the run level.
	-s	List the name, line, and time fields (the default behavior).
	-t	Report the last change of the system clock (via **date**).
	-T	Report whether terminals are writable (+), not writable (−), or unknown (?).
	-u	Report terminal usage (idle time). A dot (.) means less than one minute idle; **old** means more than 24 hours idle.
	am i	Print the username of the invoking user.

Example

This sample output was produced at 8 a.m. on April 17:

```
who -uH
NAME     LINE    TIME        IDLE   PID   COMMENTS
Earvin   ttyp3   Apr 16 08:14 16:25  2240
Larry    ttyp0   Apr 17 07:33   .    15182
```

Since **Earvin** has been idle since yesterday afternoon (16 hours), it appears that Earvin isn't at work yet. He simply left himself logged in. Larry's terminal is currently in use.

---

whodo

/bin/whodo

Determine who is doing what—produce merged, reformatted, and dated output from the **who** and **ps** commands.

---

whois

whois [*option*] *name*

TCP/IP command. Search an Internet directory for the person, login, handle, or organization specified by *name*. Precede *name* with the modifiers !, ., or *, alone or in combination, to limit the search to either (1) the name of a person or of a username, (2) a handle, or (3) an organization.

Option

  -h *host*   Search on host machine *host*.

---

write *user* [*tty*]
message

Initiate or respond to an interactive conversation with *user*. A write session is terminated with *EOF*. If the user is logged in to more than one terminal, specify a *tty* number. See also **hello** and **talk**.

---

x286emul [*arg . . .*] *prog286*

Emulate XENIX 80286. **x286emul** allows programs from XENIX System V/286 Release 2.3 or XENIX System V/286 Release 2.3.2 on the Intel 80286 to run on the Intel 80386 processor under UNIX System V Release 3.2 or later. The UNIX system automatically **execs** the 286 emulator, *arg*, with the 286 program name, **prog286**, as an additional argument.

---

xargs [*options*] [*command*]

Execute *command* (with any initial arguments), but read remaining arguments from standard input instead of specifying them directly. **xargs** passes these arguments in several bundles to *command*, allowing *command* to process more arguments than it could normally handle at once. The arguments are typically a long list of filenames (generated by **ls** or **find**, for example) that get passed to **xargs** via a pipe.

Options

  -e*string*
        Stop passing arguments when argument *string* is encountered (default is underscore).

  -i   Pass arguments to *command*, replacing instances of { } on the command line with the current line of input.

  -l*n*   Execute *command* for *n* lines of arguments.

  -n*n*   Execute *command* with up to *n* arguments.

  -p   Prompt for a y to confirm each execution of *command*.

  -s*n*   Each argument list can contain up to *n* characters (470 is the default and the maximum value).

  -t   Echo each *command* before executing.

  -x   Exit if argument list exceeds *n* characters (from -s); -x takes effect automatically with -i and -l.

Examples

grep for *pattern* in all files on the system:

```
find / -print | xargs grep pattern > out &
```

---

xargs ←	Run diff on file pairs (e.g., **f1.a** and **f1.b**, **f2.a** and **f2.b** ...):
	`echo $*	xargs -n2 diff`
	The previous line would be invoked as a shell script, specifying filenames as arguments.
	Display *file*, one word per line (same as **deroff -w**):
	`cat file	xargs -n1`
	Move files in **olddir** to **newdir**, showing each command:
	`ls olddir	xargs -i -t mv olddir/{ } newdir/{ }`
xtod	**xtod** [*filename*] > [*output.file*]
	Change file format from UNIX to MS-DOS. **xtod** adds an extra carriage return to the end of each line and a CTRL-z to the end of the file. **xtod** is not required for converting binary object files. If no filename is specified on the command line, **xtod** takes input from standard input and sends output to standard output.
xtract	**xtract** *cpio_options pattern archive*
	Extract a single file from a **cpio** archive without reading the entire archive. A file matching *pattern* will be selected from the **cpio** *archive*. The extraction is performed using the **cpio -iv** options.
yes	**yes** [*string*]
	Print **y** repeatedly, or *string*, if given. This command will continue indefinitely unless aborted. It is useful in pipes to commands that prompt for input and require a **y** response for a yes. **yes** will terminate when the command it pipes to terminates.

Part III

Shells

Part III describes the three major UNIX shells, as well as the SCO Shell. It also includes special syntax and built-in commands.

Section 4 - *The UNIX Shell: An Overview*

Section 5 - *The Bourne Shell and Korn Shell*

Section 6 - *The C Shell*

Section 7 - *The SCO Shell*

The UNIX Shell:
An Overview

For novice users, this section presents basic concepts about the UNIX shell. For advanced users, this section also summarizes the major similarities and differences between the Bourne, Korn, and C shells. Details on the three shells, plus coverage of the SCO Shell, are provided in Sections 5, 6, and 7.

The following topics are presented:

* Introduction to the shell

* Purpose of the shell

* Shell flavors

* Common features

* Differing features

Introduction to the Shell

Let's suppose that the UNIX operating system is a car. When you drive, you issue a variety of "commands": you turn the steering wheel, press the accelerator, or press the brake. But how does the car translate your commands into the action you want? Through the car's drive mechanism, which can be thought of as the car's user interface. Cars can be equipped with front-wheel drive, rear-wheel drive, four-wheel drive, and sometimes combinations of these.

The shell can be thought of as the user interface to UNIX, and by the same token, several shells are available in UNIX. Some systems provide only one shell. Many provide more than one for you to choose from. Each shell has different features, but all of them affect how commands will be interpreted and provide tools to create your UNIX environment.

The shell is simply a program that allows the system to understand your commands. (That's why the shell is often called a command interpreter.) For many users, the shell works invisibly—"behind the scenes." Your only concern is that the system do what you tell it to do; you don't care about the inner workings. In our car analogy, this is comparable to pressing the brake. Most of us don't care whether the "user interface" involves disk brakes or drum brakes, as long as the car stops.

Purpose of the Shell

There are three main uses for the shell:

- Interactive use

- Customization of your UNIX session

- Programming

Interactive Use

When the shell is used interactively, the system waits for you to type a command at the UNIX prompt. Your commands can include special symbols that let you abbreviate filenames or redirect input and output.

Customization of Your UNIX Session

A UNIX shell defines variables to control the behavior of your UNIX session. Setting these variables will tell the system, for example, which directory to use as your home directory, or the file in which to store your mail. Some variables are preset by the system; you can define others in start-up files that are read when you log in. Start-up files can also contain UNIX commands or special shell commands. These will be executed every time you log in.

Programming

UNIX shells provide a set of special (or built-in) commands that can be used to create programs called shell scripts. In fact, many built-in commands can be used interactively like UNIX commands, and UNIX commands are frequently used in shell scripts. Scripts are useful for executing a series of individual commands. This is similar to BATCH files in MS-DOS. Scripts can also execute commands repeatedly (in a loop) or conditionally (if-else), as in many high-level programming languages.

Shell Flavors

Many different UNIX shells are available. This book describes the three most popular shells:

- The Bourne (or standard) shell, the most compact shell but also the simplest

- The Korn shell, a superset of the Bourne shell that lets you edit the command line

- The C shell, which uses C syntax and has many conveniences

It also covers the SCO shell, a menu interface to the SCO operating system.

Most systems have more than one shell, and people will often use the Bourne shell for writing shell scripts and will use another shell for interactive use.

The /etc/passwd file determines which shell takes effect during your interactive UNIX session. When you log in, the system checks your entry in /etc/passwd. The last field of each entry calls a program to run as the default shell. For example:

If the program name is:	Your shell will be the:
/bin/sh	Bourne shell
/bin/rsh	Restricted Bourne shell
/bin/ksh	Korn shell
/bin/rksh	Restricted Korn shell
/bin/csh	C shell

You can change to another shell by typing the program name at the command line. For example, to change from the Bourne shell to the C shell, type:

```
$ exec csh
```

Common Features

The table below is a sampling of features that are common to the Bourne, Korn, and C shells. Note that the Korn shell is an enhanced version of the Bourne shell; therefore, the Korn shell includes all features of the Bourne shell, plus some others. The commands bg, fg, jobs, stop, and suspend are available only on systems that support job control.

Symbol/ Command	Meaning/Action
>	Redirect output.
>>	Append output to file.
<	Redirect input.
<<	"Here" document (redirect input).
|	Pipe output.
&	Run process in background.
;	Separate commands on same line
*	Match any character(s) in filename.
?	Match single character in filename.
[ ]	Match any characters enclosed.
( )	Execute in subshell.
` `	Substitute output of enclosed command.
" "	Partial quote (allows variable and command expansion).
' '	Full quote (no expansion)
\	Quote following character
$var	Use value for variable.
$$	Process id
$0	Command name
$n	nth argument ($0 < n < 9$)
$*	All arguments as a simple word
#	Begin comment.
bg	Background execution
break	Break from loop statements.
cd	Change directories.
continue	Resume a program loop.
echo	Display output.
eval	Evaluate arguments.
exec	Execute a new shell.
fg	Foreground execution
jobs	Show active jobs.
kill	Terminate running jobs.
newgrp	Change to a new group.
shift	Shift positional parameters.
stop	Suspend a background job.
suspend	Suspend a foreground job.
time	Time a command.
umask	Set or list file permissions.
unset	Erase variable or function definitions.
wait	Wait for a background job to finish.

Differing Features

The table below is a sampling of features that are different among the three shells.

sh	ksh	csh	Meaning/Action
:	:	:	Hide remarks.
$	$	%	Default prompt
		>!	Force redirection.
		>>!	Force append.
> file 2>&1	> file 2>&1	>& file	Combine stdout and stderr.
		{ }	Expand elements in list.
` `	$( )` `	` `	Substitute output of enclosed command.
$HOME	$HOME	$home	Home directory
	~	~	Home directory symbol
var=value	var=value	set var=value	Variable assignment
export var	export var=val	setenv var val	Set environment variable.
	${nn}		More than nine args can be referenced.
"$@"	"$@"		All args as separate words
$#	$#	$#argv	Number of arguments
$?	$?	$status	Exit status
$!	$!		Background exit status
$-	$-		Current options
. file	. file	source file	Read commands in file.
	alias x=y	alias x y	Name x stands for y.
case	case	switch/case	Choose alternatives.
	cd ~-	popd/pushd	Switch directories.
done	done	end	End a loop statement.
esac	esac	endsw	End case or switch.
exit [n]	exit [n]	exit [(expr)]	Exit with a status.
for/do	for/do	foreach	Loop through variables.
	print -r	glob	Ignore echo escapes.
hash	alias -t	hashstat	Display hashed commands (tracked aliases).
hash cmds	alias -t cmds	rehash	Remember command locations.
hash -r		unhash	Forget command locations.
	history	history	List previous commands.
	r	!!	Redo previous command.
	r str	!str	Redo command that starts with str.

---

sb	ksb	csb	Meaning/Action
	r x=y cmd	!cmd:s/x/y/	Edit command, then execute.
if [$i -eq 5]	if ((i==5))	if ($i==5)	Sample if statement
fi	fi	endif	End if statement.
ulimit	ulimit	limit	Set resource limits.
pwd	pwd	dirs	Print working directory.
read	read	$<	Read from terminal.
trap 2	trap 2	onintr	Ignore interrupts.
	unalias	unalias	Remove aliases.
until	until		Begin until loop.
while/do	while/do	while	Begin while loop.

The Bourne Shell
and Korn Shell

This section presents the following topics:

- Overview of features
- Syntax
- Variables
- Arithmetic expressions (Korn shell only)
- Command history (Korn shell only)
- Built-in commands
- Job control
- Invoking the shell
- Restricted shells

Overview of Features

The Bourne shell is the standard shell and provides the following features:

- Input/output redirection
- Wildcard characters (metacharacters) for filename abbreviation
- Shell variables for customizing your environment
- A built-in command set for writing shell programs

The Korn shell is a backward-compatible extension of the Bourne shell. Features that are valid only in the Korn shell are so indicated.

- Command-line editing (using vi or emacs)
- Access to previous commands (command history)
- Integer arithmetic
- More ways to match patterns and substitute variables
- Arrays and arithmetic expressions
- Command name abbreviation (aliasing)
- Job control

Syntax

This subsection describes the many symbols peculiar to the Bourne and Korn shells. The topics are arranged as follows:

- Special files
- Filename metacharacters
- Quoting
- Command forms
- Redirection forms
- Coprocesses (Korn shell only)

Special Files

/etc/profile	Executed automatically at login.
$HOME/.profile	Executed automatically at login.
/etc/passwd	Source of home directories for ~name abbreviations.
$ENV	Specifies the name of a file to read when a new Korn shell is created.

Filename Metacharacters

*	Match any string of zero or more characters.
?	Match any single character.
[abc...]	Match any one of the enclosed characters; a hyphen can be used to specify a range (e.g., a-z, A-Z, 0-9).
[!abc...]	Match any character *not* enclosed as above.

In the Korn shell:

?(pattern)	Match zero or one instance of *pattern*.
*(pattern)	Match zero or more instances of *pattern*.
+(pattern)	Match one or more instance of *pattern*.
@(pattern)	Match exactly one instance of *pattern*.
!(pattern)	Match any strings that don't contain *pattern*.
~	HOME directory of the current user
~name	HOME directory of user *name*
~+	Current working directory (PWD)
~-	Previous working directory (OLDPWD)

The *pattern* above can be a sequence of patterns separated by |, meaning that the match applies to any of the patterns. This extended syntax resembles that available to **egrep** and **awk**.

Examples

`$ ls new*`	*List* new *and* new.1.
`$ cat ch?`	*Match* ch9 *but not* ch10.
`$ vi [D-R]*`	*Match files that begin with uppercase D through R.*
`$ cp !(Junk*|Temp*)*.c ..`	*Korn shell only. Copy C source files except for* Junk *and* Temp *files.*

Quoting

Quoting disables a character's special meaning and allows it to be used literally, as itself. The following characters have special meaning to the Bourne and Korn shells:

;	Command separator
&	Background execution
( )	Command grouping
|	Pipe
> < &	Redirection symbols
* ? [ ] ~ + - @ !	Filename metacharacters
" ' \	Used in quoting other characters.
`	Command substitution

$ Variable substitution (or command substitution)

newline space tab   Word separators

The characters below can be used for quoting:

" "   Everything between " and " is taken literally, except for the following characters that keep their special meaning:

       $ Variable substitution will occur.

       `   Command substitution will occur.

       "   This marks the end of the double quote.

' '   Everything between ' and ' is taken literally except for another '.

\   The character following a \ is taken literally. Use within " " to escape ", $, and `. Often used to escape itself, spaces, or newlines.

Examples

```
$ echo 'Single quotes "protect" double quotes'
Single quotes "protect" double quotes

$ echo "Well, isn't that \"special\"?"
Well, isn't that "special"?

$ echo "You have `ls|wc -1` files in `pwd`"
You have       43 files in /home/bob

$ echo "The value of \$x is $x"
The value of $x is 100
```

Command Forms

cmd **&**	Execute *cmd* in background.
cmd1 **;** *cmd2*	Command sequence; execute multiple *cmd*s on the same line.
(*cmd1* **;** *cmd2*)	Subshell; treat *cmd1* and *cmd2* as a command group.
cmd1 **|** *cmd2*	Pipe; use output from *cmd1* as input to *cmd2*.
cmd1 `cmd2`	Command substitution; use *cmd2* output as arguments to *cmd1*.
cmd1 **$(** *cmd2* **)**	Korn-shell command substitution; nesting is allowed.
cmd1 **&&** *cmd2*	AND; execute *cmd1* and then (if *cmd1* succeeds) *cmd2*.
cmd1 **||** *cmd2*	OR; execute either *cmd1* or (if *cmd1* fails) *cmd2*.
{ *cmd1* **;** *cmd2* **}**	Execute commands in the current shell.

Examples

```
$ nroff file &                          Format in the background.
$ cd; ls                                Execute sequentially.
$ (date; who; pwd) > logfile            All output is redirected.
$ sort file | pr -3 | lp                Sort file, page output, then print.
$ vi `grep -1 ifdef *.c`                Edit files found by grep.
$ egrep '(yes|no)' `cat list`           Specify a list of files to search.
```

```
$ egrep '(yes|no)' $(cat list)        Korn shell version of previous.
$ egrep '(yes|no)' $(<list)           Same, but faster.
$ grep XX file && lp file             Print file if it contains the pattern,
$ grep XX file || echo "XX not found"  otherwise, echo an error message.
```

Redirection Forms

File Descriptor	Name	Common Abbreviation	Typical Default
0	Standard input	stdin	Keyboard
1	Standard output	stdout	Terminal
2	Standard error	stderr	Terminal

The usual input source or output destination can be changed as follows:

Simple redirection

cmd > *file*   Send standard output of *cmd* to *file* (overwrite).

cmd >> *file*   Send standard output of *cmd* to *file* (append).

cmd < *file*   Take standard input for *cmd* from *file*.

cmd << *text*   Read standard input up to a line identical to *text* (*text* can be stored in a shell variable). Input is usually typed on the screen or in the shell program. Commands that typically use this syntax include **cat**, **echo**, **ex**, and **sed**. (If <<– is used, leading tabs are ignored when comparing input with end-of-input *text* marker.) This command form is sometimes called a "Here" document.

Redirection using file descriptors

cmd >&*n*   Send *cmd* standard output to file descriptor *n*.

cmd *m*>&*n*   Same, except that output that would normally go to file descriptor *m* is sent to file descriptor *n* instead.

cmd >&–   Close standard output.

cmd <&*n*   Take input for *cmd* from file descriptor *n*.

cmd *m*<&*n*   Same, except that input that would normally come from file descriptor *m* comes from file descriptor *n* instead.

cmd <&–   Close standard input.

Multiple redirection

cmd **2>**file   Send standard error to *file*; standard output remains the same (e.g., the screen).

cmd > file **2>&1**   Send both standard error and standard output to *file*.

(*cmd* > f1) **2>**f2   Send standard output to file *f1*; standard error to file *f2*.

cmd | **tee** *files* Send output of *cmd* to standard output (usually the terminal) and to *files*. (See the example in Section 3 under **tee**.)

No space should appear between file descriptors and a redirection symbol; spacing is optional in the other cases.

Bourne and Korn

Examples

```
$ cat part1 > book
$ cat part2 part3 >> book
$ mail tim < report

$ sed 's/^/XX /g' << END_ARCHIVE
> This is often how a shell archive is "wrapped",
> bundling text for distribution.  You would normally
> run sed from a shell program, not from the command line.
> END_ARCHIVE
XX This is often how a shell archive is "wrapped",
XX bundling text for distribution.  You would normally
XX run sed from a shell program, not from the command line.
```

To redirect standard output to standard error:

```
$ echo "Usage error:  see administrator" 1>&2
```

The following command will send output (files found) to **filelist** and send error messages (inaccessible files) to file **no_access**:

```
$ (find / -print > filelist) 2>no_access
```

Coprocesses

Coprocesses are a feature of the Korn shell only.

cmd1 **|** *cmd2* **|&**	Coprocess; execute the pipeline in the background. The shell sets up a two-way pipe, allowing redirection of both standard input and standard output.
read -p *var*	Read coprocess input into variable *var*.
print -p *string*	Write *string* to the coprocess.
cmd **<&p**	Take input for *cmd* from the coprocess.
cmd **>&p**	Send output of *cmd* to the coprocess.

Examples

```
ed - memo |&            Start coprocess.
print -p /word/         Send ed command to coprocess.
read -p search          Read output of ed command into variable search.
print "$search"         Show the line on standard output.
A word to the wise.
```

Variables

This subsection describes the following:

- Variable substitution
- Built-in shell variables
- Other shell variables
- Arrays (Korn shell only)

Variable Substitution

No spaces should be used in the expressions below. The colon (`:`) is optional; if it's included, *var* must be non-null as well as set.

`var=value ...`	Set each variable *var* to a *value*.
`${var}`	Use value of *var*; braces are optional if *var* is separated.
`${var:-value}`	Use *var* if set; otherwise, use *value*.
`${var:=value}`	Use *var* if set; otherwise, use *value* and assign *value* to *var*.
`${var:?value}`	Use *var* if set; otherwise, print *value* and exit. If *value* isn't supplied, print the phrase "parameter null or not set."
`${var:+value}`	Use *value* if *var* is set; otherwise, use nothing.

In the Korn shell:

`${#var}`	Use the length of *var*.
`${#*}`	Use the number of positional parameters.
`${#@}`	Use the number of positional parameters.
`${var#pattern}`	Use value of *var* after removing *pattern* from the left. Remove the shortest matching piece.
`${var##pattern}`	Same as *#pattern*, but remove longest matching piece.
`${var%pattern}`	Use value of *var* after removing *pattern* from the right. Remove smallest matching piece
`${var%%pattern}`	Same as *%pattern*, but remove longest matching piece.

Examples

`$ u=up d=down blank=`	*Assign values to three variables (last is null).*
`$ echo ${u}root` `uproot`	*Braces are needed here.*
`$ echo ${u-$d}` `up`	*Display value of* u *or* d; *since* u *is set, it is printed.*
`$ echo ${tmp-`date`}` `Thu Feb  4 15:03:46 EST 1993`	*If* tmp *is not set, the* date *command is executed.*
`$ echo ${blank="no data"}`	blank *is set, so it is printed (a blank line).*
`$ echo ${blank:="no data"}` `no data`	blank *is set but null, so the string is printed*
`$ echo $blank` `no data`	blank *now has a new value*

Built-in Shell Variables

Built-in variables are automatically set by the shell and are typically used inside shell scripts. Built-in variables can make use of the variable substitution patterns shown above. Note that the $ is not actually part of the variable name, although the variable is always referenced this way.

`$#`	Number of command-line arguments
`$-`	Options currently in effect (arguments supplied to **sh** or to **set**)
`$?`	Exit value of last executed command
`$$`	Process number of current process
`$!`	Process number of last background command or coprocess
`$0`	First word; that is, command name
`$n`	Individual arguments on command line (positional parameters). The Bourne shell allows only nine parameters to be referenced directly (n = 1-9); the Korn shell allows n to be greater than 9 if specified as $\{n\}$.
`$*`	All arguments on command line ("$1 $2 . . .")
`"$@"`	All arguments on command line, individually quoted ("$1" "$2" . . .)

The Korn shell automatically sets these additional variables:

`$_`	Temporary variable; initialized to pathname of script or program being executed. Later, stores the last argument of previous command. Also stores name of matching MAIL file during mail checks.
ERRNO	Error number of last system call that failed
LINENO	Current line number within the script or function
OLDPWD	Previous working directory (set by **cd**)
OPTARG	Name of last option processed by **getopts**
OPTIND	Numerical index of next argument to be processed
PPID	Process number of this shell's parent
PWD	Current working directory (set by **cd**)
RANDOM[=n]	Generate a new random number with each reference; start with integer n, if given.
REPLY	Default reply used by **select** and **read**
SECONDS[=n]	Number of seconds since the shell was started, or, if n is given, number of seconds + n since the shell started

Other Shell Variables

The variables below are not automatically set by the shell. They are typically used in your **.profile** file, where you can define them to suit your needs. Variables can be assigned values by issuing commands of the form:

$ *variable=value*

The list below includes the type of value expected when defining these variables. Those that are specific to the Korn shell are marked as (K).

CDPATH=*dirs*	Directories searched by **cd**; allows shortcuts in changing directories; unset by default.

`COLUMNS=`*n*	(K) Screen's column width; used in line edit modes and **select** lists.
`EDITOR=`*file*	(K) Pathname of line edit mode to turn on (can end in **emacs** or **vi**); used when VISUAL is not set.
`ENV=`*file*	(K) Name of script that gets executed at startup; this is useful for storing alias and function definitions. For example, ENV=$HOME/.kshrc (like C shell's .cshrc).
`FCEDIT=`*file*	(K) Editor used by **fc** command (default is **/bin/ed**)
`FPATH=`*dirs*	(K) Directories to search for function definitions; undefined functions are set via **typeset -fu**; FPATH is searched when these functions are first referenced.
`HISTFILE=`*file*	(K) File in which to store command history (must be set before **ksh** first accesses history file); default is $HOME/.sh_history.
`HISTSIZE=`*n*	(K) Number of history commands available (must be set before **ksh** first accesses history file); default is 128.
`HOME=`*dir*	Home directory; set by **login** (from **passwd** file).
`IFS='`*chars*`'`	Internal field separators; default is space, tab, and newline.
`LANG=`*dir*	Directory to use for certain language-dependent programs
`LINES=`*n*	(K) Screen's line length; used for **select** lists.
`MAIL=`*file*	Default file to check for mail. Changing this will not change where your mail is delivered; set by **login**.
`MAILCHECK=`*n*	Number of seconds between mail checks; default is 10 minutes.
`MAILPATH=`*files*	One or more files, delimited by a colon, to check for mail. Each file is printed. The Korn shell prompt is ? and the default message is `You have mail in $_`. The Bourne shell prompt is % and the default message is `You have mail`.
`PATH=`*dir*	One or more pathnames, delimited by a colon, in which to search for commands to execute; default is **/usr/bin**.
`PS1=`*string*	Primary prompt string; default is **$**.
`PS2=`*string*	Secondary prompt (used in multi-line commands); default is **>**.
`PS3=`*string*	(K) Prompt string in **select** loops; default is **#?**.
`PS4=`*string*	(K) Prompt string for execution trace (**ksh -x** or **set -x**); default is **+**.
`SHACCT=`*file*	"Shell account"; file in which to log executed shell scripts. Not in Korn shell.
`SHELL=`*file*	Pathname of shell (e.g., **/bin/sh**).
`TERM=`*string*	Terminal type.
`TMOUT=`*n*	(K) If no command is typed after *n* seconds, exit the shell.
`VISUAL=`*path*	(K) Same as EDITOR, but VISUAL is checked first.

Bourne and Korn

The Bourne Shell and Korn Shell

Arrays

The Korn shell supports one-dimensional arrays of up to 1024 elements. The first element is numbered 0. An array *name* can be initialized as follows:

> **set** -A *name value0 value1* ...

where the specified values become elements of *name*. Declaring arrays is not required, however. Any valid reference to a subscripted variable can create an array.

When referencing arrays, you can use the ${ ... } syntax. This isn't needed when referencing arrays inside (( )) (the form of **let** that does automatic quoting). Note that [and] are typed literally (i.e., they don't stand for optional syntax).

${*name*[*i*]}	Use element *i* of array *name*. *i* can be any arithmetic expression as described under **let**. The expression must return a value between 0 and 1023.
${*name*[*]}	Use all elements of array *name*.
${*name*}	Use element 0 of array *name*.
${*name*[*]}	Use all elements in array *name*.
${#*name*[*]}	Use the number of elements in array *name*.
${#*name*[@]}	Use the number of elements in array *name*.

Arithmetic Expressions

The Korn shell's **let** command performs integer arithmetic. The Korn shell provides a way to substitute integer values (for use as command arguments or in variables); base conversion is also possible:

$((*expr*))	Use the value of the enclosed arithmetic expression.
B#*n*	Interpret integer *n* in numeric base *B*. For example, 8#100 specifies the octal equivalent of decimal 64.

Operators

The Korn shell uses arithmetic operators from the C programming language; they are listed below in decreasing order of precedence. Use parentheses to override precedence.

–	Unary minus
! ~	Logical negation; binary inversion (one's complement)
* / %	Multiplication; division; modulus (remainder)
+ –	Addition; subtraction
<< >>	Bitwise left shift; bitwise right shift
<= >=	Less than or equal to; greater than or equal to
< >	Less than; greater than
== !=	Equality; inequality (both evaluated left to right)

&		Bitwise AND
^		Bitwise exclusive OR
|		Bitwise OR
&&		Logical AND
||		Logical OR
*=	**/=** **%=**	Assignment
=	**+=** **-=**	
<<=	**>>=**	
&=	**^=** **|=**	

Examples

See the **let** command for more information and examples.

```
let "count=0" "i = i + 1"
let "num % 2"
(( percent >= 0 && percent <= 100 ))
```
Assign i *and* count.
Test for an even number.
Test the range of a value.

Command History

The Korn shell lets you display or modify previous commands. This is similar to the C shell's history mechanism. Commands in the history list can be modified using:

• Line-edit mode

• The **fc** command

Line-edit Mode

Line-edit mode lets you emulate many features of the vi or emacs editors. The history list is treated like a file. When the editor is invoked, you type editing keystrokes to move to the command line you want to execute. You can also change the line before executing it. When you're ready to issue the command, press RETURN.

Line-edit mode can be started in several ways. For example, these are equivalent:

```
$ VISUAL=vi
$ EDITOR=vi
$ set -o vi          Overrides value of VISUAL or EDITOR
```

Note that vi starts in input mode; to type a vi command, press ESCAPE first.

Common editing keystrokes

vi	*emacs*	*Result*
k	**CTRL-p**	Get previous command.
j	**CTRL-n**	Get next command.
/string	**CTRL-r** string	Get previous command containing *string*.
h	**CTRL-b**	Move back one character.

The Bourne Shell and Korn Shell

l	CTRL-f	Move forward one character.
b	ESC-b	Move back one word.
w	ESC-f	Move forward one word.
X	DEL	Delete previous character.
x	CTRL-d	Delete one character.
dw	ESC-d	Delete word forward.
db	ESC-h	Delete word back.
xp	CTRL-t	Transpose two characters.

The fc Command

Use fc -l to list history commands and fc -e to edit them. See the entry under built-in commands for more information.

Examples

$ history	*List the last 16 commands.*
$ fc -l 20 30	*List commands 20 through 30.*
$ fc -l -5	*List the last five commands.*
$ fc -l cat	*List the last command beginning with* cat.
$ fc -ln 5 > doit	*Save command 5 to file* doit.
$ fc -e vi 5 20	*Edit commands 5 through 20 using* vi.
$ fc -e emacs	*Edit previous command using* emacs.
$ r	*Re-execute previous command.*
$ r cat	*Re-execute last* cat *command.*
$ r doc=Doc	*Substitute (doc becomes Doc), then re-execute last command.*
$ r chap=doc c	*Re-execute last command that begins with* c, *but change string* chap *to* doc.

Built-in Commands (Bourne and Korn Shell)

Examples to be entered as a command line are shown with the $ prompt. Otherwise, examples should be treated as code fragments that might be included in a shell script. For convenience, some of the reserved words used by multi-line commands are also included.

#	#
	Ignore all text that follows on the same line. # is used in shell scripts as the comment character and is not really a command. (Take care when commenting a Bourne-shell script. A file that has # as its first character is sometimes interpreted as a C-shell script.)
#!*shell*	#!*shell*
	Used as the first line of a script to invoke the named *shell* (with optional arguments). Not supported in all shells. For example:
	`#!/bin/sh -v`

In SCO Open Desktop 2.0 (and commensurate versions of SCO UNIX), this feature was available, but not by default; one had to change a kernel parameter and rebuild the kernel to activate it. In SCO ODT 3.0 it is built in and activated by default.

#!shell

:

:

Null command. Returns an exit status of 0. Sometimes used as the first character in a file to denote a Bourne shell script. See example below and under **case**. In the Korn shell, shell variables can be placed after the : to expand them to their values.

Example

Check whether someone is logged in:

```
if who | grep $1 > /dev/null
then :                    # do nothing
                          # if pattern is found
else echo "User $1 is not logged in"
fi
```

. *file* [*arguments*]

.

Read and execute lines in *file*. *file* does not have to be executable but must reside in a directory searched by PATH. The Korn shell supports *arguments* that are stored in the positional parameters.

[[*expression*]]

[[ ]]

Korn shell only. Same as **test** *expression* or [*expression*], except that [[ ]] allows additional operators. Word splitting and filename expansion are disabled. Note that the brackets ([ ]) are typed literally.

Additional operators

&&	Logical AND of test expressions.
| |	Logical OR of test expressions.
>	First string is lexically "greater than" the second.
<	First string is lexically "less than" the second.

Bourne and Korn

---

name* () { *commands*; }

name

Define *name* as a function. Syntax can be written on one line or across many. Since the Bourne shell has no aliasing capability, simple functions can serve as aliases. The Korn shell provides the **function** command, an alternate form that works the same way.

→

name
←
	Example
	
	``
	$ count () {
	> ls
		wc -lP
		> }
		``
		
		When issued at the command line, **count** will now display the number of files in the current directory.

alias	**alias** [*options*] [*name*[='*cmd*']]
	
	Korn shell only. Assign a shorthand *name* as a synonym for *cmd*. If ='*cmd*' is omitted, print the alias for *name*; if *name* is also omitted, print all aliases. See also **unalias**. The aliases below are built into the Korn shell. Some use names of existing Bourne-shell or C-shell commands (which points out the similarities among the shells).
	
	``
	autoload='typeset -fu'
	echo='print -'
	false='let 0'
	function='typeset -f'
	hash='alias -t'
	history='fc -l'
	integer='typeset -i'
	nohup='nohup '
	pwd='print -r - $PWD'
	r='fc -e -'
	true=':'
	type='whence -v'
	``
	
	Options
	
	   -t Create a tracked alias for a UNIX command *name*. The Korn shell remembers the full pathname of the command, allowing it to be found more quickly and to be issued from any directory. If no name is supplied, current tracked aliases are listed. Tracked aliases are the same as hashed commands in the Bourne shell.
	
	   -x Export the alias; it can now be used in shell scripts and other subshells. If no name is supplied, current exported aliases are listed.
	
	Example
	
	``
	alias dir='basename `pwd`'
	``

autoload	**autoload** [*functions*] Load (define) the *functions* only when they are first used. Korn shell alias for **typeset -fu**.

bg [*jobIDs*]

Put current job or *jobIDs* in the background (Korn shell only). See "Job Control" later in this section.

break [*n*]

Exit from the innermost (most deeply nested) **for**, **while**, or **until** loop, or from the *n* innermost levels of the loop. Also exits from a **select** list.

case *value* **in**
    pattern1) *cmds1*;;
    pattern2) *cmds2*;;

    .

    .

    .

esac

Execute the first set of commands (*cmds1*) if *value* matches *pattern1*, execute the second set of commands (*cmds2*) if *value* matches *pattern2*, etc. Be sure the last command in each set ends with ;; . *value* is typically a positional parameter or other shell variable. *cmds* are typically UNIX commands, shell programming commands, or variable assignments. Patterns can use file generation metacharacters. Multiple patterns (separated by |) can be specified on the same line; in this case, the associated *cmds* are executed whenever *value* matches any of these patterns. See below and under **eval** for examples. (Note: the Korn shell allows *pattern* to be preceded by an optional open parenthesis, as in (*pattern*). It's useful for balancing parentheses inside a $( ) construct.)

Examples

Use first command-line argument to determine appropriate action:

```
case $1 in            #match the first arg
   no|yes) response=1;;
   -[tT])  table=TRUE;;
   *)      echo "unknown option"; exit 1;;
esac
```

Read user-supplied lines until user exits:

```
while :               # Null command; always true
do
   echo "Type . to finish ==> \c"
   read line
   case "$line" in
      .) echo "Message done"
         break ;;
      *) echo "$line" >> $message ;;
   esac
done
```

cd	cd [*dir*]
	cd [-]
	cd [*old new*]
	
	With no arguments, change to home directory of user. Otherwise, change working directory to *dir*. If *dir* is a relative pathname but is not in the current directory, then the CDPATH variable is searched. The last two command forms are specific to the Korn shell, where - stands for the previous directory. The third syntax modifies the current directory name by replacing string *old* with *new*, then switches to the resulting directory.
	
	Example
	
	<pre>$ **pwd**
	/usr/spool/cron
	$ **cd cron uucp** # cd prints the new directory
	/usr/spool/uucp</pre>

continue	continue [*n*] Skip remaining commands in a **for, while,** or **until** loop, resuming with the next iteration of the loop (or skipping *n* loops).
do	do Reserved word that precedes the command sequence in a **for, while, until,** or **select** statement.
done	done Reserved word that ends a **for, while, until,** or **select** statement.
echo	echo [-n] [*string*] Write *string* to standard output; if -n is specified, the output is not terminated by a newline. If no *string* is supplied, echo a newline. In the Korn shell, **echo** is just an alias for **print -**. (See also **echo** in Section 3.) **echo** understands special escape characters, which must be quoted (or escaped with a \) to prevent interpretation by the shell:

\b	Backspace
\c	Suppress the terminating newline (same as -n).
\f	Formfeed
\n	Newline
\r	Carriage return
\t	Tab character
\\	Backslash
\0*nnn*	ASCII character represented by octal number *nnn*, where *nnn* is 1, 2, or 3 digits and is preceded by a 0.

```
$ echo "testing printer" | lp
$ echo "Warning: ringing bell \007"
```

esac

Reserved word that ends a **case** statement. Omitting **esac** is a common programming error.

eval *args*

Typically, **eval** is used in shell scripts, and *args* is a line of code that contains shell variables. **eval** forces variable expansion to happen first and then runs the resulting command. This "double scanning" is useful any time shell variables contain input/output redirection symbols, aliases, or other shell variables. (For example, redirection normally happens before variable expansion, so a variable containing redirection symbols must be expanded first using **eval**; otherwise, the redirection symbols remain uninterpreted.) See the C-shell **eval** (Section 6) for another example.

Example

This fragment of a Bourne shell script shows how **eval** constructs a command that is interpreted in the right order:

```
for option
do
    case "$option" in     #define where output goes
        save) out=' > $newfile' ;;
        show) out=' | more' ;;
    esac
done
...
eval sort $file $out
```

exec [*command*]

Execute *command* in place of the current process (instead of creating a new process). **exec** is also useful for opening, closing, or copying file descriptors.

Examples

```
trap 'exec 2>&-' 0          Close standard error when
                            shell script exits (signal 0).
$ exec /bin/csh             Replace current shell with C shell.
$ exec < infile             Reassign standard input to infile.
```

exit [*n*]

Exit a shell script with status *n* (e.g., **exit 1**). *n* can be 0 (success) or nonzero (failure). If *n* is not given, exit status will be that of the most

Bourne and Korn

→

exit
←
	recent command. **exit** can be issued at the command line to close a window (log out).
	
	Example
	
	``
	if [$# -eq 0]; then
	    echo "Usage: $0 [-c] [-d] file(s)"
	    exit 1 # Error status
	fi
	``

export	**export** [*variables*] **export** [*name*=[*value*]] . . . Pass (export) the value of one or more shell *variables*, giving global meaning to the variables (which are local by default). For example, a variable defined in one shell script must be exported if its value will be used in other programs called by the script. If no *variables* are given, **export** lists the variables exported by the current shell. The second form is the Korn shell version, which is similar to the first form except that you can set a variable *name* to a *value* before exporting it. *Example* In the Bourne shell, you would type: ``` TERM=vt100 export TERM ``` In the Korn shell, you could type this instead: ``` export TERM=vt100 ```
false	**false** Korn shell alias for **let 0**.
fc	**fc** [*options*] [*first* [*last*]] **fc** -e - [*old*=*new*] [*command*] Korn shell only. Display or edit commands in the history list. (Use only one of -l or -e.) **fc** provides capabilities similar to the C shell's **history** and ! syntax. *first* and *last* are numbers or strings specifying the range of commands to display or edit. If *last* is omitted, **fc** applies to a single command (specified by *first*). If both *first* and *last* are omitted, **fc** edits the previous command or lists the last 16. The second form of **fc** takes a history *command*, replaces *old* string with *new* string, and executes the modified command. If no strings are specified, *command* is just re-executed. If no *command* is given either, the previous command is re-executed. *command* is a number or string like *first*. See examples under "Command History."

> -e [*editor*]
>> Invoke *editor* to edit the specified history commands. The default *editor* is set by shell variable FCEDIT.
>
> -e -
>> Execute (or redo) a history command; refer to second syntax line above.
>
> -l
>> List the specified command or range of commands, or list the last 16.
>
> -n
>> Suppress command numbering from the –l listing.
>
> -r
>> Reverse the order of the –l listing.

fg [*jobIDs*]

Bring current job or *jobIDs* to the foreground. See "Job Control."

fi

Reserved word that ends an **if** statement. (Don't forget to use it!)

for *x* [in *list*]
do
commands
done

For variable *x* (in optional *list* of values) do *commands*. If *list* is omitted, "$@" (positional parameters) is assumed.

Examples

Paginate files specified on the command line; save each result:

```
for file do
     pr $file > $file.tmp
done
```

Search chapters for a list of words (like **fgrep -f**):

```
for item in `cat program_list`
do
     echo "Checking chapters for"
     echo "references to program $item..."
     grep -c "$item.[co]" chap*
done
```

Extract a one-word title from each file and use as new filename:

```
for file do
     name=`sed -n 's/NAME: //p' $file`
     mv $file $name
done
```

function	function *name* { *commands;* } Korn shell alias for **typeset** -f. See *name* earlier in this listing.
getopts	**getopts** *string name* [*args*] Process command-line arguments (or *args*, if specified) and check for legal options. **getopts** is used in shell script loops and is intended to ensure standard syntax for command-line options. Standard syntax dictates that command-line options begin with a + or a –. Options can be stacked; i.e., consecutive letters can follow a single –. End processing of options by specifying –– on the command line. *string* contains the option letters to be recognized by **getopts** when running the shell script. Valid options are processed in turn and stored in the shell variable *name*. If an option is followed by a colon, the option must be followed by one or more arguments. **getopts** uses the shell variables OPTARG and OPTIND. **getopts** is available to non-Bourne shell users as **/usr/bin/getopts**.
hash	hash Korn shell alias for **alias** -t. Emulates Bourne shell's **hash**.
hash	**hash** [-r] [*commands*] Bourne shell version. Search for *commands* and remember the directory in which each command resides. Hashing causes the shell to remember the association between a "name" and the absolute pathname of an executable, so that future executions don't require a search of $PATH. With no arguments, **hash** lists the current hashed commands. The display shows *hits* (the number of times the command is called by the shell) and *cost* (the level of work needed to find the command).
history	history Show the last 16 commands. Korn shell alias for **fc** -l.
if	**if** *condition1* **then** *commands1* [**elif** *condition2* **then** *commands2*] . . . [**else** *commands3*] **fi** If *condition1* is met, do *commands1*; otherwise, if *condition2* is met, do *commands2*; if neither is met, do *commands3*. Conditions are usually specified with the **test** command. See additional examples under : and **exit**.

Insert a 0 before numbers less than 10:

```
if [ $counter -lt 10 ] then
    number=0$counter else number=$counter fi
```

Make a directory if it doesn't exist:

```
if [ ! -d $dir ]; then
    mkdir $dir chmod 775 $dir fi
```

---

integer   integer

Specify integer variables. Korn shell alias for **typeset** –i.

---

jobs [*options*] [*jobIDs*]   jobs

Korn shell only. List all running or stopped jobs, or list those specified by *jobIDs*. For example, you can check whether a long compilation or text format is still running. Also useful before logging out.
See also "Job Control" later in this section.

Options

-l   List job IDs and process group IDs.

-n   List only jobs whose status changed since last notifica-
        tion. Korn shell only.

-p   List process group IDs only.

---

kill [*options*] *IDs*   kill

Terminate each specified process *ID* or job *ID*. You must own the
process or be a privileged user. This built-in is for Korn shell only,
and is similar to **/bin/kill** described in Section 3. See also "Job Control."

Options

-l   List the signal names. (Used by itself.)

-*signal* The signal number (from **ps** -f) or name (from **kill** -l).
          With a signal number of 9, the kill is absolute.

---

let *expressions*   let
    or ((*expressions*))

Korn shell only. Perform arithmetic as specified by one or more integer *expressions*. *expressions* consist of numbers, operators, and shell
variables (which don't need a preceding $). Expressions must be
quoted if they contain spaces or other special characters. The (( ))
form does the quoting for you. For more information and examples,
see "Arithmetic Expressions" earlier in this section. See also **expr** in
Section 3.

→

let ←	*Examples* Each example below adds 1 to variable i. ``` i=`expr $i + 1` let i=i+1 let "i = i + 1" ((i = i + 1)) ```
newgrp	**newgrp** [*group*] Change your group ID to *group*, or return to your default group.
nohup	**nohup** Don't terminate a command after logout. **nohup** is a Korn shell alias: ``` nohup='nohup ' ``` The embedded space at the end lets **nohup** interpret the following command as an alias, if needed.
print	**print** [*options*] [*string* ...] Korn shell only. Display *string* (on standard output by default). **print** includes the functions of **echo** and can be used in its place on most UNIX systems. *Options* - Treat following options as strings even if they start with –. – – Same as –. -n Don't end output with a newline. -p Send *string* to the process created by |&, instead of to standard output. -r Ignore the escape sequences often used with **echo**. -R Same as -r, and treat following options as strings even if they start with – (**except -n**). -s Send *string* to the history file. -u[*n*] Send *string* to file descriptor *n* (default is 1).
pwd	**pwd** Print your present working directory on standard output. In the Korn shell, this is really an alias for **print -r - $PWD**.
r	**r** Re-execute previous command. Korn shell alias for **fc -e -**.

read *variable1* [*variable2* ...]

Bourne shell. Read one line of standard input, and assign each word (as defined by IFS) to the corresponding *variable*, with all leftover words assigned to last variable. If only one variable is specified, the entire line will be assigned to that variable. See example below and under **case**. The return status is 0 unless *EOF* is reached.

Example

```
$ read first last address
Sarah Caldwell 123 Main Street

$ echo "$last, $first\n$address"
Caldwell, Sarah
123 Main Street
```

read [*options*] [*variable1*?*string*] [*variable2* ...]

Korn shell only. Same as in the Bourne shell, except that the Korn shell version supports the options below as well as the ? syntax for prompting. If a variable is followed by ?*string*, then *string* is displayed as a user prompt. If no variables are given, input is stored in the REPLY variable.

Options

-p   Read from the output of a |& coprocess.
-r   Raw mode; ignore \ as a line continuation character.
-s   Save input as a command in the history file.
-u[*n*]   Read input from file descriptor *n* (default is 0).

Example

Prompt yourself to enter two temperatures:

```
$ read n1?"High low: " n2 High low: 65 33
```

readonly [*variable1 variable2* ...]

Prevent the specified shell variables from being assigned new values. Variables can be accessed (read) but not overwritten. In the Korn shell, the syntax *variable=value* can be used to assign a new value that cannot be changed.

return [*n*]

Used inside a function definition. Exit the function with status *n* or with the exit status of the previously executed command.

Bourne and Korn

select	select *x* [in *list*] do *commands* done

Korn shell only. Display a list of menu items on standard error, numbered in the order they are specified in *list*. If no *list* is given, items
are read from the command line (via "$@"). Following the menu is a
prompt string (set by PS3). At the PS3 prompt, users select a menu
item by typing its line number, or they redisplay the menu by typing
RETURN. (User input is stored in the environment variable REPLY.) If a
valid line number is typed, *x* is set to the item corresponding to the
number typed, then *commands* are executed.

Example

```
PS3="Select the item number:"

select event in Format Page View Exit
do
    case "$event" in
       Format) nroff $file | lp;;
       Page)   pr $file | lp;;
       View)   cat $file
       Exit)   exit 0;;
       *   )   echo "Invalid selection";;
    esac
done
```

The output of this script would look like this:

```
1. Format
2. Page
3. View
4. Exit
Select the item number:
```

set	set [*options arg1 arg2 ...*]

With no arguments, set prints the values of all variables known to the
current shell. Options can be enabled (–*option*) or disabled
(+*option*). Options can also be set when the shell is invoked, via **ksh**
or **sh**. (See "Invoking the Shell" at the end of this section.) Arguments are assigned in order to $1, $2, etc.

Options

+A *name*
> Assign remaining arguments as elements of array *name*.
> Korn shell only.

-A *name*
> Same as +A, but unset *name* before making assignments.
> Korn shell only.

-a	From now on, automatically mark variables for export after defining or changing them.
-e	Exit if a command yields a nonzero exit status. In the Korn shell, the ERR trap is issued before the command exits.
-f	Do not expand filename metacharacters (e.g., * ? [ ]).
-h	Locate commands as they are defined. The Korn shell creates tracked aliases, whereas the Bourne shell hashes function names. See **hash**.
-k	Assignment of environment variables (*var=value*) will take effect regardless of where they appear on the command line. Normally, assignments must precede the command name.
-m	Enable job control; background jobs will execute in a separate process group. -m is usually set automatically. Korn shell only.
-n	Read commands but don't execute; useful for checking errors.
-o [*m*]	List Korn shell modes, or turn on mode *m*. Many modes can be set by other options. Modes are:

allexport	Same as -a
bgnice	Run background jobs at lower priority.
emacs	Set command-line editor to **emacs**.
errexit	Same as -e
ignoreeof	Do not exit on *EOF*. To exit the shell, type **exit**.
keyword	Same as -k
markdirs	Append / to directory names during pathname expansion.
monitor	Same as -m
noclobber	Prevent overwriting via > redirection; use >| to overwrite files.
noexec	Same as -n
noglob	Same as -f
nolog	Omit function definitions from history file.
nounset	Same as -u
privileged	Same as -p
trackall	Same as -h
verbose	Same as -v
vi	Set command-line editor to **vi**.
viraw	Same as **vi**, but process each character when it's typed.
xtrace	Same as -x

-p	Start up as a privileged user (i.e., don't process $HOME/.profile).
-s	Sort the positional parameters. Korn shell only.

Bourne and Korn

set	-t	Exit after one command is executed.
←	-u	In substitutions, treat unset variables as errors.
	-v	Show each shell command line when read.
	-x	Show commands and arguments when executed, preceded by a +. This provides step-by-step debugging of shell scripts. (Same as -o xtrace.)
	-	Turn off -v and -x, and turn off option processing. Included in Korn shell for compatibility with older versions of Bourne shell.
	- -	Used as the last option; - - turns off option processing so that arguments beginning with - are not misinterpreted as options. (For example, you can set $1 to -1.) If no arguments are given after - -, unset the positional parameters.

Examples

```
set -- "$num" -20 -30     Set $1 to $num, $2 to -20, $3 to -30.
set -vx                   Read each command line; show it;
                          execute it; show it again (with arguments).
set +x                    Stop command tracing.
set -o noclobber          Prevent file overwriting.
set +o noclobber          Allow file overwriting again.
```

---

shift

shift [*n*]

Shift positional arguments (e.g., $2 becomes $1). If *n* is given, shift to the left *n* places. Used in **while** loops to iterate through command-line arguments. In the Korn shell, *n* can be an integer expression.

---

stop

stop [*jobIDs*]

Suspend the background job specified by *jobIDs*; this is the complement of **CTRL-Z** or **suspend**. Korn shell only. See "Job Control."

---

suspend

suspend

Same as **CTRL-Z**. Often used to stop an **su** command. Korn shell only.

---

test

test *condition*
      or
[*condition*]

Evaluate a *condition* and, if its value is true, return a zero exit status; otherwise, return a non-zero exit status. An alternate form of the command uses [ ] rather than the word *test*. The Korn shell allows an additional form, [[ ]]. *condition* is constructed using the expressions below. Conditions are true if the description holds true. Features that are Korn-shell-specific are marked with a (K).

File conditions

-a *file*	*file* exists. (K)
-b *file*	*file* exists and is a block special file.
-c *file*	*file* exists and is a character special file.
-d *file*	*file* exists and is a directory.
-f *file*	*file* exists and is a regular file.
-G *file*	*file* exists and its group is the effective group ID. (K)
-g *file*	*file* exists and its set-group-id bit is set.
-h *file*	*file* exists and is a symbolic link.
-k *file*	*file* exists and its sticky bit is set.
-L *file*	*file* exists and is a symbolic link. (K)
-O *file*	*file* exists and its owner is the effective user ID. (K)
-o *c*	Option *c* is on. (K)
-p *file*	*file* exists and is a named pipe (fifo).
-r *file*	*file* exists and is readable.
-s *file*	*file* exists and has a size greater than zero.
-t [*n*]	The open file descriptor *n* is associated with a terminal device; default *n* is 1.
-u *file*	*file* exists and its set-user-id bit is set.
-w *file*	*file* exists and is writable.
-x *file*	*file* exists and is executable.
f1 -ef *f2*	Files *f1* and *f2* are linked (refer to same file). (K)
f1 -nt *f2*	File *f1* is newer than *f2*. (K)
f1 -ot *f2*	File *f1* is older than *f2*. (K)

String conditions

-n *s1*	String *s1* has non-zero length.
-z *s1*	String *s1* has zero length.
s1 = *s2*	Strings *s1* and *s2* are identical. In the Korn shell, *s2* can be a regular expression.
s1 != *s2*	Strings *s1* and *s2* are *not* identical. In the Korn shell, *s2* can be a regular expression.
s1 < *s2*	ASCII value of *s1* precedes that of *s2*. (Valid only within [[ ]] construct). (K)
s1 > *s2*	ASCII value of *s1* follows that of *s2*. (Valid only within [[ ]] construct). (K)
string	*string* is not null.

Integer comparisons

n1 -eq *n2*	*n1* equals *n2*.
n1 -ge *n2*	*n1* is greater than or equal to *n2*.
n1 -gt *n2*	*n1* is greater than *n2*.
n1 -le *n2*	*n1* is less than or equal to *n2*.

→

test		
←	$n1$ -lt $n2$	$n1$ is less than or equal to $n2$.
	$n1$ -ne $n2$	$n1$ does not equal $n2$.

Combined forms

($condition$)　　True if $condition$ is true (used for grouping). The ( )'s should be preceded by a \.

! $condition$　　True if $condition$ is false.

$condition1$ -a $condition2$
　　　　　　　True if both conditions are true.

$condition1$ && $condition2$
　　　　　　　True if both conditions are true. (Valid only within [[ ]] construct.) (K)

$condition1$ -o $condition2$
　　　　　　　True if either condition is true.

$condition1$ || $condition2$
　　　　　　　True if either condition is true. (Valid only within [[ ]] construct.) (K)

Examples

Each example below shows the first line of various statements that might use a test condition:

```
while test $# -gt 0          While there are arguments ...
while [ -n "$1" ]            While the first argument is nonempty ...
if [ $count -lt 10 ]         If $count is less than 10 ...
if [ -d RCS ]                If the RCS directory exists ...
if [ "$answer" != "y" ]      If the answer is not y ...
if [ ! -r "$1" -o ! -f "$1" ]   If the first argument is not a
                                readable file or a regular file ...
```

time	

time *command*

Execute *command* and print the total elapsed time, user time, and system time (in seconds). Same as the UNIX command **time**, except that the built-in version can also time other built-in commands as well as all commands in a pipeline.

times	

times

Print accumulated process times for user and system.

trap	

trap [[*commands*] *signals*]

Execute *commands* if any of *signals* is received. Common signals include 0, 1, 2, and 15. Multiple commands should be quoted as a group and separated by semicolons internally. If *commands* is the null string (i.e., **trap** "" *signals*), then *signals* will be ignored by the shell. If *commands* are omitted entirely, reset processing of specified signals to the default action. If both *commands* and *signals* are omitted, list current trap assignments. See examples below and under **exec**.

Signals

Signals are listed along with what triggers them.

0	Exit from shell (usually when shell script finishes).
1	Hangup (usually logout)
2	Interrupt (usually CTRL-C)
3	Quit.
4	Illegal instruction
5	Trace trap.
6	IOT instruction
7	EMT instruction
8	Floating-point exception
10	Bus error
12	Bad argument to a system call
13	Write to a pipe without a process to read it.
14	Alarm timeout
15	Software termination (usually via **kill**)
ERR	Nonzero exit status of any command. Korn shell only.
DEBUG	Execution of any command. Korn shell only.

Examples

```
trap "" 2          Ignore signal 2 (interrupts).
trap 2             Obey interrupts again.
```

Remove a $tmp file when the shell program exits, or if the user logs out, presses CTRL-C, or does a **kill**:

```
trap "rm -f $tmp; exit" 0 1 2 15
```

---

type *command*

Reports absolute pathname of program invoked for *command*. In the Korn shell, this is simply an alias for **whence -v**.

Example

```
$ type mv read
mv is /bin/mv
read is a shell builtin
```

---

typeset [*options*] [*variable*[=*value* ...]]

Korn shell only. Assign a type to each variable (along with an optional initial *value*), or, if no variables are supplied, display all variables of a particular type (as determined by the options). When variables are specified, −*option* enables the type and +*option* disables it. With no variables given, −*option* prints variable names and values; +*option* prints only the names.

→

typeset	**Options**	
←	-f[*c*]	The named variable is a function; no assignment is allowed. If no variable is given, list current function names. Flag *c* can be **t**, **u**, or **x**. **t** turns on tracing (same as **set -x**). **u** marks the function as undefined, which causes autoloading of the function (i.e., a search of FPATH will locate the function when it's first used). **x** exports the function. Note the aliases **autoload** and **function**.
	-H	On non-UNIX systems, map UNIX filenames to host filenames.
	-i[*n*]	Define variables as integers of base *n*. **integer** is an alias for **typeset -i**.
	-L[*n*]	Define variables as flush-left strings, *n* characters long (truncate or pad with blanks on the right as needed). Leading blanks are stripped; leading 0's are stripped if -Z is also specified. If no *n* is supplied, field width is that of the variable's first assigned value.
	-l	Convert uppercase to lowercase.
	-R[*n*]	Define variables as flush-right strings, *n* characters long (truncate or pad with blanks on the left as needed). Trailing blanks are stripped. If no *n* is supplied, field width is that of the variable's first assigned value.
	-r	Mark variables as read-only. See also **readonly**.
	-t	Mark variables with a user-definable tag.
	-u	Convert lowercase to uppercase.
	-x	Mark variables for automatic export.
	-Z[*n*]	When used with -L, strip leading 0's. When used alone, it's similar to -R except that -Z pads numeric values with 0's and pads text values with blanks.

Examples

```
typeset              List name, value, and type of all set variables.
typeset -x           List names and values of exported variables.
typeset +r PWD       End read-only status of PWD.
typeset -i n1 n2 n   Three variables are integers.
typeset -R5 zipcode  zipcode is flush right, 5 characters wide.
```

---

ulimit

ulimit [*options*] [*n*]

Print the value of one or more resource limits, or, if *n* is specified, set a resource limit to *n*. Resource limits can be either hard (-H) or soft (-S). By default, **ulimit** sets both limits or prints the soft limit. The options determine which resource is acted on.

Options

-H	Print hard resource limit.
-S	Print soft resource limit.

umask [*nnn*]

Display file creation mask or set file creation mask to octal value *nnn*. The file creation mask determines which permission bits are turned off (e.g., **umask 002** produces **rw-rw-r--**). **umask** is also a UNIX command.

unalias *names*

Korn shell only. Remove *names* from the alias list. See also **alias**.

unset [-f] *names*

Erase definitions of functions or variables listed in *names*. In the Korn shell, functions must be specified explicitly with the -f option.

until *condition*
do
    commands
done

Until *condition* is met, do *commands*. *condition* is often specified with the **test** command.

wait [*ID*]

Pause in execution until all background jobs complete (exit status 0 will be returned), or pause until the specified background process *ID* or job *ID* completes (exit status of *ID* is returned). Note that the shell variable $! contains the process ID of the most recent background process. If job control is not in effect, *ID* can be only a process ID number. See "Job Control."

Example

    wait $!   *Wait for last background process to finish.*

Bourne
and Korn

whence [*options*] *commands*

Korn shell only. Show pathname for executables.

Options

    -p   Search for the pathname of *commands*.
    -v   Verbose output; same as **type**.

while *condition*
do
    commands
done

While *condition* is met, do *commands*. *condition* is often specified with the **test** command. See examples under **case** and **test**.

filename	filename
	Read and execute commands from executable file *filename*, or execute object file *filename* with **exec**.

Job Control

Job control lets you place foreground jobs in the background, bring background jobs to the foreground, or suspend (temporarily stop) running jobs. Job control is for Korn shell only and is enabled by any of the following commands:

```
ksh -m -i            Korn shell (same as next two)
set -m
set -o monitor
```

Many job control commands take *jobID* as an argument. This argument can be specified as follows:

%*n*   Job number *n*.

%*s*   Job whose command line starts with string *s*.

%?*s*   Job whose command line contains string *s*.

%%   Current job

%+   Current job (same as above)

%-   Previous job

The Korn shell provides the following job control commands. For more information on these commands, see "Built-in Commands" earlier in this section.

bg   Put a job in the background.

fg   Put a job in the foreground.

jobs   List active jobs.

kill   Terminate a job.

stop   Suspend a background job.

stty tostop
     Stop background jobs if they try to send output to the terminal.

wait   Wait for background jobs to finish.

CTRL-Z
     Suspend a foreground job. Then use **bg** or **fg**. (Your terminal may use something other than **CTRL-Z** as the suspend character.)

Invoking the Shell

The command interpreter for the Bourne shell (**sh**) or the Korn shell (**ksh**) can be invoked as follows:

sh [*options*] [*arguments*]
ksh [*options*] [*arguments*]

ksh and **sh** can execute commands from a terminal (when **-i** is specified), from a file (when the first *argument* is an executable script), or from standard input (if no arguments remain or if **-s** is specified).

Arguments

Arguments are assigned in order to the positional parameters $1, $2, etc. If array assignment is in effect (**-A** or **+A**), arguments are assigned as array elements. If the first argument is an executable script, commands are read from it and remaining arguments are assigned to $1, $2, etc.

Options

-c *str*	Read commands from string *str*.
-i	Create an interactive shell (prompt for input).
-p	Start up as a privileged user (i.e., don't process **$HOME/.profile**).
-r	Create a restricted shell (same as **rksh** or **rsh**).
-s	Read commands from standard input; output from built-in commands goes to file descriptor 1; all other shell output goes to file descriptor 2.

The remaining options to **sh** and **ksh** are listed under the **set** built-in command.

Restricted Shells

Restricted shells can be invoked in any of the following ways:

```
rksh                    Korn shell
ksh -r
set -r


rsh                     Bourne Shell
set -r
```

Restricted shells can also be set up by supplying **rksh** and **rsh** in the shell field of **/etc/passwd** or by using them as the value for the SHELL variable.

Restricted shells act the same as their non-restricted counterparts, except that the following are prohibited:

- Changing directory (i.e., using **cd**).

- Setting the PATH variable. **rksh** also prohibits setting ENV and SHELL.

- Specifying a / for command names or pathnames.

- Redirecting output (i.e., using > and >>).

Shell scripts can still be run, since in that case the restricted shell will call **ksh** or **sh** to run the script.

The C Shell

This section describes the C shell, so named because many of its programming constructs and symbols resemble those of the C programming language. The following topics are presented:

- Overview of features
- Syntax
- Variables
- Expressions
- Command history
- Built-in commands
- Job control
- Invoking the shell

Overview of Features

Features of the C shell include:

- Input/output redirection
- Wildcard characters (metacharacters) for filename abbreviation
- Shell variables for customizing your environment
- Integer arithmetic
- Access to previous commands (command history)
- Command-name abbreviation (aliasing)
- A built-in command set for writing shell programs
- Job control

Syntax

This subsection describes the many symbols peculiar to the C shell. The topics are arranged as follows:

- Special files
- Filename metacharacters
- Quoting
- Command forms
- Redirection forms

Special (device) Files

`~/.cshrc`	Executed at each instance of shell.
`~/.login`	Executed by login shell after .cshrc at login.
`~/.logout`	Executed by login shell at logout.
`/etc/passwd`	Source of home directories for ~*name* abbreviations.

Filename Metacharacters

`*`	Match any string of zero or more characters.
`?`	Match any single character.
`[abc...]`	Match any one of the enclosed characters; a hyphen can be used to specify a range (e.g., a-z, A-Z, 0-9).
`{abc,xxx, ...}`	Expand each comma-separated string inside braces.

| ~ | Home directory for the current user. |
| ~*name* | Home directory of user *name*. |

Examples

% **ls new***	*Match* new *and* new.1.
% **cat ch?**	*Match* ch9 *but not* ch10.
% **vi [D-R]***	*Match files that begin with uppercase D through R.*
% **ls {ch,app}?**	*Expand, then match* ch1, ch2, app1, app2.
% **cd ~tom**	*Change to* tom*'s home directory.*

Quoting

Quoting disables a character's special meaning and allows it to be used literally, as itself. The following characters have special meaning to the C shell:

;	Command separator
&	Background execution
( )	Command grouping
|	Pipe
* ? [ ] ~	Filename metacharacters
{ }	String expansion characters. Usually don't require quoting.
> < & !	Redirection symbols
! ^	History substitution, quick substitution
" ' \	Used in quoting other characters.
`	Command substitution
$	Variable substitution
newline space tab	Word separators.

The characters below can be used for quoting:

" " Everything between " and " is taken literally, except for the following characters that keep their special meaning:

$	Variable substitution will occur.
`	Command substitution will occur.
"	This marks the end of the double quote.
\	Escape next character.
!	The history character
newline	The newline character

' ' Everything between ' and ' is taken literally except for ! (history) and another ', and newline.

\ The character following a \ is taken literally. Use within " " to escape ", $, and `. Often used to escape itself, spaces, or newlines. Always needed to escape a history character (usually !).

Examples

```
% echo 'Single quotes "protect" double quotes'
Single quotes "protect" double quotes

% echo "Well, isn't that \"special\"?"
Well, isn't that "special"?

% echo "You have `ls|wc -l` files in `pwd`"
You have 43 files in /home/bob

% echo "The value of \$x is $x"
The value of $x is 100
```

Command Forms

cmd **&**	Execute *cmd* in background.
cmd1 **;** *cmd2*	Command sequence; execute multiple *cmd*s on the same line.
(*cmd1* **;** *cmd2* **)**	Subshell; treat *cmd1* and *cmd2* as a command group.
cmd1 **|** *cmd2*	Pipe; use output from *cmd1* as input to *cmd2*.
cmd1 **`** *cmd2* **`**	Command substitution; use *cmd2* output as arguments to *cmd1*.
cmd1 **||** *cmd2*	AND; execute *cmd1* and then (if *cmd1* succeeds) *cmd2*.
cmd1 **&&** *cmd2*	OR; execute either *cmd1* or (if *cmd1* fails) *cmd2*.

Examples

```
% nroff file &
% cd; ls
% (date; who; pwd) > logfile
% sort file | pr -3 | lp
% vi `grep -1 ifdef *.c`
% egrep '(yes|no)' `cat list`
% grep XX file || lp file
% grep XX file && echo XX not found
```

Format in the background.
Execute sequentially.
All output is redirected.
Sort file, page output, then print.
Edit files found by grep.
Specify a list of files to search.
Print file if it contains the pattern,
otherwise, echo an error message.

Redirection Forms

File Descriptor	Name	Common Abbreviation	Typical Default
0	Standard input	stdin	Keyboard
1	Standard output	stdout	Terminal
2	Standard error	stderr	Terminal

The usual input source or output destination can be changed as follows:

Simple redirection

cmd > file	Send output of *cmd* to *file* (overwrite).
cmd >! file	Same as above, even if **noclobber** is set.
cmd >> file	Send output of *cmd* to *file* (append).
cmd >>! file	Same as above, but create *file* even if **noclobber** is set.
cmd < file	Take input for *cmd* from *file*.
cmd << text	Read standard input up to a line identical to *text* (*text* can be stored in a shell variable). Input is usually typed on the screen or in the shell program. Commands that typically use this syntax include **cat**, **echo**, **ex**, and **sed**. If *text* is enclosed in quotes, standard input will not undergo variable substitution, command substitution, etc.

Multiple redirection

cmd >& file	Send both standard output and standard error to *file*.
cmd >&! file	Same as above, even if **noclobber** is set.
cmd >>& file	Append standard output and standard error to end of *file*.
cmd >>&! file	Same as above, but create *file* even if **noclobber** is set.
cmd1 |& cmd2	Pipe standard error together with standard output.
(cmd > f1) >& f2	Send standard output to file *f1*; standard error to file *f2*.
cmd | tee files	Send output of *cmd* to standard output (usually the terminal) and to *files*. (See the example in Section 3 under **tee**.)

Examples

```
% cat part1 > book
% cat part1 part2 >> book
% cat part2 part3 >> book
% mail tim < report
% cc calc.c >& error_out
% cc newcalc.c >&! error_out
% grep UNIX ch* |& pr
% (find / -print > filelist) >& no_access

% sed 's/^/XX /g' << "END_ARCHIVE"
This is often how a shell archive is "wrapped",
bundling text for distribution.  You would normally
run sed from a shell program, not from the command line.
"END_ARCHIVE"
XX This is often how a shell archive is "wrapped",
XX bundling text for distribution.  You would normally
XX run sed from a shell program, not from the command line.
```

Variables

This subsection describes the following:

- Variable substitution
- Variable modifiers
- Predefined shell variables
- Example .cshrc file
- Environment variables

Variable Substitution

In the following substitutions, braces ({ }) are optional, except when needed to separate a variable name from following characters that would otherwise be a part of it.

`${var}`	The value of variable *var*
`${var[i]}`	Select word or words in position *i* of *var*. *i* can be a single number, a range *m–n*, a range *-n* (missing *m* implies 1), a range *m-* (missing *n* implies all remaining words), or * (select all words). *i* can also be a variable that expands to one of these values.
`${#var}`	The number of words in *var*
`${#argv}`	The number of arguments
`$0`	Name of the program
`${#argv[n]}`	Individual arguments on command line (positional parameters); *n* = 1-9.
`${n}`	Same as ${argv[*n*]}
`${#argv[*]}`	All arguments on command line
`$*`	Same as $argv[*]
`$argv[$#argv]`	The last argument
`${?var}`	Return 1 if *var* is set; 0 if *var* is not set.
`$$`	Process number of current shell; useful as part of a filename for creating temporary files with unique names.
`$?0`	Return 1 if input filename is known; 0 if not.

Examples

Sort the third through last arguments and save the output in a unique temporary file:

```
sort $argv[3-] > tmp.$$
```

Process .cshrc commands only if the shell is interactive (i.e., the **prompt** variable must be set).

```
if ($?prompt) then
    set commands,
    alias commands,
    etc.
endif
```

Variable Modifiers

Except for $?*var*, $$, and $?0, the variable substitutions above may be followed by one of these modifiers. When braces are used, the modifier goes inside them.

:r   Return the variable's root.

:e   Return the variable's extension.

:h   Return the variable's header.

:t   Return the variable's tail.

:gr   Return all roots.

:ge   Return all extensions.

:gh   Return all headers.

:gt   Return all tails.

:q   Quote a wordlist variable, keeping the items separate. Useful when the variable contains filename metacharacters that should not be expanded.

:x   Quote a pattern, expanding it into a wordlist.

Examples using pathname modifiers

The table below shows the use of pathname modifiers on the following variable:

```
set aa=(/progs/num.c /book/chap.ps)
```

Variable Portion	Specification	Output Result
Normal variable	echo $aa	/progs/num.c /book/chap.ps
Second root	echo $aa[2]:r	/book/chap
Second header	echo $aa[2]:h	/book
Second tail	echo $aa[2]:t	chap.ps
Second extension	echo $aa[2]:e	ps
Root	echo $aa:r	/progs/num /book/chap.ps
Global root	echo $aa:gr	/progs/num /book/chap
Header	echo $aa:h	/progs /book/chap.ps
Global header	echo $aa:gh	/progs /book
Tail	echo $aa:t	num.c /book/chap.ps
Global tail	echo $aa:gt	num.c chap.ps
Extension	echo $aa:e	c /book/chap.ps
Global extension	echo $aa:ge	c ps

C Shell

Examples using quoting modifiers

```
% set a="[a-z]*" A="[A-Z]*"
% echo "$a" "$A"
[a-z]* [A-Z]*

% echo $a $A
at cc m4 Book Doc

% echo $a:x $A
[a-z]* Book Doc

% set d=($a:q $A:q)
% echo $d
at cc m4 Book Doc

% echo $d:q
[a-z]* [A-Z]*

% echo $d[1] +++ $d[2]
at cc m4 +++ Book Doc

% echo $d[1]:q
[a-z]*
```

Predefined Shell Variables

Variables can be set in one of two ways, by assigning a value:

    set var=value

or by simply turning it on:

    set var

In the table below, variables that accept values are shown with the equal sign followed by the type of value they accept; the value is then described. (Note, however, that variables such as **argv**, **cwd**, or **status** are never explicitly assigned.) For variables that are turned on or off, the table describes what they do when set. The C shell automatically sets the variables **argv**, **cwd**, **home**, **path**, **prompt**, **shell**, **status**, **term**, and **user**.

argv=(*args*)	List of arguments passed to current command; default is ( ).
cdpath=(*dirs*)	List of alternate directories to search when locating arguments for **cd**, **popd**, or **pushd**.
cwd=*dir*	Full pathname of current directory.
echo	Re-display each command line before execution; same as **csh -x** command.
histchars=*ab*	A two-character string that sets the characters to use in history-substitution and quick-substitution (default is !ˆ).
history=*n*	Number of commands to save in history list.

home=*dir*	Home directory of user, initialized from HOME. The ~ character is shorthand for this value.
ignoreeof	Ignore an end-of-file (*EOF*) from terminals; prevents accidental logout.
mail=(*n file*)	One or more files checked for new mail every five minutes or (if *n* is supplied) every *n* seconds.
noclobber	Don't redirect output to an existing file; prevents accidental destruction of files.
noglob	Turn off filename expansion; useful in shell scripts.
nonomatch	Treat filename metacharacters as literal characters, if no match; e.g., **vi ch*** creates new file **ch*** instead of printing "No match."
path=(*dirs*)	List of pathnames in which to search for commands to execute. Initialized from PATH; the default is (. **/usr/ucb /usr/bin**).
prompt='*str*'	String that prompts for interactive input; default is %.
shell=*file*	Pathname of the shell program currently in use; default is **/bin/csh.**
status=*n*	Exit status of last command. Built-in commands return 0 (success) or 1 (failure).
time='*n %c*'	If command execution takes more than *n* CPU seconds, report user time, system time, elapsed time, and CPU percentage. Supply optional %*c* flags to show other data.
verbose	Display a command after history substitution; same as the command **csh –v.**

Example .cshrc File

```
# PREDEFINED VARIABLES

set path=(~ ~/bin /usr/ucb /bin /usr/bin . )
set mail=(/usr/mail/tom)

if ($?prompt) then                    # settings for interactive use
    set echo
    set noclobber ignoreeof

    set cdpath=(/usr/lib /usr/spool/uucp)
# Now I can type cd macros
# instead of cd /usr/lib/macros

    set history=100
    set prompt='tom \!% '             # includes history number
    set time=3
```

C Shell

The C Shell

```
# MY VARIABLES

    set man1="/usr/man/man1"       # lets me do    cd $man1, ls $man1
    set a="[a-z]*"                 # lets me do    vi $a
    set A="[A-Z]*"                 # or            grep string $A

# ALIASES

    alias c "clear; dirs"          # use quotes to protect ; or |
    alias h "history|more"
    alias j jobs -l
    alias ls ls -sFC               # redefine ls command
    alias del 'mv \!* ~/tmp_dir'   # a safe alternative to rm
endif
```

Environment Variables

The C shell maintains a set of *environment variables*, which are distinct from shell variables and aren't really part of the C shell. Shell variables are meaningful only within the current shell, but environment variables are automatically exported, making them available globally. For example, C-shell variables are accessible only to a particular script in which they're defined, whereas environment variables can be used by any shell scripts, mail utilities, or editors you might invoke.

Environment variables are assigned as follows:

```
    setenv VAR value
```

By convention, environment variable names are all uppercase. You can create your own environment variables, or you can use the predefined environment variables below.

These environment variables have corresponding C-shell variables. When either one changes, the value is copied to the other:

HOME	Home directory; same as **home**.
PATH	Search path for commands; same as **path**.
TERM	Terminal type; same as **term**.

Other environment variables include the following:

EXINIT	A string of ex commands similar to those found in the startup *.exrc* file (e.g., **set ai**). Used by vi and ex.
LOGNAME	Another name for the USER variable.
MAIL	The file that holds mail. Used by mail programs. This is not the same as the C shell **mail** variable, which only checks for new mail.
PWD	The current directory; the value is copied from **cwd**.
SHELL	Undefined by default; once initialized to **shell**, the two are identical.
TERMCAP	The file that holds the cursor-positioning codes for your terminal type. Default is **/etc/termcap**.

Expressions

Expressions are used in @, **if**, and **while** statements to perform arithmetic, string comparisons, file testing, etc. **exit** and **set** can also specify expressions. Expressions are formed by combining variables and constants with operators that resemble those in the C programming language. Operator precedence is the same as in C but can be remembered as follows:

1. `*  /  %`

2. `+  -`

Group all other expressions inside ( )'s. Parentheses are required if the expression contains <, >, &, or |.

Operators

Operators can be one of the following types:

Assignment operators

`=`	Assign value.
`+=  -=`	Reassign after addition/subtraction.
`*=  /=  %=`	Reassign after multiplication/division/remainder.
`&=  ^=  |=`	Reassign after bitwise AND/XOR/OR.
`++`	Increment.
`--`	Decrement.

Arithmetic operators

`*  /  %`	Multiplication; integer division; modulus (remainder)
`+  -`	Addition; subtraction

Bitwise and logical operators

`~`	Binary inversion (one's complement)
`!`	Logical negation
`<<  >>`	Bitwise left shift; bitwise right shift
`&`	Bitwise AND
`^`	Bitwise exclusive OR
`|`	Bitwise OR
`&&`	Logical AND
`||`	Logical OR
`{ command }`	Return 1 if command is successful; 0 otherwise. Note that this is the opposite of *command*'s normal return code. The **$status** variable may be more practical.

Comparison operators

== !=	Equality; inequality
<= >=	Less than or equal to; greater than or equal to
< >	Less than; greater than

File inquiry operators

Command substitution and filename expansion are performed on *file* before the test is performed.

-d *file*	The file is a directory.
-e *file*	The file exists.
-f *file*	The file is a plain file.
-o *file*	The user owns the file.
-r *file*	The user has read permission.
-w *file*	The user has write permission.
-x *file*	The user has execute permission.
-z *file*	The file has zero size.
!	Reverse the sense of any inquiry above.

Examples

The following examples show @ commands and assume **n** = 4:

Expression	Value of $x
@ x = ($n > 10 || $n < 5)	1
@ x = ($n >= 0 && $n < 3)	0
@ x = ($n << 2)	16
@ x = ($n >> 2)	1
@ x = $n % 2	0
@ x = $n % 3	1

The following examples show the first line of **if** or **while** statements:

Expression	Meaning
while ($#argv != 0)	While there are arguments ...
if ($today[1] == "Fri")	If the first word is "Fri" ...
if (-f $argv[1])	If the first argument is a plain file ...
if (! -d $tmpdir)	If **tmpdir** is not a directory ...

Command History

Previously executed commands are stored in a history list. The C shell lets you access this list so you can verify commands, repeat them, or execute modified versions of them. The **history** built-in command displays the history list; the predefined variables **histchars** and **history** also affect the history mechanism. Accessing the history list involves three things:

- Making command substitutions (using ! and ^).
- Making argument substitutions (specific words within a command).
- Using modifiers to extract or replace parts of a command or word.

Command Substitution

`!`	Begin a history substitution.
`!!`	Previous command
`!N`	Command number *N* in history list
`!-N`	*N*th command back from current command
`!string`	Most recent command that starts with *string*
`!?string?`	Most recent command that contains *string*
`!?string?%`	Most recent command argument that contains *string*
`!$`	Last argument of previous command
`!!string`	Previous command, then append *string*.
`!N string`	Command *N*, then append *string*.
`!{s1}s2`	Most recent command starting with string *s1*, then append string *s2*.
`^old^new^`	Quick substitution; change string *old* to *new* in previous command; execute modified command.

Command Substitution Examples

The following command is assumed:

```
%3 vi cprogs/01.c ch002 ch03
```

Event Number	Command Typed	Command Executed
4	`^00^0`	`vi cprogs/01.c ch02 ch03`
5	`nroff !*`	`nroff cprogs/01.c ch02 ch03`
6	`nroff !$`	`nroff ch03`
7	`!vi`	`vi cprogs/01.c ch02 ch03`
8	`!6`	`nroff ch03`
9	`!?01`	`vi cprogs/01.c ch02 ch03`
10	`!{nr}.new`	`nroff ch03.new`
11	`!!|lp`	`nroff ch03.new	lp`
12	`more !?pr?%`	`more cprogs/01.c`

Word Substitution

Colons may precede any word specifier. After an event number, colons are optional unless shown below:

:0	Command name
:n	Argument number *n*
^	First argument
$	Last argument
:n-m	Arguments *n* through *m*
-m	Words 0 through *m*; same as :0-*m*
:n-	Arguments *n* through next-to-last
:n*	Arguments *n* through last; same as *n*-$
*	All arguments; same as ^-$ or 1-$
#	Current command line up to this point; fairly useless

Word Substitution Examples

The following command is assumed:

```
%13 cat ch01 ch02 ch03 biblio back
```

Event Number	Command Typed	Command Executed
14	ls !13^	ls ch01
15	sort !13:*	sort ch01 ch02 ch03 biblio back
16	lp !cat:3*	more ch03 biblio back
17	!cat:0-3	cat ch01 ch02 ch03
18	vi !-5:4	vi biblio

History Modifiers

Command and word substitutions can be modified by one or more of the following:

Printing, substitution, and quoting

:p	Display command but don't execute.
:s/old/new	Substitute string *new* for *old*, first instance only.
:gs/old/new	Substitute string *new* for *old*, all instances.
:&	Repeat previous substitution (:s or ^ command), first instance only.
:g&	Repeat previous substitution, all instances.
:q	Quote a wordlist.
:x	Quote separate words.

Truncation

`:r`	Extract the first available pathname root.
`:gr`	Extract all pathname roots.
`:e`	Extract the first available pathname extension.
`:ge`	Extract all pathname extensions.
`:h`	Extract the first available pathname header.
`:gh`	Extract all pathname headers.
`:t`	Extract the first available pathname tail.
`:gt`	Extract all pathname tails.

History Modifier Examples

From above, command number 17 is:

```
%17 cat ch01 ch02 ch03
```

Event Number	Command Typed	Command Executed
19	`!17:s/ch/CH/`	`cat CH01 ch02 ch03`
20	`!17g&`	`cat CH01 CH02 CH03`
21	`!more:p`	`more cprogs/01.c` *(displayed only)*
22	`cd !$:h`	`cd cprogs`
23	`vi !mo:$:t`	`vi 01.c`
24	`grep stdio !$`	`grep stdio 01.c`
25	`^stdio^include stdio^:q`	`grep "include stdio" 01.c`
26	`nroff !21:t:p`	`nroff 01.c` *(is that what I wanted?)*
27	`!!`	`nroff 01.c` *(execute it)*

Built-in C-shell Commands

#

Ignore all text that follows on the same line. # is used in shell scripts as the comment character and is not really a command. In addition, a script that uses # as its first character is interpreted as a C-shell script.

#

#!*shell*

Used as the first line of a script to invoke the named *shell* (with optional arguments). Not supported in all shells. For example:

```
#!/bin/csh -f
```

#!*shell*

:

Null command. Returns an exit status of 0. The colon command is often put as the first character of a Bourne- or Korn-shell script to act

→

: ←	as a place-holder to keep a # (hash) from accidentally becoming the first character.

---

alias

alias [*name* [*command*]]

Assign *name* as the shorthand name, or alias, for *command*. If *command* is omitted, print the alias for *name*; if *name* is also omitted, print all aliases. Aliases can be defined on the command line, but they are more often stored in **.cshrc** so that they take effect upon logging in. (See the sample **.cshrc** file earlier in this section.) Alias definitions can reference command-line arguments, much like the history list. Use \!* to refer to all command-line arguments, \!^ for the first argument, \!$ for the last, etc. An alias *name* can be any valid UNIX command; however, you lose the original command's meaning unless you type \ *name*. See also **unalias**.

Examples

Set the size for xterm windows under the X Window System:

```
alias R 'set noglob; eval `resize`; unset noglob'
```

Show aliases that contain the string *ls*:

```
alias | grep ls
```

Run nroff on all command-line arguments:

```
alias ms 'nroff -ms \!*'
```

Copy the file that is named as the first argument:

```
alias back 'cp \!^ \!^.old'
```

Use the regular **ls**, not its alias:

```
% \ls
```

---

break

break

Resume execution following the **end** command of the nearest enclosing **while** or **foreach**.

---

breaksw

breaksw

Break from a **switch**; continue execution after the **endsw**.

---

case

case *pattern* :

Identify a *pattern* in a **switch**.

---

cd [*dir*]

cd

Change working directory to *dir*; default is home directory of user. If *dir* is a relative pathname but is not in the current directory, the **cdpath** variable is searched. See the sample **.cshrc** file earlier in this section.

chdir [*dir*]

chdir

Same as **cd**. Useful if you are redefining **cd**.

continue

continue

Resume execution of nearest enclosing **while** or **foreach**.

default :

default

Label the default case (typically last) in a **switch**.

echo [-n] *string*

echo

Write *string* to standard output; if **-n** is specified, the output is not terminated by a newline. Unlike the UNIX version (**/bin/echo**) and the Bourne-shell version, the C shell's **echo** doesn't support escape characters. See also **echo** in Sections 3 and 5.

end

end

Reserved word that ends a **foreach** or **switch** statement.

endif

endif

Reserved word that ends an **if** statement.

exec *command*

exec

Execute *command* in place of current shell. This terminates the current shell, rather than creating a new process under it.

exit [(*expr*)]

exit

Exit a shell script with the status given by *expr*. A status of 0 means success; nonzero means failure. If *expr* is not specified, the exit value is that of the **status** variable. **exit** can be issued at the command line to close a window (log out).

C Shell

$\rightarrow$

exit ←	*Example* If you suspend a vi editing session (by pressing **CTRL-Z**), you might resume vi using any of these commands: ``` 8% % 8% fg 8% fg % 8% fg %vi Match initial string ```

Example
If you suspend a vi editing session (by pressing **CTRL-Z**), you might resume vi using any of these commands:

```
8% %
8% fg
8% fg %
8% fg %vi      Match initial string
```

---

foreach

foreach *name* (*wordlist*)
   commands
end

Assign variable *name* to each value in *wordlist* and execute *commands* between **foreach** and **end**. You can use **foreach** as a multi-line command issued at the C-shell prompt (first example below), or you can use it in a shell script (second example).

Examples
Rename all files that begin with a capital letter:

```
% foreach i ([A-Z]*)
? mv $i $i.new
? end
```

Check whether each command-line argument is an option or not:

```
foreach arg ($argv)
    # does it begin with - ?
    if ("$arg" =~ -*) then
        echo "Argument is an option"
    else
        echo "Argument is a filename"
    endif
end
```

---

glob

glob *wordlist*

Do filename, variable, and history substitutions on *wordlist*. This expands it much like **echo**, except that no \ escapes are recognized, and words are delimited by null characters. **glob** is typically used in shell scripts to "hardcode" a value so that it remains the same for the rest of the script.

---

goto

goto *string*

Skip to a line whose first non-blank character is *string* followed by a : and continue execution below that line. On the **goto** line, *string* can be a variable or filename pattern, but the label branched to must be a literal, expanded value and must not occur within a **foreach** or **while**.

---

login [*user* | -p]

Replace *user*'s login shell with /bin/login. -p is used to preserve environment variables.

logout

Terminate the login shell.

nice [±*n*] *command*

Change the execution priority for *command*, or, if none is given, change priority for the current shell. (See also **nice** in Section 3.) The priority range is −20 to 20, with a default of 4. The range seems backwards: −20 gives the highest priority (fastest execution); 20 gives the lowest.

+*n*   Add *n* to the priority value (lower job priority).

-*n*   Subtract *n* from the priority value (raise job priority). Privileged users only.

nohup [*command*]

"No hangup signals." Do not terminate *command* after terminal line is closed (i.e., when you hang up from a phone or log out). Use without *command* in shell scripts to keep script from being terminated. (See also **nohup** in Section 3.)

onintr *label*
onintr -
onintr

"On interrupt." Used in shell scripts to handle interrupt signals (similar to the Bourne shell's **trap 2** and **trap "" 2** commands). The first form is like a **goto** *label*. The script will branch to *label*: if it catches an interrupt signal (e.g., CTRL-C). The second form lets the script ignore interrupts. This is useful at the beginning of a script or before any code segment that needs to run unhindered (e.g., when moving files). The third form restores interrupt handling that was previously disabled with **onintr -**.

Example

```
onintr cleanup       # go to "cleanup" on interrupt
    .
    .                # shell script commands
    .
cleanup:             # label for interrupts
   onintr -          # ignore additional interrupts
   rm -f $tmpfiles   # remove any files created
   exit 2            # exit with an error status
```

rehash	**rehash**

Recompute the hash table for the **path** variable. Use **rehash** whenever a new command is created during the current session. This allows the **path** variable to locate and execute the command. (If the new command resides in a directory not listed in **path**, add this directory to **path** before rehashing.) See also **unhash**. |
| set | **set** *variable* = *value*
set *variable*[*n*] = *value*
set

Set *variable* to *value*, or if multiple values are specified, set the variable to the list of words in the value list. If an index *n* is specified, set the *n*th word in the variable to *value*. (The variable must already contain at least that number of words.) With no arguments, display the names and values of all set variables. See also "Predefined Shell Variables" earlier in this section.

Examples

```
% set list=(yes no mabye)     Assign a wordlist
% set list[3]=maybe           Assign an item in existing wordlist
% set quote="Make my day"     Assign a variable
% set x=5 y=10 history=100    Assign several variables
% set blank                   Assign a null value to blank
``` |
| setenv | **setenv** [*name* [*value*]]

Assign a *value* to an environment variable *name*. By convention, *name* is uppercase. *value* can be a single word or a quoted string. If no *value* is given, the null value is assigned. With no arguments, display the names and values of all environment variables. **setenv** is not necessary for the PATH variable because it is automatically exported from **path**. |
| shift | **shift** [*variable*]

If *variable* is given, shift the words in a wordlist variable; i.e., *name*[2] becomes *name*[1]. With no argument, shift the positional parameters (command-line arguments); i.e., **$2** becomes **$1**. **shift** is typically used in a **while** loop. See additional example under **while**.

Example

```
while ($#argv)          # while there are arguments
    if (-f $argv[1])
        wc -l $argv[1]
    else
        echo "$argv[1] is not a regular file"
    endif
    shift               # get the next argument
end
``` |

source *script*

Read and execute commands from a C-shell script. With **-h**, the commands are added to the history list but aren't executed.

Example

```
source ~/.cshrc
```

switch

Process commands depending on value of a variable. When you need to handle more than three choices, **switch** is a useful alternative to an **if-then-else** statement. If the *string* variable matches *pattern1*, the first set of *commands* is executed; if *string* matches *pattern2*, the second set of *commands* is executed; and so on. If no patterns match, execute commands under the **default** case. *string* can be specified using command substitution, variable substitution, or filename expansion. Patterns can be specified using pattern-matching symbols *, ?, and [ ]. **breaksw** is used to exit the **switch** after *commands* are executed. If **breaksw** is omitted (which is rarely done), the **switch** continues to execute another set of commands until it reaches a **breaksw** or **endsw**. Below is the general syntax of **switch**, side-by-side with an example that processes the first command-line argument.

```
switch (string)              switch ($argv[1])
   case pattern1:               case -[nN]:
       commands                     nroff $file | lp
       breaksw                      breaksw
   case pattern2:               case -[Pp]:
       commands                     pr $file | lp
       breaksw                      breaksw
   case pattern3:               case -[Mm]:
       commands                     more $file
       breaksw                      breaksw
       .                        case -[Ss]:
       .                            sort $file
       .                            breaksw
   default:                     default:
       commands                     echo "Error--no such option"
                                    exit 1
       breaksw                      breaksw
endsw                        endsw
```

time [*command*]

Execute a *command* and show how much time it uses. With no argument, **time** can be used in a shell script to time the script.

umask [*nnn*]

Display file creation mask or set file creation mask to octal *nnn*. The file creation mask determines which permission bits are turned off.

→

umask ←	umask is also a UNIX command. See the entry in Section 3 for examples.
unalias	**unalias** *name* Remove *name* from the alias list. See **alias** for more information.
unhash	**unhash** Remove internal hash table. The C shell will stop using hashed values and will spend time searching the **path** directories to locate a command. See also **rehash**.
unset	**unset** *variables* Remove one or more *variables*. Variable names may be specified as a pattern, using filename metacharacters. See **set**.
wait	**wait** Pause in execution until all child processes complete, or until an interrupt signal is received.
while	**while** (*expression*) *commands* **end** As long as *expression* is true (evaluates to non-zero), evaluate *commands* between **while** and **end**. **break** and **continue** can be used to terminate or continue the loop. See also example under **shift**. *Example* ```\nset user = (alice bob carol ted)\nwhile ($argv[1] != $user[1])\n #Cycle through each user, checking for a match\n shift user\n #If we cycled through with no match...\n if ($#user == 0) then\n echo "$argv[1] is not on the list of users"\n exit 1\n endif\nend\n```
@	**@** *variable* = *expression* **@** *variable*[*n*] = *expression* **@** Assign the value of the arithmetic *expression* to *variable*, or to the *n*th element of *variable* if the index *n* is specified. With no *variable* or *expression* specified, print the values of all shell variables (same as **set**).

Expression operators as well as examples are listed under "Expressions," earlier in this section. Two special forms are also valid:

@ *variable*++	Increment *variable* by one.
@ *variable*– –	Decrement *variable* by one.

Invoking the Shell

The C-shell command interpreter can be invoked as follows:

> **csh** [*options*] [*arguments*]

csh uses syntax resembling C and executes commands from a terminal or a file. Options -**n**, -**v**, and -**x** are useful when debugging scripts.

Options

-c	Execute commands located in first filename argument.
-e	Exit if a command produces errors.
-f	Fast start-up; start **csh** without executing .**cshrc** or .**login**.
-i	Invoke interactive shell (prompt for input).
-n	Parse commands but do not execute.
-s	Read commands from the standard input.
-t	Exit after executing one command.
-v	Display commands before executing them; expand history substitutions, but don't expand other substitutions (e.g., filename, variable, and command). Same as setting **verbose**.
-V	Same as -**v**, but also display .**cshrc**.
-x	Display commands before executing them, but expand all substitutions. Same as setting **echo**. -**x** is often combined with -**v**.
-X	Same as -**x**, but also display .**cshrc**.

C Shell

The SCO Shell

This section describes the SCO shell, a menu interface to the SCO operating system. From the SCO shell, you can run any application or utility on your system, as well as manage files and directories. The following topics are presented:

- SCO shell basics

- Main menu options

- Keystroke commands

- A map of all SCO shell menus and submenus

SCO Shell Basics

When you run the SCO shell, you get a screen from which you can run any of the programs on your system. The SCO shell differentiates between applications (computer programs, such as word processors and spreadsheets) and utilities (functions that are part of the operating system), and accesses them from separate menus.

This subsection describes how to use the SCO shell. The topics are arranged as follows:

- Starting and stopping the shell
- SCO shell screen
- Using menus
- Quick reference keys
- Using a mouse

Starting and Stopping the Shell

To start the SCO shell, type **scosh** from the operating system prompt. This will bring up the SCO shell screen.

To exit the SCO shell, select Quit from the main menu, then choose Yes.

SCO Shell Screen

The SCO shell screen (Figure 7.1) is the first thing you see in the shell. From this screen, you can run any of the utilities and applications available on your system, as well as manage files and directories.

Using Menus

The menu on the SCO shell screen contains the following items:

Item	Description
Application	Selects and runs applications.
Manager	Manages files and directories.
Print	Controls printing utilities.
Utility	Selects and runs operating system utilities.
Options	Configures SCO shell.
Quit	Exits SCO shell.

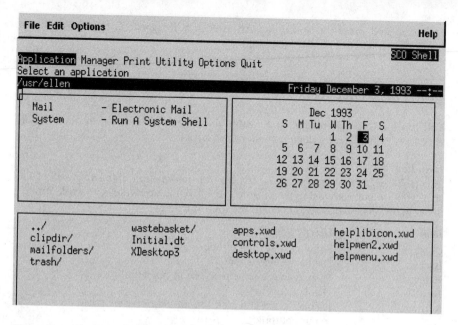

Figure 7-1: The SCO shell screen

Selecting menu items

- To move between menu items, use the space bar, left arrow, or right arrow keys. A menu item will be highlighted when the cursor is on it.

- To select a menu item, press RETURN on a highlighted item, or type the first letter of the item.

- To move down one menu level, select a menu item.

- To move up one menu level, press ESCAPE.

Forms

When you select a menu item that needs input from you, a form pops up over the screen, with fields to be filled in. After you fill in a field, press RETURN to continue to the next field. To move between fields without filling them in, use the arrow keys. If you highlight a field and see the following message at the top of your screen:

    Press <F3> for list

You can press F3 to see a list of selections.

Point and pick lists

Some menu selections offer you a list of choices. These lists are called point-and-pick lists—you point at the item using arrow keys to highlight it, then pick the item by pressing RETURN or CTRL-x. To select more than one item from a list, move to each item and press the space bar. An asterisk will appear in front of the item. After marking all your choices, press RETURN.

Quick Reference Keys

You can look up information from within the SCO shell by using the quick-reference keys, which are, by default, the function keys.

Help key

The Help key, F1, displays a help screen with information about the part of the shell you are currently using (see Figure 7-2). Use the arrow keys to scroll through the help text. The help menu contains the following items:

Item	Description
Continue	Show next section of help screen.
Back	Display previous topic.
Index	Display index of help screen in point-and-pick list.
Next	Display next topic.
Related	Display point-and-pick lists of help screens related to current topic.
Search	Search for help screens containing specific word(s).
Help	Display instructions for using Help screens.
Quit	Return to SCO shell.

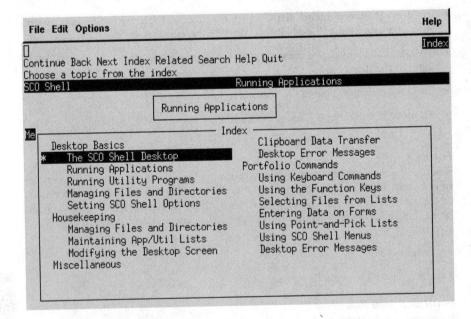

Figure 7-2: The SCO shell Help screen

Exit key

The Exit key, F2, exits the current task. From the Options menu, F2 exits the current task and prompts for a save before returning to the SCO shell screen. From other submenus, F2 puts you in the Quit menu.

List key

The List key, F3, calls up point-and-pick lists of possible entries for certain fields. A message at the top of your screen will alert you to as to whether the highlighted field has point-and-pick lists. To exit a point-and-pick list without selecting an item, press ESCAPE.

Search key

The Search key, F5, finds items in a point-and-pick list. A dialog box pops up, asking for the name of the item to search for. Enter the name and hit RETURN. The default is to scroll down the list; use the up arrow key to scroll up the list. In addition to point-and-pick lists, you can use the Search key while viewing a file in the File menu, editing and creating files with the Edit option, and reading help screens.

Calendar key

Use the Calendar key, F6, to look at past and future months in the SCO shell screen's calendar window. The right arrow key moves the calendar forward one month at a time; the left arrow key moves it backwards.

Running Commands From the SCO Shell

To run operating system commands from within the SCO shell, type ! (exclamation point), followed by the command. When the command finishes, press any key to return to the shell.

Main Menu Options

Following are descriptions of the SCO shell main menu options and what they are used for. For a complete listing of all menus, submenus, and their options, see the *SCO Shell Menu Map* at the end of this section.

File Management With the Manager Menu

The Manager menu, one of the options from the SCO shell main menu, deals with file and directory management. Most Manager menu options require two steps: first, select an option specifying the task you wish to perform; second, select the files you want to perform the tasks on.

To select a menu option, either type the first letter of the option name and press RETURN, or use the arrow keys or space bar to highlight the option name and press RETURN.

SCO Shell

Files

Selecting files

To select files, either type the filename, or highlight the filename in the point-and-pick list (using the arrow keys or Search key (F5) and press RETURN. To select more than one file from a list, move to each file and press the space bar. An asterisk will appear in front of the file. After marking all your files, press RETURN. You cannot write in more than one filename at a time. To select more than one file by typing in filenames, use wildcards to reduce the filename to one.

Viewing files

To view the contents of a file without going into editing mode, select the View option from the Manager menu. A list of the files in the current directory appears at the bottom of the screen. Select file for viewing (see "Selecting files," in this section).

Editing files

To edit a file, select the Edit option from the Manager menu. A list of the files in the current directory appears at the bottom of the screen. Select file for editing (see "Selecting files," in this section). This puts you into the file, in insert mode. For a full list of editing commands, see the table of keystroke commands at the end of this section. Commonly used editing commands are:

Arrow keys	Move cursor.
CTRL-v	Switch between insert and overstrike mode.
Backspace	Delete character to left of cursor.
CTRL-w	Delete current word, if cursor at beginning of word.
CTRL-y	Delete current line.
F8	Paste deleted line back into file.
PgUp/PgDn	Go back or forward a page, respectively.
Home	Go to beginning of current line.
End	Go to end of current line.
CTRL-n	Go to next word.
CTRL-p	Go to previous word.
F5	Search for a word.
CTRL-z/F9	Call pop-up list of extra editing and formatting options.

Copying files

To copy a file, select the Copy option from the File menu (under the Manager menu). A list of the files in the current directory appears at the bottom of the screen. Select file for copying (see "Selecting files," in this section). Next, at the prompt, enter the file to copy *to*. If you enter the name of an existing file, that file will be overwritten. If you specify a directory, a copy of the file will get put in that directory. If you specify a group of files, the destination must be a directory.

Moving/renaming files

To move or rename a file, select the Rename option from the File menu (under the Manager menu). A list of the files in the current directory appears at the bottom of the screen. Select file to be moved/renamed (see "Selecting files," in this section). Next, at the prompt, enter a destination. If you specify a file as a destination, your file is given a new name. If you specify a directory as a destination, your file moves into that directory, keeping its original name.

Removing files

To remove a file, select the Erase option from the File menu (under the Manager menu). A list of the files in the current directory appears at the bottom of the screen. Select file to be deleted (see "Selecting files," in this section). The file is then deleted and put in the wastebasket directory.

Finding files

To find a file, select the Find option from the File menu (under the Manager menu). A form appears with a fiels for specifying the filename. Wildcards may be used to specify files.

File naming conventions

- Filenames cannot be longer than fourteen characters.

- Filenames cannot be duplicated in a directory.

- Blank spaces and control characters are not allowed in filenames. Neither are the following characters:

  ! " ' ` ; / $ * & < > ( ) { } [ ] ~

Changing directories

Following are several ways to change directories:

Directory	Action
Subdirectory of current directory	Highlight directory and press RETURN
Parent directory	Use either the "less than" (<) or the ../ (dot dot slash) symbol.
Any directory	Use Manager–>Directory–>Change command

Running Applications From the Application Menu

To run applications under the SCO shell, select the Application option from the SCO shell menu. Available applications are listed in the upper left window of the screen. Application folders (groups of applications) are indicated by three dots after the name. Select the desired application. The screen then changes to display the application screen.

Printing From the Print Menu

This subsection describes the functions of the SCO shell Print menu and the Printer Configuration utility. You can use the SCO shell to print files, change printers, check print job status, and cancel print jobs.

Printing files

To print a file, select the Print option from the SCO shell menu. This gives you the Print menu. From the Print menu, select the Go option. A list of files in the current directory is displayed on the screen. Select the file(s) to print. The files are then sent to the current printer.

Selecting printers

To select a different printer, choose Select from the Print menu. A list of available printers is displayed. Select the printer desired. You are asked if you wish the new printer to become the default printer. Select Yes to do this, or No to have the printer be the default for the current SCO session only.

Checking print job status

To check on the status of a print job, choose PrintStatus from the Print menu. A list of print jobs is displayed on the screen. To leave this list and return to the Print menu, press ESCAPE.

Canceling print jobs

To cancel a print job, select Cancel from the Print menu. A list of print jobs is displayed on the screen. Select the print job you wish to cancel and press RETURN.

Running Utilities From the Utility Menu

To select a utility to run, choose Utility from the SCO shell menu. A list of available utilities is displayed in the upper left window of the screen. Select the desired utility. The screen for that utility replaces the SCO shell screen. Utility folders (groups of utilities) are indicated by three dots after the name.

Configuring the Environment From the Options Menu

Changing the SCO screen

To change the way the SCO shell screen looks, select Display from the Options menu. Use these menu options to configure the File, Application, Calendar, and Options screen windows.

Editing the applications list

To edit the application list, select Applist from the Options menu. A list of existing applications and application folders is displayed, and the cursor is in the Applist menu at the top of the screen. Use these menu options to add, edit, delete, and undelete applications, or switch applications between folders.

Editing the utilities list

To edit the utilities list, select Utillist from the Options menu. A list of existing utilities and utility folders is displayed, and the cursor is in the Utillist menu at the top of the screen. Use these menu options to add, edit, delete, and undelete utilities, or switch utilities between folders.

Keystroke Commands

Following is a list of SCO shell keystroke commands—shortcuts for performing certain functions.

Cursor Movement Commands

`CTRL-B, backspace`	Editing, Forms: backspace to erase character. Lists: move to parent directory.
`<- (left arrow)`	Editing, Forms: move left one space. Lists: move left one item.
`CTRL-h`	Editing, Forms: move left one space Lists: move to parent directory.
`CTRL-g <-`	Editing: move to leftmost column. Lists: unused.
`CTRL-p`	Editing: move to previous word. Lists: unused.
`-> (right arrow), CTRL-1`	Editing, Forms: move right one character. Lists: move right one item.
`CTRL-g ->`	Editing: move to end of line. Lists: unused.
`CTRL-n`	Editing: move to next word.
`CTRL-i, tab`	Editing: insert spaces next to tab stop. Lists: unused.
`Down arrow, CTRL-j`	Editing: move down one line. Forms: move to next field. Lists: move down one item.
`CTRL-d, PgDn`	Editing: move down one page. Forms: unused. Lists: move down one screenful.
`CTRL-g, down arrow`	Editing: move to bottom of document. Forms, Lists: unused.
`CTRL-e, End`	Editing: move to last character on line. Forms: move to last field on form. List: move to end of list.
`CTRL-k, up arrow`	Editing: move up one line. Forms: move to previous field. List: move up one item.
`CTRL-g, up arrow`	Editing: move to top of document. Forms: unused. List: unused.
`PgUp, CTRL-u`	Editing: move up one page. Forms: unused. Lists: move up one screenful.

`CTRL-t, Home`	Editing: move to left-most column. Forms: move to first field on form. Lists: move to top of list.

Insertion and Deletion Commands

`CTRL-o`	Open new line.
`CTRL-v`	Toggle between insert and overwrite modes.
`CTRL-w`	Delete word.
`CTRL-y`	Delete line.
`DELETE`	Delete character.

Other Commands

`CTRL-c`	Cancel current operation.
`CTRL-f`	Use in conjunction with a number in place of a function key.
`RETURN, CTRL-m`	Menus, Lists: select highlighted item. Forms: move to next field in form. Elsewhere: move down one line.
`ESCAPE`	Menus: move back to parent menu. Forms: exit without executing. List: exit without selecting. Editing: exit to exit menu.
`Space bar`	Lists: mark item for selection Elsewhere: move highlight.
`F1`	Call up help.
`F2`	Exit.
`F3`	Display point-and-pick list.
`F4`	Check spelling.
`F5`	Search for list entry.
`F6`	Control calendar window.
`!`	Start system command.

SCO Shell Menu Map

Following is a list of all the SCO shell menus. The main menus are in bold, the lower-level menus are indicated by arrows (one arrow for first-level menus, two arrows for second-level menus, etc.) The path column lists the shorthand menu paths for each option, consisting of the first letters of each option from the top down. For example, the shortcut for the Wastebasket option is **mfw** for manager, file, wastebasket.

SCO Shell Option	Path	Function
Application	a	Select an application.
Manager	m	Manage files and directories.
→View	mv	Display a file.
→Edit	me	Edit a file.
→File	me	Manage a file.
→→Copy	mfc	Copy a file.
→→Rename	mfr	Rename a file.
→→Find	mff	Find a file.
→→Unfind	mfu	Return to current directory's file list.
→→Permissions	mfp	Set file permissions.
→→Wastebasket	mfw	Manage files in the wastebasket.
→→→Select	mfws	Recover files from wastebasket.
→→→Delete	mfwd	Delete files from wastebasket.
→→→Clear	mfwc	Delete all files from wastebasket.
→Directory	md	Manage directory.
→→Change	mdc	Change current directory.
→→Make	mdm	Create new directory.
→→Remove	mdr	Remove directory.
→→Permissions	mdp	Set directory permissions
→Archive	ma	Save/retrieve files from floppy disk or tape.
→→Extract	mae	Retrieve files from floppy disk or tape.
→→List	mal	Display list of files on floppy disk or tape.
→→Format	maf	Prepare floppy for Create.
→→Type	mat	Specify format type.
→→Device	mad	Switch to different device.
→Transfer	mt	Transfer files to/from Clipboard.
→→Copy	mtc	Copy files to Clipboard.
→→Paste	mtp	Paste files from Clipboard.
→→Remove	mtr	Remove items from Clipboard.
→→Quit	mtq	Return to File menu.
→Preferences	mp	Set editor preferences.
→Quit	mq	Return to main menu.
Print	p	Control printers.
→Go	pq	Send files to current printer.
→Select	ps	Select current printer.
→PrintStatus	pp	Display printer status.
→Cancel	pc	Cancel print job.
→Quit	pq	Return to main menu.
Utility	u	Run a system utility.
Options	o	Specify configuration options.
→Display	od	Configure desktop display.
→→FileWindow	odf	Configure File window display.
→→AppWindow	oda	Configure Application window display.
→→CalendarWindow	oda	Configure Calendar window display.
→Applist	oa	Edit Application list.
→→Add	oaa	Add command or folder to list.
→→Edit	oae	Edit command or folder.
→→Delete	oad	Delete command or folder from list.
→→Undelete	oau	Restore command or folder.

SCO Shell

SCO Shell Option	Path	Function
→→Switch	oas	Switch to another folder.
→Utillist	ou	Edit Utility list.
→→Add	oua	Add command or folder to list.
→→Edit	oue	Edit command or folder.
→→Delete	oud	Delete command or folder from list.
→→Undelete	ouu	Restore command or folder.
→→Switch	ous	Switch to another folder.
→Save	os	Save window display configuration.
→Quit	oq	Return to main menu.
Quit	q	Leave SCO shell.
→Yes	qy	Leave SCO shell.
→No	qn	Return to main menu.

Part IV

Text Editing

Part IV summarizes the command set for the text editors and related utilities available in UNIX. Section 8 reviews pattern matching, an important aspect of text editing.

Pattern Matching

A number of UNIX text-editing utilities let you search for, and in some cases change, text patterns rather than fixed strings. These utilities include the editing programs ed, ex, vi, and sed, the awk scripting language, and the commands **grep** and **egrep**. Text patterns (also called regular expressions) contain normal characters mixed with special characters (also called metacharacters).

This section presents the following topics:

- Filenames versus patterns

- List of metacharacters available to each program

- Description of metacharacters

- Examples

Filenames Versus Patterns

Metacharacters used in pattern matching are different from metacharacters used for filename expansion (see Sections 4 and 5). When you issue a command on the command line, special characters are seen first by the shell, then by the program; therefore, unquoted metacharacters are interpreted by the shell for filename expansion. The command:

```
$ grep [A-Z]* chap[12]
```

could, for example, be interpreted by the shell as:

```
$ grep Array.c Bug.c Comp.c chap1 chap2
```

and would then try to find the pattern *Array.c* in files **Bug.c**, **Comp.c**, **chap1**, and **chap2**. To bypass the shell and pass the special characters to **grep**, use quotes:

```
$ grep "[A-Z]*" chap[12]
```

Double quotes suffice in most cases, but single quotes are the safest bet.

(Note also that in pattern matching, ? matches zero or one instance of a regular expression; in filename expansion, ? matches a single character.)

Metacharacters, Listed by UNIX Program

Some metacharacters are valid for one program but not for another. Those that are available to a UNIX program are marked by a square (■) in the table below. Full descriptions are provided after the table.

Symbol	ed	ex	vi	sed	awk	grep	egrep	Action
.	■	■	■	■	■	■	■	Match any character.
*	■	■	■	■	■	■	■	Match zero or more preceding.
^	■	■	■	■	■	■	■	Match beginning of line.
$	■	■	■	■	■	■	■	Match end of line.
\	■	■	■	■	■	■	■	Escape character following.
[ ]	■	■	■	■	■	■	■	Match one from a set.
\(\)	■	■		■				Store pattern for later replay.
\{ \}	■			■		■		Match a range of instances.
\< \>		■	■					Match word's beginning or end.
+					■		■	Match one or more preceding.
?					■		■	Match zero or one preceding.
						■		■	Separate choices to match.
( )					■		■	Group expressions to match.

In ed, ex, and sed, note that you specify both a search pattern (on the left) and a replacement pattern (on the right). The metacharacters above are meaningful only in a search pattern.

In ed, ex, and sed, the following additional metacharacters are valid only in a replacement pattern:

Symbol	ex	sed	ed	Action
\	■	■	■	Escape character following.
\n	■	■	■	Reuse pattern stored in \(\).
&	■	■		Reuse previous search pattern.
~	■			Reuse previous replacement pattern.
\u \U	■			Change character(s) to uppercase.
\l \L	■			Change character(s) to lowercase.
\E	■			Turn off previous \U or \L.
\e	■			Turn off previous \u or \l.

Metacharacters

The characters below have special meaning only in search patterns:

.   Match any *single* character except newline.

*   Match any number (or none) of the single character that immediately precedes it. The preceding character can also be a regular expression. E.g., since . (dot) means any character, .* means "match any number of any character."

^   Match the following regular expression at the beginning of the line.

$ Match the preceding regular expression at the end of the line.

[^]   Do not match enclosed character(s).

[ ]   Match any *one* of the enclosed characters.

            A hyphen (-) indicates a range of consecutive characters. A circumflex (^) as the first character in the brackets reverses the sense: it matches any one character *not* in the list. A hyphen or close bracket (]) as the first character is treated as a member of the list. All other metacharacters are treated as members of the list.

\{n,m\}   Match a range of occurrences of the single character that immediately precedes it. The preceding character can also be a regular expression. \{n\} matches exactly n occurrences, \{n,\} matches at least n occurrences, and \{n,m\} matches any number of occurrences between n and m. n and m must be between 0 and 256, inclusive.

\   Turn off the special meaning of the character that follows.

\(\)   Save the pattern enclosed between \(and \) into a special holding space. Up to nine patterns can be saved on a single line. They can be "replayed" in substitutions by the escape sequences \1 to \9.

\< \>   Match characters at beginning (\<) or end (\>) of a word.

+   Match one or more instances of preceding regular expression.

?   Match zero or one instances of preceding regular expression.

| Match the regular expression specified before or after.

( )   Group regular expressions.

The characters below have special meaning only in replacement patterns:

\   Turn off the special meaning of the character that follows.

\n   Restore the *n*th pattern previously saved by \(and \). *n* is a number from 1 to 9, with 1 starting on the left.

&   Reuse the search pattern as part of the replacement pattern.

~   Reuse the previous replacement pattern in the current replacement pattern.

\u   Convert first character of replacement pattern to uppercase.

\U   Convert replacement pattern to uppercase.

\l   Convert first character of replacement pattern to lowercase.

\L   Convert replacement pattern to lowercase.

Examples of Searching

When used with **grep** or **egrep**, regular expressions are surrounded by quotes. (If the pattern contains a $, you must use single quotes; e.g., *'pattern'*.) When used with ed, ex, sed, and awk, regular expressions are usually surrounded by / (although any delimiter works). Here are some example patterns:

Pattern	*What does it match?*
bag	The string *bag.*
^bag	*bag* at beginning of line.
bag$	*bag* at end of line.
^bag$	*bag* as the only word on line.
[Bb]ag	*Bag* or *bag.*
b[aeiou]g	Second letter is a vowel.
b[^aeiou]g	Second letter is a consonant (or uppercase or symbol).
b.g	Second letter is any character.
^...$	Any line containing exactly three characters.
^\.	Any line that begins with a dot.
^\.[a-z][a-z]	Same, followed by two lowercase letters (e.g., troff requests).
^\.[a-z]\{2\}	Same as previous, **grep** or sed only.
^[^.]	Any line that doesn't begin with a dot.
bugs*	*bug, bugs, bugss,* etc.
"word"	A word in quotes.
"*word"*	A word, with or without quotes.
[A-Z][A-Z]*	One or more uppercase letters.
[A-Z]+	Same, **egrep** or awk only.
[A-Z].*	An uppercase letter, followed by zero or more characters.
[A-Z]*	Zero or more uppercase letters.
[a-zA-Z]	Any letter.
[^0-9A-Za-z]	Any alphanumeric sequence.

egrep or awk pattern	*What does it match?*
[567]	One of the numbers *5, 6,* or *7.*
five|six|seven	One of the words *five, six,* or *seven.*

`80[23]?86`	*8086, 80286,* or *80386*
`compan(y|ies)`	*company* or *companies*

ex or vi pattern	What does it match?
`\<the`	Words like *theater* or *the*.
`the\>`	Words like *breathe* or *the*.
`\<the\>`	The word *the*.

sed or grep pattern	What does it match?
`0\{5,\}`	Five or more zeros in a row.
`[0-9]\{3\}-[0-9]\{2\}-[0-9]\{4\}`	Social security number (*nnn-nn-nnnn*).

Examples of Searching and Replacing

The following examples show the metacharacters available to sed or ex. Note that ex commands begin with a colon. A space is marked by a □; a tab is marked by *tab*.

Command	Result
`s/.*/( & )/`	Redo the entire line, but add parentheses.
`s/.*/mv & &.old/`	Change a wordlist (one word per line) into **mv** commands.
`/^$/d`	Delete blank lines.
`:g/^$/d`	Same as previous, in ex editor.
`/^[□tab]*$/d`	Delete blank lines, plus lines containing spaces or tabs.
`:g/^[□tab]*$/d`	Same as previous, in ex editor.
`s/□□*/□/g`	Turn one or more spaces into one space.
`:%s/□□*/□/g`	Same as previous, in ex editor.
`:s/[0-9]/Item &:/`	Turn a number into an item label (on the current line).
`:s`	Repeat the substitution on the first occurrence.
`:&`	Same as previous.
`:sg`	Same, but for all occurrences on the line.
`:&g`	Same as previous.
`:%&g`	Repeat the substitution globally.
`:.,$s/Fortran/\U&/g`	Change word to uppercase, on current line to last line.
`:%s/.*/\L&/`	Lowercase entire file.
`:s/\<./\u&/g`	Uppercase first letter of each word on current line. (Useful for titles.)
`:%s/yes/No/g`	Globally change a word (yes) to another word (No).
`:%s/Yes/~/g`	Globally change a different word to No (previous replacement).

Finally, here are some sed examples for transposing words. A simple transposition of two words might look like this:

```
s/die or do/do or die/                    Transpose words.
```

The real trick is to use hold buffers to transpose variable patterns. For example:

```
s/\([Dd]ie\) or \([Dd]o\)/\2 or \1/       Transpose, using hold buffers.
```

The Vi Editor

This section presents the following topics:

- Review of vi operations
- Movement commands
- Edit commands
- Saving and exiting
- Accessing multiple files
- Interacting with UNIX
- Macros
- Miscellaneous commands
- Alphabetical list of keys
- Setting up vi

Review of Vi Operations

This subsection provides a review of the following:

- Command-line syntax
- Vi modes
- Syntax of vi commands
- Status-line commands

For more information on *vi*, refer to the Nutshell Handbook *Learning the vi Editor.*

Command-line Syntax

The three most common ways of starting a vi session are:

> **vi** *file*
> **vi** *+n file*
> **vi** *+/pattern file*

You can open *file* for editing, optionally at line *n* or at the first line matching *pattern*. If no *file* is specified, vi opens with an empty buffer.

Command Mode

Once the file is opened, you are in command mode. From command mode, you can:

- Invoke insert mode
- Issue editing commands
- Move the cursor to a different position in the file
- Invoke ex commands
- Invoke a UNIX shell
- Save or exit the current version of the file

Insert Mode

In insert mode, you can enter new text in the file. Press the ESCAPE key to exit insert mode and return to command mode. The following commands invoke insert mode:

a	Append after cursor.
A	Append at end of line.

c	Begin change operation.
C	Change to end of line.
i	Insert before cursor.
I	Insert at beginning of line.
o	Open a line below current line.
O	Open a line above current line.
R	Begin overwriting text.
s	Substitute a character.
S	Substitute entire line.

Syntax of Vi Commands

In vi, commands have the following general form:

> [*n*] *operator* [*m*] *object*

The basic editing *operators* are:

c	Begin a change.
d	Begin a deletion.
y	Begin a yank (or copy).

If the current line is the object of the operation, then the operator is the same as the object: **cc**, **dd**, **yy**. Otherwise, the editing operators act on objects specified by cursor-movement commands or pattern-matching commands. *n* and *m* are the number of times the operation is performed, or the number of objects the operation is performed on. If both *n* and *m* are specified, the effect is $n \times m$.

An object can represent any of the following text blocks:

word	Includes characters up to a space or punctuation mark. A capitalized object is a variant form that recognizes only blank spaces.
sentence	Is up to ., !, ? followed by two spaces.
paragraph	Is up to next blank line or paragraph macro defined by **para=** option.
section	Is up to next section heading defined by **sect=** option.

Examples

2cw	Change the next two words.
d}	Delete up to next paragraph.
d^	Delete back to beginning of line.
5yy	Copy the next five lines by yanking them into the working buffer.
y]]	Copy up to the next section.

Status-line Commands

Most commands are not echoed on the screen as you input them. However, the status line at the bottom of the screen is used to echo input for the following commands:

/	Search forward for a pattern.
?	Search backward for a pattern.
:	Invoke an ex command.
!	Invoke a UNIX command that takes as its input an object in the buffer and replaces it with output from the command.

Commands that are input on the status line must be entered by pressing the RETURN key. In addition, error messages and output from the CTRL-G command are displayed on the status line.

Movement Commands

A number preceding a command repeats the movement. Movement commands are also objects for change, delete, and yank operations.

Character

h, j, k, l	Left, down, up, right ($\leftarrow$, $\downarrow$, $\uparrow$, $\rightarrow$).
Space bar	Right.

Text

w, W, b, B	Forward, backward by word.
e, E	End of word.
), (	Beginning of next, current sentence.
}, {	Beginning of next, current paragraph.
]], [[	Beginning of next, current section.
%	Move to matching {}, {}, or ().

Lines

0, $	First, last position of current line.
^	First nonblank character of current line.
+, -	First character of next, previous line.
RETURN	First character of next line.
n		Column n of current line.
H	Top line of screen.
M	Middle line of screen.
L	Last line of screen.
nH	n lines after top line.
nL	n lines before last line.

Screens

`CTRL-F, CTRL-B`	Scroll forward, backward one screen.
`CTRL-D, CTRL-U`	Scroll down, up one-half screen.
`CTRL-E, CTRL-Y`	Show one more line at bottom, top of window.
`z RETURN`	Reposition line with cursor: to top of screen.
`z .`	Reposition line with cursor: to middle of screen.
`z -`	Reposition line with cursor: to bottom of screen.
`CTRL-L, CTRL-R`	Redraw screen (without scrolling).

Searches

`/text`	Search forward for *text*.
`n`	Repeat previous search.
`N`	Repeat search in opposite direction.
`/ RETURN`	Repeat forward search.
`?`	Repeat previous search backward.
`?text`	Search backward for *text*.
`/text/+n`	Go to line *n* after *text*.
`?text?-n`	Go to line *n* before *text*.
`%`	Find match of current parenthesis, brace, or bracket.
`fx`	Move search forward to *x* on current line.
`Fx`	Move search backward to *x* on current line.
`tx`	Search forward before *x* in current line.
`Tx`	Search back after *x* in current line.
`,`	Reverse search direction of last f, F, t, or T.
`;`	Repeat last character search (f, F, t, or T).

Line numbering

`CTRL-G`	Display current line number.
`nG`	Move to line number *n*.
`G`	Move to last line in file.
`:n`	Move to line number *n*.
`n RETURN`	Move forward *n* lines.

Marking position

`mx`	Mark current position with character *x*.
`` `x ``	Move cursor to mark *x*.
`¬x`	Move to start of line containing *x*.
`` `` ``	Return to previous mark (or to location prior to a search).
`¬¬`	Like above, but return to start of line.

Edit Commands

Recall that **c**, **d**, and **y** are the basic editing operators.

Inserting new text

a	Append after cursor.
A	Append to end of line.
i	Insert before cursor.
I	Insert at beginning of line.
o	Open a line below cursor.
O	Open a line above cursor.
ESCAPE	Terminate insert mode.
CTRL-J	Move down one line.
RETURN	Move to the first character position on the next line.
CTRL-I	Insert a tab.
CTRL-T	Move to next tab setting.
Backspace	Move back one character.
CTRL-H	Move back one character.
CTRL-U	Delete current line.
CTRL-V	Quote next character.
CTRL-W	Move back one word.

CTRL-H and CTRL-U are set by **stty**. Your terminal settings may differ.

Changing and deleting text

cw	Change word.
cc	Change line.
C	Change text from current position to end of line.
dd	Delete current line.
*n*dd	Delete *n* lines.
D	Delete text from cursor position to end of line.
dw	Delete a word.
d}	Delete up to next paragraph.
d^	Delete back to beginning of line.
d/*pat*	Delete up to first occurrence of pattern.
dn	Delete up to next occurrence of pattern.
df*a*	Delete up to and including *a* on current line.
dt*a*	Delete up to (not including) *a* on current line.
dL	Delete up to last line on screen.
dG	Delete to end of file.
p	Insert last deleted text after cursor.
P	Insert last deleted text before cursor.
r*x*	Replace character with *x*.
R*text*	Replace *text* beginning at cursor.
s	Substitute character.
4s	Substitute four characters.
S	Substitute entire line.
u	Undo last change.
U	Restore current line.
x	Delete current cursor position.
X	Delete back one character.
5X	Delete previous five characters.
.	Repeat last change.
~	Reverse case.

`>>`	Shift current line one tab space to the right.
`<<`	Shift current line one tab space to the left.

Copying and moving

`Y`	Copy current line to new buffer.
`yy`	Copy current line.
`"xyy`	Yank current line to buffer *x*.
`"xd`	Delete into buffer *x*.
`"Xd`	Delete and append into buffer *x*.
`"xp`	Put contents of buffer *x*.
`y]]`	Copy up to next section heading.
`ye`	Copy to end of word.

Saving and Exiting

Writing a file means saving the edits and updating the file's modification time.

`ZZ`	Quit vi, writing the file only if changes were made.
`:x`	Same as **ZZ**.
`:wq`	Write and quit file.
`:w`	Write file.
`:w file`	Save copy to *file*.
`:n1,n2w file`	Write lines *n1* to *n2* to new *file*.
`:F(CIN1FP,n2w >> file`	Append lines *n1* to *n2* to existing *file*.
`:w!`	Write file (overriding protection).
`:w! file`	Overwrite *file* with current buffer.
`:w %.new`	Write current buffer named *file* as *file.new*.
`:q`	Quit file.
`:q!`	Quit file (discarding edits).
`Q`	Quit vi and invoke ex.
`:vi`	Return to vi after **Q** command.
`:e file2`	Edit *file2* without leaving vi.
`:n`	Edit next file.
`:e!`	Return to version of current file at time of last write.
`:e#`	Edit alternate file.
`%`	Current filename.
`#`	Alternate filename.

Accessing Multiple Files

`:e file`	Edit another *file*; current file becomes alternate.
`:e!`	Restore last saved version of current file.
`:e + file`	Begin editing at end of *file*.
`:e +n file`	Open *file* at line *n*.
`:e #`	Open to previous position in alternate file.
`:ta tag`	Edit file at location *tag*.
`:n`	Edit next file.
`:n!`	Forces next file.
`:n files`	Specify new list of *files*.
`CTRL-G`	Show current file and line number.

| `:args` | Display multiple files to be edited. |
| `:rew` | Rewind list of multiple files to top. |

Interacting with UNIX

`:r file`	Read in contents of *file* after cursor.
`:r !command`	Read in output from *command* after current line.
`:nr !command`	Like above, but place after line *n* (0 for top of file).
`:!command`	Run *command*, then return.
`!object command`	Send buffer *object* to UNIX *command*; replace with output.
`:n1,n2! command`	Send lines *n1* – *n2* to *command*; replace with output.
`n!!command`	Send *n* lines to UNIX *command*; replace with output.
`!!`	Repeat last system command.
`:sh`	Create subshell; return to file with *EOF*.
`CTRL-Z`	Suspend editor, resume with **fg** (not in all versions).
`:so file`	Read and execute commands from *file*.

Macros

`:ab in out`	Use *in* as abbreviation for *out*.
`:unab in`	Remove abbreviation for *in*.
`:ab`	List abbreviations.
`:map c sequence`	Map character *c* as *sequence* of commands.
`:unmap c`	Disable map for character *c*.
`:map`	List characters that are mapped.
`:map! c sequence`	Map character *c* to insert mode *sequence*.
`:unmap! c`	Disable input mode map (you may need to quote the character with CTRL-V).
`:map!`	List characters that are mapped to input mode.

The following characters are unused in command mode and can be mapped as user-defined commands.

Letters:	g K q V v
Control keys:	^A ^K ^O ^T ^W ^X
Symbols:	_ * \ =

(Note: The = is used by vi if Lisp mode is set.)

Miscellaneous Commands

`J`	Join two lines.
`:j!`	Join two lines, preserving blank spaces.
`<<`	Shift this line left one shift width (default is 8 spaces).
`>>`	Shift this line right one shift width (default is 8 spaces).
`>}`	Shift right to end of paragraph.
`<%`	Shift left until matching parenthesis, brace, bracket, etc. (Cursor must be on the matching symbol.)

Alphabetical List of Keys

For brevity, control characters are marked by ^.

a	Append text after cursor.
A	Append text at end of line.
^A	Unused.
b	Back up to beginning of word in current line.
B	Back up to word, ignoring punctuation.
^B	Scroll backward one window.
c	Change operator.
C	Change to end of current line.
^C	Unused in command mode; ends insert mode.
d	Delete operator.
D	Delete to end of current line.
^D	Scroll down half-window.
e	Move to end of word.
E	Move to end of word, ignoring punctuation.
^E	Show one more line at bottom of window.
f	Find next character typed forward on current line.
F	Find next character typed backward on current line.
^F	Scroll forward one window.
g	Unused.
G	Go to specified line or end of file.
^G	Print information about file on status line.
h	Move cursor left.
H	Move cursor to home position.
^H	Move cursor left; Backspace key in insert mode.
i	Insert text before cursor.
I	Insert text before first nonblank character on line.
^I	Unused in command mode; in insert mode, same as TAB key.
j	Move cursor down.
J	Join two lines.
^J	Move cursor down; in insert mode, move down a line.
k	Move cursor up.
K	Unused.
^K	Unused.
l	Move cursor right.
L	Move cursor to last position in window.
^L	Redraw screen.
m	Mark the current cursor position in register (a-z).
M	Move cursor to middle position in window.
^M	Carriage return.
n	Repeat the last search command.
N	Repeat the last search command in reverse direction.
^N	Down arrow cursor key.

o	Open line below current line.
O	Open line above current line.
^O	Unused.
p	Put yanked or deleted text after or below cursor.
P	Put yanked or deleted text before or above cursor.
^P	Up arrow cursor key.
q	Unused.
Q	Quit vi and invoke ex.
^Q	Unused (on some terminals, resume data flow).
r	Replace character at cursor with the next character you type.
R	Replace characters.
^R	Redraw the screen.
s	Change the character under the cursor to typed characters.
S	Change entire line.
^S	Unused (on some terminals, stop data flow).
t	Move cursor forward to character before next character typed.
T	Move cursor backward to character after next character typed.
^T	Unused in command mode; in insert mode, move right one tab space if **autoindent** is set.
u	Undo the last change made.
U	Restore current line, discarding changes.
^U	Scroll the screen upward half-window.
v	Unused.
V	Unused.
^V	Unused in command mode; in insert mode, quote next character.
w	Move to beginning of next word.
W	Move to beginning of next word, ignoring punctuation.
^W	Unused in command mode; in insert mode, back up to beginning of word.
x	Delete character under cursor.
X	Delete character before cursor.
^X	Unused.
y	Yank or copy operator.
Y	Make copy of current line.
^Y	Show one more line at top of window.
z	Reposition line containing cursor. z must be followed either by: RETURN (reposition line to top of screen), . (reposition line to middle of screen), or - (reposition line to bottom of screen).
ZZ	Exit the editor, saving changes.
^Z	Suspend vi (only on systems that have job control).

Setting Up Vi

This subsection describes the following:

- The :set command

- Options available with :set

- Example .exrc file

The :set Command

The :set command allows you to specify options that change characteristics of your editing environment. Options may be put in the .exrc file or set during a vi session.

The colon should not be typed if the command is put in .exrc.

:set x	Enable option x.
:set nox	Disable option x.
:set x=val	Give value to option x.
:set	Show changed options.
:set all	Show all options.
:set x?	Show value of option x.

Options Used by :set

The following table describes the options to :set. The first column includes the optional abbreviation, if there is one, and uses an equal sign to show that the option takes a value. The second column gives the default, and the third column describes the behavior of the enabled option.

Option	Default	Description
autoindent (ai)	noai	In insert mode, indent each line to the same level as the line above or below. Use with shiftwidth option.
autoprint (ap)	ap	Display changes after each editor command. (For global replacement, display last replacement.)
autowrite (aw)	noaw	Automatically write (save) file if changed before opening another file with :n or before giving UNIX command with :!.
beautify (bf)	nobf	Ignore all control characters during input (except tab, newline, or formfeed).
directory= (dir)	/tmp	Name the directory in which ex stores buffer files. (Directory must be writable.)

Option	Default	Description
edcompatible	noed-compatible	Use ed-like features on substitute commands.
errorbells (eb)	noeb	Sound bell when an error occurs.
hardtabs= (ht)	8	Define boundaries for terminal hardware tabs.
ignorecase (ic)	noic	Disregard case during a search.
lisp	nolisp	Insert indents in appropriate Lisp format. ( ), { }, [[, and]] are modified to have meaning for Lisp.
list	nolist	Print tabs as ^I; mark ends of lines with $. (Use **list** to tell if end character is a tab or a space.)
magic	magic	Wildcard characters . (dot), * (asterisk), and [ ] (brackets) have special meaning in patterns.
mesg	nomesg	Permit system messages to display on terminal while editing in vi.
number (nu)	nonu	Display line numbers on left of screen during editing session.
optimize (opt)	noopt	Abolish carriage returns at the end of lines when printing multiple lines, speeds output on dumb terminals when printing lines with leading white space (blanks or tabs).
paragraphs= (para)	IPLPPPQP LIpplpipbp	Define paragraph delimiters for movement by { or }. The pairs of characters in the value are the names of nroff/troff macros that begin paragraphs.
prompt	prompt	Display the ex prompt (:) when vi's **Q** command is given.
readonly (ro)	noro	Any writes (saves) of a file will fail unless you use ! after the write (works with **w**, **ZZ**, or **autowrite**).
redraw (re)	noredraw	Terminal redraws screen whenever edits are made (in other words, insert mode pushes over existing characters, and deleted lines immediately close up). Default depends on line speed and terminal type. **noredraw** is useful at slow speeds on a dumb terminal: deleted lines show up as @, and inserted text appears to overwrite existing text until you press ESCAPE.
remap	remap	Allow nested map sequences.

Option	Default	Description
report=	5	Display a message on the prompt line whenever you make an edit that affects at least a certain number of lines. For example, **6dd** reports the message 6 lines deleted.
scroll=	<1/2 window>	Amount of screen to scroll.
sections= (sect)	SHNHH HU	Define section delimiters for [[ ]] movement. The pairs of characters in the value are the names of nroff/troff macros that begin sections.
shell= (sh)	/bin/sh	Pathname of shell used for shell escape (:!) and shell command (:sh). Default value is derived from SHELL variable, which varies on different systems.
shiftwidth= (sw)	8	Define number of spaces in backward (^D) tabs when using the **autoindent** option.
showmatch (sm)	nosm	In vi, when) or } is entered, cursor moves briefly to matching (or {. (If match is not on the screen, rings the error message bell.) Very useful for programming.
showmode	noshowmode	In insert mode, displays a message on the prompt line indicating the type of insert you are making. For example, "Open Mode," or "Append Mode."
slowopen (slow)		Hold off display during insert. Default depends on line speed and terminal type.
tabstop= (ts)	8	Define number of spaces that a tab indents during editing session.
taglength= (tl)	0	Define number of characters that are significant for tags. Default (zero) means that all characters are significant.
tags=	tags /usr/lib/tags	Define pathname of files containing tags (see the UNIX **ctags** command.) By default, the system looks for files **tags** (in the current directory) and **/usr/lib/tags**.
term=	$TERM	Set terminal type.
terse	noterse	Display shorter error messages.
timeout (to)	timeout	Keyboard maps "time out" after 1 second.
ttytype=		Set terminal type.
warn	warn	Display the message, "No write since last change."

Option	Default	Description
window= (w)		Show a certain number of lines of the file on the screen. Default depends on line speed and terminal type.
wrapmargin= (wm)	0	Define right margin. If greater than zero, automatically inserts carriage returns to break lines.
wrapscan (ws)	ws	Searches wrap around either end of file.
writeany (wa)	nowa	Allow saving to any file.

Example .exrc File

```
set nowrapscan wrapmargin=7
set sections=SeAhBhChDh nomesg
map q :w^M:n^M
map v dwElp
ab ORA O'Reilly & Associates, Inc.
```

The Ex Editor

Ex is a line editor that serves as the foundation for the screen editor vi. Ex commands work on the current line or on a range of lines in a file. Most often, you use ex from within vi. In vi, ex commands are preceded by a colon and entered by pressing RETURN.

But you can invoke ex on its own—from the command line—just as you would invoke vi. (You could execute an ex script this way.) You can also use the vi command Q to quit the vi editor and enter ex.

This section presents the following topics:

- Syntax of ex commands

- Alphabetical summary of commands

For more information, see the Nutshell Handbook *Learning the vi Editor.*

Syntax of Ex Commands

To enter an ex command from vi, type:

:[*address*] *command* [*options*]

An initial : indicates an ex command. As you type the command, it is echoed on the status line. Enter the command by pressing RETURN. *address* is the line number or range of lines that are the object of *command*. *options* and *addresses* are described below. Ex commands are described in the alphabetical summary.

You can exit ex in several ways:

:x	Exit (save changes and quit).
:q!	Quit without saving changes.
:vi	Quit and enter the vi editor.

Options

!	Indicates a variant command form, overriding the normal behavior.
count	The number of times the command is to be repeated. Unlike in vi commands, *count* cannot precede the command, because a number preceding an ex command is treated as a line address. For example, d3 deletes three lines beginning with the current line; 3d deletes line 3.
file	The name of a file that is affected by the command. % stands for current file; # stands for previous file.

Addresses

If no address is given, the current line is the object of the command. If the address specifies a range of lines, the format is:

x,y

where *x* and *y* are the first and last addressed lines (*x* must precede *y* in the buffer). *x* and *y* may be line numbers or symbols. Using ; instead of , sets the current line to *x* before interpreting *y*. The notation 1,$ addresses all lines in the file, as does %.

Address Symbols

1,$	All lines in the file.
%	All lines; same as 1,$.
x,y	Lines *x* through *y*.
x;y	Lines *x* through *y*, with current line reset to *x*.
0	Top of file.
.	Current line.
n	Absolute line number *n*.
$	Last line.

x-n	*n* lines before *x*.
x+n	*n* lines after *x*.
-[n]	One or *n* lines previous.
+[n]	One or *n* lines ahead.
¬*x*	Line marked with *x*.
¬¬	Previous mark.
/*pattern*/	Forward to line matching *pattern*.
?*pattern*?	Backward to line matching *pattern*.

See Section 8 for more information on using patterns.

Alphabetical Summary of Ex Commands

Ex commands can be entered by specifying any unique abbreviation. In this listing, the full name appears in the margin, and the shortest possible abbreviation is used in the syntax line. Examples are assumed to be typed from vi, so they include the : prompt.

---

ab [*string text*]   **abbrev**

Define *string* when typed to be translated into *text*. If *string* and *text* are not specified, list all current abbreviations.

Examples

Note: ^M appears when you type CTRL-V followed by RETURN.

```
:ab ora O'Reilly & Associates, Inc.
:ab id Name:^MRank:^MPhone:
```

[*address*] **a**[!]   **append**
text
.

Append *text* at specified *address*, or at present address if none is specified. Add a ! to switch the **autoindent** setting that will be used during input. E.g., if **autoindent** was enabled, ! disables it.

---

ar   **args**

Print filename arguments (the list of files to edit). The current argument is shown in brackets ([]).

[*address*] **c**[!]   **change**
text
.

Replace the specified lines with *text*. Add a ! to switch the **autoin-dent** setting during input of *text*.

---

copy	[*address*] co *destination*
	Copy the lines included in *address* to the specified *destination* address. The command t is a synonym for **copy**.
	Example
| | ```
:1,10 co 50
``` |
delete	[*address*] d [*buffer*]
	Delete the lines included in *address*. If *buffer* is specified, save or append the text to the named buffer.
	Examples
| | ```
:/Part I/,/Part II/-1d    Delete to line above "Part II"
:/main/+d                 Delete line below "main"
:.,$d                     Delete from this line to last line
``` |
edit	e[!] [+*n*] [*file*]
	Begin editing *file*. Add a ! to discard any changes to the current file. If no *file* is given, edit another copy of the current file. With the +*n* argument, begin editing on line *n*.
	Examples
| | ```
:e file
:e#
:e!
``` |
file	f [*filename*]
	Change the name of the current file to *filename*, which is considered "not edited." If no *filename* is specified, print the current status of the file.
	Example
| | ```
:f %.new
``` |
global	[*address*] g[!]/*pattern*/[*commands*]
	Execute *commands* on all lines that contain *pattern* or, if *address* is specified, on all lines within that range. If *commands* are not specified, print all such lines. If ! is used, execute *commands* on all lines that *don't* contain *pattern*. See v.
	Examples
| | ```
:g/Unix/p
:g/Name:/s/tom/Tom/
``` |
```

[*address*] i[!]
text

.

Insert *text* at line before the specified address, or at present
address if none is specified. Add a ! to switch the **autoindent** setting during input of *text*.

insert

[*address*] j[!] [*count*]

Place the text in the specified range on one line, with white space
adjusted to provide two blank characters after a period (.), no
blank characters after a), and one blank character otherwise. Add
a ! to prevent white space adjustment.

join

Example

```
:1,5j!                Join first five lines, preserving white space
```

[*address*] k *char*

Mark the given *address* with *char*. Return later to the line with 'x.

k

[*address*] l [*count*]

Print the specified lines so that tabs display as ^I and the ends of
lines display as $. l is a temporary version of :**set list**.

list

map[!] [*char commands*]

Define a keyboard macro named *char* as the specified sequence of
commands. *char* is usually a single character, or the sequence #*n*,
representing a function key on the keyboard. Use a ! to create a
macro for input mode. With no arguments, list the currently
defined macros.

map

Examples

```
:map K dwwP             Transpose two words
:map q :w^M:n^M         Write current file; go to next
:map! + ^[bi(^[ea)      Enclose previous word in parentheses
```

[*address*] ma *char*

Mark the specified line with *char*, a single lowercase letter. Return
later to the line with 'x. Same as k.

mark

[*address*] m *destination*

Move the lines specified by *address* to the *destination* address.

move

→

move ←	*Example* `:.,/Note/m /END/` *Move text block after line containing "END"*
next	n[!] [[+*command*] *filelist*] Edit the next file from the command-line argument list. Use **args** to list these files. If *filelist* is provided, replace the current argument list with *filelist* and begin editing on the first file; if *command* is given (containing no spaces), execute *command* after editing the first such file. *Example* `:n chap*` *Start editing all "chapter" files*
number	[*address*] nu [*count*] Print each line specified by *address*, preceded by its buffer line number. Use **#** as an alternate abbreviation for **number**. *count* specifies the number of lines to show, starting with *address*.
open	[*address*] o [/*pattern*/] Enter vi's open mode at the lines specified by *address*, or at the lines matching *pattern*. Enter and exit open mode with **Q**. Open mode lets you use the regular vi commands, but only one line at a time. May be useful on slow dialup lines.
preserve	pre Save the current editor buffer as though the system had crashed.
print	[*address*] p [*count*] Print the lines specified by *address*. *count* specifies the number of lines to print, starting with *address*. **P** is another abbreviation. *Example* `:100;+5p` *Show line 100 and the next five lines*
put	[*address*] pu [*char*] Restore the lines that were previously deleted or yanked from named buffer *char*, and put them after the line specified by *address*. If *char* is not specified, restore the last deleted or yanked text.

q[!]

Terminate current editing session. Use ! to discard changes made since the last save. If the editing session includes additional files in the argument list that were never accessed, quit by typing **q!** or by typing **q** twice.

[*address*] **r** *file*

read

Copy in the text from *file* on the line below the specified *address*. If *file* is not specified, the current filename is used.

Example

```
:0r $HOME/data          Read file in at top of current file
```

[*address*] **r** !*command*

read

Read the output of UNIX *command* into the text after the line specified by *address*.

Example

```
:$r !cal                Place a calendar at end of file
```

---

rec [*file*]

recover

Recover *file* from system save area.

---

rew[!]

rewind

Rewind argument list and begin editing the first file in the list. The ! flag rewinds, discarding any changes to the current file that haven't been saved.

---

se *parameter1 parameter2* ...

set

Set a value to an option with each *parameter*, or if no *parameter* is supplied, print all options that have been changed from their defaults. For Boolean-valued options, each *parameter* can be phrased as *option* or **no***option*; other options can be assigned with the syntax *option=value*. Specify **all** to list current settings.

Examples

```
:set nows wm=10
:set all
```

---

sh

shell

Create a new shell. Resume editing when the shell is terminated.

---

source	so *file* Read and execute ex commands from *file*. ***Example*** `:so $HOME/.exrc`

substitute	[*address*] s [/*pattern*/*replacement*/] [*options*] [*count*]
	
	Replace each instance of *pattern* on the specified lines with *replacement*. If *pattern* and *replacement* are omitted, repeat last substitution. *count* specifies the number of lines on which to substitute, starting with *address*. See additional examples in Section 8.
	
	Options
	
	  c Prompt for confirmation before each change.
	  g Substitute all instances of *pattern* on each line.
	  p Print the last line on which a substitution was made.
	
	Examples
	
	`:1,10s/yes/no/g` *Substitute on first 10 lines*
	`:%s/[Hh]ello/Hi/gc` *Confirm global substitutions*
	`:s/Fortran/\U&/ 3` *Uppercase first instance of "Fortran"*
	                              on next three lines

t	[*address*] t *destination* Copy the lines included in *address* to the specified *destination* address. t is an alias for **copy**. ***Example*** `:%t$` *Copy the file and add it to the end*
tag	[*address*] ta *tag* Switch the editing session to the file containing *tag*. ***Example*** Run **ctags**, then switch to the file containing *myfunction*: `:!ctags *.c` `:tag` *myfunction*
unabbreviate	una *word* Remove *word* from the list of abbreviations.
undo	u Reverse the changes made by the last editing command.

unm[!] char

Remove *char* from the list of keyboard macros. Use ! to remove a macro for input mode.

unmap

[*address*] v/*pattern*/[*commands*]

Execute *commands* on all lines *not* containing *pattern*. If *commands* are not specified, print all such lines. v is equivalent to g!.

Example

```
:v/#include/d          Delete all lines except "#include" lines
```

v

---

ve

Print the editor's current version number.

version

[*address*] vi [*type*] [*count*]

Enter visual mode (vi) at the line specified by *address*. Exit with Q. *type* can be one of -, ^, or . (See the z command). *count* specifies an initial window size.

visual

---

vi [+*n*] file

Begin editing *file* in visual mode (vi), optionally at line *n*.

visual

[*address*] w[!] [[>>] *file*]

Write lines specified by *address* to *file*, or write full contents of buffer if *address* is not specified. If *file* is also omitted, save the contents of the buffer to the current filename. If >> *file* is used, write contents to the end of an existing *file*. The ! flag forces the editor to write over any current contents of *file*.

write

[*address*] w !*command*

Write lines specified by *address* to *command*.

Examples

```
:1,10w name_list        Copy first 10 lines to name_list
:50w >> name_list       Now append line 50
```

write

---

wq[!]

Write and quit the file in one command. The ! flag forces the editor to write over any current contents of *file*.

wq

---

xit	**x** Write the file if it was changed since the last write; then quit.
yank	[*address*] **ya** [*char*] [*count*] Place lines specified by *address* in named buffer *char*. If no *char* is given, place lines in general buffer. *count* specifies the number of lines to yank, starting with *address*. **Example** `:101,200 ya a`

z	[*address*] **z** [*type*] [*count*]
	
	Print a window of text, with the line specified by *address* at the top. *count* specifies the number of lines to be displayed.
	
	Type
	   + Place specified line at top of window (the default).
	   - Place specified line at bottom of window.
	   . Place specified line in center of window.
	   ^ Print the previous window.
	   = Place specified line in center of window, and leave this line as the current line.

!	[*address*] **!***command*
	
	Execute UNIX *command* in a shell. If *address* is specified, apply the lines contained in *address* as standard input to *command*, and replace the lines with the output.
	
	Examples
	
	   `:!ls` *List files in the current directory*
	   `:11,20!sort -f` *Sort lines 11-20 of current file*

=	[*address*] **=** Print the line number of the next line matching *address*. If no address is given, print the number of the last line.
< >	[*address*] **<** [*count*] or [*address*] **>** [*count*] Shift lines specified by *address* either left (<) or right (>). Only blanks and tabs are shifted in a left shift. *count* specifies the number of lines to shift, starting with *address*.

address

Print the line specified in *address*.

RETURN

Print the next line in the file.

[*address*] & [*options*] [*count*]

Repeat the previous substitution (**s**) command. *count* specifies the number of lines on which to substitute, starting with *address*.

Examples

```
:s/Overdue/Paid/    Substitute once on current line
:g/Status/&         Redo substitution on all "Status" lines
```

[*address*] ~ [*count*]

Replace the previous regular expression with the previous replacement pattern from a substitute (**s**) command.

The Sed Editor

This section presents the following topics:

- Command-line syntax
- Conceptual overview of sed
- Syntax of sed commands
- Group summary of sed commands
- Alphabetical summary of sed commands

For more information, see the Nutshell Handbook *sed & awk*.

Command-line Syntax

The syntax for invoking sed has two forms:

> **sed** [*options*] '*command*' *file(s)*
> **sed** [*options*] -f *scriptfile file(s)*

The first form allows you to specify an editing command on the command line, surrounded by single quotes. The second form allows you to specify a *scriptfile*, a file containing sed commands. If no files are specified, sed reads from standard input.

The following *options* are recognized:

-n	Suppress the default output; sed displays only those lines specified with the **p** command, or with the **p** flag of the **s** command.
-e *cmd*	Next argument is an editing command; not needed unless specifying two or more editing commands.
-f *file*	Next argument is a file containing editing commands.

Conceptual Overview

Sed is a non-interactive, or stream-oriented, editor. It interprets a script and performs the actions in the script. Sed is stream-oriented because, like many UNIX programs, input flows through the program and is directed to standard output. For example, **sort** is stream-oriented; vi is not. Sed's input typically comes from a file, but can be directed from the keyboard. Output goes to the screen by default, but can be captured in a file instead.

Typical uses of sed include:

- Editing one or more files automatically

- Simplifying repetitive edits to multiple files

- Writing conversion programs

Sed operates as follows:

- Each line of input is copied into a pattern space.

- All editing commands in a sed script are applied in order to each line of input.

- Editing commands are applied to all lines (globally) unless line addressing restricts the lines affected.

- If a command changes the input, subsequent command-addresses will be applied to the current line in the pattern space, not the original input line.

- The original input file is unchanged because the editing commands modify a copy of the original input line. The copy is sent to standard output (but can be redirected to a file).

Syntax of Sed Commands

Sed commands have the general form:

> [*address*][,*address*][!]*command* [*arguments*]

Sed commands consist of *addresses* and editing *commands*. *commands* consist of a single letter or symbol; they are described later, alphabetically and by group. *arguments* include the label supplied to **b** or **t**, the filename supplied to **r** or **w**, and the substitution flags for **s**. *addresses* are described below.

Pattern Addressing

A sed command can specify zero, one, or two addresses. An address can be a line number, the symbol $ (for last line), or a regular expression enclosed in slashes (/*pattern*/). Regular expressions are described in Section 8, *Pattern Matching*. Additionally, \n can be used to match any newline in the pattern space (resulting from the N command), but not the newline at the end of the pattern space.

If the command specifies:	*Then the command is applied to:*
No address	Each input line
One address	Any line matching the address. Some commands accept only one address: **a**, **i**, **r**, **q**, and =.
Two comma-separated addresses	First matching line and all succeeding lines up to and including a line matching the second address.
An address followed by !	All lines that do *not* match the address.

Examples

`s/xx/yy/g`	Substitute on all lines (all occurrences).
`/BSD/d`	Delete lines containing BSD.
`/^BEGIN/,/^END/p`	Print between BEGIN and END, inclusive.
`/SAVE/!d`	Delete any line that doesn't contain SAVE.
`/BEGIN/,/END/!s/xx/yy/g`	Substitute on all lines, except between BEGIN and END.

Braces ({}) are used in sed to nest one address inside another or to apply multiple commands at the same address:

> [/*pattern*/][,/*pattern*/]{
> *command1*
> *command2*
> }

The opening curly brace must end a line, and the closing curly brace must be on a line by itself. Be sure there are no blank spaces after the braces.

Group Summary of Sed Commands

In the lists below, the sed commands are grouped by function and are described tersely. Full descriptions, including syntax and examples, can be found afterward in the alphabetical summary.

Basic editing

a\	Append text after a line.
c\	Replace text (usually a text block).
i\	Insert text after a line.
d	Delete lines.
s	Make substitutions.
y	Translate characters (like a UNIX **tr**).

Line information

=	Display line number of a line.
l	Display control characters in ASCII.
p	Display the line.

Input/output processing

n	Skip current line and.go to line below.
r	Read another file's contents into the input.
w	Write input lines to another file.
q	Quit the sed script (no further output).

Yanking and putting

h	Copy pattern space into hold space; wipe out what's there.
H	Copy pattern space into hold space; append to what's there.
g	Get the hold space back; wipe out the pattern space.
G	Get the hold space back; append to pattern space.
x	Exchange contents of hold space and pattern space.

Branching commands

b	Branch to *label* or to end of script.
t	Same as **b**, but branch only after substitution.
:*label*	Label branched to by **t** or **b**.

Multiline input processing

N	Read another line of input (creates embedded newline).
D	Delete up to the embedded newline.
P	Print up to the embedded newline.

:*label*

Label a line in the script for the transfer of control by **b** or **t**. *label* may contain up to seven characters.

[*/pattern/*]=

Write to standard output the line number of each line addressed by *pattern*.

[*address*]a\
text

Append *text* following each line matched by *address*. If *text* goes over more than one line, newlines must be "hidden" by preceding them with a backslash. The *text* will be terminated by the first newline that is not hidden in this way. The *text* is not available in the pattern space, and subsequent commands cannot be applied to it. The results of this command are sent to standard output when the list of editing commands is finished, regardless of what happens to the current line in the pattern space.

Example

```
$a\
This goes after the last line in the file\
(marked by $).  This text is escaped at the\
end of each line, except for the last one.
```

[*address1*][,*address2*]b[*label*]

Transfer control unconditionally to :*label* elsewhere in script. That is, the command following the *label* is the next command applied to the current line. If no *label* is specified, control falls through to the end of the script, so no more commands are applied to the current line.

Example

Ignore lines between .TS and .TE; resume script after TE:

```
/^\.TS/,/^\.TE/b
```

[*address1*][,*address2*]c\
text

Replace the lines selected by the address with *text*. When a range of lines is specified, all lines as a group are replaced by a single copy of *text*. The newline following each line of *text* must be escaped by a backslash, except the last line. The contents of the pattern space are, in effect, deleted and no subsequent editing commands can be applied.

$\rightarrow$

c ←	**Example** Replace first 100 lines in a file: ``` 1,100c\ \ <First 100 names to be supplied> ```
d	**[*address1*][,*address2*]d** Delete the addressed line (or lines) from the pattern space. Thus, the line is not passed to standard output. A new line of input is read, and editing resumes with the first command in the script. **Example** Delete all blank lines: ``` /^$/d ```

D	**[*address1*][,*address2*]D**
	
	Delete first part (up to embedded newline) of multi-line pattern space created by N command and resume editing with first command in script. If this command empties the pattern space, then a new line of input is read, as if the **d** had been executed.
	
	Example
	Strip multiple blank lines, leaving only one:
	
	``
	/^$/{
	N
	/^\n$/D
	}
	``

g	**[*address1*][,*address2*]g** Paste the contents of the hold space (see **h** or **H** command) back into the pattern space, wiping out the previous contents of the pattern space. The example shows a simple way to copy lines. **Example** This script collects all lines containing the word *Item:* and copies them to a place marker later in the file. The place marker is overwritten. ``` /Item:/H /<Replace this line with the item list>/g ```
G	**[*address1*][,*address2*]G** Same as **g**, except that the hold space is pasted below the address instead of overwriting it. The example shows a simple way to "cut and paste" lines.

SCO UNIX in a Nutshell

Example

This script collects all lines containing the word *Item*: and moves them after a place marker later in the file. The original *Item*: lines are deleted.

```
/Item:/{
H
d
}
/Summary of items:/G
```

[*address1*][,*address2*]h

Copy the pattern space into the hold space, a special temporary buffer. The previous contents of the hold space are obliterated. You can use **h** to save a line before editing it.

Example

```
# Edit a line; print the change; replay the original
/UNIX/{
h
s/.* UNIX \(.*\) .*/\1:/
p
x
}
```

Sample input:

```
This describes the UNIX ls command.
This describes the UNIX cp command.
```

Sample output:

```
ls:
This describes the UNIX ls command.
cp:
This describes the UNIX cp command.
```

[*address1*][,*address2*]H

Append the contents of the pattern space (preceded by a newline) to the contents of the hold space. Even if the hold space is empty, **H** still appends a newline. **H** is like an incremental copy. See examples under **g** and **G**.

[*address1*]i\
text

Insert *text* before each line matched by *address*. (See **a** for details on *text*.)

Example

```
/Item 1/i\
The five items are listed below:
```

l	**[*address1*] [,*address2*] l** List the contents of the pattern space, showing nonprinting characters as ASCII codes. Long lines are wrapped.

n	**[*address1*] [,*address2*] n**
	
	Read next line of input into pattern space. The current line is sent to standard output, and the next line becomes the current line. Control passes to the command following **n** instead of resuming at the top of the script.
	
	Example
	
	In the ms macros, a section header occurs on the line below an .NH macro. To print all lines of header text, invoke this script with **sed -n**:
	
	<pre>/^\.NH/{
	n
	p
	}</pre>

N	**[*address1*] [,*address2*] N**
	
	Append next input line to contents of pattern space; the two lines are separated by an embedded newline. (This command is designed to allow pattern matches across two lines.) Using \n to match the embedded newline, you can match patterns across multiple lines. See example under **D**.
	
	Examples
	
	Like previous example, but print .NH line as well as header title:
	
	<pre>/^\.NH/{
	N
	p
	}</pre>
	Join two lines (replace newline with space):
	
	<pre>/^\.NH/{
	N
	s/\n/ /
	p
	}</pre>

p	**[*address1*] [,*address2*] p** Print the addressed line(s). Unless the **-n** command-line option is used, this command will cause duplicate lines to be output. Also, it is typically used before commands that change flow control (**d, N, b**) and that might prevent the current line from being output. See examples under **h, n,** and **N**.

[*address1*][,*address2*]P

Print first part (up to embedded newline) of multi-line pattern created by **N** command. Same as **p** if **N** has not been applied to a line.

[*address*]q

Quit when *address* is encountered. The addressed line is first written to output (if default output is not suppressed), along with any text appended to it by previous **a** or **r** commands.

Example

Delete everything after the addressed line:

```
/Garbled text follows:/q
```

Print only the first 50 lines of a file:

```
50q
```

[*address*]r *file*

Read contents of *file* and append after the contents of the pattern space. Exactly one space must be put between the **r** and the filename.

Example

```
/The list of items follow:/r item_file
```

[*address1*][,*address2*]s/*pattern*/*replacement*/[*flags*]

Substitute *replacement* for *pattern* on each addressed line. If pattern addresses are used, the pattern // represents the last pattern address specified. The following flags can be specified:

n	Replace *n*th instance of /*pattern*/ on each addressed line. *n* is any number in the range 1 to 512; the default is 1.
g	Replace all instances of /*pattern*/ on each addressed line, not just the first instance.
p	Print the line if a successful substitution is done. If several successful substitutions are done, multiple copies of the line will be printed.
w *file*	Write the line to a *file* if a replacement was done. A maximum of 10 different *files* can be opened.

Examples

Here are some short, commented scripts:

```
# Change third and fourth quote to ( and ):
/function/{
s/"/(/3
s/"/)/4
}
```

$\rightarrow$

```
# Remove all quotes on a given line:
/Title/s/"//g

# Remove first colon or all quotes; print resulting lines:
s/://p
s/"//gp

# Change first "if" but leave "ifdef" alone:
/ifdef/!s/if/   if/
```

t

[*address1*][,*address2*]t [*label*]

Test if any substitutions have been made on addressed lines, and if so, branch to line marked by :*label*. (See b and :.) If *label* is not specified, control falls through to bottom of script. The t command is like a case statement in the C programming language or the shell programming languages. You test each case: when it's true, you exit the construct.

Example

Suppose you want to fill empty fields of a database. You have this:

```
ID: 1    Name: greg    Rate: 45
ID: 2    Name: dale
ID: 3
```

You want this:

```
ID: 1    Name: greg    Rate: 45    Phone: ??
ID: 2    Name: dale    Rate: ??    Phone: ??
ID: 3    Name: ????    Rate: ??    Phone: ??
```

You need to test the number of fields already there. Here's the script (fields are tab-separated):

```
/ID/{
s/ID: .* Name: .* Rate: .*/&   Phone: ??/p
t
s/ID: .* Name: .*/&   Rate: ??   Phone: ??/p
t
s/ID: .*/&   Name: ??   Rate: ??   Phone: ??/p
}
```

w

[*address1*][,*address2*]w *file*

Append contents of pattern space to *file*. This action occurs when the command is encountered, rather than when the pattern space is output. Exactly one space must separate the w and the filename. A maximum of ten different files can be opened in a script. This command will create the file if it does not exist; if the file exists, its contents will be overwritten each time the script is executed. Multiple write commands that direct output to the same file append to the end of the file.

Example

```
# Store tbl and eqn blocks in a file:
/^\.TS/,/^\.TE/w troff_stuff
/^\.EQ/,/^\.EN/w troff_stuff
```

[*address1*][,*address2*]x

Exchange contents of the pattern space with the contents of the hold space. See **h** for an example.

[*address1*][,*address2*]y/*abc*/*xyz*/

Translate characters. Change every instance of *a* to *x*, *b* to *y*, *c* to *z*, etc.

Example

```
# Change item 1, 2, 3 to Item A, B, C ...
/^item [1-9]/y/i123456789/IABCDEFGHI/
```

Sed

The Awk Scripting Language

This section presents the following topics:

- Conceptual overview
- Command-line syntax
- Patterns and procedures
- System variables
- Operators
- Variable and array assignment
- Group listing of commands
- Alphabetical summary of commands

For more information, see the Nutshell Handbook *sed & awk*.

Conceptual Overview

Awk is a powerful pattern-matching program for processing text files that may be composed of fixed or variable length records separated by some delineator (by default, a newline character). Awk may be used from the command line or in awk scripts. On SCO UNIX systems, you may find that awk is linked to oawk (old awk) and nawk (new awk); this is for historical reasons and for backward compatability with shell scripts that might have used those names. The awk supplied with SCO UNIX embodies all the features of oawk and nawk.

With awk, you can:

- Conveniently process a text file as though it were made up of records and fields in a textual database.

- Use variables to change the database.

- Execute UNIX commands from a script.

- Perform arithmetic and string operations.

- Use programming constructs such as loops and conditionals.

- Define your own functions.

- Process the result of UNIX commands.

- Process command-line arguments more gracefully.

- Produce formatted reports.

Command-line Syntax

The syntax for invoking awk has two forms:

> **awk** [*options*] '*script*' *var=value file(s)*
> **awk** [*options*] -f *scriptfile var=value file(s)*

You can specify a *script* directly on the command line, or you can store a script in a *scriptfile* and specify it with -f. Variables can be assigned a value on the command line. The latter method is preferred for very long awk programs, as it avoids the possible `arg list too long` error message that might otherwise be returned by the shell. The value can be a literal, a shell variable (*$name*), or a command substitution (`` `cmd` ``), but the value is available only after a line of input is read (i.e., after the **BEGIN** statement). Awk operates on one or more *files*. If none are specified (or if - is specified), awk reads from the standard input.

The recognized *options* are:

-F*c* — Set the field separator to character *c*. This is the same as setting the system variable **FS**. Nawk allows *c* to be a regular expression. Each input line, or record, is divided into fields by white space (blanks or tabs) or by some other user-definable record separator. Fields are referred to by the variables $1, $2, ..., $*n*. $0 refers to the entire record.

-v *var=value*　Assign a *value* to variable *var*. This allows assignment before the script begins execution. (Available in nawk only.)

For example, to print the first three (colon-separated) fields on a separate line:

```
awk -F: '{print $1; print $2; print $3}' /etc/passwd
```

Numerous examples are shown later in this section under "Patterns and Procedures."

Patterns and Procedures

Awk scripts consist of patterns and procedures:

> *pattern* {*procedure*}

Both are optional. If *pattern* is missing, {*procedure*} is applied to all lines. If {*procedure*} is missing, the matched line is printed.

Patterns

A pattern can be any of the following:

> /*regular expression*/
> *relational expression*
> *pattern-matching expression*
> **BEGIN**
> **END**

- Expressions can be composed of quoted strings, numbers, operators, functions, defined variables, or any of the predefined variables described later under "Awk System Variables".

- Regular expressions use the extended set of metacharacters and are described in Section 8.

- In addition, ^ and $ can be used to refer to the beginning and end of a field, respectively, rather than the beginning and end of a line.

- Relational expressions use the relational operators listed under "Operators" later in this section. Comparisons can be either string or numeric. For example, **$2 > $1** selects lines for which the second field is greater than the first.

- Pattern-matching expressions use the operators ~ (match) and !~ (don't match). See "Operators" later in this section.

- The **BEGIN** pattern lets you specify procedures that will take place *before* the first input line is processed. (Generally, you set global variables here.)

- The **END** pattern lets you specify procedures that will take place *after* the last input record is read.

- If there are more than one **BEGIN** and/or **END** patterns, they are matched and their associated actions taken in the order in which they appear in the script.

Except for BEGIN and END, patterns can be combined with the Boolean operators ||
(or), s-1&& (and), and ! (not). A range of lines can also be specified using
comma-separated patterns:

pattern, pattern

Procedures

Procedures consist of one or more commands, functions, or variable assignments,
separated by newlines or semicolons, and contained within curly braces. Commands fall into four groups:

- Variable or array assignments

- Printing commands

- Built-in functions

- Control-flow commands

Simple Pattern-Procedure Examples

1. Print first field of each line:

   ```
   { print $1 }
   ```

2. Print all lines that contain *pattern*:

   ```
   /pattern/
   ```

3. Print first field of lines that contain *pattern*:

   ```
   /pattern/{ print $1 }
   ```

4. Print records containing more than two fields:

   ```
   NF > 2
   ```

5. Interpret input records as a group of lines up to a blank line:

   ```
   BEGIN { FS = "\n"; RS = "" }
   ```

6. Print fields 2 and 3 in switched order, but only on lines whose first field matches
   the string "URGENT":

   ```
   $1 ~ /URGENT/ { print $3, $2 }
   ```

7. Count and print the number of *pattern* found:

   ```
   /pattern/ { ++x } END { print x }
   ```

8. Add numbers in second column and print total:

```
{total += $2 }; END { print "column total is", total}
```

9. Print lines that contain fewer than 20 characters:

```
length($0) < 20
```

10. Print each line that begins with *Name:* and that contains exactly seven fields:

```
NF == 7 && /^Name:/
```

11. Reverse the order of fields:

```
{ for (i = NF; i >= 1; i--) print $i }
```

Awk System Variables

Variable	Description
n	nth field in current record; fields are separated by FS.
$0	Entire input record
ARGC	Number of arguments on command line
ARGV	An array containing the command-line arguments
ENVIRON	An associative array of environment variables
FILENAME	Current filename
FNR	Like NR, but relative to the current file
FS	Field separator (default is any white space)
NF	Number of fields in current record
NR	Number of the current record
OFMT	Output format for numbers (default is %.6g)
OFS	Output field separator (default is a blank)
ORS	Output record separator (default is a newline)
RLENGTH	Length of the string matched by **match** function
RS	Record separator (default is a newline)
RSTART	First position in the string matched by **match** function
SUBSEP	Separator character for array subscripts (default is \034)

Operators

The table below lists the operators, in order of increasing precedence, that are available in awk.

Symbol	Meaning
= =+ -= *= /= %= ^=	Assignment
?:	C conditional expression)
||	Logical OR
&&	Logical AND
~ !~	Match regular expression and negation
< <= > >= != ==	Relational operators
(blank)	Concatenation
+ -	Addition, subtraction
* / %	Multiplication, division, and modulus
+ - !	Unary plus and minus, and logical negation

Symbol	Meaning
^	Exponentiation
++ --	Increment and decrement, either prefix or postfix
$	Field reference

Variables and Array Assignments

Variables can be assigned a value with an = sign. For example:

```
FS = ","
```

Expressions using the operators +, -, /, and % (modulo) can be assigned to variables.

Arrays can be created with the **split** function (see below), or they can simply be named in an assignment statement. ++, +=, and -= are used to increment or decrement an array, as in the C language. Array elements can be subscripted with numbers (*array*[1], ..., *array*[*n*]) or with names. For example, to count the number of occurrences of a pattern, you could use the following script:

```
/pattern/ { array["/pattern/"]++ }
END { print array["/pattern/"] }
```

In awk, variables need not be declared previous to their use, nor do arrays need to be dimensioned; they are activated upon first reference. All variables are stored as strings, but may be used either as strings or numbers. Awk will use the program script context to determine whether to treat a variable as a string or a number, but the distinction can also be forced by the user. To force a variable to be treated as a string, catenate a null to the variable:

```
var ""
```

To force a variable to be treated as a number, add zero to it:

```
var + 0
```

Group Listing of Awk Commands

Awk commands may be classified as follows:

Arithmetic Functions	String Functions	Control Flow Statements	Input/Output Processing	Miscellaneous
atan2	gsub	break	close	delete
cos	index	continue	getline	function
exp	length	do/while	next	system
int	match	exit	print	
log	split	for	printf	
rand	sub	if	sprintf	
sin	substr	return		
sqrt	tolower	while		
srand	toupper			

Alphabetical Summary of Commands

The following alphabetical list of statements and functions includes all that are available in awk in SCO UNIX. Nawk includes all old awk commands, plus some additional commands (marked as {N}). Gawk includes all nawk commands, plus some additional commands (marked as {G}). Commands that aren't marked with a symbol are available in all versions.

atan2(*y,x*) Return the arctangent of *y/x* in radians.	**atan2**
break Exit from a **while** or **for** loop.	**break**
close(*filename–expr*) **close**(*command-expr*) In most implementations of awk, you can only have ten files open simultaneously and one pipe. Therefore, nawk provides a **close** statement that allows you to close a file or a pipe. It takes as an argument the same expression that opened the pipe or file.	**close**
continue Begin next iteration of **while** or **for** loop without reaching the bottom.	**continue**
cos(*x*) Return the cosine of *x*, an angle in radians.	**cos**
delete(*array*[*element*]) Delete element of array.	**delete**
do *body* **while** (*expr*) Looping statement. Execute statements in *body*, then evaluate *expr*. If **expr** is true, execute *body* again.	**do**
exit Do not execute remaining instruction and read no new input. END procedures will be executed.	**exit**

exp	**exp**(*arg*) Return the natural exponent of *arg* (the inverse of **log**).
for	**for** (*i=lower*; *i<=upper*; *i++*) *command* While the value of variable *i* is in the range between *lower* and *upper*, do *command*. A series of commands must be put within braces. **<=** or any relational operator can be used; **++** or **--** can be used to increment or decrement the variable.
for	**for** (*item* **in** *array*) *command* For each *item* in an associative *array*, do *command*. More than one command must be put inside braces. Refer to each element of the array as *array*[*item*]. Elements of awk arrays are stored in an order that enables access of any element in essentially equivalent time. This order may appear to be indiscriminate; if the output is desired in sorted order, you must pipe it through the **sort** command.

function	**function** *name*(*parameter–list*) {
	   statements
	}
	
	Create *name* as a user-defined function consisting of awk *statements* that apply to the specified list of parameters.

getline	**getline** [*var*] [<*file*] or *command*	**getline** [*var*] Read next line of input. Original awk does not support the syntax to open multiple input streams. The first form reads input from *file* and the second form reads the output of *command*. Both forms read one line at a time, and each time the statement is executed it gets the next line of input. The line of input is assigned to $0 and is parsed into fields, setting **NF**, **NR**, and **FNR**. If *var* is specified, the result is assigned to *var* and the $0 is not changed. Thus, if the result is assigned to a variable, the current line does not change. It is actually a function, and it returns 1 if it reads a record successfully, 0 if end-of-line is encountered, and −1 if for some reason it is otherwise unsuccessful.
gsub	**gsub**(*r,s,t*) Globally substitute *s* for each match of the regular expression *r* in the string *t*. Return the number of substitutions. If *t* is not supplied, defaults to $0.

if *(condition)*
    command
[else]
    [command]

If *condition* is true, do *command(s)*, otherwise do *command* in **else** clause. Condition can be an expression using any of the relational operators <, <=, ==, !=, >=, or >, as well as the pattern-matching operator ~ (e.g., "if $1 ~ /[Aa].*/"). A series of commands must be put within braces.

---

index(*substr,str*)

Return the position of substring in string.

---

int(*arg*)

Return the integer part of *arg*.

---

length(*arg*)

Return the length of *arg*. If *arg* is not supplied, $0 is assumed. Therefore, **length** can be used as a predefined variable that contains the length of the current record.

---

log(*arg*)

Return the natural logarithm of *arg* (the inverse of **exp**).

---

match(*s,r*)

Function that matches the pattern, specified by the regular expression *r*, in the string *s* and returns either the position in *s* where the match begins, or 0 if no occurrences are found. Sets the value of RSTART and RLENGTH.

---

next

Read next input line and start new cycle through pattern/procedures statements.

---

print [*args*] [*destination*]

Print *args* on output. Literal strings must be quoted. Fields are printed in the order they are listed. If separated by commas in the argument list, they are separated in the output by the character specified by OFS. If separated by spaces, they are concatenated in the output. *destination* is a UNIX redirection or pipe expression (e.g., > *file*) that redirects the default output.

	if
	index
	int
	length
	log
	match
	next
	print

Awk

printf	**printf** [*format* [, *expression(s)*]]

Formatted print statement. Expressions or variables can be formatted according to instructions in the *format* argument. The number of arguments must correspond to the number specified in the format sections.

format follows the conventions of the C-language *printf* statement. Here are a few of the most common formats:

%s	A string
%d	A decimal number
%*n.m*f	A floating point number; *n* = total number of digits. *m* = number of digits after decimal point.
%[-]*n*c	*n* specifies minimum field length for format type *c*, while - justifies value in field; otherwise value is right-justified.

format can also contain embedded escape sequences: \n (newline) or \t (tab) being the most common.

Spaces and literal text can be placed in the *format* argument by quoting the entire argument. If there are multiple expressions to be printed, there should be multiple formats specified.

Example

Using the script:

```
{printf ("The sum on line %s is %d \n", NR, $1+$2)}
```

the following input line:

```
5    5
```

produces this output, followed by a newline:

```
The sum on line 1 is 10.
```

rand	**rand()**

Generate a random number between 0 and 1. This function returns the same number each time the script is executed, unless the random number generator is seeded using the **srand()** function.

return	**return** [*expr*]

Used at end of user-defined functions to exit function, returning value of expression.

sin	**sin(***x***)**

Return the sine of x, an angle in radians.

split(*string,array*[*,sep*])

Split *string* into elements of array *array*[1],...,*array*[*n*]. The string is split at each occurrence of separator *sep*. If *sep* is not specified, **FS** is used. The number of array elements created is returned.

split

sprintf [*format* [, *expression(s)*]]

Return the value of one or more *expressions*, using the specified *format* (see **printf**). Data is formatted but not printed.

sprintf

sqrt(*arg*)

Return square root of *arg*.

sqrt

srand(*expr*)

Use *expr* to set a new seed for random number generator. Default is time of day.

srand

sub(*r,s,t*)

Substitute *s* for first match of the regular expression *r* in the string *t*. Return 1 if successful; 0 otherwise. If *t* is not supplied, defaults to $0.

sub

substr(*string,m,*[*n*])

Return substring of *string* beginning at character position *m* and consisting of the next *n* characters. If *n* is omitted, include all characters to the end of string.

substr

system(*command*)

Function that executes the specified *command* and returns its status. The status of the command that is executed typically indicates its success (1), completion (0) or unexpected error (–1). The output of the command is not available for processing within the awk script. Use "*command* | **getline**" to read the output of the command into the script.

system

tolower(*str*)

Translate all uppercase characters in *str* to lowercase and return the new string.

tolower

toupper(*str*)

Translate all lowercase characters in *str* to uppercase and return the new string.

toupper

Awk

while (*condition*)
command

Do *command* while *condition* is true (see **if** for a description of allowable conditions). A series of commands must be put within braces.

Part V

Software Development

The UNIX operating system earned its reputation by providing an unexcelled environment for software development. Section 13 provides tables of commonly-used commands. Section 14 is an alphabetical listing of software development commands.

Section 13 - *Overview*

Section 14 - *Programming Commands*

Programming Overview

This section lists tables of commonly used programming commands.

Common Commands

Following are tables of commonly used software development commands. These commands, and more, are covered in detail in the next section.

Creating Programs

cc	C compiler
ld	Link editor
m4	Macro processor
make	Create programs
lex	Lexical analyzer
yacc	Compiler used with lex

Debugging Programs

adb	Assembly level or absolute debugger
cb	C program beautifier
cflow	Identify nesting levels of functions in a program.
CodeView	Visual debugger

ctrace	C program debugger
cscope	Examine functions contained in a program.
cxref	Create cross reference of functions and symbols used within a program.
dbxtra	dbx-based screen-oriented debugger
dbXtra	Graphical symbolic debugger with Motif user interface
lint	C program checker based on cc compiler
rlint	C program checker based on rcc compiler
sdb	Symbolic debugger.

Maintaining Programs

make	Maintain, update, and regenerate related programs and files.
imake	CPP interface to make
SCCS	Source code control system

Software Development
Commands

This section presents the SCO UNIX programming commands.

adb

adb *options* [*objfile* [*corefile*]]

General purpose debugger. *objfile* is normally an executable file of either XENIX or COFF format with the default filename **a.out**. *corefile* is assumed to be a core image file produced after executing *objfile*; default is *core*.

Options

-w   Create both *objfile* and *corefile* and open for reading and writing.

-p *prompt*
    Define *prompt* string, which may be any combination of characters. Default is an asterisk (*).

Commands

Requests to **adb** are of the form:

[*address*] [,*count*] [*command*] [;]

For most commands, *count* specifies how many times the command will be executed (default is one.) If *address* is present, the current position in the file, called *dot*, is set to the value given by *address*. *address* is a special expression with the form:

[*segment*:]*offset*

where *segment* gives the address of a specific text or data setment, and *offset* gives an offset from the beginning of that segment.

Initially, *dot* is set to zero. Most commands consist of a verb followed by a modifier. The *format*s listed with the verbs below consist of one or more characters specifying a style of printing. The following verbs are available:

?f   Locations starting at text *address* in *objfile* are printed according to the format f.

/f   Locations starting at data *address* in *corefile* are printed according to format f. Value of *address* itself is printed in the styles indicated by format f.

Commands available are:

newline If the previous command temporarily incremented *dot*, the increment is permanent. Repeat previous command with a count of 1.

[?/]l *value* **mask**
    Words starting at *dot* are masked with **mask** and compared with *value* until a match is found. If **L** is used, the match is for four bytes at a time instead of two.

[?/]w *value*...

Write the two-byte *value* into the addressed location. If W is used, write four bytes.

[?/]m *segnum fpos size*...

Set new values for the given segment's file position and size. If *size* is not set, only the file position is changed. *segnum* must be the segment number of a segment already in the memory map. If ? is given, a text segment is affected; if /, a data segment.

[?/]M *segnum fpos size*...

Create a new segment in the memory map. The segment is given file position *fpos* and physical size *size*. If ? is given, a text segment is affected; if /, a data segment.

>*name*   *dot* is assigned to the variable or register named by *name*.

!   A shell is called to read the rest of the line following !.

$ *modifier*

Miscellaneous commands. Available modifiers are:

c   C stack backtrace. This command is case-insensitive.
d   Set input and output default format to decimal.
e   Print names and values of external variables.
<f   Read commands from the file f, and return.
>f   Send output to file f.
b   Print all breakpoints and their associated counts and commands.
f   Print floating registers in single or double length.
m   Print the address map.
o   Set input and output default format to octal.
q   Exit adb.
r   Print general registers and the instruction addressed by *ip*. *dot* is set to *ip*.
s   Set limit for symbol matches to *address*. Default is 255.
v   Print all non-zero variables in octal.
w   Set page width for output to *address*. Default is 80.
x   Set input and output default format to hexadecimal.

: *modifier*

Manage a subprocess. Available modifiers are:

br   Set breakpoint at *address*. Breakpoint is executed *count*–1 times before causing a stop.
br   Delete breakpoint at *address*.
co   Subprocess is continued and signal s is passed to it.
k   Subprocess is terminated.

→

adb	
←	

r[*arguments*]
    Run *objfile* as a subprocess.

R[*arguments*]
    Same as **r** except that *arguments* are passed through a shell before being passed to the program, so that shell metacharacters can be used in filenames.

s   Same as **co** except that the subprocess is single stepped *count* times.

---

admin

admin [*options*] *files*

Add *files* to SCCS or change *options* of SCCS *files*.

Options

-a[*user* | *groupid*]
    Assign *user* or *groupid* permission to make deltas; a ! before *user* or *groupid* denies permission. If no list is given, anyone has permission.

-d*flag* Delete *flag* previously set with -f. Applicable *flags* are:

    b   Enable the -b option in a **get** command; this allows branch deltas.

    c*n*   Set highest release to *n* (default is 9999).

    d*n*   Set **get** default delta number to *n*.

    f*n*   Set lowest release to *n* (default is 1).

    i[*string*] Treat No id keywords (ge6) message as a fatal error. *string*, if present, forces a fatal error if keywords do not exactly match *string*.

    j   Allow multiple concurrent **get**s.

    l*list*   Releases in *list* cannot accept changes; use the letter **a** to specify all releases.

    m*name* Substitute %M% keyword with module *name*.

    n   Create a null delta from which to branch.

    q*string* Substitute %Q% keyword with *string*.

    t*type* Substitute %Y% keyword with module *type*.

    v[*prog*] Force **delta** command to prompt for modification request numbers as the reason for creating a delta. Run program file *prog* to check for valid numbers.

-e[*user* | *groupid*]
    Permission to make deltas is denied to each *user* or *groupid*.

-f*flag* Set *flag* (see -d above).

-h   Check an existing SCCS file for possible corruption.

-i[*file*]	Create a new SCCS file, using the contents of *file* as the initial delta. If *file* is omitted, use standard input.	**admin**
-m[*list*]	Insert *list* of modification request numbers as the reason for creating the file.	
-n	Create a new SCCS file that is empty.	
-r*n.n*	Set initial delta to release number *n.n*. Default is 1.1. Must be used with -i.	
-t[*file*]	Replace SCCS file description with contents of *file*. If *file* is missing, the existing description is deleted.	
-y[*text*]	Insert *text* as comment for initial delta (valid only with -i or -n).	
-z	Recompute the SCCS file checksum and store in first line.	

Example

Create a new SCCS file and initialize it with the contents of **ch01**, which will become *delta 1.1*.

```
admin -ich01 s.ch01
```

---

ar [-V] *key* [*args*] [*posname*] *archive* [*files*]   ar

Maintain a group of *files* that are combined into a file *archive*. Used most commonly to create and update library files as used by the link editor (**ld**). Only one key letter may be used, but each can be combined with additional *args* (with no separations between). *posname* is the name of a file in *archive*. When moving or replacing *files*, you can specify that they be placed before or after *posname*. See **lorder** for another example. -V prints the version number of **ar** on standard error.

Key

d	Delete *files* from *archive*.
m	Move *files* to end of *archive*.
p	Print *files* in *archive*.
q	Append *files* to *archive*.
r	Replace *files* in *archive*.
t	List the contents of *archive* or list the named *files*.
x	Extract contents from *archive* or only the named *files*.

Args

a	Use with **r** or **m** key to place *files* in the archive after *posname*.
b	Same as **a** but before *posname*.
c	Create *archive* silently.
i	Same as **b**.
l	Place temporary files in local directory rather than **/tmp** (SVR3 only).

Programming Commands

$\rightarrow$

ar ←	**s** Force regeneration of *archive* symbol table (useful after running **strip** or **mcs**).
	u Use with **r** to replace only *files* that have changed since being put in *archive*.
	v Verbose; print a description.

Example

Replace **mylib.a** with object files from the current directory:

```
ar r mylib.a `ls *.o`
```

---

as

as [*options*] *files*

Generate an object file from each specified assembly language source *file*. Object files have the same root name as source files but replace the .s suffix with .o. There may be some additional system-specific options. See also **dis**.

Options

- **-df**   Do not produce line number information in object file.
- **-m**   Run **m4** on *file*.
- **-n**   Turn off optimization of long/short addresses.
- **-o** *obj/^file*
      Place output in object file *obj/^file* (default is *file*.o).
- **-R**   Remove *file* upon completion.
- **-V**   Display the version number of the assembler.
- **-Y** [*key*,] *dir*
      Search directory *dir* for the **m4** preprocessor (if *key* is **m**), for the file containing predefined macros (if *key* is **d**), or for both (if *key* is omitted).

---

cb

cb [*options*] [*files*]

C program "beautifier" that formats *files* using proper C programming structure.

Options

- **-j**   Join split lines.
- **-l** *length*   Split lines longer than *length*.
- **-s**   Standardize code to style of Kernighan and Ritchie in *The C Programming Language*.

Example

```
cb -l 70 calc.c > calc_new.c
```

---

cc

cc [*options*] *files*

Compile one or more C source files (*file*.c), assembler source files (*file*.s), or preprocessed C source files (*file*.i). **cc** automatically

---

invokes the link editor **ld** (unless −c is supplied). In some cases, **cc** generates an object file having a .o suffix and a corresponding root name. By default, output is placed in **a.out**. **cc** accepts additional system-specific options.

Note: This command runs the ANSI C compiler; use **/usr/bin/cc** if you want to run the compiler for Kernighan and Ritchie's C.

Options

−**ansi**   Enforce full ANSI conformance.

−**B1** *path/filename*
>Define alternate pass 1 (p1) for the compiler.

−**B2** *path/filename*
>Define alternate pass 2 (p2) for the compiler.

−**B3** *path/filename*
>Define alternate pass 3 (p3) for the compiler.

−**C**   Preserve comments when preprocessing a file with −E, −P, or −EP.

−**c**   Create linkable object file for each source file, but do not call linker.

−**compat**
>Make executable file that is binary compatible across the following systems:
>
>386 UNIX System V Release 3.2
>UNIX-286 System V
>UNIX-386 System V
>UNIX-286 3.0
>UNIX-8086 System V
>
>Use XENIX libraries and create OMF object files.

−**CSON**, −**CSOFF**
>Enable/disable common subexpression optimization, when optimization (−O) is specified.

−**d**   Display compiler passes and their arguments before they are executed.

−**dos**   Create an executable program for MS-DOS systems.

−**D***name*[=*string*]
>Define *name* to the preprocessor as if defined by a **#define** statement in each source file.

−**E**   Preprocess each source file as described for −P, sending results to standard output. Place a **#line** directive with the current input line number and source-file name at beginning of output for each file.

−**EP**   Preprocess each source file as described for −P, sending results to a file and standard output. This option does not place a **#line** directive at the beginning of the file.

−**F***num*
>Set size of program stack to *num* bytes, specified in hexadecimal.

→

-Fa, -Fa*filename*
> Create an assembly source listing in source.*asm* or *filename* in MASM format.

-Fc, -Fc*filename*
> Create a merged assembler and C listing in source.*L* or in *filename*.

-Fe*filename*
> Name executable program file *filename*.

-Fl, -Fl*filename*
> Create a listing file in source.*L* or *filename* with assembly source and object code.

-Fm, -Fm*filename*
> Instruct linker to direct a map listing to *a.map* or to *filename*.

-Fo*object–filename*
> Preceding a source filename, this option causes the object file created from that source to be called *object-filename* instead of the default name, source.*o*. There may be multiple **Fo** options on the command line.

-FPa, -FPc, -FPc87, -FPi, -FPi87
> Used in conjunction with **-dos** or **-os2** to control the type of floating-point code generated and which library support to use.

-g
> Generate more symbol-table information needed for debuggers **sdb**, **dbxtra**, and **CodeView**.

-Gc
> Specifies alternative calling sequences and naming conventions used in System V 386 Pascal and System V 386 FORTRAN.

-Gs
> Remove stack probe routines to reduce binary size and speed execution slightly.

-H*len* Set maximum length of external symbols to *len*.

-help, -HELPC
> Print help menu.

-i
> Create separate instruction and data spaces for small model programs (8086/186/286 compilations only).

-I *dir* Search for include files in directory *dir* (in addition to standard locations). Supply a **-I** for each new *dir* to be searched.

-iBCS2
> Enforce strict Intel Binary Compatibility Standard 2 conformance.

-J
> Change default mode for *char* type from signed to unsigned.

-K Remove stack probes from a program.

-L Create an assembler listing containing assembled code and assembly source instructions in the file source.*L*.

-1 *name*

> Search library lib*name*.a for unresolved function references.

-LARGE

> Invoke large model passes of the compiler (included for backward compatibility only).

-link All options and filenames that follow -link are passed directly to ld.

-m *name*

> Create map file called *name*. This option is used only to produce XENIX-compatible binaries.

-M *string*

> Set program configuration. *string* may be any combination of the following:

> 0   8086 code generation.
> 1   186 code generation.
> 2   286 code generation.
> 3   386 code generation.
> b   Reverse word order for *long* types, putting high order word first.
> c   Create compact model program (for 186/286 compilations only).
> d   Instruct compiler not to assume register SS=DS.
> e   Enable far, near, huge, pascal, and fortran keywords.
> f   Enable software floating point that does not exist in UNIX.
> h   Create huge model program (use for 186/286 compilations only).
> l   Create large model program (use for 8086/186/286 compilations only).
> m   Create medium model program (use for 8086/186/286 compilations only).
> s   Create small model program (default).
> t *num*
>> Set threshold for size of largest data item in data group to *num*. Default is 32,767. This option can only be used in large model programs.

-n Set pure text model—only model supported for 80386 binaries.

-nl *len*

> Set maximum length of external symbols to *len*.

-nointl

> Create a binary that does not include international functionality.

-ND *name*

> Set data segment name for each compiled or assembled source file to *name*.

-NM *name*
> Set module name for each compiled or assembled source file to *name*.

-NT *name*
> Set text segment name for each compiled or assembled source file to *name*.

-O   Optimize object code (produced by .c or .i files).

-o *file* Send object output to *file* instead of to **a.out**.

-O *string*
> Invoke object code optimizer. *string* consists of one or more of the the following characters:

> 3   Disable pass 3 (p3) optimization.

> a   Relax alias checking.

> c   Enable default (block-level) local common expressions.

> d   Turn off the following optimizations:
> a, c, e, g, i, l, s, t.

> e   Enable global register allocation.

> g   Enable global optimizations and global common expressions.

> h   Optimize code for functions returning type *char* or *short*.

> i   Enable generation of intrinsic routines.

> l   Perform loop optimizations (386 only).

> n   Disable unsafe loop optimizations (default).

> p   Improve consistency in floating-point calculations.

> r   Disable in-line returns from functions.

> s   Optimize code for space.

> t   Optimize code for speed (default).

> x   Perform maximum optimization.

> z   Enable maximum loop and global-register allocation of optimization.

-os2 Create an executable program for OS/2, using OS/2 libraries.

-P   Run only the preprocessor and place the result in *file*.i.

-p   Generate benchmark code to count the times each routine is called. File **mon.out** is created, so **prof** can later be used to produce an execution profile.

-pack Pack structures.

-posix Enforce strict POSIX conformance.

-ql   Invoke the basic block analyzer and produce code to count the times each source line is executed. Use **lprof** to list the counts.

-qp   Same as -p.

-quiet Turn off echoing of source filenames to standard error during compilation.

-r   Perform an incremental link.

-S   Create assembly source listing in source.*asm.* This file is in **masm** format.

-s   Instruct linker to strip symbol-table information from executable output file.

-Sl *linewidth*
> Set maximum number of characters per line in the source listing.

-Sp *pagelength*
> Set number of lines per page in the source listing.

-Ss *string*, -St *string*
> Set subtitle (-Ss) and title (-St) for source listings and bypass **cc**'s linking operation.

-strict   Restrict language to ANSI specifications.

-svid   Enforce SVID Issue 2 conformance.

-Tc *filename*
> Tell **cc** that *filename* is a C source file.

-u   Eliminate all manifest defines.

-U*definition*
> Remove or undefine the given manifest define.

-unix   Generate SCO UNIX COFF files (default).

-V*string*
> Place a text string in the object file. *string* must be enclosed in double quotes if it contains quotation marks or blank spaces, and a backslash must precede any quotation marks within the *string*.

-w   Prevent compiler warning messages from being issued.

-W*num*
> Set output level for compiler warning messages:
>
> 0   No warning messages are issued.
> 1   Most warning messages are issued (default).
> 2   More warning messages are issued, including use of functions with no declared return type, failure to put **return** statements in functions with non-**void** return types, and data conversion that would cause loss of data or precision.
> 3   All of the above warning messages are issued.

-WX   Cause all warnings to be fatal.

-xenix Produce XENIX programs using XENIX libraries and #include files.

-x2.3   Equivalent to -**xenix**, but also includes the extended functions that are available with XENIX System V 386 release 2.3.

-xout   Like -**x2.3**, but also includes the functionality of SCO UNIX 3.2.

→

cc	
←	**-xpg3** Enforce strict XPG3 conformance.

-xpg3plus
> Closely represents a true X/Open-conforming implementation with SCO-added value.

-X Remove standard directories from list of directories to be searched for **#include** files.

-z Display various compiler passes and their arguments, but do not execute them.

-Za Restrict language to ANSI specifications.

-Zd Include line-number information in object file.

-Ze Enable **far**, **near**, **huge**, **pascal**, and **fortran** keywords.

-Zg Generate function declarations from function definitions, and write declarations to standard output.

-Zi Include information for the **sdb**, **dbxtra**, and **CodeView** debuggers in the output file.

-Zl Remove default library information from the object file.

-Zp_n_ Pack structure members in memory. _n_ can be one of:

  1 Allocate alignment to 1 (for 8086 processors).
  2 Allocate alignment to 2 (default for 80286 processors).
  4 Allocate alignment to 4 (default for 80386 processors).

-Zs Perform syntax check only.

---

cdc

cdc -r_sid_ [_options_] _files_

Change the delta comments of the specified _sid_ (SCCS ID) of one or more SCCS _files_.

Options

-m[_list_] Add the _list_ of modification request numbers (use a ! before any number to delete it). **-m** is useful only when **admin** has set the **v** flag for _file_. If **-m** is omitted, the terminal displays MRs? as an input prompt.

-y[_string_] Add _string_ to the comments for the specified delta. If **-y** is omitted, the terminal displays comments? as an input prompt.

Example

For delta 1.3 of file **s.prog.c**, add modification numbers x01-5 and x02-8 and then add comments:

```
cdc -r1.3 s.prog.c
MRs? x01-5 x02-8
comments? this went out to review
```

cflow [*options*] *files*

Produce an outline (or flowchart) of external function calls for the C, lex, yacc, assembler, or object *files*. **cflow** also accepts the **cc** options -D, -I, and -U.

Options

- -d*n* Stop outlining when nesting level *n* is reached.
- -i_ Include functions whose names begin with _.
- -ix Include external and static data symbols.
- -r Invert the listing; show the callers of each function and sort in lexicographical order by callee.

chkshlib [*options*] *file1* [*file2 file3* ...]

Check for compatibility between files. Files are compatible if every library symbol in one that should be matched is matched in the second. The pathname for the target shared library in both files must be identical. *file1* may be compatible with *file2* without the reverse being true. Exit status is 0 if no incompatibilities are found, 1 if incompatibility is found, and 2 if a processing error occurs.

Options

- -b If symbols found in *file1* are not in the bounds of *file2*, report warning messages to standard output.
- -i Turn off restriction that calls for pathnames for target shared library to be identical in order for two files to be compatible.
- -n Indicate that there are exactly two input files that are target shared libraries, where the first references symbols in the second. The -i option must be used with this option.
- -v Cause verbose reporting of all incompatibilities to standard output.

Input files

Valid combinations of input files are:

Executable	[Target shared library(1)...Target shared library(n)]
Executable	[Host shared library(1)...Host shared library(n)]
Host shared library	Target shared library
Host shared library	Host shared library
Target shared library	Host shared library
Target shared library	Target shared library

codeview [*options*] [*executable_file* [*arguments*]]

Visual debugger. CodeView provides a window-type environment in which to debug C and assembly language programs. The

→

Programming Commands

codeview

←

optional *arguments* are parameters passed to the *executable_file*. CodeView provides the ability to browse source or assembly code, and can debug programs written in C, FORTRAN, BASIC, Pascal, and assembly language. It can debug both COFF and *x.out* executable files. To use CodeView, you first create an executable file from compiled object files. This executable file must be compiled and linked with the correct options for generating symbolic debug and line number records (when compiling with **cc**, use the **-g** or **-Zd** and **-Zi** options).

Options

    -c *command-list*
        Execute *command-list* on startup.

    -C *corefile* | -
        Load *corefile* instead of the default *core* in the current directory.

    -I *dir* Include *dir* in the default list of directories to be searched while looking for a source file.

    -r   Use 80386 hardware debug registers for breakpoints set in data.

    -tsf   Ignore statefile.

CodeView windows

Source window	Displays source code.
Command window	Accepts debugging commands.
Watch window	Displays current value of variables.
Local window	Displays values of variables local to current function.
Memory window	Displays contents of memory.
Register window	Displays contents of microprocessor's registers, as well as processor flags.
8087 window	Displays registers of coprocessor or its software emulator.

---

comb

comb [*options*] *files*

Reduce the size of the specified SCCS *files*. This is done by pruning selected deltas and combining those that remain, thereby reconstructing the SCCS file. The default behavior prunes all but the most recent delta in a particular branch and keeps only those ancestors needed to preserve the tree structure. **comb** produces a shell script on standard output. Actual reconstruction of the SCCS files is done by running the script.

Options

    -c*list* Preserve only those deltas whose SCCS IDs are specified in the comma-separated *list*. Use a hyphen (–) to supply a range; e.g., 1.3,2.1-2.5.

-o   Access the reconstructed *file* at the release number of the delta that is created, instead of at the most recent ancestor. This option may change the tree structure.

-p*sid*   In reconstructing *file*, discard all deltas whose SCCS identification string is older than *sid*.

-s   Generate a shell script that calculates how much the file has been reduced in size. -s is useful as a preview of what **comb** will do when actually run.

conv [*options*] -t *target* [– | *files*]

Convert object files in the Common Object File Format (COFF) from their current byte ordering to the byte ordering of the *target* machine. The converted file is written to *file.v*. **conv** can be used on either the source or target machine. Legal values for *target* are: pdp, vax, ibm, x86, b16, mc68, and m32. If source and target machines have the same byte ordering, use the **convert** command instead of **conv**.

Options

-    Names of *files* should be read from standard input.

-a   If input file is an archive, produce output file in System V Release 2.0 portable archive format.

-o   If input file is an archive, produce output file in old (pre-System V) archive format.

-p   If input file is an archive, produce output file in System V Release 1.0 random access archive format.

-s   "Preswab" all characters in the object file. This is useful only for 3B20 computer object files which are to be "swab-dumped" from a DEC machine to a 3B20 computer.

Example

To ship object files from a VAX system to a 3B2 computer, execute the following commands:

```
conv -t m32 *.out uucp *.out.v my3b2!~/rje/
```

convert [*options*] *infile outfile*

Convert archive files to common formats. *infile* must be an archive file and *outfile* will be the equivalent System V archive file. All other types of **convert** input will be passed unmodified from *infile* to *outfile*. *infile* must be different from *outfile*.

Options

-5   Convert a non-System V archive file.

-x   Required for XENIX archives. -x will convert the general archive structure but leave archive members unmodified.

cpp [*options*] [*ifile* [*ofile*]]

AT&T C language preprocessor. **cpp** is invoked as the first pass of any C compilation by the **rcc** command. The output of **cpp** is a form acceptable as input to the next pass of the C compiler. *ifile* and *ofile* are, respectively, the input and output for the preprocessor; they default to standard input and standard output.

Options

- **-C**   Pass along all comments (except those found on **cpp** directive lines). By default, **cpp** strips C-style comments.

- **-D***name*[*=def*]
     Define *name* with value *def* as if by a **#define**. If no *=def* is given, *name* is defined with value 1. **-D** has lower precedence than **-U**.

- **-H**   Print pathnames of included files, one per line, on standard error.

- **-I***dir*   Search in directory *dir* for **#include** files whose names do not begin with **/** before looking in directories on standard list. **#include** files whose names are enclosed in double quotes and do not begin with **/** will be searched for first in the current directory, then in directories named on **-I** options, and last in directories on the standard list.

- **-P**   Preprocess input without producing line control information used by next pass of C compiler.

- **-S***n*   Set size of the *sbf* buffer. *n* is number of bytes to be dynamically allocated to sbf buffer. The sbf buffer is used, among other things, to store values of **#defines**. Without **-S**, a default statically allocated buffer is set up.

- **-T**   Use only the first eight characters to distinguish preprocessor symbols. This option is included for backward compatibility.

- **-U***name*
     Remove any initial definition of *name*, where *name* is a reserved symbol predefined by the preprocessor or a name defined on a **-D** option. Names predefined by **cpp** are **unix** and **i386**.

- **-Y***dir*   Use directory *dir* in place of standard list of directories when searching for **#include** files.

Special names

cpp understands two special names:

LINE   Current source line number (as a decimal integer)
FILE   Current filename (as a C string)

These special names can be used anywhere, including macros, just like any other defined names. **cpp**'s understanding of the line number and filename may be changed using a **#line** directive.

Directives

All **cpp** directive lines start with # in column 1. Any number of blanks and tabs is allowed between the # and the directive. The directives are:

#define *name token–string*

Defines a macro called *name*, with a value of *token-string*. Subsequent instances of *name* are replaced with *token-string*.

#define *name(arg, . . . , arg) token–string*

This allows substitution of a macro with arguments. *token-string* will be substituted for *name* in the input file. If *name* is followed by an argument list, each token in the list replaces the corresponding *arg* in the macro definition.

#undef *name*

Remove definition of the macro *name*. No additional tokens are permitted on the directive line after *name*.

#ident *string*

Put *string* into the comment section of an object file.

#include

Include contents of *filename* at this point in the program. No additional tokens are permitted on the directive line after the final " or >.

#line *integer–constant*

Causes **cpp** to generate line-control information for the next pass of the C compiler. The compiler behaves as if *integer-constant* is the line number of the next line of source code and *filename* (if present) is the name of the input file. No additional tokens are permitted on the directive line after the optional *filename*.

#endif End a section of lines begun by a test directive (**#if**, **#ifdef**, or **#ifndef**). No additional tokens are permitted on the directive line.

#ifdef *name*

Lines following this directive and up to matching **#endif** or next **#else** or **#elif** will appear in the output if *name* is not currently defined. No additional tokens are permitted on the directive line after *name*.

#if *constant–expression*

Lines following this directive and up to matching **#endif** or next **#else** or **#elif** will appear in the output if *constant-expression* evaluates to non-zero.

#elif *constant–expression*

An arbitrary number of **#elif** directives is allowed between a **#if**, **#ifdef**, or **#ifndef** directive and a **#else** or **#endif** directive. The lines following the **#elif** and up to

→

---

cpp ←	the next **#else**, **#elif**, or **#endif** directive will appear in the output if the preceding test directive and all intervening **#elif** directives evaluate to zero, and the *constant-expression* evaluates to non-zero. If *constant-expression* evaluates to non-zero, all succeeding **#elif** and **#else** directives will be ignored.
	#else Lines following this directive and up to the matching **#endif** will appear in the output if the preceding test directive evaluates to zero and all intervening **#elif** directives evaluate to zero. No additional tokens are permitted on the directive line.

---

cprs

cprs [*option*] *infile outfile*

Compress a common object file. **cprs** reduces the size of *infile* by removing duplicate structure and union descriptors, producing *outfile* as output. Only COFF files are supported by this activity.

Option

-p   Print statistical messages including total number of tags, total duplicate tags, and total reduction of *infile*.

---

cscope

cscope [*options*] *files*

Interactive utility for finding code fragments in one or more C, lex, or yacc source *files*. **cscope** builds a symbol cross-reference (named **cscope.out** by default) and then calls up a menu. The menu prompts the user to search for functions, macros, variables, preprocessor directives, etc. Type **?** to list interactive commands. Subsequent calls to **cscope** rebuild the cross-reference if needed (i.e., if filenames or file contents have changed). Source filenames can be stored in a file **cscope.files**. This file can then be specified instead of *files*. Options -I, -p, and -T are also recognized when placed in **cscope.files**.

Options

-d   Don't update the cross-reference.

-e   Don't show the CTRL-E prompt between files.

-f *out*   Give the cross-reference file the name *out* instead of **cscope.out**.

-I *dir*   Search for include files in *dir* before searching the default (**/usr/include**). **cscope** searches the current directory, then *dir*, then the default.

-i *in*   Check source files whose names are listed in *in* rather than in **cscope.files**.

ctags [options] files

Create a list of function and macro names that are defined in the specified C, Pascal, FORTRAN, yacc, or lex source *files*. The output list (named **tags** by default) contains lines of the form:

name   *file*   *context*

where *name* is the function or macro name, *file* is the source file in which *name* is defined, and *context* is a search pattern that shows the line of code containing *name*. After the list of tags is created, you can invoke vi on any file and type:

```
:set tags=tagsfile
:tag name
```

This switches the vi editor to the source file associated with the *name* listed in *tagsfile* (which you specify with -f).

Options

-a   Append tag output to existing list of tags.

-u   Update tags file to reflect new locations of functions (e.g., when functions are moved to a different source file). Old tags are deleted; new tags are appended.

-v   Print to standard output a listing (index) of each function, source file, and page number (1 page = 64 lines).

-w   Suppress warning messages.

-x   Produce a listing of each function, its line number, source file, and context.

---

ctrace [options] [file]

Debug a C program. **ctrace** reads the C source *file* and writes a modified version to standard output. Common options are -f and -v. **ctrace** also accepts the cc options -D, -I, and -U.

Options

-e   Print variables as floating point.

-f *functions*
    Trace only the specified *functions*.

-l *n*   Follow a statement loop *n* times (default is 20).

-o   Print variables in octal.

-p '*s*'   Print trace output via function *s* (default is **printf**).

-P   Run the C preprocessor before tracing.

-r*file*   Change the trace function package to *file* (default is **runtime.c**).

-s   Suppress certain redundant code.

-t*n*   Trace *n* variables per statement (default is 10; maximum is 20).

-u   Print variables as unsigned.

$\rightarrow$

ctrace ←	-v *functions* Do not trace the specified *functions*. -x Print variables as hexadecimal.

cxref

cxref [*options*] *files*

Build a cross-reference table for each of the C source *files*. The table lists all symbols, providing columns for the name and the associated function, file, and line. In the table, symbols are marked by = if assigned, − if declared, or * if defined. **cxref** also accepts the **cc** options −D, −I, and −U.

Options

-A   Turn off macro cross-referencing.

-c   Print a combined cross-reference of all input files.

-D*name=def*
       Define *name* with value *def* as if by a #**define**.

-E   Turn off constant cross-references.

-F   Turn off function cross-references.

-i   Turn off all cross-referencing, except that specified using the following flags (-i must be specified first on the command line):

       -a Turn on macro cross-references.

       -e Turn on constant cross-references.

       -f Turn on function cross-references.

       -l Turn on label cross-references.

       -m Turn on manifest cross-references.

       -v Turn on variable cross-references.

       -y Turn on typedef cross-references.

-I *pathname*
       Add *pathname* to list of directories to be searched when an #**include** file is not found in the directory containing the current source file, or whenever angle brackets enclose the filename.

-L   Turn off label cross-references.

-M   Turn off manifest cross-references.

-N   Enable cross-referencing of symbols in **/usr/include**.

-o*file* Direct output to *file* instead of standard output.

-s   Operate silently; do not print input filenames.

-t   Format for 80-column listing.

-U*name*, -U*definition*
       Remove any initial definition of *name*, where *name* is a reserved symbol that is predefined by the particular preprocessor.

-V   Turn off variable cross-references.

-w[*n*]	Format for maximum width of *n* columns (default is 80; *n* must be more than 50).	**cxref**
-Y	Turn off typedef cross-references.	

dbXtra [*X11 flag* | *dbXtra flag*] ... [*objfile* [*coredump* | *processid*]]

dbXtra

Screen-oriented, windowed-environment source level debugger for C and assembly language programs. **dbXtra** invokes the Motif version of the **dbxtra** debugger.

Options

-F   Assume that file-scoped structure/union/enum definitions with the same name are identical. The default is to assume they have different definitions.

-C   Request C debugging only.

-C++   Assume C++ mode.

-c *file*   Execute **dbXtra** commands in *file* before reading from standard input.

-I *dir*   Add *dir* to the list of directories that are searched when looking for a source file.

-r   Execute *objfile* immediately.

-x   Ignore cross-reference file when initializing **dbXtra**.

dbxtra [*options*] [*objfile* [*corefile*]]

dbxtra

Screen-oriented, windowed-environment source level debugger for C and assembly language programs. **dbxtra** is a superset of the **dbx** and **sdb** debuggers available with most UNIX systems. The object file *objfile* contains the executable instructions for the program to be debugged. If not specified, **dbxtra** prompts for the name of the file. The core file *corefile* determines the state of the program when it faulted. If not specified, the file named *core* in the current directory is used, if it exists.

dbxtra invokes the **curses** version of the debugger, suitable for use with most common alphanumeric terminals as well as within X windows. The second form of the command, **dbXtra** (see **dbXtra**, above), can only be used within the X windowing system and invokes the Motif version of the debugger.

Options

-C   Request C debugging only.

-C++   Assume C++ mode.

-c *file*   Execute **dbxtra** commands in *file* before reading from standard input.

-F   Assume that file-scoped structure/union/enum definitions with the same name are identical.

Programming Commands

→

-I *dir* Add *dir* to the list of directories that are searched when looking for a source file.

-i Force **dbxtra** to act as though standard input is a terminal.

-r Execute *objfile* immediately.

-s Do not invoke screen manager—work in line mode only.

-x Ignore cross-reference file when initializing **dbxtra**.

Alphabetical summary of commands

alias *name command/string*

Define *name* to be an alias for *command* or *string*. For example:

```
alias s(n) "stop at n"
```

means that the command s(20) expands to stop at 20. See also **unalias**.

assign *var = expr*

Assign the value of *expr* to variable *var*.

backward *n*

Scroll source window backward *n* lines.

bindkey [*key* [*string*]]

Bind *key* with contents of *string*.

catch [*signals*]

Start trapping signals before they are sent to the program. Specify one or more *signals* by number or by name. By default all signals are trapped except SIGCONT, SIGCHILD, SIGALRM, and SIGKILL. See also **ignore**.

cc Toggle between C++ and C output modes. If -C option of **dbxtra** was specified, this command is not enabled.

cont *integer/signal-name*

Continue execution from the point at which it was stopped. If a *signal-name* is specified, resume process as if it had received the signal; otherwise, continue process as though it had not been stopped.

dbxref [*options*] [*files*]

Generate cross-reference file necessary for the **xref**, enhanced **whatis**, and **whereis** commands. *files* is the list of C files. **dbxref** options include:

-D *name*[=*def*]

Supply a #**define** directive, defining *name* to be *def* or, if no *def* is given, the value 1.

-I *dir* Search for include files in directory *dir* (in addition to standard locations). Supply a -I for each new *dir* to be searched.

-i Do an incremental cross-reference. An incremental cross-reference is used to update the cross-reference when only some files have been modified. The old information relevant to those files is forgotten, the files are rescanned, and the information integrated with the old data.

-o*file* Place output in *file*. An extension of .**xref** is added if necessary.

-U *name*

Remove definition of name, as if through an **#undef** directive.

delete *event–number*

Remove traces, stops, and whens corresponding to each *event-number*, given by **status**.

detach If version of UNIX supports the **ptrace detach** request, the process being debugged has all breakpoints removed and is allowed to execute at full speed. Otherwise, the process is killed.

disable [*event–number*]

Disable traces, stops, and whens corresponding to each *event-number*, given by **status**.

display [*expressions*]

Show the value of one or more *expressions* in a special-purpose window. Values are updated each time execution stops.

down [n]

Move current function down *n* levels on stack. Default is 1. See also **up**.

enable *event–number*

Enable traces, stops, and whens corresponding to each *event-number*.

edit [*file*]/*func*

Invoke editor either on *file*, on current source file (if no *file* is given), or on file containing *func*. The EDITOR environment variable determines which editor is used.

exec [*file*]

If the process being debugged does an **exec** system call, this tells **bdxtra** that a new symbol table should be read in.

file [*file*]

Change name of current source file to *file* or, if no *file* is given, print name of current source file.

forward *n*

Scroll source window forward *n* lines.

fpregs *n*

Display contents of 80387 floating-point registers in a human-readable form.

func [*func*]

Change current function to *func* or, if no *func* is given, print current function.

$\rightarrow$

---

goto *line–number*

> Continue execution and stop before the first instruction at the specified *line-number* is executed.

help [*command*]

> Print a synopsis of all **dbxtra** commands or of the given *command*. For commands including non-alphanumeric characters, the command name must be quoted.

ignore [*signals*]

> Stop trapping signals before they are sent to the program. Specify one or more *signals* by number or by name. Omit signal to display the currently ignored signal. See also **catch**.

jump *line–number*

> Continue execution from *line-number*.

keys [on | off]

> Turn on/off interpretations of keys into screen functions. Default is **on**.

kill   Stop execution or debugging of current program.

list [*n1* [,*n2*]]/*func*

> List the source text between lines *n1* and *n2*, or on lines surrounding the first statement of *func*. With no arguments, list the next ten lines.

more [on | off]

> Turn on/off **more**-like features for **dbxtra** and the debugged program's output. Default is **on**.

next [*n*]

> Execute next *n* source lines. Default is 1. **next** doesn't go into functions.

nexti   Same as **next**, but do a single instruction instead of a source line.

print *expressions*

> Print the values of one or more comma-separated *expressions*.

quit   Exit **dbxtra**.

regs   Display contents of the 80386 registers in a human-readable form.

rerun [*arguments*]

> Without *arguments*, redo the previous **run** command (and its arguments). Otherwise, this command is the same as **run**.

return [*procedure*]

> Continue until a return to *procedure* (or current procedure) is called.

run [*arguments*]

> Begin executing the object file, passing optional command-line *arguments*. The arguments can include input or output redirection to a named file.

screen [on | off]

Turn screen mode on/off. Default is **on**.

set *var* [= *expr*]

Define value *expr* for variable *var*. See also **unset**. Built-in variables include:

$frame If set to an address, use the stack frame it points to. (Useful for kernel debugging.)

$hex*item* When set, print hexadecimal values for specified *item*. *item* can be **chars**, **ints**, **off-sets**, or **strings**.

$listwindow

Default number of lines to show using **list** command (default is 10).

$mapaddrs

When set, start mapping addresses; when unset, stop. (Useful for kernel debugging.)

$unsafecall

When set, turn off type checking of parameters in **call** statements.

$unsafeassign

When set, turn off type checking in **assign** statements.

setenv *VAR string*

Set environment variable *VAR* to *string*.

sh *command*

Pass *command* to the shell for execution.

skip [*n*]

Continue execution from where it stopped. *n* number of breakpoints are ignored before the program stops.

source *file*

Read commands for **dbxtra** from *file*.

status [> *file*]

Show active **trace**, **stop**, and **when** commands; store output in *file*.

step [*n*]

Execute *n* source lines. Default is 1. **step** goes into functions.

stepi Same as **step**, but do a single instruction instead of a source line.

stop *restriction* [**if** *cond*]

Stop execution if specified *restriction* is true. See **trace** about *cond*. Restrictions include:

at *n* Source line *n* is reached.

if *cond* Condition *cond* is true.

in *func* Procedure or function *func* is called.

inclass *class*

Each method of C++ class is called.

$\rightarrow$

---

infunction *func*

Top-level function in a C++ module is
called.

inmethod *member*

Named *member* of any C++ class is called.

var   Variable *var* has changed.

trace [*restriction*] [**if** *cond*]

Report tracing information as program is executed,
according to the *restriction*. With no arguments, all
source lines are printed before being executed. *cond* is
a Boolean expression; if it evaluates to false, then the
tracing information is not printed. Restrictions include:

in *func*   Report while executing *func*.

inclass *class*

Print name of function that called any member of *class*.

infunction *func*

Print name of function that called any top-
level C++ *func*.

inmethod *member*

Print name of function that called *member*
of any class.

expr **at** *n*   Print value of *expr* each time line *n* is
reached.

func   Print name of function that called *func*.

n   Show source line *n* before executing it.

var   Print value of *var* each time it changes.

var [**in** *func*]

Same as above, but print information only
while executing from within the specified
procedure or function.

unalias *name*

Remove the alias *name*. See also **alias**.

unbindkey *key*

Unbind *key*.

undisplay [*expressions*]

Stop displaying *expressions* (see **display**). *expression* can
be a number, in which case it refers to the item-number
in a **display** list.

unset *var*

Remove the debugger variable *var*. See also **set**.

up [*n*]   Move current function up *n* levels on stack. Default is
1. See also **down**.

use [*directories*]

Define one or more *directories* to search when looking
for source files. With no argument, print the current
search directories.

        Print version information for **dbxtra**.

vt100 [on | off]

        Turn on/off **vt100** emulator for the debugged program's output. Default is **on**.

whatis [-r] *name*

        Print the declaration of the identifier, class, or type *name*. -**r** recursively prints the declarations of inherited classes.

when *restriction commands*

        Execute one or more **dbxtra** *commands* (separated by semi-colons) when *restriction* is true. See **stop** for list of restrictions.

where [*n*]

        List all active functions on the stack, or only the top *n*.

whereis *identifier*

        Print the fully-qualified name of symbols that match *identifier*.

which *identifier*

        Print the fully-qualified name of *identifier*.

xref *identifier*

        If cross-reference information has been loaded, print a cross-reference for the given symbol.

addr1/ Print contents of memory starting at the address *addr1*. Stop printing when a second address is reached or when *n* items have been printed, as shown by the syntax lines below:

> *addr1, addr2/*[*mode*]
> *addr1/*[*n*] [*mode*]

mode specifies the output format. The default is **X**. Addresses may be **.** (next address), &*addr* (symbolic address), and $**r***n* (register *n*). They may include the symbols +, −, and * (indirection). Modes include:

b	Print a byte in octal.
c	Print a byte as a character.
d	Print a short word in decimal.
D	Print a long word in decimal.
f	Print a single-precision real number.
F	Print a double-precision real number.
i	Print a machine instruction.
o	Print a short word in octal.
O	Print a long word in octal.
s	Print a string as characters terminated by a null byte.
x	Print a short word in hexadecimal.
X	Print a long word in hexadecimal.

→

dbxtra	*address* = [*mode*]
←	Display the value of *address*.

delta	**delta** [*options*] *files*
	Incorporate changes (add a delta) to one or more SCCS *files*. **delta** is used to store changes made to a text file that was retrieved by **get** -e and then edited. **delta** normally removes the text file.

Options

- **-g***list*   Ignore deltas whose SCCS IDs (version numbers) are specified in the comma-separated *list*. Use – to supply a range; e.g., 1.3,2.1-2.5.

- **-m**[*list*]   Supply a *list* of modification request numbers as reasons for creating new deltas. **-m** is useful only when **admin** has set the **v** flag for *file*. If **-m** is omitted, the terminal displays **MRs?** as an input prompt.

- **-n**   Do not remove the edited file (extracted by **get** -e) after execution of **delta**.

- **-p**   Print a **diff**-style listing of delta changes to *file*.

- **-r***SID*   Delta version number that identifies *file*. **-r** is needed only when more than one version of an SCCS file is being edited simultaneously.

- **-s**   Suppress printing of new SID and other delta information.

- **-y**[*string*]   Insert *string* as a comment describing why the delta was made. If **-y** is omitted, the terminal displays **comments?** as an input prompt.

dis	**dis** [*options*] *files*
	Disassemble the object or archive *files*. See also **as**.

Options

- **-d** *section*   Disassemble only the specified *section* of data, printing its offset.

- **-da** *section*   Same as **-d**, but print the data's actual address.

- **-F** *func*   Disassemble only the specified function; reuse **-F** for additional functions.

- **-l** *string*   Disassemble only the library file *string* (e.g., *string* would be *x* for **lib***x*.a).

- **-L**   Look for C source labels in files containing debug information (e.g., files compiled with **cc** -g).

- **-o**   Print octal output (default is hexadecimal).

- **-t** *section*   Same as **-d**, but print text output.

- **-V**   Print version information on standard error.

dosld [options] file ...

MS-DOS cross linker. **dosld** links the object *file*(s) to create a program for execution under MS-DOS. Files passed to **dosld** may be either UNIX-style libraries or ordinary 8086 files. Unless **-u** is used, at least one of the files passed must be an ordinary object file.

Options

-C   Case sensitivity on.

-D   Perform DS allocation. Generally used in conjunction with **-H**.

-F *num*

    Set stack size to hexadecimal value *num*. Stack segment will be set to to *num* bytes in the output file.

-G   Ignore group associations. Provided for compatibility with old versions of MS-LINK.

-H   Set a field in the header of the executable file telling MS-DOS to load the program at the highest available position in memory.

-L   Include line numbers.

-M   Include public symbols in the list file. Symbols are sorted twice: lexicographically and by address.

-m *filename*

    Create file *filename* including information about the segments and groups.

-nl *num*

    Set name length to a decimal number, *num*. All public and external symbols longer than *num* characters will be truncated.

-o *filename*

    Create output file *filename* instead of the default name **a.out**.

-S *num*

    Set segment limit to a decimal number, *num*, between 1 and 1024. Default is 128.

-u *num*

    Name undefined symbol, *name*. This option may appear more than once on the command line.

---

dump [options] files

Dump selected parts of a common object file. Output can be directed via standard redirection tools. **dump** operates only on COFF executables. *file*(s) are processed according to the following options:

Options

-a   Dump archive header of each member of each archive file argument.

→

Programming Commands

dump	-c	Dump string table.
	-f	Dump file header.
←	-g	Dump global symbols in symbol table of an archive.
	-h	Dump section headers.
	-L	Interpret and print contents of .lib sections.
	-l	Dump line number information.
	-o	Dump each optional header.
	-r	Dump relocation information.
	-s	Dump section contents.
	-t	Dump symbol-table entries.
	-V	Print **dump** version number.

-z *name*
> Dump line number entries for named function.

Modifiers

Following is a list of modifiers that can be used in conjuction with the options listed above to modify their capabilities. Blanks separating an *option* and its *modifier* are optional.

-d *number*
> Dump section *number*, or range of sections starting at *number* and ending at *number* specified by +d.

+d *number*
> Dump sections in range either beginning with first section or beginning with section specified by -d.

-n *name*
> Dump information pertaining only to named entity. This modifier is used with -h, -l, -r, -s, and -t.

-p   Suppress printing the headers.

-t *index*
> Dump only indexed symbol-table entry. -t used in conjunction with +t specifies a range of symbol-table entries.

+t *index*
> Dump symbol-table entries in range ending with indexed entry. Range begins at first symbol-table entry or entry specified by -t.

-u   Underline name of file for emphasis.

-v   Dump information in symbolic representation, rather than numeric. This modifier can be used with all options except -0 and -s.

-z *name,number*
> Dump line-number entry or range of line numbers starting at *number* for the named function.

+z *number*
> Dump line numbers starting at either function *name* or *number* specified by -z, up to *number* specified by +z.

dumpmsg [*options*] [*catfile* | –] *msgfile*

Generate a message source file. **dumpmsg** reads the formatted message catalogue *catfile* and generates a message source file *msgfile*. To read from standard input or write to standard output, use – instead of *catfile*.

Options

-C   Converts all non-ASCII characters of the message text to escape sequences representing the character.

-X   Inhibit production of only X/Open-compatible sources.

findstr [*options*] *file* ...

findstr

Find strings in C source code and write them on standard output in the form:

```
filename pos len "...message text..."
```

where *filename* is the name of the C source file, *pos* is the character position of the message within the source file and *len* is the message length in bytes.

Options

-b   Source file directory name truncation within the string file.

-p [*cpp_option*]
     Preprocess source file before performing find. Arguments following –p are interpreted as **cpp** options.

fixhdr *options files*

fixhdr

Change header of output files created by link editors or assemblers. Modifications include changing the format of the header, the fixed stack size, the standalone load address, and symbol names. **fixhdr** takes one option at a time. To make more than one modification to a file, use **fixhdr** on the original, then use it again on the **fixhdr** output, specifying the next option.

Options

-5x [-n]
     Change 5.2 (UNIX System V Release 2) **a.out** format of header to **x.out** format. -n causes leading underscores on symbol names to be passed with no modifications.

-86x   Add **x.out** header format to **86rel** object module format.

-A *num*
     Add or change standalone load addresss specified in **x.out** format of header. *num* must be a hexadecimal number.

Programming
Commands

→

Software Development Commands

311

fixhdr ←	**-ax -c** [11,86] Change **a.out** format of header to **x.out** format. **-c** specifies the target CPU; **11** specifies a PDP-11 CPU; **86** specifies one of the 8086 family of CPUs.
	-bx Change **b.out** format of header to **x.out** format.
	-C *cpu* Set CPU type.
	-F *num* Add or change fixed stack size specified in **x.out** format of header. *num* must be a hexadecimal number.
	-M[smlh] Change model of **x.out** or **86rel** format. Model refers to compiler model specified when creating binary; **s** for small model, **m** for medium model, **l** for large model, **h** for huge model.
	-r Ensure that resolution table is non-zero size.
	-s *s1=s2* [**-s** *s3=s4*] Change symbol names, where symbol name of *s1* is changed to *s2*.
	-v [2,3,5,7] Change version of XENIX specified in header. XENIX Version 2 was based on UNIX Version 7.
	-x4 Change **x.out** format of header to the 4.2BSD **a.out** format.
	-x5 Change **x.out** format of header to the 5.2 SVR2 **a.out** format.
	-xa Change **x.out** format of header to the **a.out** format.
	-xb Change **x.out** format of header to the **b.out** format.

gencat	**gencat** [*option*] *database msgfiles*

Append (or merge) messages contained in one or more *msgfiles* to the formatted message *database* file. If *database* doesn't exist, it is created. Each message in *msgfile* is preceded by a numerical identifier. Comment lines can be added by using a dollar sign at the beginning of a line, followed by a space or tab.

Options

-     Use standard output or standard input in place of *database* or *msgfile*, respectively.
- **-X**   Inhibit check for portability to X/Open.

gencc	**gencc** [*options*]

Create a frontend to the **rcc** command. The frontend generated is a one-line shell script which calls **rcc** with the proper **-Y** options (specifying new locations of pieces of the compilation system). **gencc** prompts for the location of each tool and directory which can be respecified. If no location is specified, it assumes that piece of the system has not been relocated.

---

get [*options*] *files*

Retrieve a text version of an SCCS *file*. The retrieved text file (also called the g-file) has the same name as the SCCS file but drops the **s.** prefix. For each SCCS *file*, **get** prints its version number and the number of lines retrieved. See "Identification Keywords" for a list of keywords that can be placed in text files.

Options

-a*n*　　Retrieve delta sequence number *n*; not very useful (used by **comb**).

-b　　　Create new branch (use with -e).

-c*date*　Retrieve a version that includes only those changes made before *date*. *date* is a series of two-digit numbers indicating the year, followed by an optional month, day, hour, minute, and second. Symbolic characters can be used as field separators.

-e　　　Retrieve a text file for editing; this is the most commonly-used option.

-g　　　Suppress the text and just retrieve the SCCS ID (version number), typically to check it.

-i*list*　Incorporate into the retrieved text file any deltas whose SCCS IDs (version numbers) are specified in the comma-separated *list*. Use a hyphen (-) to supply a range (e.g., 1.3,2.1-2.5).

-k　　　Do not expand ID keywords to their values; use in place of -e to regenerate (overwrite) a text file that was ruined during editing.

-l[p]　　Create a delta summary (saved to a file or, with -lp, displayed on standard output).

-m　　　Precede each text line with the SCCS ID of the delta it relates to.

-n　　　Precede each text line with the %M% keyword (typically the name of the text file).

-p　　　Write retrieved text to standard output instead of to a file.

-r*sid*　Retrieve SCCS ID (version number) *sid*.

-s　　　Suppress normal output (show error messages only).

-t　　　Retrieve the top (most recent) version of a release.

-w*string*
　　　　Replace the %W% keyword with *string*; %W% is the header label used by **what**.

-x*list*　Exclude the *list* of deltas from the retrieved text file; the inverse of -i.

→

---

get ←	*Examples* Retrieve file **prog.c** for editing; a subsequent **delta** creates a branch at version 1.3: ``` get -e -b -r1.3 s.prog.c ``` Retrieve file **prog.c**; contents exclude changes made after 2:30 p.m. on June 1, 1990 (except for deltas 2.6 and 2.7, which are included): ``` get -c'90/06/01 14:30:00' -i'2.6,2.7' s.prog.c ``` Display the contents of **s.text.c** (all revisions except 1.1 - 1.7): ``` get -p -x1.1-1.7 s.text.c ```
help	**help** [*commands* | *error_codes*] Online help facility to explain SCCS commands or error messages. With no arguments, **help** prompts for a command name or an error code. To display a brief syntax, supply the SCCS command name. To display an explanation of an error message, supply the code that appears after an SCCS error message. The **help** files usually reside in **/usr/ccs/lib**. Error messages produced by aborted SCCS commands are of the form: ``` ERROR filename: message (code) ``` The *code* is useful for finding out the nature of your error. To do this, type: ``` help code ``` *Example* When everything else fails, try this: ``` help stuck ```
imake	**imake** *options* C preprocessor (**cpp**) interface to the **make** utility. **imake** (for *include make*) solves the portability problem of **make** by allowing machine dependencies to be kept in a central set of configuration files, separate from the descriptions of the various items to be built. The targets are contained in the *Imakefile*, a machine-independent description of the targets to be built, written as **cpp** macros. **imake** uses **cpp** to process the configuration files and the *Imakefile*, and generate machine-specific *Makefiles*, which can then be used by **make**. One of the configuration files is a template file, a master file for **imake**. This template file (default is **Imake.tmpl**) #include's the other configuration files that contain machine dependencies such as

variable assignments, site definitions, and **cpp** macros, and directs the order in which the files are processed. Each file affects the interpretation of later files and sections of **Imake.tmpl**.

Comments may be included in **imake** configuration files, but the initial # needs to be preceded with an empty C comment:

```
/**/#
```

For more information, see **cpp** and **make**.

Options

-D*define*

> Set directory-specific variables. This option is passed directly to **cpp**.

-e

> Execute the generated *Makefile*. Default is to leave this to the user.

-f *filename*

> Name of per-directory input file. Default is *Imakefile*.

-I*directory*

> Directory in which **imake** template and configuration files may be found. This option is passed directly to **cpp**.

-s *filename*

> Name of **make** description file to be generated. If filename is a dash, the output is written to stdout. The default is to generate, but not execute, a *Makefile*.

-T*template*

> Name of master template file used by **cpp**. This file is usually located in the directory specified with the -I option. The default file is **Imake.tmpl**.

-v

> Print the **cpp** command line used to generate the *Makefile*.

Tools

Following are a list of tools used with **imake**:

imboot [*options*] [*topdir* [*curdir*]]

> Bootstrap a *Makefile* from an *Imakefile*. By default, **imboot** looks for configuration files in the **config** directory under the project root directory. The -c *name* or -C *name* options tell **imboot** to use a set of publicly-installed configuration files instead of, or in addition to, respectively, any files in the project's **config** directory. *topdir* specifies the location of the project root. *curdir* (usually omitted) specifies the name of the current directory, relative to the project root.

imdent [*options*] [*files*]

> Indent **cpp** directives to show nesting level. **imdent** reads the named input *files*, or standard input if no files are specified, and adds indentation to **cpp** directives based on the nesting level of conditionals. The -n

---

option is a number specifying indentation increments per nesting level. Default is two spaces. -0 removes all indentation.

makedepend [*options*] [*files*]

Create header file dependencies in *Makefiles*. **mak-edepend** reads the named input source *files* in sequence and parses them to process **#include, #define, #undef, #ifdef, #ifndef, #endif, #if,** and **#else** directives so it can tell which **#include** directives would be used in a compilation. **makedepend** determines the dependencies and writes them to the *Makefile*. **make** then knows which object files must be recompiled when a dependency has changed. **makedepend** has the following options:

-- *options* --

Ignore any unrecognized options following double hyphen. A second double hyphen terminates this action. Recognized options between the hyphens are processed normally.

-a   Append dependencies to any existing ones instead of replacing existing ones.

-D*name=value*

-D*name*   Define *name* with the given value (first form) or with value 1 (second form.)

-f*filename* Write dependencies to *filename* instead of to *Makefile*.

-I*dir*   Add directory *dir* to the list of directories searched

mkdirhier *dir* . . .

Create directory *dir* during file installation operations.

msub [*options*] [*file*]

Substitute **make** variables into a template to produce a script. **msub** reads the *Makefile* in the current directory to find all variable definition lines of the form `var=value`. Then it reads any *files* on the command line, searches them for references to the *Makefile* variables, and replaces the references with the corresponding variable values. The result is written to the standard output. *msub* has the following options:

-f *file*   Extract variable values from *file* instead of *Makefile*.

+/-R*str* Specify variable reference indicators within templates. +R and -R are used in pairs: +R specifies the string that initiates a variable reference, and -R specifies the string that terminates it.

xmkmf [*option*] [*topdir*] [*curdir*]

> Bootstrap a *Makefile* from an *Imakefile*. *topdir* specifies the location of the project root directory. *curdir* (usually omitted) is specified as a relative pathname from the top of the build tree to the current directory. The -a option is equivalent to the following command sequence:

```
% xmkmf
% make Makefiles
% make includes
% make depend
```

Configuration files

Following is a list of the **imake** configuration files:

Imake.tmpl
> Master template for **imake**. **Imake.tmpl** includes all the other configuration files, plus the *Imakefile* in the current directory.

```
#include <Imake.vb>
#include VendorFile (.cf files)
#include <site.def>
#include <Imake.params>
#include <Imake.rules>
#include INCLUDE_IMAKEFILE
```

Imake.vb
> Contains vendor blocks that define Vendorfile as the name of a parameter file for a particular vendor. For example:

```
#ifdef VendorA
#define VendorFile <A.cf>
#endif

#ifdef VendorB
#define VendorFile <B.cf>
#endif
```

VendorFile
> Vendor file, from **Imake.vb**, to be used. See .cf files, below.

Imake.params
> Parameter file that contains default variable assignments for machine dependencies such as programs, options, libraries, header files, and installation locations.

Imake.rules
> Contains **cpp** macro definitions that are configured for the current platform. The macro definitions are fed into **imake**, which runs **cpp** to process the mac-

$\rightarrow$

---

ros. Newlines (line continuations) are indicated by
the string @@\ (double at sign, backslash).

site.def   Contains site-specific (as opposed to vendor-specific)
information, such as installation directories, what set
of programs to build, and any special versions of programs to use during the build. The *site.def* file
changes from machine to machine.

.cf*   The .cf files are the vendor-specific *VendorFiles* that
live in **Imake.vb**. A .cf file contains platform-specific
definitions, such as version numbers of the operating
system and compiler, and workarounds for missing
commands. The definitions in .cf files override the
defaults, defined in **Imake.params**.

The Imakefile

The *Imakefile* is a per-directory file that indicates targets to be
built and installed, and rules to be applied. **imake** reads the
Imakefile and expands the rules into *Makefile* target entries. An
Imakefile may also include definitions of make variables, and
list the dependencies of the targets. The dependencies are
expressed as *cpp* macros, which are defined in **Imake.rules**.
Whenever you change an *Imakefile*, you need to rebuild the
Makefile and regenerate header file dependencies. For more
information on **imake**, see the Nutshell Handbook *Software Portability with imake*.

---

insertmsg

insertmsg [*options*] [*strfile*] ...

Separate strings from program logic. Given a list of C strings contained in the inputfile *strfile*, **insertmsg** prepares the identified C
source files for message catalogue localization. *strfile* is a data file
containing lines in the format:

```
filename pos len "...message text..."
```

All string constants are replaced with calls to the **catgets()** subrou-
tine, which retrieves localized files from a natural message catalogue at run time. A new version of each C source file is produced
with the character **nl_** prepended to the original file names. In
addition to calls of *catgets( )*, the new source files will also have the
following lines inserted:

```
# include <nl_types.h>
#define NL_SETN setnum
extern nl_catd m_catd;
extern char *catgets();
```

In addition to creating a new source file, **insertmsg** writes a message source file on the standard output, which can be used as the
input to **gencat**, or for natural language localizations of the message
text.

-m *message_number*

Set first message number to *message_number*. Default value is 1.

-v   Set verbose mode.

Example

Given an input file, *test.c*, the command

```
findstr test.c > strfile.test
```

will generate a string list for *test.c*. The command

```
insertmsg strfile.test
```

will generate a new file nl_test.c with **catgets()** subroutines, and output the string list used in the catalogue on standard output.

---

ld [*options*] *objfiles*

Combine several *objfiles*, in the specified order, into a single executable object module (**a.out** by default). **ld** is the link editor and is often invoked automatically by compiler commands such as **cc**.

Options

-a   Create an absolute (executable) file. If **-r** is used, allocate memory for common symbols.

-e *symbol*

Set *symbol* as the address of the output file's entry point.

-f *Fill*   Set default fill patterns for holes within an output section as well as initialize *.bss* sections.

-l*x*   Search a library named **lib***x***.so** or **lib***x***.a** (the placement of this option on the line affects when the library is searched).

-L *dir*   Search directory *dir* before standard search directories (this option must precede -l).

-m *mapfile*

Produce a map of the input/output sections and store in *mapfile*.

-M   Output a message for each multiply-defined external definition.

-N   Put the data section immediately after the text section. (SVR3 only.)

-o*file*   Send the output to *file* (default is **a.out**).

-Q*c*   List version information about **ld** in the output (*c* = **y**, the default) or do not list (*c* = **n**).

-r   Allow output to be subject to another **ld**.

$\rightarrow$

ld		
←	-s	Remove symbol table and relocation entries.
	-strict	Suppress generation of symbols **edata**, **etext** and **end** (which are aliases used for compatibility with previous releases) to _edata, _etext and _end.
	-t	Suppress warning about multiply-defined symbols of unequal size.
	-u *symbol*	
		Enter *symbol* in symbol table; useful when loading from an archive library. *symbol* must precede the library that defines it (so -u must precede -l).
	-V	Print the version of **ld**.
	-VS *num*	
		Use *num* as decimal version stamp identifying **a.out** file produced.
	-x	Do not preserve local symbols in output symbol table.
	-YP, *dirlist*	
		Specify a comma-separated list of directories to use in place of the default search directories (see also -L).
	-z	Do not bind anything to address zero.

---

lex	**lex** [*options*] [*files*]

Generate a lexical analysis program (named **lex.yy.c**) based on the regular expressions and C statements contained in one or more input *files*. See also **yacc** and the Nutshell Handbook *lex & yacc*.

Options

	-c	*file*'s program statements are in C (default).
	-n	Suppress the output summary.
	-Q*c*	Print version information in **lex.yy.c** (if *c* = **y**) or suppress information (if *c* = **n**, the default).
	-t	Write program to standard output, not **lex.yy.c**.
	-v	Print a summary of machine-generated statistics.
	-V	Print version information on standard error.

---

lint	**lint** [*options*] *files*

Detect bugs, portability problems, and other possible errors in the specified C programs. By default, **lint** uses definitions in the C library **llib-lc.ln**. If desired, output from .c files can be saved in "object files" having a **.ln** suffix. A second **lint** pass can be invoked on **.ln** files and libraries for further checking. **lint** also accepts the **cc** options -D, -I, -U, and -X. See also the Nutshell Handbook, *Checking C Programs with lint*.

Note: This command checks programs written in ANSI C; use **/usr/ucb/lint** if you want to check programs written in Kernighan

and Ritchie's C. Note also that options **-a**, **-b**, **-h**, and **-x** have
exactly the opposite meaning in the BSD and System V versions.

Options

-a	Ignore long values assigned to variables that aren't long.
-b	Ignore break statements that cannot be reached.
-c	Don't execute the second pass of **lint**; save output from first pass in .ln files. (Same as BSD **-i** option.)
-F	Print files using full pathname, not just the filename.
-h	Don't test for bugs, bad style, or extraneous information.
-k	Re-enable warnings that are normally suppressed by directive /* LINTED [*message*] */, and print the additional *message* (if specified).
-l*x*	Use library **llib-l***x***.ln** in addition to **llib-lc.ln**.
-n	Do not check for compatibility.
-o *lib*	Create a **lint** library named **llib-l.***lib***.ln** from the output of the first pass of **lint**.
-p	Check for portability to variants of C.
-u	Ignore functions or external variables that are undefined or unused.
-v	Ignore unused arguments within functions; same as specifying the directive /* ARGSUSED */.
-x	Ignore unused variables referred to by **extern** declarations.

---

list [*options*] *source-file* ... [*object-file*]

Produce C source listing, with line number information attached,
from a common object file. Object files given to **list** must have
been compiled with the **-g** option of **cc**. If no object file is specified, the default object file, **a.out** will be used.

Options

-F*function*	List only the named function. This option may be specified more than once on the command line.
-h	Suppress heading output.
-V	Print, on standard error, version number of the **list** command executing.

Error messages

```
list: name: cannot open
```
        name cannot be read.
```
list: name: invalid C source name
```
        Source file names do not end in .c.
```
list: name: bad magic
```
        Invalid object file.

Programming Commands

→

list
←
	`list: name: symbols have been stripped, cannot`
	    `proceed`
	      Some or all of symbolic debugging information missing.
	`list: name: cannot read line numbers`
	      Some or all of symbolic debugging information missing.
	`list: name: not in symbol table`
	      Some or all of symbolic debugging information missing.
	`list: name: cannot find function in symbol table`
	      list confused by #ifdef's in source file.
	`list: name: out of sync: too many }`
	      list confused by #ifdef's in source file.
	`list: name: unexpected end-of-file`
	      list confused by #ifdef's in source file.
	`list: name: missing or inappropriate line numbers`
	      Either symbol debugging information is missing or list
	      confused by C preprocessor statements.

---

lorder

lorder *objfiles*

Take object filenames (e.g., files with .o suffix) and output a list of related pairs. The first file listed includes references to external identifiers that are defined in the second. **lorder** output can be sent to **tsort** to make link editing of an archive more efficient.

Example

To produce an ordered list of object files and replace them in the library **program_arch** (provided they are newer):

```
ar cru program_arch `lorder *.o | tsort`
```

---

lprof

lprof [*options*]
lprof -m *files* [-T] -d *out*

Display a program's profile data on a line-by-line basis. Data includes a list of source files, each source code line (with line numbers), and the number of times each line was executed. This file is generated by specifying **cc -ql** when compiling a program or when creating a shared object named *prog* (default is **a.out**). See also **prof** and **gprof**.

Options

   -c *file* Read input profile *file* instead of *prog*.cnt.

   -d *out* Store merged profile data in file *out*. Must be used with -**m**.

   -I *dir* Search for include files in *dir* as well as in the default place (/usr/include).

   -m *files* Merge several profile *files* and total the execution counts. *files* are of the form *f1*.cnt, *f2*.cnt, *f3*.cnt , etc., where each file contains the profile data from a different run of the same program. Used with -**d**.

-o *prog* Look in the profile file for a program named *prog* instead of the name used when the profile file was created. -o is needed when files have been renamed or moved.

-p   Print the default listing; useful with -r and -s.

-r *list*   Used with -p to print only the source files given in *list*.

-s   For each function, print the percentage of code lines that are executed.

-T   Ignore timestamp of executable files being profiled.

-x   Omit execution counts. For lines that executed, show only the line numbers; for lines that didn't execute, print the line number, the symbol [U], and the source line.

m4 [*options*] [*files*]

Macro processor for RATFOR, C, and other program *files.*

Options

-B*n*   Set push-back and argument collection buffers to *n* (default is 4,096).

-D*name*[=*value*]

        Define *name* as *value* or, if *value* is not specified, define *name* as null.

-e   Operate interactively, ignoring interrupts.

-H*n*   Set symbol-table hash array to *n* (default is 199).

-s   Enable line-sync output for the C preprocessor.

-S*n*   Set call-stack size to *n* (default is 100 slots).

-T*n*   Set token buffer size to *n* (default is 512 bytes).

-U*name* Undefine *name.*

make [*options*] [*targets*] [*macro definitions*]

Update one or more *targets* according to dependency instructions in a description file in the current directory. By default, this file is called **makefile** or **Makefile**. Options, targets, and macro definitions can appear in any order. Macros definitions are typed as:

    `name=string`

For more information on **make**, see the Nutshell Handbook *Managing Projects with make.*

Options

-e   Override **makefile** assignments with environment variables.

-f *makefile*

        Use *makefile* as the description file; a filename of – denotes standard input.

→

-i   Ignore command error codes (same as .IGNORE).

-k   Abandon the current entry when it fails, but keep working with unrelated entries.

-n   Print commands but don't execute (used for testing).

-p   Print macro definitions and target descriptions.

-q   Query; return 0 if file is up-to-date; nonzero otherwise.

-r   Do not use default rules.

-s   Do not display command lines (same as .SILENT).

-t   Touch the target files, causing them to be updated.

Description file lines

Instructions in the description file are interpreted as single lines. If an instruction must span more than one input line, use a backslash (\) at the end of the line so that the next line is considered as a continuation. The description file may contain any of the following types of lines:

blank lines

Blank lines are ignored.

comment lines

A pound sign (#) can be used at the beginning of a line or anywhere in the middle. **make** ignores everything after the #.

dependency lines

Depending on one or more targets, certain commands that follow will be executed. Possible formats include:

```
targets : prerequisites
targets :: prerequisites
```

In the first form, subsequent commands are executed if the prerequisites are met. The second form is a variant that lets you specify the same targets on more than one dependency line. In both forms, if no prerequisites are supplied, then subsequent commands are *always* executed (whenever any of the targets are specified). No tab should precede any *targets*.

suffix rules

These specify that files ending with the first suffix can be prerequisites for files ending with the second suffix (assuming the root filenames are the same). Either of these formats can be used:

```
.suffix.suffix:
.suffix:
```

The second form means that the root filename depends on the filename with the corresponding suffix.

commands

Commands are grouped below the dependency line and are typed on lines that begin with a tab. If a command is preceded by a hyphen (–), **make** ignores any error returned. If a command is preceded by an at-sign (@), the command line won't echo on the display (unless **make** is called with -n).

macro definitions

These have the following form:

```
name = string
```

Blank space is optional around the =.

include statements

Similar to the C include directive, these have the form:

```
include file
```

Internal macros

$? The list of prerequisites that have been changed more recently than the current target. Can be used only in normal description file entries—not suffix rules.

$@ The name of the current target, except in description file entries for making libraries, where it becomes the library name. Can be used both in normal description file entries and in suffix rules.

$< The name of the current prerequisite that has been modified more recently than the current target. Can be used only in suffix rules and in the .DEFAULT: entry.

$* The name—without the suffix—of the current prerequisite that has been modified more recently than the current target. Can be used only in suffix rules.

$% The name of the corresponding .o file when the current target is a library module. Can be used both in normal description file entries and in suffix rules.

Macro modifiers

Macro modifiers are not available in all variants of **make**.

D The directory portion of any internal macro name except $?. Valid uses are:

```
$(*D)    $$(@D)
$(<D)    ${%D}
$(@D)
```

F The file portion of any internal macro name except $?. Valid uses are:

```
$(*F)    $$(@F)
$(<F)    ${%F}
$(@F)
```

Macro string substitution

String substitution is not available in all variants of **make**.

${*macro:s1=s2*}

Evaluates to the current definition of **${*macro*}**, after substituting the string *s1* for every occurrence of *s2* that

make
←

occurs either immediately before a blank or tab, or at the end of the macro definition.

Special target names

.DEFAULT: Commands associated with this target are executed if **make** can't find any description file entries or suffix rules with which to build a requested target.

.IGNORE: Ignore error codes. Same as the **-i** option.

.PRECIOUS: Files you specify for this target are not removed when you send a signal (such as interrupt) that aborts **make**, or when a command line in your description file returns an error.

.SILENT: Execute commands but do not echo them. Same as the **-s** option.

.SUFFIXES: Suffixes associated with this target are meaningful in suffix rules. If no suffixes are listed, the existing list of suffix rules is effectively "turned off."

---

mar

mar *key* [*option*] *afile names* ...

Message catalogue archive and library maintainer. **mar** maintains groups of message catalogue files created by **gencat**, combined into a single archive file, *afile. names* are constituent files in the archive file. *key* is one character from the set **drtpx**, optionally concatenated with **v**.

The meanings of the *key* characters are:

d   Delete named file(s) from archive file. If no names given, all files in archive will be deleted.

p   Print named files to standard output. If no names given, all files will be printed.

r   Replace named files in the archive file or append them to archive file if they are not already part of the archive. Archive file will be created if it does not already exist.

t   Print table of contents of archive file. If no names given, all files in archive are printed.

x   Extract named files. If no names given, all files in archive will be extracted.

v   Verbose. Used with **dxtr** keys, **v** gives a file-by-file description of the making of a new archive file from the old archive and the constituent files. When used with **t**, it gives a long listing of all information about the files, including name, last update, size, and name of message catalogue as referenced by **catopen**, **catgets**, and **catgetmsg**.

masm is the Microsoft 8086/286/386 assembler. It reads and
assembles 8086/80286/80386 assembly language instructions from
sourcefile to create a linkable object file *sourcefile*.o, or an executable program **a.out**.

Options

- -a   Alphabetize assembled output segments before copying
        them to object file.

- -c   Output cross-reference data for each assembled file to
        filename.**crf**

- -d   Add a pass 1 listing to assembly listing *filename*.**lst**

- -D*sym*[*=value*]

        If the optional *=value* is present, the symbol *sym* is
        defined to be *value*. *value* should not contain blanks,
        commas, or semicolons. If *=value* is not present, *sym* is
        defined as a null TEXTMACRO.

- -e   Generate floating-point code to emulate the 8087 or 80287
        coprocessor.

- -h   List command-like syntax and all valid assembler options.

- -I*path*

        Define *path* appended to –I as the search path for
        #include files. Up to 10 **#include** *path*s are allowed in
        one invocation of **masm**.

- -l*listfile*

        Create an assembly listing file with the same base name
        as the *sourcefile* but with a **.lst** extension. The file lists the
        source instructions, assembled (binary) code for each
        instruction, and any assembly errors. If filename is **-**,
        listing is written to standard output. If *listfile* argument
        given, listing file is called *listfile*.

- Ml   Leave case of symbols alone (default).

- Mu   Disable case sensitivity.

- Mx   Preserve lowercase letters in public and external names
        only when copying these names to the object file, other-
        wise **masm** converts lowercase to uppercase.

- -n   Suppress symbol tables in listing files. –l must also be
        used for this option to take effect.

- -o*obj/ˆfile*

        Copy assembled instructions to the file named *obj/ˆfile*.
        This file can be linked to form an executable file only if
        no errors occurred during the assembly.

- -p   Check for pure code.

- -r   Do not generate floating-point code to emulate 8087 or
        80287

- -s   Write segments in source-code order (default).

→

masm ←	-t Suppress messages for successful assembly.
	-v Print verbose error statistics on console. Default is to display only error counts.

-w[012]
   Set error-display level, where:
   0   No error messages
   1   Serious error messages (default)
   2   Advisory error messages

-x- Prevent error messages from being written to screen

-X Copy to assembly listing all statements forming the body of an **IF** directive whose expression evaluates to false.

-Zd Put line-number information in the object file.

-Zi Put symbolic and line-number information in the object file.

-Z Display source line for each error message (default).

Return value

The **masm** exit codes have the following meanings:

0	No error
1	Argument error
2	Unable to open input file.
3	Unable to open listing file.
4	Unable to open object file.
5	Unable to open cross-reference file.
6	Unable to open include file.
7	Assembly errors. If fatal, the object file is deleted.
8	Memory allocation error
9	Real number input not allowed in this version.
10	Unable to define symbol from command line.
11	Assembler interrupted.

---

mcs

mcs [*options*] *files*

Manipulate the comment section. **mcs** is used to add to, compress, delete, or print a section of one or more ELF object *files*. The default section is **.comment**.

Options

-a *string*	Append *string* to the comment section of *files*.
-c	Compress the comment section of *files* and remove duplicate entries.
-d	Delete the comment section (including header).
-n *name*	Act on section *name* instead of .comment.
-p	Print the comment section on standard output.

Example

```
mcs -p kernel.o
```
                    Print the comment section of kernel.o

Create a shared library. **mkshlib** builds both the host and target shared libraries. The host shared library is an archive used to link-edit user programs with the shared library. The target shared library is an executable module that is bound into the user's address space during execution of a program using the shared library. The user interface to **mkshlib** consists of command-line options and a shared library specification file. **mkshlib** invokes other tools, such as the archiver (**ar**), the assembler (**as**), and the link editor (**ld**). Tools are invoked through the use of **execvp**, which searches directories in the user's PATH.

Options

-h *host*

> Output filename of host shared library being created. If −**n** used, new target shared library will not be generated.

-L *dir* [-L *dir* ...]

> Change algorithm of searching for the host shared libraries specified with the **#objects noload** directive to look in *dir* before looking in the default directories.

-n

> Do not generate a new target shared library. −**t** must still be supplied, since a version of the target shared library is needed to build the host shared library.

-q   Quiet warning messages.

-t *target*

> Output filename of the target shared library being created.

-s *specfil*

> Shared library specification file, *specfil*, that contains all the information necessary to build both the host and target shared libraries. The contents and format of the specification file are given by the directives listed below:

> **#address** *sectname address*

> > Start address, *address*, of section *sectname* for the target.

> **#target** *pathname*

> > Absolute pathname, *pathname*, at which the target shared library will be installed on the target machine.

> **#branch**

> > Start of branch table specifications. Lines following this directive are taken to be branch table specification lines, having the following format:

> > ```
> > funcname <white space> position
> > ```

→

mkshlib
←

where *funcname* is the name of the symbol given a branch table entry and *position* specifies the position of *funcname*'s branch table entry. This directive must be specified exactly once per shared library specification file.

#objects

Lines following this directive are taken to be the list of input object files in the order they are to be loaded into the target. This directive must be specified exactly once per shared library specification file.

#objects noload

The **#objects noload** directive is followed by a list of host shared libraries.

#hide linker [*]

This directive changes symbols that are normally *external* into *static* symbols, local to the library being created. However, all symbols specified in **#init** and **#branch** directives are assumed to be *external* symbols and cannot be changed into *static* symbols using this directive.

#export linker [*]

Symbols given in this directive are *external* symbols that, because of a regular expression in a **#hide** directive, would otherwise have been made *static*.

#init *object*

Object file, *object*, requires initialization code. The lines following this directive are taken to be initialization specification lines, with the following format:

```
ptr <white space> import
```

where *ptr* is a pointer to the associated imported symbol, *import*, and must be defined in the current specified object file, *object*. All initializations for a particular object file must be given once, and multiple specifications of the same object file are not allowed.

#ident *string*

String, *string*, to be included in the .*comment* section of the target shared library.

Specifies a comment.

mkstr

mkstr [–] [*messagefile*] [*prefix*] *file* . . .

Create an error message file from C source. **mkstr** processes each specified *file*, placing a massaged version of the input file in a file whose name consists of the specified *prefix* and the original name. The optional dash causes the error messages to be placed at the

end of the specified *messagefile* for recompiling part of a large
mkstred program.

Example

The command

```
mkstr pistrings xx *.c
```

causes all the error messages from the C source files in the current directory to be placed in the file *pistrings* and causes processed copies of the source for these files to be placed in files
whose names are prefixed with *xx*.

---

nm [*options*] *objfiles*

Print the symbol table (name list) in alphabetical order for one or
more object files (usually ELF or COFF files). Output includes each
symbol's value, type, size, name, etc. A key letter categorizing the
symbol can also be displayed.

Options

-e	Report only external and static symbols; obsolete.
-f	Report all information; obsolete.
-h	Suppress the header.
-n	Sort the external symbols by name.
-o	Report values in octal.
-p	Precede each symbol with its key letter (used for pars-ing).
-r	Report the object file's name on each line.
-T	Truncate the symbol name in the display; obsolete.
-u	Report only the undefined symbols.
-v	Sort the external symbols by value.
-V	Print **nm**'s version number on standard error.
-x	Report values in hexadecimal.

Key letters

A	Absolute symbol
C	Common symbol
D	Data object symbol
F	File symbol
N	Symbol with no type
S	Section symbol
T	Text symbol
U	Undefined symbol

---

os2ld [*options*] *file* ...

OS/2 cross linker. **os2ld** links the object *file*(s) to create a program
for execution under OS/2. Files passed to **os2ld** may be either

→

UNIX-style libraries or ordinary 8086 object files. Unless using −u, at least one of the files passed must be an ordinary object file.

Options

- −B Produce an executable .COM file.
- −C Treat uppercase and lowercase characters in symbol names as identical.
- −D Perform DS allocation; generally used in conjuction with −H.
- −F *num*

  Set stack size to hexadecimal number *num*. os2ld will set the stack segment to *num* bytes in the output file.
- −H *num*

  Load high—set a field in the header of the executable file to tell OS/2 to load the program at the highest available position in memory.
- −L Include line numbers in the listing file (if any).
- −M Include public symbols in the list file.
- −m *filename*

  Create a map file, *filename*, with information about the segments and groups in the executable. Public symbols and line numbers will be listed in *filename* if −M and −L options are given.
- −n *num*

  Set name length to the decimal number *num*. os2ld truncates all public and external symbols longer than *num* characters.
- −o *filename*

  Name output file to *filename* (default is **a.out**).
- −P Pack code segments.
- −Pc[<dec#>]

  Pack code segments; default limit for a segment is 64K minus 36.
- −Pd[<dec#>]

  Pack data segments; default limit is 64K.
- −Q Don't pack code segments. This is the default for segmented-executable pack code.
- −S *num*

  Set segment limit to *num*, a decimal number between 1 and 1024 (default is 128).
- −u *name* [−u *name*] . . .

  Name undefined symbol *name*. os2ld will enter the given name into its symbol table as an undefined symbol.

---

prof

prof [*options*] [*object_file*]

Display the profile data for an object file. The file's symbol table is compared with profile file **mon.out** (previously created by the monitor function). Choose only one of the sort options -a, -c, -n, or -t . See also lprof and gprof.

Options

-a	List output by symbol address.
-c	List output by decreasing number of calls.
-g	Include non-global (static) function symbols.
-h	Suppress the report heading.
-m*pf*	Use *pf* as the input profile file instead of **mon.out**.
-n	List by symbol name.
-o	Show addresses in octal (invalid with -**x**).
-s	Print a summary on standard error.
-t	List by decreasing total time percentage (the default).
-x	Show addresses in hexadecimal (invalid with -**o**).
-z	Include zero usage calls.

---

prs [*options*] *files*

Print formatted information for one or more SCCS *files*.

Options

-a	Include information for removed deltas.
-c*date*	Cutoff *date* used with -**e** or -**l** (see **get** for format of *date*).
-d[*format*]	Specify output *format* by supplying text and/or SCCS keywords.
-e	With -**r**, list data for deltas earlier than or including *sid*; with -**c**, list data for deltas not newer than *date*.
-l	Like -**e**, but later than or including *sid* or *date*.
-r[*sid*]	Specify SCCS ID *sid*; default is the most recent delta.

Example

The following command:

```
prs -d"program :M: version :I: by :P:" -r s.yes.c
```

might produce this output:

```
program yes.c version 2.4.6 by daniel
```

---

rcc [*options*] *files*

Invoke the AT&T compiler. The AT&T compilation tools consist of a preprocessor, compiler, optimizer, assembler, and link editor. **rcc** processes the supplied options, then executes the various tools with the proper arguments.

→

Files whose names end with .c are taken to be C source programs and may be preprocessed, compiled, optimized, assembled, and linked. If compilation runs through the assembler, an object file is produced called *source*.o, with .o substituted for .c. The .o file is normally deleted if a single C program is compiled and then immediately linked. In the same way, files whose names end in .s are taken to be assembly source programs and may be assembled and linked; files whose names end in .i are taken to be preprocessed C source programs and may be compiled, optimized, assembled, and linked. Files not ending in .c, .s, or .i are passed to the linker.

Options

-c   Suppress linking phase of compilation and do not remove object files.

-dl   Do not generate symbolic debugging line-number information.

-ds   Do not generate symbol attribute information for the symbolic debugger.

-E   Run only **cpp** on the named C programs and send the result to standard output.

-g   Generate additional information needed for debuggers like **dbxtra**, **codeview**, and **sdb**.

-H   Print out (on standard error) the pathname of each file included during current compilation.

-o *outfile*
Produce an output object file, *outfile* (default name is **a.out**).

-P *outfile*
Run only **cpp** on the named C source files and leave the results in corresponding files suffixed .i.

-p *outfile*
Produce code that counts number of times each routine is called. Also, if linking takes place, link profiled versions of **lib.a** and **libm.a** and call **monitor** automatically. **mon.out** will be created on normal termination of the object program.

-qp   Produce profiled code where the **p** argument produces identical results to the -**p** option.

-S   Compile, but do not assemble, the named C source files, and leave the assembly-language output in corresponding files suffixed .s.

-V   Print the version(s) of the compiler, optimizer, assembler, and/or linker invoked.

-Wc,*arg1*[,*arg2* ...]
Hand off the argument(s) *arg1* to pass *c* where *c* is one of [*p02al*] indicating the preprocessor, compiler, optimizer, assembler, or link editor, respectively.

-Y[*p02alSILU*],*dirname*

Specify new path name, *dirname*, for the locations of the tools and directories designated in the first argument. [*p02alSILU*] represents:

p   Preprocessor

0   Compiler

2   Optimizer

a   Assembler

l   Link editor

S   Directory containing start-up routines

I   Default include directory searched by **cpp**.

L   First default library directory searched by **ld**

U   Second default library directory searched by **ld**

Zp[1|2|4]

Pack structure members in memory. Specifying an option to -**Zp** will force alignment on the given byte boundary. If no option is used with -**Zp**, structure members will be packed on one-byte boundaries.

Files

LIBDIR is usually **/lib**. BINDIR is usually **usr/tmp** but can be redefined by setting the environment variable TMPDIR.

file.c	C source file
file.c	Preprocessed C source file
file.o	Object file
file.s	Assembly language file
a.out	Link-edited output
LIBDIR/*rcrt1.o	Start-up routine
LIBDIR/*rcrtn.o	Start-up routine
TMPDIR/*	Temporary files
LIBDIR/rcpp	Preprocessor, **cpp**
LIBDIR/rcomp	Compiler
LIBDIR/roptim	Optimizer
BINDIR/as	Assembler, **as**
BINDIR/ld	Link editor, **ld**
LIBDIR/	Standard C library
LIBDIR/libc_s.a	Standard C shared library

---

rcflow [*options*] *files*

Generate C flowgraph. **rcflow** analyzes a collection of C, yacc, lex, assembler, and object files and attempts to build a graph charting the external references. Each line of output begins with a reference number, followed by tabs indicating the level, then the name of the global symbol followed by a colon and the symbol's definition.

$\rightarrow$

Programming Commands

rcflow
←

Options

In addition to the -D, -I, and -U options (see cc and cpp), the following options are interpreted by **rcflow**:

-d*num*
Set depth at which flowgraph is cut off. *num* is a decimal integer; by default a very large number.

-i_
Include names beginning with an underscore. Default is to exclude these functions.

-ix
Include external and static data symbols. Default is to include only functions in the flowgraph.

-r
Reverse the "caller:callee" relationship, producing an inverted listing showing the callers of each function.

Examples

Given the following in *file.c*:

```
int  i;

main()
{
    f();
    g();
    f();
}

f()
{
    i = h();
}
```

The command:

```
rcflow -ix file.c
```

produces the output:

```
1    main: int(), <file.c 4>
2         f: int(), <file.c 11>
3            h: <>
4            i: int, ,file.c 1>
5         g: <>
```

rcxref

rcxref [*options*] *files*

Generate C-program cross-reference table. **rcxref** uses a special version of **cpp** to include #**define**'d information in its symbol table. It produces a listing on standard output of all symbols (auto, static, and global) in each file separately or in combination.

Options

In addition to the -D, -I, and -U options (see cc and cpp), the following options are interpreted by **rcxref**:

-c	Print a combined cross-reference of all input files	**rcxref**

-D*name=def*
Define *name* with value *def* as if by a **#define**. If no =*def* is given, *name* is defined with value 1.

-o *file* Direct output to *file*.

-s Operate silently; do not print input file names.

-t Format listing for 80-column width.

-w <*num*>
Width option. Formats output no wider than <*num*> (decimal) columns. This option defaults to 80 if <*num*> is not specified or is less than 51.

---

regcmp [-] *files*

regcmp

Stands *for regular expression compile*. Compile the regular expressions in one or more *files* and place output in *file*.i (or in *file*.c if - is specified). The output is C source code, while the input entries in *files* are of the form:

```
C variable    "regular expression"
```

---

rlint [*option*] ... *file* ...

rlint

Detect bugs, portability problems, and other possible errors in the specifed C programs. **rlint** is based on the AT&T compiler **rcc**, and does not accept either the ANSI or Microsoft dialects of the C language. To check programs written with either of these dialects, use the **lint** command.

Options

-a Suppress complaints about assignments of long values to variables that are not long.

-b Suppress complaints about break statements that cannot be reached.

-c Produce a **.rln** file for every .c file on the command line.

-h Do not apply heuristic tests that attempt to intuit bugs, improve style, and reduce waste.

-l*x* Include additional **rlint** library **llib-lx.rln**.

-n Do not check compatibility against either standard or portable **rlint** library.

-o *lib* Create an **rlint** library with the name **llib-llib.rln**. -c nullifies any use of this option.

-p Attempt to check portability to other dialects (IBM and GCOS) of C.

-u Suppress complaints about functions and external variables used and not defined, or defined and not used.

$\rightarrow$

Programming Commands

rlint
←

    −v   Suppress complaints about unused arguments in functions.

    −x   Do not report variables referred to by external declarations but never used.

The −D, −I, and −U options of **cpp** and the −g and −O options of **rcc** are also recognized as separate arguments.

Comments

Certain conventional comments in the C source will change the behavior of **rlint**:

/*ARGSUSED*/
    Turns on −v option for next function.

/*LINTLIBRARY*/
    Placed at beginning of a file, turns off complaints about unused functions and function arguments in file.

/*NOTREACHED*/
    Placed at appropriate points, stops comments about unreachable code.

/*VARARGSn*/
    Suppresses usual checking for variable numbers of arguments in the following function declaration. Data types of first n arguments are checked. When placed at appropriate points, stops comments about unreachable code.

Files

LIBDIR Directory where rlint libraries specified by −l**x** must exist, usually **/usr/lib**.

LIBDIR/rlint[12]
    First and second passes.

LIBDIR/llib−lc.rln
    Declarations for C Library functions.

LIBDIR/llib−port.rln
    Declarations for portable functions.

LIBDIR/llib−lm.rln
    Declarations for Math Library functions.

TMPDIR/*rlint*
    Temporaries.

TMPDIR
    Usually **/usr/tmp** but can be redefined by setting the environment variable TMPDIR.

---

rmdel

rmdel −r*sid files*

SCCS command. Remove a delta from one or more SCCS *files*, where *sid* is the SCCS ID. The delta must be the most recent in its branch.

---

sact *files*

For the specified SCCS *files*, report which deltas are about to change (i.e., which files are currently being edited via **get -e**, but haven't yet been updated via **delta**). **sact** lists output in five fields: SCCS ID of the current delta being edited, SCCS ID of the new delta to create, user who issued the **get -e**, date and time it was issued.

SCCS *command sccs.file*

The Source Code Control System (SCCS) lets you keep track of each revision of a document. SCCS *commands* are applied to SCCS files, named s.*file*. Each time a file is *entered* into SCCS, SCCS notes which lines have been changed or deleted since the most recent version. From that information, SCCS can regenerate the file on demand.

Each set of changes is called a *delta* and is assigned an SCCS identification string (*sid*). The *sid* consists of either two components, release and level numbers (in the form *a.b*), or of four components: the release, level, branch, and sequence numbers (in the form *a.b.c.d*). The branches and sequences are for situations when two on-running versions of the same file are recorded in SCCS. For example, *delta 3.2.1.1* refers to release 3, level 2, branch 1, sequence 1.

To create and initialize an SCCS file, use the **admin** command with the **-i** option. For example:

```
admin -ich01 s.ch01
```

creates a new SCCS file and initializes it with the contents of **ch01**, which becomes *delta 1.1*.

Once changes have been made to the SCCS file, return it to SCCS with the command:

```
delta s.ch01
```

To retrieve any version of a file from SCCS, use the **get** command. Using the example above, retrieve **ch01** by entering:

```
get s.ch01
```

Identification keywords

The keywords below may be used in an SCCS file. A **get** command will expand these keywords to the value described.

%A%	Shorthand for providing **what** strings for program files; %A% = %Z%%Y% %M% %I%%Z%
%B%	Branch number
%C%	Current line number, intended for identifying where error occurred
%D%	Current date (YY/MM/DD)
%E%	Date newest applied delta was created (YY/MM/DD)

→

Programming Commands

%F%	SCCS filename
%G%	Date newest applied delta was created (MM/DD/YY)
%H%	Current date (MM/DD/YY)
%I%	*sid* of the retrieved text (%R%.%L%.%B%.%S%)
%L%	Level number
%M%	Module name (filename without .s prefix)
%P%	Fully qualified SCCS filename
%Q%	Value of *string*, as defined by **admin -fq***string*
%R%	Release number
%S%	Sequence number
%T%	Current time (HH:MM:SS)
%U%	Time newest applied delta was created (HH:MM:SS)
%W%	Another shorthand like %A%; %W% = %Z%%M% *tab* %I%
%Y%	Module type, as defined by **admin -ft***type*
%Z%	String recognized by **what**; that is, @(#)

Data keywords

Data keywords specify which parts of an SCCS file are to be retrieved and output using the **-d** option of the **prs** command.

:A:	Form of **what** string
:B:	Branch number
:BD:	Body
:BF:	Branch flag
:C:	Comments for delta
:CB:	Ceiling boundary
:D:	Date delta created (:Dy:/:Dm:/:Dd:)
:Dd:	Day delta created
:Dg:	Deltas ignored (sequence number)
:DI:	Sequence number of deltas (:Dn:/:Dx:/:Dg:)
:DL:	Delta line statistics (:Li:/:Ld:/:Lu:)
:Dm:	Month delta created
:Dn:	Deltas included (sequence number)
:DP:	Predecessor delta sequence number
:Ds:	Default sid
:DS:	Delta sequence number
:Dt:	Delta information
:DT:	Delta type
:Dx:	Deltas excluded (sequence number)
:Dy:	Year delta created
:F:	SCCS filename
:FB:	Floor boundary
:FD:	File descriptive text
:FL:	Flag list
:GB:	Gotten body
:I:	SCCS ID string (sid) (:R:.:L:.:B:.:S:)
:J:	Joint edit flag
:KF:	Keyword error/warning flag
:KV:	Keyword validation string
:L:	Level number

:Ld:	Lines deleted by delta
:Li:	Lines inserted by delta
:LK:	Locked releases
:Lu:	Lines unchanged by delta
:M:	Module name
:MF:	Modification validation flag
:MP:	Modification validation program name
:MR:	Modification numbers for delta
:ND:	Null delta flag
:P:	Username of programmer who created delta
:PN:	SCCS file pathname
:Q:	User-defined keyword
:R:	Release number
:S:	Sequence number
:T:	Time delta created (:Th:::Tm:::Ts:.)
:Th:	Hour delta created
:Tm:	Minutes delta created
:Ts:	Seconds delta created
:UN:	Usernames
:W:	Form of **what** string
:Y:	Module type flag
:Z:	**what** string delimiter

SCCS commands

Following is a table of SCCS commands. For full syntax and options, see the individual SCCS commands in this section. File arguments to SCCS commands can be either filenames or directory names. Naming a directory will cause all the files in that directory to be processed, with nonapplicable and nonreadable files ignored. If, in place of a file argument, a dash (–) is entered, the command will read from standard input for the names of files to be processed, one on each line.

admin	Create and administer SCCS files.
cdc	Change delta comments of an SCCS ID.
comb	Reduce size of SCCS files.
delta	Make a change (delta) to an SCCS file.
get	Retrieve a text version of an SCCS file.
help	Online help for SCCS.
prs	Print an SCCS file.
rmdel	Remove a delta from an SCC0 file.
sact	Report current SCCS file editing activity.
sccsdiff	Compare two versions of an SCCS file.
unget	Cancel a previous get of an SCCS file.
val	Validate SCCS file.
what	Print identification strings.

→

Programming
Commands

sccs and pseudo-commands

The compatibility packages include **sccs**, a front-end to the SCCS utility. This command provides a user-friendly interface to SCCS and has the following command-line syntax:

/usr/ucb/sccs [*options*] *command* [*SCCS_flags*] [*files*]

In addition to providing all of the regular SCCS commands, **sccs** offers pseudo-commands. These are easy-to-use, prebuilt combinations of the regular SCCS commands. *options* apply only to the **sccs** interface. *command* is the SCCS command or pseudo-command to run, and *SCCS_flags* are specific options passed to the SCCS command being run.

sccs makes it easier to specify files, because it automatically prepends SCCS/s. to any filename arguments. For example:

```
sccs get -e file.c
```

would be interpreted as:

```
get -e SCCS/s.file.c
```

Options

-d*prepath*   Locate files in *prepath* rather than in current directory. For example:

```
sccs -d/home get file.c
```

is interpreted as:

```
get /home/SCCS/s.file.c
```

-p*endpath*   Access files from directory *endpath* instead of SCCS. For example:

```
sccs -pVERSIONS get file.c
```

is interpreted as:

```
get VERSIONS/s.file.c
```

-r   Invoke **sccs** as the real user instead of as the effective user.

Pseudo-commands

Equivalent SCCS actions are indicated in parentheses:

check   Like **info**, but return nonzero exit codes instead of filenames.

clean   Remove from current directory any files that aren't being edited under SCCS (via **get -e**, for example).

create   Create SCCS files (**admin -i** followed by **get**).

deledit	Same as **delta** followed by **get** -e.	SCCS
delget	Same as **delta** followed by **get**.	
diffs	Compare file's current version and SCCS version (like **sccsdiff**).	
edit	Get a file to edit (**get** -e).	
enter	Like **create**, but without the subsequent **get** (**admin** -i).	
fix	Same as **rmdel** (must be followed by -r).	
info	List files being edited (similar to **sact**).	
print	Print information (like **prs** -e followed by **get** -p -m)	
tell	Like **info**, but list one filename per line.	
unedit	Same as **unget**.	

sccsdiff -r*sid1* -r*sid2* [*options*] *files*

sccsdiff

Report differences between two versions of an SCCS *file*. *sid1* and *sid2* identify the deltas to be compared. This command invokes **bdiff** (which in turn calls **diff**).

Options

-p   Pipe output through **pr**.

-s*n*   Use file segment size *n* (*n* is passed to **bdiff**).

sdb [*options*] [*objfile* [*corefile* [*dir*]]]

sdb

Symbolic debugger used for checking assembly programs, executable C and FORTRAN programs, and core image files resulting from aborted programs. *objfile* contains an executable program, and *corefile* contains the core image produced when *objfile* was executed. **a.out** is the default *objfile*. **core** is the default *corefile*. The *dir_list* argument specifies the source directory for the files compiled to create *objfile*. A - in place of *corefile* will force **sdb** to ignore any core image file.

Options

-w   All addresses refer to the executing program; otherwise they refer to **objfile** or **corefile**.

-W   Suppress warning messages about older files.

Command specifiers

In the "Commands" section below, commands use the specifiers *m*, *l*, and *n*. *m* is the display format of an address. (Addresses are specified by a variable or a line number.) *l* is the address length. *n* stands for the line number.

→

Values for m

a	Characters starting at variable's address
c	Character
d	Decimal
f	32-bit floating
g	64-bit double precision floating
i	Disassemble machine-language instructions; print address using numbers and symbols.
I	Same as i, but print address using numbers only.
o	Octal
p	Pointer to procedure
s	Print character(s) at address pointed to by (string pointer) variable.
u	Unsigned decimal
x	Hexadecimal

Values for l

Length specifiers are meaningful only with *m* values of c, d, o, u, or x.

b	One byte
h	Two bytes (half word)
l	Four bytes (long word)

Commands

Refer to the previous specifiers when reviewing the **sdb** commands, which are grouped below:

Formatted printing

t	Print a stack trace
T	Print the top line of the stack trace

variable/clm

Print variable according to length *l* and format *m*. Number *c* specifies how much memory (in units of *l*) to display.

n?lm

variable:?lm

Print from **a.out** and procedure *variable* according to length *l* and format *m*. Default *lm* is i.

variable=lm

n=lm

number=lm

Print address of *variable* or line number *n*, in the format specified by *l* and *m*. Use the last form to convert *number* to the format specified by *l* and *m*. Default *lm* is lx.

variable!value

Assign *value* to *variable*.

x	Display the machine registers and the machine instructions.
X	Display the machine instructions.

Examining the source

e	Print name of current file.
e*proc*	Set current file to file containing procedure *proc*.
e*file*	Set current file to *file*.
e*dir/*	Append directory *dir* to directory list.
p	Print current line.
w	Print ten lines surrounding the current line.
z	Print ten lines (starting at current); reset current line to last line.

/*regexp*/
    Search ahead for regular expression *regexp*.

?*regexp*?
    Search back for regular expression *regexp*.

n	Set current line to *n* and print it.

count+
    Advance *count* lines; print new current line.

count-
    Go back *count* lines; print new current line.

Executing the source

n a   Set a breakpoint at line number *n* and inform the user.

[*n*] b *commands*
    Set breakpoint at line number *n* and optionally execute **sdb** *commands* (separated by ;) at breakpoint.

[*n*] c *count*
    Continue after a breakpoint or, if *count* is given, stop after *count* breakpoints. If *n* is specified, set a temporary breakpoint at line number *n*.

[*n*] C *count*
    Same as **c**, but reactivate any signal that stopped program.

n g *count*
    Continue at line number *n* after a breakpoint. If *count* is given, ignore *count* breakpoints.

[*count*] r *args*
    Run the program with the specified arguments. Ignore *count* breakpoints.

[*count*] r
    Rerun the program with the previously specified arguments. Ignore *count* breakpoints.

[*count*] R
    Run the program with no arguments. Ignore *count* breakpoints.

Programming
Commands

→

f1 [*level*] [**v**]

This command is used when single-stepping via **s**, **S**, or **m**. **v** turns off verbose mode; omit **v** to turn on verbose mode. If *level* is omitted, print only source file or function name when either changes; otherwise, set *level* to 1 (print C source lines before execution) or 2 or higher (print C source lines and assembler statements).

:*proc*(*a1,a2,...*)

Execute procedure *proc* with arguments *a1*, *a2*, etc. Arguments can be constants, local variable names, or register names. Append **/m** in order to print the returned value in format *m* (default is **d**).

Breakpoint and program control

B   Print active breakpoints.

[*n*] **d**   Delete breakpoint at line number *n*.

D   Remove all breakpoints.

i *count*

Single-step *count* machine-language instructions. Same as **i**, but reactivate any signal that stopped program.

k   Kill the program you're debugging.

l   Print the previous line executed.

M   Print the address maps.

*var***$m** *count*

Single-step *count* lines until the specified variable or address is modified. Omitting *count* specifies an infinite count.

q   Exit **sdb**.

s [*count*]

Single-step *count* lines.

S [*count*]

Same as **s**, but skip called functions.

Miscellaneous commands

#*text*   Supply a text comment ignored by **sdb**.

!*cmd*   Execute *cmd* with **sh**.

newline

Display the next line or memory location, or disassemble the next instruction.

EOF   Scroll the display ten lines.

< *file*   Execute commands contained in *file*.

M   Print address maps.

Q   Print list of procedures and files being debugged.

q   Exit **sdb**.

string   Print a quoted *string*; recognizes C escape characters.

V   Print the **sdb** version number.

size [*options*] [*objfile* . . .]

Print the (decimal) number of bytes of each *objfile*. If *objfile* is not specified, **a.out** is used.

Options

-f   Print size of any loaded section, followed by section name in parentheses.

-n   Print sizes for nonallocatable sections or for nonloadable segments.

-o   Print output in octal.

-V   Report the **size** program version number.

-x   Print output in hexadecimal.

---

strip [*options*] *files*

Remove information from COMMON object *files* or archive *files*, thereby reducing file sizes and freeing disk space. The following items can be removed:

1. Symbol table
2. Debugging information
3. Line number information
4. Static symbol information
5. External symbol information
6. Block delimiters
7. Relocation bits

Options

-b   Don't strip items 4, 5, and 6.

-l   Strip only item 3 (line number information).

-r   Don't strip items 4, 5, and 7.

-V   Print the version number of **strip** on standard error.

-x   Strip only items 2 and 3.

---

tsort [*file*]

Perform a topological sort on *file*. Typically used to reorganize an archive library for more efficient handling by **ar** or **ld**.

Example

Find the ordering relationship of all object files and sort them for access by **ld**:

```
lorder *.o | tsort
```

---

unget [*options*] *files*

Cancel a previous **get -e** for one or more SCCS *files*. If a file is being edited via **get -e**, issuing **delta** will process the edits (creating

→

unget ←	a new delta), whereas **unget** will delete the edited version (preventing a new delta from being made).

	Options
	   -n Do not remove file retrieved with **get -e**.
	   -r*sid* The SCCS ID of the delta to cancel; needed only if **get -e** was issued more than once for the same SCCS file.
	   -s Suppress display of the intended delta's *sid*.

val	**val** [*options*] *files* Validate that the SCCS *files* meet the characteristics specified in the options. **val** produces messages on the standard output for each file and returns an eight-bit code upon exit.

	Options
	   - Read standard input and interpret each line as a **val** command-line argument. Exit with an EOF. This option is used by itself.
	   -m*name*
	        Compare *name* with %M% keyword in *file*.
	   -r*sid* Check whether the SCCS ID is ambiguous or invalid.
	   -s Silence any error message.
	   -y*type* Compare *type* with %Y% keyword in *file*.

vc	**vc** [*options*] [*keyword=value* ...] Version control (SCCS). Copy lines from standard input to standard output under control of the **vc** keywords and arguments within the standard input.

	Options
	   -a Replace control keywords in all lines, including text lines.
	   -c*k* Use *k* instead of : as the control character.
	   -s Suppress warning messages.
	   -t If any control characters are found before the first tab in the file, remove all characters up to the first tab.

what	**what** [*option*] *files* Search *files* for the pattern @(#) and print the text that follows it. Actually, the pattern searched for is the value of %Z%, but the **get** command expands this keyword to @(#). The main purpose of **what** is to print identification strings.
	Option -s Quit after finding the first occurrence of a pattern.

xstr [*arguments*]

Extract strings from C programs. The strings are hashed to a file, **strings**, and are replaced with references to **strings**. The command

    xstr *-c filename*

will extract the strings from the C source in *name*, and replace string references by expressions of the form (&xstr[number]) for some number. An appropriate declaration of **xstr** is prepended to the file. The resulting C text is placed in the file **x.c**, to be compiled. The strings from this file are placed in the **strings** data base if they are not there already. After all components of a large program have been compiled, a file **xs.c**, declaring the common **xstr** space, can be created by a command of the form:

    xstr *name1 name2 name3*

xstr can also be used on a single file. The command

    xstr *name*

creates files **x.c** and **xs.c** without using or affecting any *strings* file in the same directory.

Arguments

    -   Read from standard input.

    -c *filename*

           Take C source text from *filename.*

Files

    strings   Database of strings.

    x.c   Massaged C source.

    x.c   C source for definition of array **xstr**.

    /tmp/xs* Temporary file when **xstr** *name* doesn't touch **strings**.

---

yacc [*options*] *file*

Given a *file* containing context-free grammar, convert *file* into tables for subsequent parsing and send output to **y.tab.c**. This command name stands for yet another compiler-compiler. See also **lex** and the Nutshell Handbook *lex & yacc.*

Options

    -d   Generate **y.tab.h**, producing **#define** statements that relate **yacc**'s token codes to the token names declared by the user.

    -l   Exclude **#line** constructs from code produced in **y.tab.c**. (Use after debugging is complete.)

    -S   Increase allocation of various resources.

→

yacc
←

	-t	Compile runtime debugging code by default.
	-v	Generate **y.output**, a file containing diagnostics and notes about the parsing tables.

Part VI

System and Network Administration

Part VI contains infomation about SCO UNIX system administration. It starts with an overview and tables of commonly used commands, moves to a chapter on the sysadmsh shell, and ends with an alphabetical listing of commands.

Many useful system administration and network administration commands are actually user-level commands. If you can't find a command here, check in Sections 2 and 3 of this book.

Section 15 - *Overview*

Section 16 - *The sysadmsh Shell*

Section 17 - *System Administration Commands*

System Administration Overview

System administration tasks in SCO UNIX can be accomplished with commands, or with the menu driven **sysadmsh** utility. For detailed information on **sysadmsh**, see Section 16.

Common Commands

Following are tables of commonly used system administration commands.

Archiving

backup	Perform UNIX backup functions.
cpio	Copy file archives.
dd	Convert files with different data formats.
restore	Restore backups.
tar	Copy files to or restore files from an archive medium.
volcopy	Make literal copy of UNIX filesystem.

Daemons

auditd	Audit daemon
ftpd	File Transfer Protocol daemon
gated	Gateway routing daemon
inetd	Internet services daemon
lockd	Network lock daemon
lpd	Printer lock daemon
named	Internet domain name server
nfsd	NFS daemon
pppd	Point-to-point protocol daemon
rarpd	Reverse Address Resolution Protocol daemon
routed	Network routing daemon
snmp	SNMP daemon
timed	Time server daemon
uucpd	UUCP daemon

Hardware

badtrk	Find bad tracks.
divvy	Disk dividing utility.
dparam	Display/change hard disk characteristics currently in effect.
fdisk	Maintain disk partitions.
fdswap	Swap default boot floppy drive.
hwconfig	Return hardware configuration information.
kbmode	Set keyboard mode or test keyboard support.
mkdev	Create device file(s) associated with a peripheral device.

Installation

btldinstall	Install boot-time loadable device drivers into Link Kit.
custom	Install software products and components.
installpkg	Install AT&T-style UNIX system software package.
pkgadd	Add software package to the system.
pkgchk	Check accuracy of installation.
swconfig	List system software modifications.

Managing Filesystems

dcopy	Copy UNIX filesystems for optimal access time.
dfsck	Check and repair filesystems (plural).
divvy	Disk-dividing utility
fsck	Check and repair filesystem.
fsdb	Filesystem debugger

link	Link files and directories.
mkfs	Construct a filesystem.
mount	Mount a filesystem.
restore	Back up filesystem.
umount	Unmount a filesystem.
unlink	Unlink files and directories.
volcopy	Make literal copy of UNIX filesystem.

Miscellaneous

asktime	Prompt for the correct time of day.
badtrk	Scan media surface for bad tracks.
configure	Kernel configuration program.
displaypkg	Display installed AT&T packages.
enable/disable	Put logins on terminals.
idbuild	Build a new UNIX system kernel.
idconfig	Build system kernel configuration files.
idspace	Investigate free space in the root.
infocmp	Compare/print terminfo descriptions.
login	Sign onto system.
netconfig	Configure networking products.
netutil	Administer the Micnet network.
pkginfo	Display software package information.
pkgrm	Remove package from a system.
removepkg	Remove installed package.
setclock	Set system real-time clock.

Printing

accept/reject	Accept/reject print requests.
enable/disable	Turn on/off line printers.
lpadmin	Configure print service.
lpfilter	Administer filters to be used with print service.
lpforms	Administer forms used with print service.
lpmove	Move print requests.
lpsched	Start print service.
lpsh	Menu-driven **lp** print service administration utility.
lpshut	Shut down print service.

Security and System Integrity

fixperm	Correct or initialize file permissions and ownership.
goodpw	Check passwords for non-obviousness.
integrity	Examine system files against authentication database.
makekey	Generate an encryption key.

pwarn	Issue a warning about password expiration.
pwck	Check a password file.
relax	Change system security defaults.
tcbck	Trusted computing base checker.

Starting and Stopping the System

autoboot	Automatically boot the system.
brc/bcheckrc	Check root filesystem at boot time.
haltsys	Close out filesystems and shut down the system.
reboot	Shut down, then reboot system.
runacct	Run daily accounting.
shutdown	Shut down system.

sysadmsh

atcronsh	Menu-driven at and cron administration utility.
auditsh	Menu-driven audit administration utility.
authsh	Menu-driven authorization administration utility.
backupsh	Menu-driven backup administration utility.
lpsh	Menu-driven lp print service administration utility.

System Activity and Process Management

crash	Examine memory image of live or crashed system kernel.
fuser	Identify processes using file or filesystem.
kill	Terminate process *IDs*.
last	Indicate last logins of users and teletypes.
netstat	Show network status.
ps	Report on active processes.
sag	System activity graph
sar	System activity report package
w	Print summaries of system usage, currently logged-in users, and what they are doing.
who	Display information about the current status of the system.

Users

idleout	Log out idle users.
rmuser	Remove user accounts from the system.
wall	Write to all users.

Networking Overview

Networks connect computers so that the different systems can share information. For users and system administrators, UNIX has traditionally provided a set of simple, but valuable, network services. They let you check whether systems are running, refer to files residing on remote systems, communicate via electronic mail, and so on.

Networking commands generally come in bundles. When a vendor provides a certain package, such as Network File System (NFS), it also tends to provide a set of commands that share the same underlying protocols and libraries. So this book presents commands in such groups.

For most commands to work over a network, each system must be continuously running a server process in the background, silently waiting to handle the user's request. This kind of process is called a *daemon*, and it represents the first group of commands in our list. Daemons are covered in Section 17 of this book, *System Administration Commands*.

Most UNIX networking commands are based on the Internet Protocols. These are standardized ways of communicating across a network on hierarchical layers. The protocols range from the addressing and packet routing at a relatively low layer, to finding users and executing user commands at a higher layer.

The basic user commands that most systems support over the Internet Protocols are generally called TCP/IP commands, named after the two most common protocols. You can use all of these commands to communicate with other UNIX systems besides SCO systems. Many can be used to communicate with non-UNIX systems too, because a wide variety of systems support TCP/IP.

NFS, NIS, and ONC allow for transparent file sharing across networks. They come with a number of commands, mostly for system administration, but a few of value to users as well. A few useful RPC-based commands stand on their own, but most are used to administer NFS and NIS.

UUCP (which stands for UNIX-to-UNIX Copy) is a file-transfer protocol that is unrelated to the Internet protocols and is useful over phone lines.

MMDF and **sendmail** are also covered in this section.

TCP/IP Administration Commands

biff	Notify of mail arrival.
finger	Look up user information.
ftp	File transfer program
ifconfig	Configure network interface parameters.
mkhosts	Make node name commands.
netconfig	Configure network devices.
netutil	Administer Micnet network.
ping	Send ICMP ECHO_REQUEST packets to network hosts.
rcp	Remote file copy
rdate	Notify time server that date has changed.

rlogin	Remote login
slattach	Attach serial lines as network interfaces.
slink	Streams linker
snmp	SNMP start/stop script
talk	Talk to another user
tcp	TCP start/stop script
telnet	Use TELNET to interface with remote system.

NFS and NIS Administration Commands

automount	Automatically mount NFS filesystems.
domainname	Set or display name of current NIS domain.
lckclnt	Create lock manager client handles.
makedbm	Make an NIS dbm file.
nfs	NFS start/stop script
nfsstat	NFS statistics
portmap	DARPA port to RPC program number mapper
rpcinfo	Report RPC information.
ypinit	Build and install NIS databases.
ypmake	Rebuild NIS databases.
yppush	Force propagation of a changed NIS map.
ypserv	NIS server and binder processes
ypwhich	Return hostname of NIS server or map master.
ypxfr	Transfer NIS map from NIS server to here.

UUCP Administration Commands

uuchat	Dial a modem.
uucheck	Check UUCP directories and permissions files.
uucico	File transport program for the UUCP system.
uuclean	UUCP spool directory clean-up
uudemon	UUCP administrative scripts
uuinstall	Administer UUCP control files.
uulist	Convert UUCP routing file to MMDF format.
uulog	Query log file of UUCP transactions.
uusched	Scheduler for the UUCP file transport system
uustat	Provide information about uucp requests.
uutry	Try to contact remote system with debugging on.
uux, uuxqt	Execute commands on remote machines.

MMDF Commands

checkaddr	Check validity of an address within the local mail system (MMDF).
checkque	Report on amount of mail waiting in the MMDF distribution queue.
checkup	Check aspects of MMDF system configuration.

cleanque	Clean **tmp** and **msg** subdirectories of MMDF home queue directory.
cnvtmbox	Convert mailboxes between XENIX-style and MMDF format.
dbmbuild	Rebuild MMDF hashed database.
dbmedit	Edit MMDF database file.
deliver	MMDF mail-delivery process
list	List processor channel for MMDF.
mmdfalias	Convert XENIX-style aliases file to MMDF format.
mnlist	Convert a XENIX-style Micnet routing file to MMDF format.
rmail	Submit remote mail received via UUCP.
submit	MMDF mail queue manager
uulist	Convert a UUCP routing file to MMDF format (see section on UUCP).

Overview of TCP/IP

TCP/IP is a set of communications protocols that define how different types of computers talk to each other. Two of the protocols in the set give TCP/IP its name: the Transmission Control Protocol and the Internet Protocol. The Internet Protocol moves data between hosts in the form of datagrams. It splits data into packets, which are then forwarded to machines via the network. The Transmission Control Protocol ensures that the datagrams in a message are reassembled in the correct order at their final destination, and that any missing datagrams are resent until they are correctly received. The standard model for networking protocols and distributed applications is the International Standards Organization (ISO) seven-layer model shown in the following table.

The ISO Seven-layer Model

Layer	Name	Physical Layer
7	Application	NFS and NIS
		rlogin, telnet, ftp, etc.
6	Presentation	XDR
5	Session	RPC
		sockets
4	Transport	TCP, UDP
3	Network	IP
2	Data Link	Ethernet
1	Physical	

TCP/IP protocols

Two of the protocols in the set give TCP/IP its name: the Transmission Control Protocol and the Internet Protocol. The Internet Protocol moves data between hosts in the form of datagrams. It splits data in to packets, which are then forwarded to machines via the network. The Transmission Control Protocol ensures that the datagrams in a message are reassembled in the correct order at their final destination, and that any missing datagrams are resent until they are correctly received. Other protocols provided as part of TCP/IP include:

Address Resolution Protocol (ARP)
Translates between Internet and Ethernet addresses.

Internet Control Message Protocol (ICMP)
Error-message and control protocol.

Point-to-Point Protocol (PPP)
Provides both synchronous and asynchronous network connections.

Reverse Address Resolution Protocol (RARP)
Translates between Ethernet and Internet addresses (opposite of ARP).

Serial Line Internet Protocol (SLIP)
Enables IP over serial lines.

Simple Mail Transport Protocol
Used by MMDF to send mail via TCP/IP.

Simple Network Management Protocol (SNMP)
Performs distributed network management functions via TCP/IP.

User Datagram Protocol (UDP)
Provides data transfer, without the reliable delivery capabilities of TCP/IP.

In the architecture of TCP/IP protocols, data is passed down the stack (toward the Network Access Layer) when it is being sent to the network, and up the stack when it is being received from the network (see Figure 15-1).

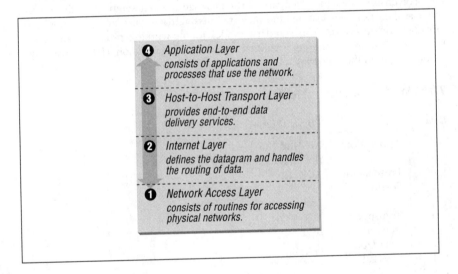

Figure 15-1: Layers in the TCP/IP Protocol Architecture

IP Addresses

The IP (Internet) address is a 32-bit binary number that differentiates your machine from all others on the network. Each machine must have a unique IP address. An IP address contains two parts: a network part and a host part. The number of address bits used to identify the network and host differ according to the class of the address. There are three main address classes: A, B, and C (see Figure 15-2).

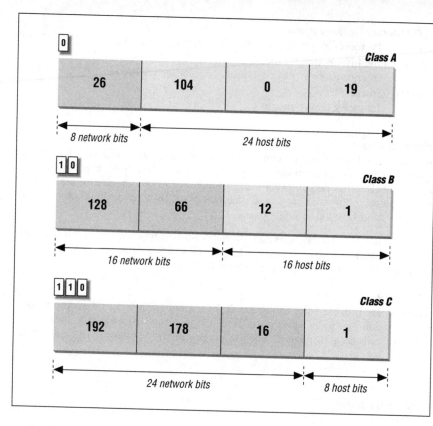

Figure 15-2: IP Address Structure

If you wish to connect to the DARPA Internet, contact the Network Information Center and have them assign you a network address. If you are not connecting to an outside network, you can choose your own network address, as long as it conforms to the IP address syntax. An IP address is different than an Ethernet address, which is assigned by the physical Ethernet card manufacturer.

Gateways and Routing

Gateways are hosts responsible for exchanging routing information and forwarding data from one network to another. Each portion of a network that is under a separate local administration is called an autonomous system (AS). Autonomous systems connect to each other via exterior gateways. An AS may also contain its own system of networks, linked via interior gateways.

Gateway protocols
Gateway protocols include:

    EGP (Exterior Gateway Protocol)

BGP (Border Gateway Protocol)
Protocols for exterior gateways to exchange information.

RIP (Routing Information Protocol)
Interior gateway protocol; most popular for LANs.

HELLO protocol
Interior gateway protocol.

Routing daemons

gated and **routed**, the routing daemons, can be run on a host to make it function as a gateway. Only one of them can run on a host at any given time. **gated** is the gateway routing daemon, and allows a host to function as both an exterior and interior gateway. It simplifies the routing configuration by combining the protocols RIP, Hello, BGP, and EGP into a single package.

routed, the network routing daemon, allows a host to function as an interior gateway only. **routed** manages the Internet Routing tables. For more details on **gated** and **routed**, see the TCP/IP commands in Section 17.

Routing tables

Routing tables provide information needed to route packets to their destinations. This information includes destination network, gateway to use, route status, and number of packets transmitted. Routing tables can be displayed with the **netstat** command.

Name Service

Each host on a network has a name that points to information about the host. Hostnames can be assigned to any device that has an IP address. Name service translates the hostnames (easy for people to remember) to IP addresses (the numbers the computer deals with).

DNS and BIND

DNS (the Domain Name System) is a distributed database of information about hosts on a network. Its structure is similar to that of the UNIX filesystem, an inverted tree with the root at the top. The branches of the tree are called domains (or subdomains), and correspond to IP addresses. The most popular implementation of DNS is the BIND (Berkeley Internet Name Domain) software.

DNS works as a client-server model. The *resolver* is the client, the software that asks questions about host information. The *name server* is the process that answers the questions. The server side of BIND is the **named** daemon. You can interactively query name servers for host information with the **nslookup** command. For more details on **named** and **nslookup**, see the TCP/IP commands in Section 17.

As a domain in the network, you just have to keep your domain up-to-date. The name servers make your domain data available to all the other name servers on the network.

Domain names

The full domain name is the sequence of names from the current domain back to the root, with a period separating the names. For instance, ora.com indicates the domain ora (for O'Reilly & Associates) which is under the domain com (for commercial). The standard form for including an end user in a domain address is user@domain. For instance, ellie@ora.com indicates the user ellie at ora.com. Top-level domains include:

COM   Commercial organizations

GOV   Government organizations

MIL   Military departments

ORG   Miscellaneous organizations

Countries also have top-level domains.

Registering domains

If you are setting up a domain that is going to be on a public network, you need to register your domain with the network. For the Internet, contact HOSTMASTER@NIC.DDN.MIL. For BITNET, contact INFO@BITNIC.

Configuring TCP/IP

netconfig

The SCO TCP/IP configuration program is called **netconfig**. **netconfig** installs the device drivers, configures the kernel, and modifies the startup files to support the newly installed device. **netconfig** views the layers of the TCP/IP architecture as links in a chain, flowing from the applications level through the basic TCP/IP services to the physical network. **netconfig** represents these chains as a list of software and hardware linked together by -> symbols. For example, the chain of SCO NFS, SCO TCP/IP, and a Western Digital Ethernet card is written as:

```
sco_nfs->sco_tcp->wdn0
```

netconfig allows you to install and uninstall these chains. It can be used either interactively or from the command line. For more information on **netconfig**, see the TCP/IP commands in Section 17.

ifconfig

The network interface represents the way that the networking software uses the hardware—the driver, the IP address, and so forth. To configure a network interface, use the **ifconfig** command. With **ifconfig**, you can assign an address to a network interface, setting the netmask, broadcast address, and IP address at boot time. You can also set network interface parameters, including: the use of ARP, the use of driver dependent debugging code, the use of one-packet mode, and the address of the correspondent on the other end of a point-to-point link. For more information on **ifconfig**, see the TCP/IP commands in Section 17.

Serial line communication

There are two protocols for serial line communication: Serial Line IP (SLIP) and Point-to-Point Protocol (PPP). These protocols let computers transfer information using the serial port, instead of a network card, and a serial cable in place of an Ethernet cable.

SLIP is included with the SCO TCP/IP package; it is automatically installed when you install TCP/IP. PPP is supplied as a separate installation package. You can install it automatically with TCP/IP, or separately. PPP is a proposed Internet standard and was developed to enhance the functionality of SLIP, adding error detection, process authentication, and the ability to send data either asynchronously or synchronously.

To configure a direct SLIP connection between machines, use **netconfig**. To configure a dialup SLIP connection, use PPP. To configure PPP, use the **netconfig** command. For more information about SLIP, see **slattach** in the TCP/IP commands at the end of this section

Ethernet cards

A physical network interface is required on the SCO system. There are many Ethernet interfaces available for SCO systems. The following table lists some of them:

Ethernet Cards Supported by SCO

Interface Name	Description
e3A	3Com 501 EtherLink I
e3B	3Com 503 EtherLink II
e3C	3Com 523 EtherLink/MC
e3D	3Com 507 EtherLink 16
hpi	HP ISA card (various models)
hpe	HP 27248A EISA
i6E	Racal InterLan NI6510 ISA
i3B	Racal InterLan ES3210 EISA
tok	IBM Token Ring Adapter (various models)
exos	Excelan 205 Ethernet
wdn	Western Digital EtherCard PLUS (various models)

Troubleshooting TCP/IP

The following commands can be used to troubleshoot TCP/IP. For more details on these commands, see the TCP/IP commands in Section 17.

ifconfig	Provides information about the basic configuration of the network interface.
netstat	Displays network status.
ping	Indicates whether a remote host can be reached.
nslookup	Queries the DNS name service.
dig	Queries the DNS name service.

ripquery   Queries RIP gateways.
traceroute
    Traces route taken by packets to reach network host.

Overview of NFS

NFS is a distributed filesystem that allows users to mount remote filesystems as if they were local. NFS uses a client-server model where a server exports directories to be shared, and clients mount the directories to access the files in them. NFS eliminates the need to keep copies of files on several machines by letting the clients all share a single copy of a file on the server. NFS is an RPC-based application-level protocol. For more information on the architecture of network protocols, see the TCP/IP section.

Administering NFS

Setting up NFS clients and servers involves starting the NFS daemons, exporting filesystems from the NFS servers, and mounting them on the clients. The **/etc/exports** file is the NFS server configuration file, controlling which files and directories are exported and what kinds of access are allowed. Names and addresses for clients receiving services are kept in the **/etc/hosts** file.

Daemons

NFS server daemons, called **nfsd** daemons, run on the server and accept RPC calls from clients. NFS servers also run the **mountd** daemon to handle mount requests. On the client, caching and buffering are handled by **biod**, the block I/O daemon. The **portmap** daemon maps RPC calls to the appropriate TCP/IP port numbers. To start the NFS daemons, check the NFS starter script, **/etc/nfs**.

Exporting filesystems

To set up an NFS server, first check **/etc/hosts** to make sure the name, network address, and aliases of all NFS client or server hosts are there. Next, edit the **/etc/exports** file to include the mount-point pathname of the filesystem to be exported. Check the NFS starter script, **/etc/nfs**, to ensure that the **mountd** daemon is running. Export the files in **/etc/exports** with the **exportfs** command.

Mounting filesystems

To enable an NFS client, mount a remote filesystem after NFS is started, either by using the **mount** command or by specifying default remote filesystems in **/etc/default/filesys**. A **mount** request calls **mountd**, which checks access permissions of the client and returns a pointer to a filesystem. Once a directory is mounted, it remains attached to the local filesystem until it is dismounted with the **umount** command, or until the local system is rebooted.

Usually, only the superuser can mount filesystems with NFS. However, you can enable users to mount and unmount selected filesystems using the **mnt** and **umnt** commands. This can reduce traffic by having filesystems mounted only when needed. To enable user mounting, create an entry in **/etc/default/filesys** for each filesystem to be mounted.

Starting and stopping NFS

NFS is started and stopped with the **/etc/nfs start** and **/etc/nfs stop** scripts. It will start automatically at system startup time if **/etc/nfs** is linked to **/etc/rc2.dS***name*. It will stop automatically at system shutdown time if **/etc/nfs** is linked to **/etc/rc2.d K***name*.

Overview of NIS

NIS refers to the service formerly know as Sun Yellow Pages (YP). It is used to make configuration information consistent on all machines in a network. It does this by designating a single host as the master of all the system administration files and databases, and distributing this information to all other hosts on the network. The information is compiled into databases called maps. NIS is built on the RPC protocol.

Servers

In SCO NIS, there are three types of servers: master, slave, and copy-only. Master servers are responsible for maintaining the maps and distributing them to the slave and client-only servers. The files are then available locally to requesting processes. Slave and copy-only servers differ in that slave servers may satisfy requests to transfer maps if the master server becomes unavailable.

Domains

An NIS domain is a group of hosts that use the same set of maps. The maps are contained in a subdirectory of **/etc/yp** having the same name as the domain. The machines in a domain share password, hosts, and group file information. NIS domain names are set with the **domainname** command.

NIS maps

NIS stores information in database files called maps. Each map consists of a pair of **dbm** database files, one containing a directory of keys (a bitmap of indices), the other containing data values. ASCII files are converted into **dbm** files by selecting the key field and separating it from the value field by spaces or a tab. The non-ASCII structure of **dbm** files neccessitates using NIS tools such as **ypxfr** and **yppush** to move maps between machines. When maps land at their destination servers, they are translated back into ASCII files.

The file **/etc/yp/YP_MAP_X_LATE** contains a complete listing of active NIS maps, as well as NIS aliases for NIS maps. All maps must be listed here in order for NIS to serve them.

Map manipulation utilities

The following SCO utilities are used to adminster NIS maps:

ypmake
> Modifies default maps listed in **YP_MAP_X_LATE**. **ypmake** also runs **yppush** by default to distribute newly updated maps.

makedbm
> Makes **dbm** files. Modifies only *ypservers* map and any non-default maps.

---

ypinit   Builds and installs NIS databases. Manipulates maps when NIS is being initialized. Should not be used when NIS is already running.

ypxfr   Transfers updated maps from the master server.

Administering NIS

SCO NIS is enabled by setting up NIS servers, initializing NIS, and starting the NIS daemons.

Setting up an NIS server

Setting up an NIS server involves: creating local user accounts; editing YP_MAP_X_LATE to add or remove files you do/don't want NIS to service; making sure that the NIS domain name is set to **unknown**; checking that the **passwd**, **hosts**, **ethers**, **group**, **networks**, **protocols**, and **services** files are current on your master server; and adding the entry:

```
/etc/yp
```

To your /.profile or /.cshrc file.

Initializing NIS

Use the **ypinit** command to initalize NIS.

Starting NIS

When you initialize NIS, /etc/nfs is modified to enable the automatic starting of NIS daemons, so they are started and stopped whenever NFS is started or stopped.

Adding NIS servers

To add NIS servers, edit the **ypservers** map on the master server, distribute it to other servers, and install and initialize NIS on the new server. To remove a slave or copy-only server from an NIS domain, use **custom** to remove the NIS package from the server, and edit the **ypservers** map on the master server and distribute it to other servers.

NIS user accounts

NIS networks have two kinds of user accounts: distributed, and local. Distributed accounts must be administered from the master machine, and they provide information that is uniform on each machine in an NIS domain. Changes made to distributed accounts are distributed via NIS maps. Local accounts are administered from the local computer, and they provide account information unique to a specific machine. They are not affected by NIS maps and changes made to local accounts do not affect NIS. When NIS is installed, pre-existing accounts default to local accounts.

RPC and XDR

RPC (Remote Procedure Call) is the session protocol used by both NFS and NIS. It allows a host to make a procedure call that appears to be local, but is really executed remotely, on another machine on the network. RPC is implemented as a library of procedures, plus a network standard for data byte-ordering called XDR (eXternal Data Representation).

Automounter

The automounter (the **automount** program) allows remote NFS filesystems to be mounted automatically and transparently. Mount information is kept in automounter maps, which are usually maintained in NIS maps. Automounter mounts all file hierarchies under the directory **/tmp_mnt**, then acts as a symbolic link server, associating the actual mount point with the one in **/tmp_mnt**. For more details, see the **automount** command in Section 17.

Automounter maps

Automounter information is kept in map files. These maps can reside on the local machine, or on remote machines, managed by NIS. There are three types of automounter maps:

direct   Lists complete directories and their locations. Each directory listed is automatically mounted as needed.

indirect
   Lists individual directory entries and their locations.

master   Lists all indirect and direct maps, options, and mount points.

A simple map entry takes the form:

   directory [*–mount-options*] *location...*

Where *directory* is the full pathname of the directory to mount when used in direct map, or the basename of a subdirectory in an indirect map. *mount-options* is a comma-separated list of NFS **mount** options, and *location* specifies a remote filesystem from which the directory may be mounted.

auto.master map

automount normally consults the *auto.master* NIS configuration map for a list of initial **automount** maps, and sets up automatic mounts for them in addition to those given on the command line. Maps given on the command line, or those given in a local **auto.master** file, override those in the NIS *auto.master* map.

UUCP

This section presents UUCP, *U*nix-to-*U*nix *C*o*P*y, a collection of programs that provide networking capabilities for UNIX systems. With these programs, you can transfer files between and execute commands on remote computers. UUCP requests are spooled for execution when communication has been established between two systems. Depending on how the configuration files are set up, the connection could be established immediately, or put off till a later time.

UUCP is designed to use standard serial cables, modems, and telephone service. If your network consists of an Ethernet LAN, with or without an Internet connection, you do not need to use UUCP, as it duplicates many features found in LAN Manager Client and TCP/IP.

Some of the UUCP programs are specific to UUCP, others are standard UNIX programs. Two standard UNIX programs that can be used with UUCP are **cu** and **mail**. The main UUCP-specific programs are **uucp**, used to request file transfers to or from remote machines, and **uux**, used to request execution of a command on a remote machine. The **uucico** daemon does most of the work transferring files and remote execution requests between systems. Another daemon, **uuxqt**, is invoked on the remote system to process the remote execution requests. The UUCP programs are listed in detail in Section 17.

File Transfer

Sending and retrieving files (including electronic mail) between networked UNIX systems is the most frequently used function of UUCP. Restricted access to directories on remote filesystems is the biggest block to easy file transfer. To avoid problems with filesystem access, you can use a special directory accessible by everyone called the Public Directory (PUBDIR). The full pathname to this directory is **/usr/spool/uucppublic**. **uuco**, **uuto**, and **uupick** are the commands used to copy files to and from PUBDIR. Administrative scripts may periodically clear PUBDIR and delete the files in it, so it's a good idea to get files out of this directory as soon as possible.

In a **uucp** pathname, the tilde character followed by a slash (~/) is an abbreviation for the pathname **/usr/spool/uucppublic**. The tilde character followed by a user id (~user) is an abbreviation for the user's login directory. When identifying remote files, you must include the names of remote system names. System names are followed by an exclamation point.

Administering UUCP

To set up a UUCP network, you need to:

- Connect and configure a modem or direct wire.

- Configure the UUCP software, using **uuinstall**.

- Create login accounts for any sites that will be calling your system.

- Test the connections with each remote site.

UUCP directories

There are three primary directories associated with UUCP:

/usr/spool/uucp

> Working directory for UUCP. Work files, lock files, and log files are stored here and in subdirectories.

/usr/spool/uucppublic

> Public directory (PUBDIR); is readable and writable by everyone.

/usr/lib/uucp

> Most UUCP programs are stored here, along with the supporting database or control files.

User programs like **uucp** and **uux** are kept in **/usr/bin**.

UUCP control files

Systems file

The **Systems** file (**/usr/lib/uucp/Systems**) contains information needed by the **uucico** daemon to establish a communications link to a remote computer. Each entry in the file represents a computer than can be called by your computer. More than one entry may exist for a specific computer. Each entry in the **Systems** file has the following format:

> *sitename schedule device speed phone login-script*

where:

sitename contains node name of the remote computer.

schedule is a string indicating day-of-week and time-of-day when the remote computer can be called.

device is the device type to be used to establish the communications link to the remote computer.

speed is the transfer speed of the device used in establishing the communications link.

phone is the phone number of remote computer for automatic dialers.

login-script contains login information (chat script). The chat script defines the login "conversation" that will occur between the two systems. It consists of "expect-send" pairs, separated by spaces, with optional "subexpect-subsend" pairs separated by hyphens, as in the following example:

```
         expect                 send    expect
    send                          |       |      |
      |                 |         |       |      |
    ogin:-BREAK-ogin: nuucp ssword: external
                  |    |
               subsend  subexpect
```

This line defines what the local system *expects* from the remote system and what it should *send* as a reply to the remote system, if the correct string is received.

Permissions file

The **Permissions** file (**/usr/lib/uucp/Permissions**) specifies the permissions (login, file access, command execution) that remote computers have with your system.

Entries

> A line in the **Permissions** file may be terminated by a backslash (\) to indicate continuation. Entries are made up of options delimited by spaces. The options are name-value pairs. There are two types of entries:

LOGNAME   Permissions that take effect when a remote computer calls your computer.

MACHINE   Permissions that take effect when your computer calls a remote computer.

Options

Following are the options for the **Permissions** file:

REQUEST   Whether a remote.computer can request to set up file transfers from your computer. The options are REQUEST=yes, and REQUEST=no (default).

SENDFILES   Whether your computer can send the work queued for the remote computer. The options are SENDFILES=yes, and SENDFILES=call (default, specifies that queued files be sent only when your computer calls the remote computer).

READ and WRITE
                 Various parts of the filesystem that **uucico** can read from/write to. Default is the **uucppublic** directory (READ=**/usr/spool/uucppublic**; WRITE=**/usr/spool/uucppublic**). READ and WRITE options do not affect the actual permissions of a file or directory.

NOREAD and NOWRITE
                 Specify exceptions to READ and WRITE options.

CALLBACK   Specifies, in LOGNAME entries, whether transaction takes place until the calling system is called back. Options are CALLBACK=yes and CALLBACK=no (default).

COMMANDS   Specifies commands in MACHINE entries that a remote computer can execute on your computer. The default commands are **rnews** and **uucp**.

VALIDATE   Requires that privileged computers have a unique login or password for UUCP transactions.

Example

```
MACHINE=site LOGNAME=login \
COMMANDS=rmail:rnews:uucp \
READ=/usr/spool/uucppublic:/usr/tmp \
WRITE=/usr/spool/uucppublic:/usr/tmp \
SENDFILES=yes REQUEST-yes
```

Devices file

The **Devices** file (**/usr/lib/uucp/Devices**) holds information for all the devices that can be used to make a link to a remote computer. Devices are: Automatic Call Units, direct links, or network connections. Each entry in the **Devices** file has the following format:

   type ttyline dialerline speed dialer-token

where:

type contains one of two keywords (direct or ACU), the name of a LAN switch, or a system name.

ttyline contains device name of port associated with the *Devices* entry.

dialerline is useful only for 801-type dialers. Unless you have an 801 dialer, enter a hyphen as a placeholder.

speed is the speed or speed range of device.

dialer-token contains pairs of dialers and tokens (arguments passed to tokens).

Dialers file
The **Dialers** file (/usr/lib/uucp/Dialers) specifies the initial conversation that must take place on a line before it can be made available for transferring data.

Dialcodes file
The **Dialcodes** file (/usr/lib/uucp/Dialcodes) contains the dial-code abbreviations that can be used in the *Phone* field of the **Systems** file. This is useful if you want to create a standard **Systems** file for distribution among several sites.

Sysfiles file
The **Sysfiles** file (/usr/lib/uucp/Sysfiles) lets you assign different files to be used by **uucp** and **cu** as the **Systems**, **Devices**, and **Dialers** files.

Create login accounts for remote sites
UUCP login accounts are the same as regular user accounts, but they use a special login directory and login program:

Login shell: */usr/lib/uucp/uucico*
Home directory: */usr/spool/uucppublic*

Use the **sysadmsh** selection Accounts–>User–>Create to create the new account.

Atdialers

Starting with version 3.2.4, SCO supplies the **atdialer** suite of programs (/usr/lib/uucp/atdial*) to replace the dialer programs. Dialers require the existence of a compiler and the atdialers do not. For more information on the **atdialer** programs, see the **atdialer** command in Section 3, *SCO UNIX User Commands*.

Security with /etc/passwd

Like all users, **uucico** must log in to your system. By assigning a password, you can keep unauthorized users from logging in. The **/etc/passwd** file has one *administrative login* for UUCP maintenance and one *working login*. The administrative login is the owner of all UUCP programs, directories, and files. It is used by the **cron** program when it runs the UUCP maintenance shell scripts. This login should not be used when dialing into the system. The working login is the login id that a remote **uucico** will use to actually log in to your system. There can be a general access login for all systems, or you can add a number of system-specific logins.

```
        password
         | group ID  home dir
         |    |         |
uucp::5:1::/usr/lib/uucp:
nuucp::6:1::/usr/spool/uucppublic:/usr/lib/uucp/uucico
  |        |  |                                  |
login      |  user info
ID         |                      shell
                |
         user ID
```

Field	Function in /etc/passwd
login id	*uucp* or *uucpadm* for administrative logins; any login name for working logins. It can also be a specific system name.
password	Initially blank. A password should be assigned with the **passwd** command, after which the encrypted password will appear here.
user id	Usually **5**, for **uucp**.
group id	Group to which the user belongs; you may use the same group number as your UNIX administrative files.
user info	Optional string describing the login name.
home dir	Home directory for this id; **/usr/lib/uucp** for the administrative login, **/usr/spool/uucppublic** for working logins.
shell	Command interpreter the remote system gets when it logs in; use **/usr/lib/uucp/uucico** for working logins. The administrative login uses **/bin/sh** by default. Specify the pathname of the C shell or Korn shell if you want to use one of these shells instead.

For maximum security, you should not use the general access working login shipped with the system. You should instead create individual UUCP logins for specific systems. This allows greater control over the files that can be accessed by these systems.

MMDF

MMDF (Multichannel Memorandum Distribution Facility) is the default mail router on SCO UNIX. MMDF routes mail locally and over Micnet, UUCP, or other networks that provide MMDF support.

Configuring MMDF

The **custom** utility installs MMDF and configures a basic system for sending mail on a local machine. To change MMDF configuration, log in as **mmdf** and edit the configuration files. Whenever you change MMDF alias or routing information in any way, you must rebuild the hashed database.

MMDF Configuration files

/usr/mmdf/mmdftailor
>   Defines all mail attributes for local machine.

/usr/mmdf/table/alias.list
>   Defines aliases for mailing lists.

/usr/mmdf/table/alias.user
>   Defines aliases for users.

/usr/mmdf/table/alias.ali
>   Defines aliases for system accounts.

/usr/mmdf/table/*.dom
>   Domain files match hostnames to fully-qualified hostnames.

/usr/mmdf/table/*.chn
>   Channel files expand fully-qualified hostnames to specify the addressing information necessary to reach the host or domain.

The sysadmsh Shell

This section describes **sysadmsh**, the SCO system administration shell. **sysadmsh** is a menu interface for system administration tasks that allows you to bypass the command line to run system administration commands. The following topics are presented:

- **sysadmsh** basics

- Main menu options

- Map of all **sysadmsh** menus and submenus.

sysadmsh Basics

Starting and Stopping sysadmsh

To start **sysadmsh** from the command line, type **sysadmsh**. To start **sysadmsh** from the Open Desktop, select the Controls icon, then select the Administration icon from the Controls window.

To exit **sysadmsh**, select Quit from the **sysadmsh** main menu, or select Exit from the File menu at the top of the **sysadmsh** screen.

The sysadmsh Screen

The **sysadmsh** screen is a blank screen with a menu bar across the top. Selecting a menu item replaces the top level menu with a secondary level menu bar. For a complete **sysadmsh** menu tree, see the end of this section. The top level menu items are:

- System—administer and configure system resources and report system status.

- Backups—perform backups of files and filesystems.

- Accounts—manage user accounts.

- Printers—administer the print system.

- Media—read, copy, compare, and format floppy disks and tapes.

- Jobs—authorize, report on, or terminate jobs.

- Dirs/Files—manage files and directories.

- Filesystems—check, add, create, mount, or unmount filesystems.

- User—user-specific applications.

- Quit—quit **sysadmsh**

Selecting Menu Items

sysadmsh menus are navigated in any of the following ways:

- Move through menu options with either the space bar or the arrow keys, then press RETURN on the desired option.

- Press the first letter of the desired option.

- Using a mouse, click the left button to select an option.

Forms

If you select an option that requires additional information, a *form* appears on the screen for you to fill in with the information.

The following tables list shortcuts for using forms. For brevity, control characters are marked by ^.

Form operations

Keyboard	Mouse	Action
ESCAPE	Right button	Abort—do not finish filling in form.
Up/down arrows	Left button	Move to other fields in form.
Left/right arrows	—	Move left and right in current field.
RETURN	Middle button	Complete data entry to a field and move to next field.
^x	—	Exit and execute form.
F4	—	Call spell checker.
F10	—	Exit and execute form (same as ^x).

Edit keystrokes

Keystroke	Action
CTRL-y	Delete current line.
CTRL-w	Delete current word.
CTRL-g, CTRL-h	Move to beginning of line.
CTRL-g, CTRL-l	Move to end of line.
CTRL-v	Toggle overstrike mode.
DELETE	Delete character over cursor.
Backspace	Delete character to left of cursor.
CTRL-u	Move up one page.
CTRL-d	Move down one page.
CTRL-n	Go to next word.
CTRL-p	Go to previous word.

Point-and-pick operations

Keyboard	Mouse	Action
RETURN	Middle button	Select item.
ESCAPE	Right button	End selection process.
CTRL-v	—	Toggle selecting all or none of list items.
Up, down arrow	Move mouse up or down	Move to other items in list.
Left, right arrow	Move mouse right or left	Move across multicolumn display.
Space bar	Left button	Mark an item.
F5	—	Search key—find items in long listing.
First letter	—	Select item by first letter.

Radio Buttons

sysadmsh

Radio buttons are rows of selection boxes in a form. You select them like menu items, and they provide a second level of selections from within the form.

Scan Windows

When you select a **sysadmsh** menu option, the result of the command is displayed in a a pop-up type of window called a *scan window*. The following operations are used to navigate scan windows:

Scan Window Operations

Keyboard	Mouse	Action
ESCAPE	Right button	Exit file.
Up arrow	—	Move up one line.
Down arrow	—	Move down one line.
RETURN	—	Move down one line.
PgDn	Middle button	Move down a page.
Space	Middle button	Move down a page.
PgUp	Left button	Move up a page.
Home	—	Move to top of display.
End	—	Move to bottom of display.
F5	—	Search for pattern in display.
F7	—	Print output of command or file currently in scan window.

Help

Context-sensitive help is available from any menu via the F1 key. An initial Help window appears on your screen. For the complete Help menu, press F1 again. Following are the Help menu options:

Help Menu Options

Option	Action
Continue	Continue to next page of help text.
Back	Move back to previous topics.
Next	Move forward to next topics.
Index	Choose new topic from list.
Related	Choose new topic related to current one.
Search	Search for new topic by matching a pattern.
Help	Explain how help facility is used.
Quit	Exit Help and return to **sysadmsh**.

Function Keys

The following function keys provide **sysadmsh** shortcuts:

Key	Action
F1	Help key—displays help for current context.
F2	Exit key—activates Quit option on top menu.
F3	Pop-up key—displays list of items acceptable for current form in field.
F4	Spell key—displays list of possible correct spellings of word in current form field.
F5	Search key—prompts for a search string.

Environment Variables

sysadmsh uses the following environment variables, which can be defined in user .login or .profile files:

SA_EDITOR	If not set, default editor is Lyrix, if installed; otherwise is vi.
SA_PRINT	If set, **sysadmsh** sends output directly to **/dev/lp** printer device. If not set, output is piped to **/bin/lp** program.
SA_USERAPPS	If not set, default user application file is $HOME/.sysadmmenu.

Menu Options

Following is a list of the **sysadmsh** main menu options and what they are used for:

System	Get system reports, configure system files, add or remove hardware and software, and administer and examine system auditing data.
Backups	Perform backup of files.
Accounts	Control functions of user accounts such as logins and passwords.
Printers	Administer the print system.
Media	Floppies and tapes: format, read, copy, and compare.
Jobs	Control jobs: report on, terminate, schedule, and authorize.
Dirs/Files	Files and directories: list, view, edit, remove, print, and change permissions.
Filesystems	Filesystems: check(**fsck**), mount and unmount, create on a floppy, and add support for DOS filesystems.
User	Read user-specific applications from $HOME/.sysadmmenu.
Quit	Quit **sysadmsh**.

sysadmsh

Menu Map

Following is a table listing all the **sysadmsh** menus. The main menus are in bold, the lower level menus are indicated by arrows (one arrow for first-level menus, two arrows for second-level menus etc.) The path column lists the shorthand menu path for each option, consisting of the first letters of each option from the top down. For example, the shortcut for the Users option is **sru** for system, report, user.

sysadmsh Option	Path	Function
System	s	System-wide reports, configurations
→Report	sr	Report on current state of system.
→→Activity	sra	Report on current system activity.
→→Users	sru	Report on users currently logged in.
→→Printers	srp	Report on current printer status.
→→Disk	srd	Report on current disk usage.
→→Network	srn	Report on current network files.
→→→Xnet	srnx	Report on XENIX-NET status.
→→→UUCP	srnu	Report on UUCP status.
→→Messages	srm	Read system messages.
→→Software	srs	Check installed software/package status.
→Configure	sc	Configure system files.
→→Security	scs	Change system security level
→→→Relax	scsr	Reset security to default UNIX system levels.
→→Kernel	sck	Change kernel parameters or capabilities.
→→→Parameters	sckp	Configure tuneable kernel parameters.
→→→Rebuild	sckr	Relink kernel according to current settings.
→→→DOS	sckd	Add DOS filesystem support to kernel.
→→→Streams	scks	Add streams support to kernel.
→→→Layers	sckl	Add shell layers support to kernel.
→→Logout	scl	Set idle time before user is logged out.
→→Defaults	scd	Modify system default parameters.
→→→Home	scdh	Modify default home directory for users.
→→→Message	scdm	Modify message-of-the-day file.
→→→Checklist	scdc	List filesystems checked at startup.
→→→Other	scdo	Modify other default files.
→→International	sci	Configure system for international use.
→→→System	scis	Set system local variables.
→→→Individual	scii	Change user's default locale.
→→→Display	scid	Change mapping of terminal character set.
→→→Keyboard	scik	Change mapping of console keyboard.
→→Network	scn	Configure networking files.
→→→UUCP	scnu	Configure UUCP files, enable/disable tty.
→→→Time	scnt	Set system time.
→→→Menus	scnm	Customize **sysadmsh** menus.
→→→Other	scno	Execute third-party **sysadmsh** extensions.
→Hardware	sh	Add/remove hardware from system.
→→HardDisk	shh	Add hard disk to system.
→→Tape	sht	Add/remove tape drive from system.
→→Printer	shp	Add/remove printer from system.
→→Card_Serial	shs	Add serial card to system.
→→Mouse	shm	Add mouse to system.

sysadmsh Option	Path	Function
→→Video	shv	Configure video card graphics parameters.
→Software	ss	Add/remove software from system.
→Audit	sa	Administer/examine system auditing data.
→→Enable	sae	Enable audit using existing parameters file.
→→Disable	sad	Disable audit.
→→Collection	sac	Display/modify audit collection rules.
→→→Directories	sacd	Display/modify audit directory list.
→→→→List	sacdl	Display audit directory list.
→→→→Create	sacdc	Create new audit directory.
→→→→Delete	sacdd	Delete existing audit directory.
→→→→Add	sacda	Add entry to audit directory list.
→→→→Remove	sacdr	Remove entry from audit directory list.
→→→Events	sace	Display/modify list of audited events.
→→→→View	sacev	Display system audit collection mask.
→→→→Modify	sacem	Modify system audit collection mask.
→→→IDs	saci	Display/modify list of users/groups audited.
→→→→View	saciv	Display list of users/groups audited.
→→→→Modify	sacim	Modify list of users/groups audited.
→→→Parameters	sacp	Display/modify audit parameters.
→→→→View	sacpv	Display audit parameters.
→→→→Modify	sacpm	Modify audit parameters.
→→→Reset	sacr	Change collection rules to default values.
→→→Statistics	sacs	Display statistics of current audit session.
→→Report	sar	Report on stored audit session data.
→→→List	sarl	List report templates available.
→→→View	sarv	View parameters in a report template.
→→→Create	sarc	Create new report template.
→→→Modify	sarm	Modify existing report template.
→→→Delete	sard	Delete existing report template.
→→→Generate	sarg	Generate report of audit session.
→→Files	saf	Manipulate audit session files.
→→→List	safl	List audit session files on system.
→→→Backup	safb	Back up audit session file to removable media.
→→→Delete	safd	Remove audit session file.
→→→Restore	safr	Restore audit file from removable media.
→Execute	se	Execute programs that are system specific.
→Terminate	st	Shut down system to remove power or reboot.
Backups	b	Perform backup of files.
→Create	bc	Create backups.
→→Scheduled	bcs	Perform scheduled filesystem backups.
→→Unscheduled	bcu	Perform unscheduled filesystem backup.
→Restore	br	Restore filesystem and files.
→→Partial	brp	Restore specific directories and files.
→→Full	brf	Restore entire filesystem.
→Schedule	bs	Modify scheduled backup frequency.
→View	bv	View contents of a backup.
→Integrity	bi	Check integrity of a backup.

sysadmsh

The sysadmsh Shell

sysadmsh Option	Path	Function
Accounts	a	Control functions of user accounts.
→User	au	Alter/create/retire user accounts.
→→Examine	aue	Set password/ID/authorization/audit parameters.
→→Create	auc	Make new user account.
→→Retire	aur	Close existing user account.
→Defaults	ad	Set system-wide parameters.
→→Authorizations	ada	View/modify default kernel subsystem privileges.
→→Password	adp	View/modify default password life/choice.
→→Logins	adl	View/modify default login attempt controls.
→Terminal	at	Manage terminal database entries.
→→Examine	ate	View/modify existing terminal entry.
→→Create	atc	Make new terminal entry.
→→Delete	atd	Delete existing terminal entry.
→→Lock	atl	Lock a specific terminal.
→→UnLock	atu	Unlock a specific terminal.
→→Assign	ata	Manage device-name equivalences database.
→→→Examine	atae	View/modify existing device entry.
→→→Create	atac	Make new device entry.
→→→Delete	atad	Delete existing device entry.
→Report	ar	Report on passwords/terminals/login activity.
→→Password	arp	Report on accounts by password status.
→→→Impending	arpi	Report on accounts with passwords near expiration.
→→→Expired	arpe	Report on accounts with expired passwords.
→→→Dead	arpd	Report on accounts with dead passwords.
→→→User	arpu	Report on single user's password.
→→→Group	arpg	Report on single group's password.
→→→Full	arpf	List all entries in password database.
→→Terminal	art	Report on access status by terminals.
→→Login	arl	Report login activity by user/group/terminal.
→→→User	arlu	Report logins of one/range of/all users.
→→→Group	arlg	Report logins of a group or range of groups.
→→→Terminal	arlt	Report logins of one/range of/all terminals.
→Check	ac	Check contents of **tcb** files for errors.
→→Databases	acd	Check consistency of subsystem databases.
→→Password	acp	Check **/etc/passwd** and **/etc/group**.
Printers	p	Administer print system.
→Configure	pc	Configure printers on print service.
→→Add	pca	Add printer to system.
→→Modify	pcm	Modify printer configuration.
→→Remove	pcr	Remove printer destination from print service.
→→Default	pcd	Change default destination printer.
→→Parameters	pcp	Modify printer controls and parameters.
→→Errors	pce	Set error warning notification/recovery modes.
→→Content	pcc	Type of content printable on printer
→→Users	pcu	Who can use printer
→Schedule	ps	Start/stop printer service, handle requests.
→→Begin	psb	Start printer service.
→→Stop	pss	Shut down printer service.
→→Accept	psa	Allow requests for destination.

sysadmsh Option	Path	Function
→→Reject	psr	Reject requests for destination.
→→Enable	pse	Enable printers.
→→Disable	psd	Disable printers.
→Request	pr	Move or cancel requests on print service.
→→Move	prm	Move requests between destinations.
→→Cancel	prc	Cancel requests made to print service.
→Auxiliary	pa	Handle print-wheels/filters/preprinted forms.
→→Alert	paa	Set/list an alert for print-wheel.
→→Filter	paf	Administer filters used with print service.
→→→Change/Add	pafc	Add/change filter used with print service.
→→→Remove	pafr	Remove filter from print service.
→→→List	pafl	List description of filter.
→→→Original	pafo	Restore original filter description.
→PPforms	pap	Administer preprinted forms of print service.
→→Configure	papc	Modify printer settings for preprinted forms.
→→Modify	papm	Add/change preprinted forms.
→→Remove	papr	Remove preprinted forms.
→→List	papl	List attributes of existing form.
→→Users	papu	Allow/deny user access to a form.
→→Alerts	papa	Modify alert method for mounted form.
→→→Specify	papas	Specify alerting method.
→→→List	papal	List current alert.
→→→Terminate	papat	Terminate active alert.
→→→Remove	papar	Remove alert definition.
→Priorities	pp	Set printing queue priorities.
→→Default	ppd	Set system-wide priority default.
→→Highest	pph	Set default highest priority level for users.
→→Remove	ppr	Remove users from specified priority level.
→→List	ppl	List default priority level and limits.
Media	m	Read/copy/compare/format floppies and tapes.
→List	ml	List contents of floppy or tape.
→Extract	me	Extract contents of floppy or tape.
→Archive	ma	Store files/directories/filesystems on media.
→Format	mf	Format UNIX or DOS floppy.
→Duplicate	md	Make copy of floppy or tape.
→Tapedump	mt	Display physical contents of tape.
Jobs	j	View/control processes.
→Report	jr	Report on current processes.
→Terminate	jt	Terminate currently running process.
→Authorize	ja	Authorize users to run jobs.
→→Scheduled	jas	Authorize creating regularly scheduled jobs.
→→→Default	jasd	Set default authorization for scheduled jobs.
→→→User	jasu	Allow/prohibit user-scheduled jobs.
→→→View	jasv	Check who can create scheduled jobs.
→→Delayed	jad	Authorize users to create delayed jobs.
→→→Default	jadd	Set default authorization for delayed jobs.
→→→User	jadu	Allow/prohibit user from creating delayed jobs.
→→→View	jadv	Check who is authorized to create delayed jobs.

sysadmsh Option	Path	Function
→→Environment	jae	Modify delayed job environment.
→→→At	jaea	Modify environment for **at**-controlled jobs.
→→→Batch	jaeb	Modify environment for **batch** jobs.
Dirs/Files	d	Files and directories.
→List	dl	List files in current directory.
→View	dv	View contents of file.
→Copy	dc	Copy directory or file.
→Edit	de	Edit file(s).
→Modify	dm	Change file parameters.
→→Permissions	dmp	Change file permissions.
→→Ownership	dmo	Change file ownership.
→→Group	dmg	Change group ownership.
→→Name	dmn	Rename or move files.
→→Size	dms	Compact files.
→→Format	dmf	Change file formats.
→Print	dp	Print files.
→Archive	da	Store files.
→Differences	dd	Compare two text files or directories.
→Remove	dd	Remove files or directories.
→UseDOS	du	Use DOS utilities to manipulate DOS files.
→→List	dul	List DOS files in current directory.
→→Remove	dur	Remove DOS file or directory.
→→MakeDir	dum	Create DOS directory.
→→Copy	duc	Copy files between DOS and UNIX systems.
→→View	duv	Display DOS files.
→→Format	duf	Format DOS media.
Filesystems	f	Check/act on filesystems.
→Check	fc	Check and repair filesystem (**fsck**).
→Mount	fm	Mount filesystem.
→Unmount	fu	Unmount filesystem.
→Add	fa	Add information for a new filesystem.
→Floppy	ff	Create filesystem on a floppy.
→DOS	fd	Add support for DOS filesystem.
User	u	User-specific applications read from **$HOME/.sysadmmenu**
Quit	q	Quit **sysadmsh**.
→Yes	qy	Leave **sysadmsh**.
→No	qn	Cancel Quit command.

17

System Administration Commands

This section presents the SCO UNIX System Administration commands.

acctcms

/usr/lib/acct/acctcms [*options*] *files*

Command summary from per-process accounting records.

Options

-a	Print output in ASCII rather than internal summary format.
-c	Sort by total CPU time rather than total kcore-minutes.
-j	Combine all commands invoked only once under ***other.
-n	Sort by number of command invocations.
-o	With -a, output a non-prime-time-only command summary.
-p	With -a, output a prime-time-only command summary.
-s	Any filenames encountered hereafter are already in internal summary format.
-t	Process all records as total accounting records.

Example

A typical sequence for performing daily command accounting and for maintaining a running total is:

```
acctcms file ...>today
cp total previoustotal
acctcms -s today previoustotal >total
acctcms -a -s today
```

acctcom

/usr/lib/acct/acctcom [[*options*] [*file*]] ...

Search and print process accounting file(s). **acctcom** reads *file*, the standard input, or **/usr/adm/pacct**, and writes selected records to the standard output. **acctcom** reports only on processes that have terminated; use **ps** for active processes.

Options

-a	Show some average statistics about the processes selected.
-b	Read backwards, showing latest commands first.
-C *sec*	Show only processes with total CPU time, system plus user, exceeding *sec* seconds.
-E *time*	Select processes ending at or after *time*.
-e *time*	Select processes existing at or before *time*.
-f	Print the **fork/exec** flag and system exit status columns in the output.
-g *group*	Show only processes belonging to *group*.

-H *factor*
> Show only processes exceeding *factor*, where factor is (total CPU time)/(elapsed time).

-h
> Instead of mean memory size, show the fraction of total available CPU time consumed by the process during its execution (total CPU time)/(elapsed time).

-I *chars*
> Show only processes transferring more characters than the cutoff number given by *chars*.

-i
> Print columns containing the I/O counts in the output.

-k
> Instead of memory size, show total kcore minutes.

-l *line*
> Show only processes belonging to terminal /dev/*line*.

-m
> Show mean core size (default).

-n *pattern*
> Show only commands matching *pattern*.

-O *sec*
> Show only processes with CPU system time exceeding *sec* seconds.

-o *ofile*
> Copy selected process records in the input data format to *ofile*; suppress standard output printing.

-q
> Do not print any output records; just print the average statistics.

-r
> Show CPU factor: user time/(system-time + user-time).

-S *time*
> Select processes starting at or after *time*.

-s *time*
> Select processes existing at or after *time*, given in the format *hr*[:*min*[:*sec*]].

-u *user*
> Show only processes belonging to *user* that may be specified by: a user ID, a login name converted to a user ID, a # designating only those processes executed with superuser privileges, or a ? designating only those processes associated with unknown user IDs.

-v
> Exclude column headings from the output.

/usr/lib/acct/acctcon1 [*options*]

Generate per login accounting records.

Options

-l *file*
> Create *file* to contain a summary of line usage.

-o *file*
> *file* is filled with an overall record for the accounting period.

-p
> Print input only.

-t
> Instead of using current file (and current time) as input, use last time found in input.

acctcon2	**/usr/lib/acct/acctcon2** Generate per-login accounting records. **acctcon2** expects a sequence of login session records as input and converts them into total accounting records.
acctdisk	**/usr/lib/acct/acctdisk** Gather user disk block data—read lines containing user ID, login name, and number of disk blocks, and convert them to total accounting records that can be merged with other accounting records.

acctdusg	**/usr/lib/acct/acctdusg**
	
	Calculate disk consumption for accounting records.
	
	Options
	
	   -u *file* Place in *file* records consisting of those filenames for which **acctdusg** charges no one.
	   -p *file* *file* is name of password file.

acctmerg	**/usr/lib/acct/acctmerg** [*options*] [*files*] Merge or add total accounting files. **acctmerg** reads its standard input and up to nine additional files, all in *tacct* format. ***Options*** Produce output in ASCII version of *tacct*. Input files are in ASCII version of *tacct*. Print input with no processing. Produce a single record that totals all input. Summarize by user ID rather than user ID and name. Produce output in verbose ASCII format, with more precise notation for floating-point numbers.
accton	**/usr/lib/acct/accton** [*file*] Turn process accounting on and off. If no *file* is given, accounting is turned off. If *file* is given, the kernel appends process accounting records.
acctprc1	**/usr/lib/acct/acctprc1** [*ctmp*] Generate per process accounting records. If *ctmp* is given, it is expected to contain a list of login sessions in the form described in **acctcon.** If *ctmp* is not given, **acctprc1** obtains login names from the password file.
acctprc2	**/usr/lib/acct/acctprc2** Generate accounting total records. Read records in the form written by **acctprc1,** summarize them by user ID and name, then write the

sorted summaries to the standard output as total accounting records.

acctsh

Shell procedures for accounting.

/usr/lib/acct/chargefee *login–name number*

Charge a *number* of units to *login-name*.

/usr/lib/acct/ckpacct [*blocks*]

Periodically check the size of **/usr/adm/pacct**. If size exceeds *blocks* (1000 by default), **turnacct** will be invoked with argument **switch**. If number of free disk blocks in **/usr** filesystem falls below 500, **ckpacct** will automatically turn off the collection of process accounting records via the **off** argument to **turnacct**. **ckpacct** should be initiated via **cron**.

/usr/lib/acct/dodisk [-o] [*files*]

Perform disk accounting functions. By default, will do disk accounting on special files in **/etc/default/filesys**. With **-o**, will do a slower version of disk accounting by login directory. If *files* are used, accounting will be done on those filesystems only. **dodisk** should be invoked by **cron**.

/usr/lib/acct/lastlogin

Invoked by **runacct** to update **/usr/adm/acct /sum/loginlog**, which shows the last date on which each person logged in.

/usr/lib/acct/monacct [*number*]

Should be invoked once a month or each accounting period. *number* indicates which month or period it is. With no *number*, defaults to current month.

/usr/lib/acct/nulladm *file*

Create *file* with mode 664 and ensure that owner and group are *adm*. **nulladm** is called by various accounting shell procedures.

/usr/lib/acct/prctmp [*file*]

Print session record file. Take one or more filenames as arguments; otherwise read from the standard input.

/usr/lib/acct/prdaily [-1] [-c] [*mmdd*]

Invoked by **runacct** to format a report of the previous day's accounting data. Print current daily accounting reports by typing **prdaily**. Print previous day's accounting reports by using the *mmdd* option to specify month and day. **-1** prints a report of exceptional usage by login ID for the specified date. **-c** prints a report of exceptional resource usage by command and can be used only on current day's accounting data.

acctsh ←	/usr/lib/acct/prtacct *file* [*"heading"*] 　　Format and print any total accounting (*tacct*) file. /usr/lib/acct/runacct [mmdd] [*mmdd state*] 　　Perform accumulation of connect, process, fee, and 　　disk accounting on a daily basis. **runacct** also creates 　　summaries of command usage. /usr/lib/acct/shutacct [*"reason"*] 　　Invoked during system shutdown to turn process 　　accounting off and append a *"reason"* record to 　　/etc/wtmp. /usr/lib/acct/startup 　　Called by /etc/init.d/acct to turn the accounting on 　　whenever the system is brought to a multiuser state. /usr/lib/acct/turnacct on | off | switch 　　Interface to **accton** that turns process accounting **on** or 　　**off**. **switch** turns accounting off, moves the current 　　/usr/adm/pacct file to the next free name in 　　/usr/adm/pacct *incr* (where *incr* is a number starting 　　with 1 and incrementing by one for each additional 　　*pacct* file), then turns accounting back on again.
aioinfo	aioinfo [*raw–device*] Print out AIO statistics. By default, **aioinfo** opens /dev/rroot to get a file descriptor for the AIO ioctl. If this is not accessible, or sup- port for AIO is not linked into the kernel, an alternate AIO disk partition name must be specified.
aiolkinit	/etc/aiolkinit/ [*raw–device*] Set up AIO memory locking permissions. **aiolkinit** reads the /usr/lib/aiomemlock file and sets up an internal kernel table entry for each line. Typically, **aiolkinit** is called by a script in the /etc/rc2.d directory (this script should be invoked before starting up any program that uses AIO). **aiolkinit** defaults to opening /dev/rroot to call the appropriate AIO I/O control command (ioctl). If /dev/rroot does not support AIO, an alternate AIO device must be provided as an argument. **aiolkinit** can be run only by the superuser.
ale	/tcb/bin/ale *file program* [*arguments*] Lock and update authentication files—allow authentication adminis- trator to execute shell scripts that update authentication files while in multiuser mode. The **auth** subsystem and **chown** kernel authori- zations are required to run **ale**. *file* is the absolute pathname of the authentication file to be locked during the update. *program* is the name of the shell script to perform the update; it must reside in the /tcb/lib/auth_scripts directory. *arguments* are the arguments to be passed to the script.

ap [options] [usernames]

Generate account profile for *usernames*, or, if not specified, to all users listed in the password file, for propagation to other machines.

Options

-d   Write an account profile entry to standard output.

-f *file*   File to restore account profile information from.

-o   Overwrite an existing account profile that has the same username and user ID as the one being restored.

-r   Restore account profile information from the file specified by the -f *file* option.

-v   Output a message to the standard error for each account profile dumped or restored.

Example

To dump the account profiles for users *root* and *guest* to a file called **profiles** and display a message after each account profile is dumped:

```
ap -dv root guest > profiles
```

/tcb/bin/asroot command [arguments]

Run a *command* as root, along with optional *arguments*.

/etc/asktime

Prompt for the correct time of day. Enter a legal time according to the proper format:

```
[ [yy]mmdd]hhmm
```

where the first *mm* is the month number; *dd* is the day number in the month; *hh* is the hour number; second *mm* is the minute number; *yy* is the last two digits of the year number (optional). If no year is mentioned, defaults to current year. This command can be run only by the superuser. **/etc/asktimerc** is a link to **/etc/asktime**.

---

assign [options] [device]

Assign devices. *device* must be an assignable device not currently assigned. No devices will be assigned unless all can be assigned. With no arguments, **assign** prints a list of assignable devices and names of users to whom assigned.

→

assign
←
	Options
	
	  -d Deassign devices (see also **deassign** command).
	  -u Suppress assignment, but perform error checking.
	  -v Give verbose output.

atcronsh	**/usr/lib/sysadm/atcronsh**
	
	at and **cron** administration utility. **atcronsh** is the screen interface invoked by the **sysadmsh** *Jobs->Authorize* selection (it is not recommended to invoke **atcronsh** directly). **atcronsh** is used to specify which users are allowed to use the **cron**, **at**, and **batch** commands. It also allows the **at** and **batch** prototype files to be edited.
	
	atcronsh allows a system default for **cron**, **at**, and **batch** to be given. Defaults can be:
	  none No user authorized.
	  allow All users allowed to use commands unless specifically denied.
	  deny All users denied permission to use commands unless specifically authorized.

auditcmd	**/tcb/bin/auditcmd** [*options*]
	
	Command interface for audit subsystem activation, termination, statistic retrieval, and subsystem notification. **auditcmd** may only be executed by processes with the **configaudit** kernel authorization, since the audit device is used.
	
	Options
	
	  -c Retrieve audit subsystem statistics from the audit device.
	  -d Disable audit subsystem.
	  -e Enable audit subsystem for audit record generation.
	  -m Inform audit subsystem that multiuser run state has been achieved and that alternate audit directories specified by the administrator using **sysadmsh** are now mounted and available.
	  -q Perform specified option silently.
	  -s Inform audit subsystem that a system shutdown is in progress.

auditd	**/tcb/bin/auditd** [*options*] Audit subsystem daemon that reads audit collection files generated by the audit subsystem and compacts the records.

Options

-y, -n   Invoke (-y) or avoid (-n) an interactive query of
whether to recover records from abnormally terminated audit sessions.

/usr/lib/sysadm/auditsh

Menu-driven audit administration utility. **auditsh** is the screen interface invoked by the **sysadmsh** *System–>Audit* selection (it is not
recommended to invoke **auditsh** directly). **auditsh** controls the audit
subsystem, allowing: establishment of audit subsystem initialization
parameters, specification of criteria for selecting output records
during reduction, report generation, dynamic changing of subsystem parameters, and backup and restore of compacted audit output
files.

/tcb/bin/authck [*options*]

Check internal consistency of authentication database. **authck**
requires the invoking user to be root or have **auth** subsystem
authorization.

Options

-a   Shorthand for turning on all the -p, -t, and -s options.
-p   Check Protected Password database and /etc/passwd
such that neither contains entries not in the other, and
fields common to both agree.
-s [-n | -y]]
Check Protected Subsystem database files to ensure
that they correctly reflect the subsystem authorization
entries in the Protected Password database. If any
inconsistencies are found, and neither the -n or -y
flags have been given, the administrator is asked
whether **authck** should repair the Subsystem database.
-y calls for repair without asking, -n makes **authck**
abort the repair phase.
-t   Check fields in Terminal Control database for reason-
able values.
-v   Provide running diagnostics as program proceeds.

---

authckrc [*options*]

Multiuser mode tcb check script. See **tcbck** for more details on
using **authckrc**.

---

auths [*options*]

List and/or restrict kernel authorizations. With no arguments, **auths**
returns the kernel authorizations associated with the current process.

$\rightarrow$

Options

-a *authlist*

Allow user to alter kernel authorizations. Requires list of comma-separated authorizations, *authlist*, which becomes the absolute set of kernel authorizations for the new process. To start a process with a null set of kernel authorizations, use the empty string "".

-c *command*

command is passed to user's shell, as specified in user's **/etc/passwd** entry, and is run as a single command.

-r *authlist*

Allow user to alter kernel authorizations. Requires list of comma-separated authorizations, *authlist*, which is removed from the authorization set of the invoking process when forming the kernel authorizations for the new process.

-v

List new kernel authorizations before new command or shell is run. With -a options, warn when more authorizations are attempted to be set than already exist; or, with -r option, when more authorizations are attempted to be removed than already exist.

Examples

Execute a shell without the **execsuid** kernel authorization:

```
auths -r execsuid
```

List the current kernel authorizations:

```
auths
```

Execute *yourprog* with no kernel authorizations:

```
auths -a "" -c yourprog
```

Execute *myprog* with **chmodsugid** and **execsuid**:

```
auths -a chmodsugid,execsuid -c myprog
```

---

authsh

/usr/lib/sysadm/authsh

authsh is a full screen menu-driven interface, invoked by the sysadmsh *Accounts* selection, that provides the functions necessary to control the generation and maintenance of user and system passwords, the terminal database configuration, terminal and account locking, and the generation of administrator reports on system activity. For more information, see Section 16, *The sysadmsh Shell*.

autoboot

Automatically boot the system when the computer is turned on, provided no key is pressed at the **boot** prompt. **autoboot** checks the **etc/default/boot** file for the following instructions on autobooting:

AUTOBOOT=YES or NO
> Whether or not **boot** times out and loads the kernel.

MULTIUSER=YES or NO
> Whether or not **init** invokes **sulogin** or proceeds to multi-user mode.

PANICBOOT=YES or NO
> Whether or not the system reboots after a **panic**.

RONLYROOT=YES or NO
> Whether or not the root filesystem is mounted **readonly**.

DEFBOOTSTR=_bootstring_
> Set default bootstring to _bootstring_.

SYSTTY=_x_
> If _x_ is **1**, system console device is set to serial adapter at COM. If _x_ is **0**, system console is set to main display adapter.

SLEEPTIME=_n_
> Set time (in seconds) between calls to **sync**.

TIMEOUT=_n_
> _n_ is number of seconds to timeout at the Boot: prompt before booting the kernel. If TIMEOUT unspecified, _n_ defaults to one minute.

If either **etc/default/boot** or the variable needed cannot be found, the variable is assumed to be **NO**. However, if filesystem cannot be found, **PANICBOOT** is set to **YES**. If **mail** is installed on the system, the output of the boot sequence is mailed to _root_, otherwise, check **/etc/bootlog** for output.

---

automount [_options_] [_directory map_]

NFS daemon that automatically and transparently mounts NFS filesystems. **automount** uses an **automount** map to locate an appropriate NFS file server, exported filesystem, and mount options. It then mounts the filesystem in a temporary location and replaces the filesystem entry for the directory or subdirectory with a symbolic link to the temporary location. If the filesystem is not accessed within a certain interval (default is five minutes), **automount** unmounts the filesystem and removes the symbolic link. If the indicated directory has not already been created, **automount** creates it and removes it upon exiting.

Maps may be assigned to a directory using an entry in a direct **auto-mount** map, or by specifying an indirect map on the command line. If *directory* is a pathname, *map* points to an indirect map, a list of the subdirectories contained in *directory*.

Map entry format

A simple map entry takes the form:

directory [*-mount-options*] *location*...

Where *directory* is the full pathname of the directory to mount when used in direct map, or the basename of a subdirectory in an indirect map. *mount-options* is a comma-separated list of NFS **mount** options, and *location* specifies a remote filesystem from which the directory may be mounted.

Options

-D envar=*value*
: Assign *value* to the indicated **automount** (environment) variable.

-f *master–file*
: Read local file *master-file* for initialization, ahead of the *auto.master* NIS map.

-M *mount–directory*
: Mount temporary filesystems in directory *mount-directory* instead of **/tmp_mnt**.

-m
: Suppress initialization of *directory-map* pairs listed in the **auto.master** NIS database.

-n
: Disable dynamic mounts.

-T
: Trace—expand each NFS call and display on standard output.

-tl *duration*
: *duration*, in seconds, that a filesystem is to remain mounted when not in use. Default is 300 seconds.

-tm *interval*
: *interval*, in seconds, between attempts to mount a filesystem. Default is 30 seconds.

-tw *interval*
: *interval*, in seconds, between attempts to unmount filesystems that have exceeded their cached times. Default is 60 seconds.

-v
: Verbose—log status messages to the console.

automount maps

Direct maps

Contains mappings for any number of directories. Each directory listed in the map is automatically mounted as needed.

Indirect maps

> Allows specification of mappings for subdirectories you wish to mount under the *directory* indicated on the command line.

Included maps

> Contents of a map can be included in another map with an entry of the form:

> +*mapname*

> where *mapname* can be either a filename, the name of an NIS map, or one of the special maps described below.

Special maps

> There are three special maps currently available:

> -hosts   Uses the hostname resolution facilities available on the system to locate a remote host when the hostname is specified.

> -null   Cancel a previous map for the directory indicated.

> -passwd   Uses the **passwd** database to attempt to locate the home directory of a user.

auto.master map

> **automount** normally consults the **auto.master** NIS configuration map for a list of initial **automount** maps and sets up automatic mounts for them in addition to those given on the command line. Maps given on the command line, or those given in a local **auto.master** file override those in the NIS **auto.master** map.

---

backup [*options*]

Perform UNIX backup functions. **backup** is a frontend to the **cpio** utility. It is not recommended for routine system backups; use **sysadmsh** for system backups.

Options

> -c   Complete backup.

> -d*device*

> > Device to be used. Default is **/dev/rdsk/f0q15d** (the 1.2M floppy).

> -f *files*   Back up files specifed by *files*.

> -h   Give backup history—when the last complete and partial backups were done.

> -p   Incremental/partial backup. Back up only files modified since date of last backup.

> -t   Used when device is a tape. Must be used with -d when tape device is specified.

> -u *user*   Back up a user's home directory. If more than one user is specified, the *user* arguments must be in quotes.

backupsh	Screen interface invoked by the **sysadmsh** Backups selection to administer the backup subsystem (it is not recommended to invoke **backupsh** directly). **backupsh** allows scheduled and non-scheduled backups to be taken, the **/usr/lib/sysadmin/schedule** file to be edited, and complete filesystems or single files or directories to be restored. **backupsh** can be used with both UNIX and XENIX filesystems. If a UNIX filesystem is used, **cpio** is called; if XENIX is used, **xbackup** or **xrestore** is called.

badtrk

/etc/badtrk [*options*]

Used chiefly during system installation, **badtrk** scans the media surface for flaws, creates a new bad track table, prints the current table, and adds and deletes entries in the table. Bad tracks listed in the table are aliased to good tracks. **badtrk** only applies to standard disk controllers, not to SCSI host adapters or IDA controllers, and can only be used in single-user mode.

Options

-e   Change size of bad track table.

-f *device*
Open the partition *device* and read the bad track table associated with that partition. *device* must be a UNIX partition of a fixed disk: **/dev/rhd0a** for the first drive, **/dev/rhd1a** for the second, and so on.

-m *max*
Set maximum number of bad tracks to *max*. Use only in non-interactive mode, in conjunction with -e:

[-e [-m *max*]]

-s *arguments*
Invoke **badtrk** non-interactively. *arguments* specify either quick or thorough, destructive or non-destructive scan:

[q]uick [t]horough [d]estructive [n]on-destructive

User should specify either q or t, and either d or n.

-v   Display progress messages indicating how much of the disk has been scanned. This option is used only in non-interactive mode in conjunction with -e.

bcheckrc

/etc/bcheckrc [*option*]

System initialization procedure. **bcheckrc** checks the root filesystem. This shell procedure is executed via entries in **/etc/inittab** by **init** whenever the system is booted (or rebooted). First, the status of the root filesystem is checked. If it is found to be bad, **bcheckrc** repairs it. Then, a second procedure, **brc**, clears the mount

filesystem table, **etc/mnttab**, and puts the entry for the root
filesystm into the mounted table. After these two procedures have
executed, **init** checks for the "initdefault" value in **/etc/inittab**,
which tells **init** in which run-level to place the system.

Option

-a   Run without operator intervention. **init** calls **bcheckrc**
              with **-a** when the system autoboots.

bcheckrc

/etc/biod [*nservers*]

NFS daemon—starts *nservers* asynchronous block I/O daemons that
do read-ahead and write-behind of blocks from the client's buffer
cache. **biod**'s primary function is to increase the performance of
block I/O operations on remote filesystems.

biod

---

bootpd [*options*] [*configfile* [*dumpfile*]]

TCP/IP command. Internet Boot Protocol server. **bootpd** is normally run by **/etc/inetd** by including the following line in the file
/etc/inetd.conf:

    bootps dgram udp wait root /etc/bootpd bootpd

This causes **bootpd** to be started only when a boot request arrives.
Upon startup, **bootpd** first reads its configuration file, **/etc/bootptab**
(or the *configfile* listed on the command line), then begins listening
for BOOTREQUEST packets.

bootpd looks in **/etc/services** to find the port numbers it should
use. Two entries are extracted: **bootps**—the bootp server listening
port, and **bootpc**—the destination port used to reply to clients.

If **bootpd** is compiled with the -DDEBUG option, receipt of a
SIGUSR1 signal causes it to dump its memory-resident database to
the file **/etc/bootpd.dump** or the command-line specified *dumpfile*.

Options

-d   Each instance of this switch increases the level of
              debugging output.

-s   Run **bootpd** in a standalone configuration. In this case,
              the **-t** switch has no effect.

-t*timeout*
              Specify a different timeout value in minutes. A timeout
              value of zero means forever.

Configuration file

The **bootpd** configuration file has a format in which two-charac-
ter, case-sensitive tag symbols are used to represent host

bootpd

bootpd ←	parameters. These parameter declarations are separated by colons. The general format is: hostname:tg=value...:tg=value...:tg=value... where *hostname* is the actual name of a bootp client and *tg* is a tag symbol. The currently recognized tags are listed below. ***Tags*** bf Bootfile bs Bootfile size in 512-octet blocks cs Cookie server address list ds Domain name server address list gw Gateway address list ha Host hardware address hd Bootfilehome directory hn Send hostname ht Host hardware type (see Assigned Numbers RFC) im Impress server address list ip Host IP address lg Log server address list lp LPR server address list ns IEN-116 name server address list rl Resource location protocol server address list sm Host subnet mask tc Table continuation to Time offset in seconds from UTC ts Time server addresss list vm Vendor magic cookie selector There is also a generic tag, T*n*, where *n* is an RFC 1048 vendor field tag number. Generic data may be represented as either a stream of hexadecimal numbers or as a quoted string of ASCII characters.

brc	**/etc/brc** [*option*]
	
	System initialization procedure. **brc** clears mounted filesystem table and adds an entry for root filesystem. This shell procedure is executed via entries in **/etc/inittab** by **init** whenever the system is booted (or rebooted). **brc** works after **bcheckrc** has checked the status of the root filesystem. See also **bcheckrc**.
	
	Option
	
	  -a Run without operator intervention. **init** calls **brc** with
	            -a when the system autoboots.

btldinstall	**/etc/btldinstall** *mount_dir* Install packages from boot-time loadable device drivers (btld) into the Link Kit. *mount_dir* is expected to be the root directory of a

mounted btld disk. **btldinstall** is typically run by a Bourne shell script which is always present on a btld disk.

Environment variables

The following environment variables are available for use in scripts run by **bldinstall**:

$pkg   Current package being installed
$pkginst   All packages to be installed
$okdrivers All drivers to be installed for this package

---

captoinfo [*options*] [*file*]

Convert the termcap terminal description entries given in *file* into terminfo source entries and write them to the standard output along with any comments found. If no *file* is given, the TERMCAP environment variable is used for the filename or entry.

Options

-1   Print fields one per line. Otherwise, fields are printed several to a line, up to a maximum width of 60 characters.

-V   Display the version of the program on the standard error, and exit.

-v   Verbose—print tracing information on the standard error as the program runs.

-w *width*

Change output to *width* characters.

/usr/mmdf/bin/checkaddr [−*w*] [*addresses* ...]

Check validity of an address within the local mail system (MMDF). **checkaddr** can be given either addresses on the command line (one address per argument), or a list of addresses on the standard input (one address per line).

Option

-w   Cause **submit** to generate a detailed submission tracing.

/usr/mmdf/bin/checkque [options]

Report on the amount of mail waiting in the MMDF distribution queue. **checkque** indicates the total number of messages and the size of the queue directory, then lists the number of messages waiting for each transmission channel. Because the mail queue is usually protected from access by any uid except MMDF, **checkque** should be run under the *root* or *mmdf* uid.

→

checkque
←
	Options
	
	   -c Specify one or more channel names. If this option is used, **checkque** restricts its report to the named channels.
	
	   -f Print name of oldest queued message for each channel.
	
	   -p List only channels with problems—channels with mail waiting for over some "problem threshold" (default is 24 hours).
	
	  -t*age* [m]
	
	           Change problem threshold. A number of hours (or minutes, if **m** is appended) should appear without a space after the -t.
	
	   -s Force an abbreviated summary listing instead of the normal multiline report.
	
	   -z Skip channels with no messages queued.

checkup	**/usr/mmdf/bin/checkup** [*options*]
	
	Check aspects of MMDF system configuration. **checkup** reports on all problems encountered, including correct states. Displayed problems are prefixed by two asterisks; information that is advisory is enclosed in square brackets.
	
	Options
	
	   -p Report only problems detected by **checkup**.
	   -v [*digit*]
	
	           Display *digit* level of information. *digit* goes from 1 (same as -p) to level 7, which displays all information.

chg_audit	**/tcb/lib/chg_audit** [on] Enable and disable auditing for the next session. This command is normally invoked by the **auditsh**. The **on** argument enables auditing.
chroot	**chroot** *newroot command* Change root directory for a command. The given *command* is executed relative to the new root. The meaning of any initial / in pathnames is changed to *newroot* for a command and any of its children. In addition, the initial working directory is *newroot*. This command is restricted to the superuser.
chtype	**/tcb/lib/auth_scripts/chtype** Script called by **unretire** when changing the usertype of an account. For more details, see the **unretire** command.

cleanque [option]

MMDF command—remove extraneous files from the **tmp** and **msg** subdirectories of the MMDF home queue directory. **cleanque** also sends warnings for mail that has not been fully delivered after *warntime*—time in hours that a message can remain in a queue before a warning message about delayed delivery is sent to sender; and returns mail that has not been fully delivered after *failtime*—time a message can remain in a queue before a failed mail message is sent to sender and the message purged from the queue.

Option

-w   This option can be used if you are running **cleanque** manually and want to see what the program is doing.

/usr/lib/cleantmp

Remove the temporary files in the directories specified in /etc/default/cleantmp under the variable **TMPDIRS**. By default, /tmp and /usr/tmp are examined. Files in these directories that are not accessed within the last *n* days will be removed, where *n* is the number of days specified (default is 7) under the variable **FILEAGING** in /etc/default/cleantmp.

/usr/mmdf/bin/cnvtmbox [options] old_mailbox [new_mailbox]

Convert mailboxes between XENIX-style and MMDF format. If *new_mailbox* is specified, **cnvtmbox** places the converted mailbox in this folder; otherwise, converted mailbox is written to standard output.

Options

-c   Convert XENIX-style or mixed-format mailbox to MMDF format. If not options are specified, -c is the default.

-o   Convert MMDF or mixed-format mailbox to XENIX-style (or old UNIX-style) format.

/etc/comsat

TCP/IP command—biff server. **comsat** receives reports of incoming mail and notifies users if they have requested this service. It receives the messages on a datagram port associated with the **biff** service specification and **inetd**. The one-line messages are of the form:

user@ mailbox-offset

If *user* is logged into the system, *offset* is used as a seek offset into the appropriate mailbox file, and the first seven lines or 560 characters of the messages are printed on the user's terminal.

configure | **configure** [*options*] [*resource=value* ...]

Kernel configuration program. Resources are modified interactively or with command-line options. Adding or deleting device-driver components requires command-line options.

Syntax

> **cd /etc/conf/cf.d**
> **. /configure** [*options*][*resource=value*]

Options

Command-line options are designed for writing driver-installation shell scripts.

-A *address address*
> Return the name of the device with the I/O address conflict. *address*es are hexadecimal I/O addresses.

-a [*func1 func2* ...]
> Add functions (*func1*, etc.). These are the names of functions appearing within **bdevsw** or **cdevsw**, as appropriate, plus the names of the initialization, clock poll, halt, and interrupt routines, if present, plus the name of the tty structure pointer.

-b   Indicate that a block driver is being referenced.

-C *channel*
> Used with **-a**, indicates the DMA *channel* (an integer) used by the device. Default is to not use DMA.

-c   Indicate that a character driver is being referenced.

-d [*func1 func2* ...]
> Delete functions (*func1*, etc.). These are the names of functions appearing within **bdevsw** or **cdevsw**, as appropriate, plus the names of the initialization, clock poll, halt, and interrupt routines, if present, plus the name of the tty structure pointer.

-D   With **-a**, enable device driver able to share its DMA channel; with **-d**, delete this characteristic. Default is to not share.

-f *file*   Much of the configuration data is maintained in two files, whose default names are **mdevice** and **mtune**. **-f** can be used to specify alternate names. If **-f** is the only option present, **configure** is still interactive.

-G   With **-a**, add the **G** characteristic to the driver. With **-d**, delete the **G** characteristic. The **G** characteristic indicates whether or not the device uses an interrupt, even though an interrupt is specified in the **sdevice** file. The default is to not set this characteristic.

-g *dev_name handler* | *dev_name*
> Add or remove graphics input (GIN) device handlers. Given just the *dev_name* argument, the GIN device is removed from the configuration files. If **-g** has two

arguments, the second is a handler for *dev_name*, and the device is added to the files.

- **-H** With **-a** or **-d**, add or delete the characteristic that the driver supports hardware distinguishing it from those that are entirely software (pseudo-devices). Default is to set this characteristic.

- **-h** *dev_name*

    Give the driver or streams module name when the name is different from the prefix, or when no prefix is specified, as in the case of the streams module. The name can be 1-8 characters long.

- **-I** *address address*

    Hexadecimal start and end I/O *address*es. Default values are zero.

- **-i** With **-a** or **-d**, add or delete the characteristic that the device is a tty. Default is off.

- **-J** *address address*

    Hexadecimal start and end controller memory *address*es. Default values are zero.

- **-j** [*prefix* [**NEXTMAJOR**]

    When followed by a *prefix* used by a driver, the major device number is displayed. When followed by the string **NEXTMAJOR**, the smallest unused major device number is displayed.

- **-l** *priority level*

    Set interrupt priority level of device, which is almost always the same as the type of **spl** call used; a driver that interlocks using **spl5** almost always has an interrupt priority level of 5.

- **-m** *major_dev_number*

    Major device number of the driver.

- **-M** *maximum minimum*

    Maximum and minimum number of devices that can be specified in the **sdevice** file. Default is a maximum of one and minimum of zero.

- **-m** *major_dev_number*

    Major device number of the driver.

- **-O** With **-a** or **-d**, indicate whether or not the IOA range of the device can overlap that of another device. Default is no.

- **-o** Override flag. When invoked non-interactively, it overrides the minimum and maximum values that are otherwise enforced.

- **-P** With **-a** or **-d**, add or delete an ignore I flag in the device *mdevice* entry. The I flag allows the configuration build utilities to ignore a device's **pack.d** directory driver.

-p   With **-a** or **-d**, add or delete the characteristic that the device is an SCSI peripheral. Default is off.

-q   With **-a** or **-d**, add or delete the characteristic that the device is a SCSI host adapter. Default is off.

-R   With **-a** or **-d**, indicate whether or not the driver is required in the kernel all the time. Default is yes.

-S   With **-a** or **-d**, indicate whether or not the driver has one *sdevice* entry only. Default is no.

-s   When adding or deleting a streams module, use this option with the **-h** option and instead of **-m**, **-b**, and **-c**. For a streams driver, use it with **-m** and **-c**.

-t   Displays nothing except possibly error messages. However, it has a return value of 1 if a driver corresponding to the given combination of **-m**, **-b**, and **-c** options is already configured and 0 if no such driver is present.

-T *interrupt_scheme*
     Type of interrupt scheme the device uses. Default is zero. Possible arguments are:

    0   Device does not require an interrupt line.

    1   Device requires an interrupt line. If the device supports more than one controller, each controller requires a separate interrupt.

    2   Device requires an interrupt line. If the device supports more than one controller, controllers share same interrupt.

    3   Device requires an interrupt line. If the device supports more than one controller, the controllers share the same interrupt.

-U *number_of_subdevices*
     Encode a device-dependent numeric value in the *sdevice* file to indicate the number of subdevices on a controller or pseudo-device.

-V *interrupt_vector*
     Name of the device with the vector conflict.

-v *interrupt_vector* [*interrupt_vector2* . . .]
     Modify system notion of vectors on which this device can interrupt.

-w   When specifying a parameter value, this option works in the same way as **-p**, but suppresses all warning messages when a parameter is set outside current maximum and minimum values.

-X *offset*
     Add (**-a**) or delete (**-d**) an extended minor device number entry from *mdevice*.

-x	Dump all resource prompts known to **configure**. These reveal the name, description, and current value of each parameter capable of being reconfigured.	configure
-Y	With -**a** or -**d**, indicate whether or not to configure a driver into the kernel.	
-y *resource*	Display current value of requested parameter.	
-Z	Indicate that a device can have more than one entry in *mdevice*. Using -**d** with -**Z** removes only the *mdevice* entry; using -**d** without -**Z** removes the *mdevice* entry and the *sdevice* entry.	

---

consoleprint [*file*]

consoleprint

Print **/usr/adm/messages** or any file to a serial printer attached to the printer port of a serial console. **consoleprint** is normally run by a system administrator to get a hardcopy of the system console messages.

/etc/cpd

cpd

TCP/IP command—copy-protection daemon that monitors license usage on the local network. The SCO TCP/IP products register with this service at startup time.

---

cpio *flags* [*options*]

cpio

Copy file archives in from or out to tape or disk, or to another location on the local machine. Each of the three flags -**i**, -**o**, or -**p** accepts different options.

Flags

cpio -**i** [*options*] [*patterns*]

Copy in (extract) files whose names match selected *patterns*. Each pattern can include filename metacharacters from the Bourne shell. (Patterns should be quoted or escaped so they are interpreted by **cpio**, not by the shell.) If no pattern is used, all files are copied in. During extraction, existing files are not overwritten by older versions in the archive (unless -**u** is specified).

cpio -**o** [*options*]

Copy out a list of files whose names are given on the standard input.

cpio -**p** [*options*] *directory*

Copy files to another directory on the same system. Destination pathnames are interpreted relative to the named *directory*.

→

Comparison of valid options

Options available to the -i, -o, and -p flags are shown respectively in the first, second, and third row below. (The – is omitted for clarity.)

```
i: 6   b B c C d E f H I k K   m M   r R s S t u v V
o:   a A   B c C       H       L M O           v V
p:   a         d           l L m       R         u v V
```

Options

-a	Reset access times of input files.
-A	Suppress absolute pathnames.
-b	Swap bytes and half-words. Words are 4 bytes.
-B	Block input or output using a blocksize of 5120 bytes per record (default is 512 bytes per record).
-c	Read or write header information as ASCII characters; useful when source and destination machines are of differing types.
-C *n*	Like B, but blocksize can be any positive integer *n*.
-d	Create directories as needed.
-E *file*	Extract filenames listed in *file* from the archives.
-f	Reverse the sense of copying; copy all files *except* those that match *patterns*.
-I *file*	Read *file* as an input archive.
-k	Skip corrupted file headers and I/O errors.
-K *volumesize*	Specify *volumesize* as size of media volume.
-l	Link files instead of copying.
-L	Follow symbolic links.
-m	Retain previous file modification time.
-M *msg*	Print *msg* when switching media. Use variable %d in the message as a numeric ID for the next medium. -M is valid only with -I or -O.
-O *file*	Direct the output to *file.*
-r	Rename files interactively.
-R *ID*	Reassign file ownership and group information to the user's login *ID* (privileged users only).
-s	Swap bytes.
-S	Swap half-words.
-t	Print a table of contents of the input (create no files). When used with the -v option, resembles output of **ls** -l.
-u	Unconditional copy; old files can overwrite new ones.
-v	Print a list of filenames.

-V   Print a dot for each file read or written (this shows **cpio**
      at work without cluttering the screen).

-6   Process a UNIX 6th Edition archive format file.

Examples

Generate a list of old files using **find**; use list as input to **cpio**:

```
find . -name "*.old" -print | cpio -ocBv\
    > /dev/rst8
```

Restore from a tape drive all files whose name contains **save**
(subdirectories are created if needed):

```
cpio -icdv "save" < /dev/rst8
```

To move a directory tree:

```
find . -depth -print | cpio -padm /mydir
```

/tcb/bin/cps [*option*]

Make specific sytem files consistent with the authentication database. **cps** is used primarily by the crash recovery script to ensure
that files critical to TCB exist and have the correct owner, group,
and access permissions specified in the File Control database. If no
parameters are supplied, pathnames are read from the standard
input. **cps** converts the supplied pathnames to canonical pathnames, enabling them to be looked up in the File Control database.
cps can be used only by superusers.

Option

absolute_pathnames
      Absolute pathnames of directories and files to be
      created. An entry for each component of each path-
      name must be present in the File Control database,
      otherwise a fatal error is returned.

/etc/crash [*options*]

Examine memory image of a live or a crashed system kernel. **crash**
displays the values of system control structures, tables, and other
pertinent information.

Options

-d *dumpfile*
      File containing the system memory image. Default is
      /dev/mem.

-n *namelist*
      Text file containing the symbol table for symbolic
      access to the memory image. Default is **/unix**.

-w *outputfile*
      File for crash output. Default is the standard output.

→

Commands

? [-w *filename*]
> List available commands.

!command
> Escape to the shell to execute a command.

adv [-ep] [-w *filename*] [*table_entry*] ...
> Print the advertise table.

base [-w *filename*] *number* ...
> Print number in binary, octal, decimal, and hexadecimal.

buffer [-w *filename*] [*–format*] *bufferslot*

buffer [-p] [-w *filename*] [*–format*] *start_addr*
> Alias: **b**. Print the contents of a buffer in the designated format. The following format designations are recognized: -b, byte; -c, character; -d, decimal; -x, hexadecimal; -o, octal; -r, directory; and -i, inode. If no format is given, the previous format is used. The default format at the beginning of a crash session is hexadecimal.

bufhdr [-fp] [-w *filename*] [*table_entry*] ...
> Alias: **buf**. Print system buffer headers.

callout [-w *filename*]
> Alias: **c**. Print the callout table.

dballoc [-w *file*][*class* ...]
> Print dballoc table.

dbfree [-w *filename*]
> Print free streams data block headers.

dblock [-ep] [-w *filename*] [*dblk_addr*] ...
> Print allocated streams data block headers.

defproc [-c] [-w *filename*]

defproc [-w *filename*] [*slot*]
> Set the value of the process slot argument.

ds [-w *filename*] *virtual_address* ...
> Print the data symbol whose address is closest to, but not greater than, the address entered.

file [-ep] [-w filename] [*table_entry*] ...
> Alias: **f**. Print the file table.

findaddr [-w *filename*] *tableslot*
> Print the address of *slot* in *table*.

findslot [-w *filename*] *virtual_address*
> Print table, entry slot number, and offset for the address entered.

fs [-w *filename*] *table_entry*
> Print filesystem information table.

gdp [-dfp] [-w *filename*] *table_entry*
> Print the gift descriptor protocol table.

gdt [-e] [-w *filename*] [-p] *table_entry*
    Print global descriptor table.

help [-w *filename*] command ...
    Print a description of the named command, including
    syntax and aliases.

crash

---

custom [*options*]

custom

Install software products and components. **custom** is executable
only by the superuser and is either interactive (enter **custom** at the
command line) or can be invoked from the command line with
several options.

Syntax

    custom [-od] [-abilrv [*package*]] [-s *set*] [-m *device*] [-f[*file*]]

Three arguments are required for a completely non-interactive
use of **custom**:

1. A set identifier: -o or -d. Only one of -o or -d may be
   specified.
2. A command: -i, -r, -l, -f, -a, -v, -b, -s. Only one of these
   commands may be specified, followed by an argument of
   the appropriate type (one or more package names, or a
   filename).
3. Either one or more package names, or a filename.

Options

    -a   Add a new product.

    -b   Enforce product dependencies specified in the bundle
           file for bundled products.

    -d   Development system

    -f   Install specified file.

    -i   Install specified package(s).

    -l   List files in specified package(s).

    -m   Specify media device. Default is **/dev/rinstall**.

    -o   Operating System

    -r   Remove specified package(s).

    -s *set* Install a specified *set*—a collection of packages listed in
           a **permsfile** entry for a product.

    -v   Verbose output for installing and removing packages.

/usr/mmdf/table/dbmbuild [*options*] [*database* [*table* ...]]

dbmbuild

Rebuild MMDF hashed database. Whenever you change MMDF alias
or routing information, rebuild the hashed database by logging in
as **mmdf** and running **dbmbuild** from the **/usr/mmkf/table** directory.
If no database file is specified, the default database **mmdfdbm** is
used. If no table files are specified, all tables listed in the tailor file

$\rightarrow$

are used. **dbmbuild** must be run as "usr mmdf" or the build will not work.

Options

-d   Run in debug mode.

-k   Keep going. If a file is mentioned that does not exist, ignore it.

-n   Create new database. If this option is omitted, **dbmbuild** updates an existing database. If no options are specified, -n is assumed; however, if you give any options, you must specify the -n option if you want to create a new database.

-v   Run in verbose mode.

dbmedit

/usr/mmdf/table/dbmedit [*options*] [*cmd* ...]

Edit MMDF database file.

Options

-d*database*
         Specify alternate database. Default is given by the **tbldbm** configuration variable or by the MDBM **usr/mmdf/mmdftailor** variable.

-v   Get verbose description of program's activities.

Commands

If no arguments are given, **dbmedit** goes into interactive mode, prompting user for each command. Otherwise, arguments are taken as one command. Commands in **dbmedit** refer to keys, tables, and values. Tables are hashed into the database using **dbmbuild**. Keys appear on the left side of the tables and values on the right side. The command lines in interactive mode are parsed using standard MMDF string-to-argument routines, so the same quoting and escape conventions apply. All commands may be shortened to their first character only. The commands are:

add<key> *table value*
         Add key/table entry with the given value.

change<key> *table* [*old value*] *newvalue*
         Change value of specifed key/table pair to *newvalue*. If *oldvalue* is specified, change the entry matching that value. Otherwise, change the value of the first occurrence or add a new key/table pair if none already exists.

delete<key> [*table* [*value*]]
         Delete values for specified key. If a table is specified, delete only values for specified key/table pair. If a value is also specified, delete only entries for the pair with that value.

print<key> [*table*]	**dbmedit**

Print value of key/table pair. If table is omitted, print value of any table entry with this key.

help   Give brief summary of commands.

quit   Exit program.

/etc/dcopy [*options*] *inputfs outputfs*	**dcopy**

Copy UNIX filesystems for optimal access time. **dcopy** copies *inputfs*, the device file for the existing filesystem, to *outputfs*, the device file to hold the reorganized result. This utility is for UNIX filesystems only. For the most effective optimization, *inputfs* should be the raw device and *outputfs* the block device. Both should be unmounted filesystems. With no options, **dcopy** copies files from *inputfs*, compressing directories by removing vacant entries and spacing consecutive blocks in a file by the optimal rotational gap. To terminate **dcopy**, send a quit signal, followed by an interrupt or quit.

Options

-a*n*   Place files not accessed in *n* days after the free blocks of the destination file system (default is 7 days).

-d   Leave order of directory entries as is (default is to move subdirectories to beginning of directories).

-f*fsize* [:*isize*]

Specify *outputfs* filesystem and inode list sizes. If this option, or :*isize*, is not given, values from *inputfs* are used.

-s*X*   Supply device information for creating an optimal organization of blocks in a file. Forms of *X* are same as -s option of **fsck**.

-v   Currently report how many files were processed and size of source and destination freelists.

---

deassign [*options*] [*device*]	**deassign**

Deassign devices: either *device*, or, if no arguments are given, all devices assigned to the user.

Options

-u   Suppress deassignment but perform error checking.

-v   Give verbose output.

/usr/mmdf/bin/deliver [*options*] [*message1 ... messageN*]	**deliver**

MMDF mail delivery process. **deliver** handles management of all mail delivery under the MMDF mail system. It does not deliver mail directly, rather it calls on MMDF channels to handle actual delivery. **deliver**'s actions are guided by the MMDF tailoring file,

→

deliver ←	/usr/mmdf/mmdftailor, and by the command-line options. It can run as either a deamon or a user-invoked program.

Options

    -b   Background mode—cause **deliver** to run as a background daemon, making periodic sweeps over the mail queues looking for undelivered mail and attempting delivery.

    -c_channel1,channel2_...
        Comma-separated list of channels to be processed.

    -d   Causes **deliver** to assume it is already in the mail queue—do not issue an explicit **chdir**. This is useful if you wish to have **deliver** operate on an alternate mail queue hierarchy, mainly for testing.

    -L_logfile_
        Set logfile to _logfile_. Default is to log into the file **msg.log** in the MMDF log directory. This option is available only to the superuser and MMDF.

    -l_minutes_
        Set time-to-live, in minutes, for entries in the dead-host cache. Time defaults to two hours.

    -m_maxsort_
        Set sort threshold. If there are more than _maxsort_ messages in a given channel's queue, they are processed in directory order without first sorting by submission time. If this option is not specified, the value of _maxsort_ is given in the tailor file by **MMAXSORT**.

    -p   Pickup-only mode. Indicates that invoker would like to pickup a passive mail channel.

    -s   Force linear search of mail queue.

    -T_seconds_
        Set sleep time between background sweeps of the mail queue. Default is 10 seconds.

    -t_hrs_   Prevent **deliver** from attempting to deliver messages that have been in the queue for more than _hrs_ hours. This option only applies when the queue is being sorted.

    -w   Watch delivery. Print informative messages on the standard output while attempting delivery.

    -V_loglevel_
        Set logging level to the level specified. _loglevel_ should be a valid MMDF logging-level string, such as FTR. This option is only available to the superuser and MMDF.

devnm	**/etc/devnm/** [_names_]

Identify device name, the special file associated with the mounted filesystem where _name_ resides. This command is most commonly used by the **/etc/rc2** scripts to construct a mount table entry for the _root_ device.

Example

Be sure to type full pathnames in this example: If **/dev/hd1** is mounted on **/u**:

```
/etc/devnm /u
```

produces:

```
/dev/hd1 /u
```

/etc/dfsck [*options1*] *filesys1* ... −[*options2*] *filesys2* ...

Check and repair filesystems. **dfsck** allows two filesystem checks on two different drives simultaneously. *options1* and *options2* are passed to **fsck** for the two sets of filesystems. A dash is the separator between filesystem groups. **dfsck** displays the filesystem name for each message to the operator. When answering a question from **dfsck**, the operator must preface the response with a **1** or a **2**, indicating that the answer refers to the first or second filesystem group. Do not use **dfsck** to check the *root* filesystem.

Options

For options, see the listing for the **fsck** command.

/usr/lib/uucp/dialX *ttyname telno speed*
/usr/lib/uucp/dialX **−h** [**−c**] *ttyname speed*
/usr/lib/uucp/uuchat *ttyname speed chat-script*

Dial a modem. **dial**X dials a modem attached to *ttyname*. X is a dialer name, such as "HA1200." **uucico** invokes **dial** with a *ttyname*, *telno* (telephone number), and *speed*. **dial** attempts to dial the phone number on the specified line at the given speed. When using **dialHA12** or **dialHA24**, *speed* can be a range of baud rates. The range is specified with the form: *lowrate–highrate*, where *lowrate* is the minimum acceptable connection baud rate and *highrate* is the maximum. The **dial** program to be used on a particular line is specified in the fifth field of the entry for that line in **/usr/lib/uucp/Devices**. If there is no **dial** program of that name, then **uucico**, **ct**, and **cu** use a built-in dialer, together with the chat-script of that name, in **/usr/lib/uucp/Dialers**.

Options

−c   Tell dialer to wait for a connection and adjust the line rate to match before returning.

−h   Hang up the modem.

Dialer programs

Several dialer programs are provided. Source for these is provided in their respective .c files.

Binary File	Modem
dialHA12	Hayes Smartmodem 1200 or compatible
dialHA24	Hayes Smartmodem 2400 or compatible
dialHA96V	Hayes Smartmodem 9600 or compatible
dialMUL	Multitech Multimodem 224 EH
dialVA3450	Racal Badic 3451 modem
dialVA96	Racal Badic 9600 modem
dialTBIT	Telebit Trailblazer Modem

dial

←

Return codes

dial returns the status of the attempt through the following **dial** return codes:

bit 0x80 = 1
> Connection attempt failed.

bits 0x0f = *n*
> If bit 0x80 is a 1, the following bits are the dialer error code *n*:

0	General or unknown error code
1	Line being used
2	A signal has aborted the dialer
3	Dialer arguments are invalid
4	Phone number is invalid
5	Baud rate is invalid or dialer could not connect at requested baud rate
6	Can't open the line
7	ioctl error on the line
8	Timeout waiting for connection
9	No dial tone detected.
10	Unused
11	Unused
12	Unused
13	Phone is busy.
14	No carrier is detected.
15	Remote system did not answer.

> Error codes 12-15 indicate that the problem is at the remote end.

dig

dig [*options*]

TCP/IP command—Domain Information Groper. **dig** can be used to gather information from the DNS servers. It has two modes: a simple interactive mode that makes a single query and a batch mode that executes a query for each in a list of several query lines.

Options

> % *ignored_comment*
>> Include an argument that should not be parsed.

<-*dig_option*>

> Options affecting the operation of **dig**. The following are currently available:
>
> -c *query-class*
>> Specify class of query: either an integer value to be included in the class field, or use the abbreviated mnemonic (**in = C_IN**).
>
> -envsav
>> Save **dig** environment, after all arguments are parsed, to a file to become the default environment. If the shell environment variable **LOCAL-DEF** is set to the name of a file, this is where the default **dig** environment will be saved. If not, the file **DiG.env** will be created in the current working directory.
>
> -f *file*
>> File for **dig** batch mode that contains a list of query specifications to be executed sequentially. Lines beginning with colons (;), commas (,), hash marks (#), or backslash n (\n) are ignored.
>
> -P *ping-string*
>> After query returns, execute a **ping** command for a response-time comparison.
>
> -p *port*
>> Port number: query a name server listening to a non-standard Port number. Default is 53.
>
> -T *time*
>> Time in seconds between start of successive queries when running in batch mode. Default is zero.
>
> -t *query-type*
>> Specify type of query: either an integer value to be included in the type field, or use the abbreviated mnemonic (**mx = T_MX**).
>
> -x *dot-notation-address*
>> A convenient form to specify inverse address mapping.

domain

> Domain name for which information is requested.

server

> Specify either a domain name or a dot-notation Internet address. Default is the default name server for your machine.

<*query-type*>

> Type of information requested. Default is **a**. The following types will be recognized (see RFC 1035 for the complete list):

a	T_A	Network address
any	T_ANY	All/any information about specified domain
mx	T_MX	Mail exchanger from the domain
ns	T_NS	Name servers

dig			
←	soa	T_SOA	Zone of authority record
	hinfo	T_HINFO	Host information
	axfr	T_AXFR	Zone transfer
	txt	T_TXT	Arbitrary number of strings

<query-class>
    Network class requested in query. Default is **in**. The fol-
    lowing classes are recognized (see RFC 1035 for the com-
    plete list):

in	C_IN	Internet class domain
any	C_ANY	All/any class information

+*<query-option>*
    Use **+** to specify an option to be changed in the query
    packet or to change some **dig** output specifics. If an option
    requires a parameter, the format will be:

        +*keyword*[=*value*]

---

disable

disable *tty* . . .
disable [*options*] *printers*

Turn off terminals and printers, respectively. For terminals, manipulate the **/etc/conf/cf.d/init.base** file and signal **init** to disallow
logins on a particular terminal. For printers, stop print requests
from being sent to *printer*.

Options

   -c   Cancel any requests currently printing.

   -r[*reason*]
    Associate a *reason* with disabling the printer. *reason*
    applies to all printers listed up to next -r option.

   -W   Disable *printers* when print requests currently printing
    have finished.

Examples

A printer named *linepr* is disabled because of a paper jam:

```
disable -r"paper jam" linepr
```

---

diskusg

/usr/lib/acct/diskusg [*options*] [*files*]

Generate disk accounting data by user ID from data in *files*, or standard input, if no *files* are indicated.

The output of **diskusg** is normally the input to **acctdisk**, which generates total accounting records that can be merged with other
accounting records. **diskusg** is normally run in **dodisk**.

-i*fnmlist*   Ignore data on filesystems whose filesystem name is in *fnmlist*, a list of filesystem names separated by commas or enclosed within quotes. **diskusg** compares each name in this list with the filesystem name stored in the volume ID.

-p*file*   Use *file* as the name of the password file to generate login names. Default is **/etc/passwd**.

-s   Input data is already in **diskusg** output format (all lines for a single user combined into a single line).

-u*file*   Write records to *file* of files that are charged to no one. Records consist of the special filename, inode number, and user ID.

-v   Verbose. Print a list on standard error of all files charged to no one.

Example

The following will generate daily disk accounting information:

```
for i in /dev/dsk/0s1 /dev/dks/0s3; do
    diskusg $i > dtmp. `basename $i` &
done
wait
diskusg -s dtmp.* | sort +0n +1 | acctdisk > disktacct
```

displaypkg

Display installed packages—list the names of all the AT&T-style UNIX packages that were installed using the **installpkg** command.

divvy [*options*] [*device*]

Disk dividing utility. **divvy** divides an **fdisk** partition into a number of divisions, identified by unique major and minor device numbers, and used for a filesystem, swap area, or for isolating bad spots on the device. You can specify a *device* on the command line; default *device* is **/dev/hd0a**. When **divvy** is invoked from the command line, you see a main menu with a list of commands to choose from. Besides dividing disks, you can use **divvy** to create new filesystems, change the size of filesystems, or remove filesystems.

Options

-C *#1 #2 #3*

    Create division number *#1* starting at block number *#2* and ending at block number *#3*.

-D *#*   Delete division number *#*.

-i   Installation only. Disk being divided will contain a **root** filesystem on division 0. Only to be done from a non-active partition on the root floppy.

→

divvy ←	-m	Make disk being divided into a number of mountable filesystems.
	-n	Non-interactive installation; automatic option. Disk being divided will contain the following: **root** filesystem on division 0; **swap** on division 1; **/u** filesystem on division 2; and **scratch** on division 5.
	-P #	Print start block number and end block number of division number # (or all divisions, if # is missing).

dkinit

dkinit [*device*]

dkinit provides a menu-driven frontend to the **dparam** command, which displays or changes the hard disk characteristics currently in effect.

dlvr_audit

/etc/auth/dlvr_audit [*option*] *tstamp event record pid cmd*

Produce audit records for subsystem events. **dlvr_audit** sends the data over a message queue to the audit daemon, which appends the record to the audit trail. *tstamp* is the time in seconds past Jan 1, 1970 that the audit record was produced; *event* is the number of the event type as described in **sys/audit.h**; *record* is the audit record format type as described in **sys/audit.h**; *pid* is the process ID of the event process; *cmd* is the name of the protected subsystem command; and *code* is specific to the *event* type being generated.

Option

    -v   Force program to report all of its actions. Normally, this is not used, so audit records can be made without the knowledge of the program user.

dmesg

dmesg [-]

Display the system messages on the console.

Option

    -    Display only messages generated since the last time **dmesg** was performed. **dmesg** is included for backward compatibility only. The device **/dev/error** is recommended instead.

domainname

domainname [*name*]

NFS/NIS command—set or display name of current NIS domain. With no argument, **domainname** dislays the name of the current NIS domain. Only the superuser can set the domainname by giving an argument; this is usually done in the startup script **/etc/nfs**.

dparam [*option*]
dparam/dev/rhd [0 | 1] 0 [*characteristics*]

Display/change hard disk characteristics currently in effect.

Option

-w   Copy **/etc/masterboot** to disk to ensure that nonstandard hard disks are supported for the specified drive.

When writing characteristics for the specified hard disk, **dparam** changes the current disk controller status and updates the masterboot block. The argument ordering is critical and must be entered as specified below. In respective order, hard disk characteristics are:

Characteristics

number of cylinders
Total number of cylinders on the hard disk.

number of heads
Number of heads.

reduced write current cylinder
Hardware-specific; consult your hardware manual.

write precompensation cylinder
Hardware-specific; consult your hardware manual.

ecc   Number of bits of error correction on I/O transfers; consult your hardware manual.

control
Hardware-specific; consult your hardware manual.

landing zone cylinder
Where to park heads after shutting down system

number of sectors per track
Number of sectors per track on hard disk

/etc/ecc [*options*]

Add/delete entries from the bad-page table. The Memory Error Correction Code (ECC) utilities periodically check RAM for single and double-bit errors to increase data integrity. ECC errors are reported via the system console and **/usr/adm/messages** and are mapped and stored in a bad page table using **ecc**. This utility works only with Corollary smp RAM and compatibles.

eccd is the ECC daemon, or background program.

/etc/eisa [*slots* | *option*]

Report on boards installed on the EISA bus. By default, **eisa** reports on the motherboard and 15 slots. You can specify a number of *slots* for which you want a report. **eisa** reports only EISA boards installed on an EISA system, not the 8- or 16-bit ISA (XT/AT) boards. Only root can execute this command. Return values are: 0 indicates

$\rightarrow$

eisa ←	success, 1 indicates a command-line error, 2 indicates motherboard was not located, greater than 2 indicates an unspecified error. **Option** H, h To get usage information if you do not specify slot information.
fdswap	**fdswap** [*options*] Swap default boot floppy drive—tell the CMOS to swap the default floppy drive used to read boot information at boot time. With no arguments, **fdswap** reports the current **fdswap** state, on or off. Change takes effect at next system boot. Note: **fdswap** requires BIOS support that exists in only a few machines. **Options** on Change default drive setting. off Switch drive setting back to default.
ff	**/etc/ff** [*options*] *special* List filenames and statistics for a filesystem. **ff** reads the i-list and directories of the *special* file, assuming it is a filesystem. Inode data are saved for each file that matches selection criteria. Output consists of the pathname for each saved inode plus other file information requested by the options listed below. Output fields are positional and separated by tabs. The default line produced by **ff** is: *pathname i-number* With all options enabled, the output would be: *pathname i-number size uid* **Options** The argument *n* in the following options is used as a decimal integer, where +*n* means more than *n* and –*n* means less than *n*. A day is defined as a 24-hour period. -a*n* Select if inode has been accessed in *n* days. -c*n* Select if inode has been changed in *n* days. -i*inode–list* Generate names for only those inodes specified in *inode-list.* -I Do not print inode number after each filename. -l Generate supplementary list of all pathnames for multiple-linked files. -m*n* Select if inode has been modified in *n* days. -n*file* Select if inode has been modified more recently than the argument *file.*

> -p*prefix*
>> *prefix* will be added to each generated pathname. Default is . (dot).
>
> -s   Print file size, in bytes, after each pathname.
> -u   Print owner's login name after each pathname.

/etc/fingerd

TCP/IP command—remote user information server. **fingerd** provides a network interface to the **finger** program. It listens for TCP connections on the **finger** port, and, for each connection, reads a single input line, passes the line to **finger**, and copies the output of **finger** to the user on the client machine. **fingerd** is started by **inetd**, and must have an entry in **inetd**'s configuration file, **/etc/inetd.conf**.

---

fixhdr *options files*

Change header of output files created by link editors or assemblers. Modifications include changing the format of the header, fixed stack size, standalone load address, and symbol names. **fixhdr** takes one option at a time. To make more than one modification to a file, use **fixhdr** on the original, then use it again on the **fixhdr** output, specifying the next option.

Options

> -5x [-n]
>> Change 5.2 (UNIX System V Release 2) **a.out** format of header to **x.out** format. -n causes leading underscores on symbol names to be passed with no modifications.
>
> -86x   Add **x.out** header format to **86rel** object module format.
> -A *num*
>> Add or change standalone load addresss specified in **x.out** format of header. *num* must be a hexadecimal number.
>
> -ax -c [11,86]
>> Change **a.out** format of header to **x.out** format. -c specifies the target CPU; **11** specifies a PDP-11 CPU; **86** specifies one of the 8086 family of CPUs.
>
> -bx   Change **b.out** format of header to **x.out** format.
> -C *cpu*
>> Set CPU type.
>
> -F *num*
>> Add or change fixed stack size specified in **x.out** format of header. *num* must be a hexadecimal number.
>
> -M[smlh]
>> Change model of **x.out** or **86rel** format. Model refers to compiler model specified when creating binary; **s** for small model, **m** for medium model, **l** for large model, **h** for huge model.

→

fixhdr
←
	-r Ensure that resolution table is non-zero size.
	
	-s *s1=s2* [-s *s3=s4*]
	     Change symbol names, where symbol name of *s1* is changed to *s2*.
	
	-v [2,3,5,7]
	     Change version of XENIX specified in header. XENIX Version 2 was based on UNIX Version 7.

---

fixmog

/tcb/bin/fixmog [*options*]

Make all system files consistent with authentication database. **fixmog** attemts to correct inconsistencies found by the **integrity** command by changing the owner, group, and access permissions of files to those in the File Control database. **fixmog** can only be used by superusers.

Options

-i   Interactive option. **fixmog** requrests confirmation before making changes. -i overrides -v.

-v   Verbose option. **fixmog** displays a line detailing each change made.

---

fixperm

/etc/fixperm [*options*] *specfile*

Correct or initialize file permissions and ownership. For each line in the specification file *specfile*, **fixperm** makes the listed pathname conform to a specification. It can be invoked only by a superuser and works only from the root directory.

Options

-a   Ensure that all files specified in the list exist on the hard disk.

-C   Compress all types of files that have the additional C permission specification.

-c   Create empty files and missing directories. Also create (or modify) device files.

-D   List directories only on standard output.

-d *pkg* Process input lines beginning with given package specifier string.

-f   List files only on standard output. Do not modify target files.

-g   List devices as specified in permlist. No changes are made as a result of this flag.

-i   Available from a program or shell script only. Check only if the selected packages are installed. Return values are:
     0:     Package completely installed
     3:     Not found

4:     Package not installed
5:     Package partially installed

- **-L**   List files on standard output, but any compressed files are printed with .Z suffix.

- **-l**   List files and directories on standard output.

- **-n**   Report errors only. Do not make any changes.

- **-O**   Omit link names from lists when used with the following list options: **-D, -f, -l, -L,** or **-w**.

- **-p**   Override default uid/gid found in **/etc/passwd** and **etc/group** with the value found in the permlist.

- **-S**   Issue a complaint if files are not in **x.out** format.

- **-s**   Modify special device files in addition to the rest of the permlist.

- **-U**   Uncompress all types of files that have the additional **C** permission specification.

- **-u** *pkg*   Like **-d**, but processes items that are not part of the given package.

- **-v**   Verbose—in particular, issues a complaint if executable files are word-swapped, not fixed stack, not separate I and D, or not stripped.

- **-w**   Lists where (what volume) the specified files or directories are located.

- **-X**   Print only files and/or directories not installed.

---

fsave *filesystem* [*dumpinfo*] [*mediainfo*] [*sitename*]

Interactive, error-checking *filesystem* backup. **fsave** is used by **fsphoto** to provide a semi-automated interface to **xbackup** and **cpio** for backing up filesystems. **fsave** can be executed only by the superuser.

Arguments

dumpinfo

Set of blank-separated strings that give optional information about backup:

dumplevel size savetime importance marker

Each of these strings may be quoted and can thus contain spaces.

dumplevel

Level of dump to be performed—single digit from 0 to 9, or the letter *x*, which means no backup to be done.

size   Size of media volumes to be used—feet for tapes and kilobytes for floppies. Default is -, which means first size listed in *mediainfo*.

savetime

How long backup is to be saved. Default is 1 year.

→

importance

How important is backup? For example, **critical** or **precautionary**. Those which are **critical** have their format checked by **xdumpdir**. Default is important.

marker

Either **none** (default) or an additional label you wish to place on each volume.

mediainfo

Set of blank-separated strings giving optional information about media to be used:

drive **d** *density sizes*... [*format*]
drive **k** *sizes*... [*format*]

drive Name of backup device to use. Default is **/dev/rmt0**.

k *sizes*

If **k** specified, *drive* is assumed to be a floppy, and the list of *sizes* that follows defines the allowable capacities of the floppies that can be used.

d *density sizes*

Otherwise, **d** must be specified. In this case, *drive* is assumed to be a magtape at *density* BPI, in one of the possible *sizes*

format

Command used to format the tape or floppy described.

sitename

Where backup was made. Note that the **uucp** nodename from **/etc/systemid** is automatically placed on the volume labels.

---

fsck

/etc/fsck [*options*] [*filesystem*] ...

Check and repair filesystems. If a filesystem is consistent, the number of files, number of blocks used, and number of blocks free are reported. If a filesystem is inconsistent, the operator **fsck** prompts for concurrence before each correction is attempted. If no *filesystem* is specified, **fsck** reads a list of default filesystems from the file **/etc/checklist**.

Options

-a   (Autoboot). Examine FSCKFIX flag in **/etc/default/boot**. If FSCKFIX is set to YES, **fsck** behaves as if it had been called with the -y flag.

-b   Reboot (S51K and AFS filesystems only.)

-C[*clustersize*]

(S51K filesystem only.) Convert named S51K filesystem into an AFS (Acer Fast Filesystem.) -s option must also be present. *clustersize* must be a power of 2 and less than 16 (recommended value 8).

-D   Check directories for bad blocks.

-E   Convert named AFS filesystem to EAFS (Extended Acer Fast Filesystem), which includes support for long filenames and symbolic links. Can be combined with -C option to convert an S52K filesystem to EAFS.

-f   Fast check. Check block and sizes (Phase 1) and check free list (Phase 5). Free list will be reconstructed (Phase 6) if necessary.

-n   Assume a *no* response to all questions asked by **fsck**.

-q   Quiet **fsck**. Do not print size-check messages in Phase 1. Unreferenced FIFO files will selectively be removed.

-rr   Recover root filesystem (XENIX filesystems only). -rr implies -y and overrides -n.

-sb:c

      Ignore actual free list and unconditionally reconstruct a new one by rewriting the super-block of the filesystem. Filesystem must be unmounted while this is done.

-S   Conditionally reconstruct the free list. This option forces a *no* response to all questions asked by **fsck**.

-t   If **fsck** cannot obtain enough memory to keep its tables, it uses a scratch file. -t specifies the file named in the next argument as this scratch file. Make sure you leave a space between -t and the filename, or **fsck** will use the entire filesystem as a scratch file and erase the entire disk.

-y   Assume a *yes* response to all questions asked by **fsck**.

/etc/fsdb *special* [*option*]

Filesystem debugger. **fsdb** can be used to patch up a damaged filesystem after a crash. *special* is filesystem to debug. **fsdb** has conversions to translate block and inumbers into their corresponding disk addresses. Also included are mnemonic offsets to access different parts of an inode. **fsdb** reads a block at a time and will therefore work with raw as well as block I/O. Should be used only on unmounted filesystems.

Option

-     Disable error-checking routines.

Symbols recognized by fsdb

#	Absolute address
!	Escape to shell.
,	General print facilities
+, -	Address arithmetic
>, <	Save, restore an address.
=	Numerical assignment
=+	Incremental assignment
=-	Decremental assignment
=	Character string assignment
B	Byte mode

→

fsdb	b	Convert to block address.
←	D	Double word mode
	d	Directory slot offset
	f	File print facility
	i	Convert from inumber to inode address.
	O	Error-checking flip-flop
	p	General print facilities
	q	Quit.
	W	Word mode

Print options

b	Print as octal bytes.
c	Print as characters.
d	Print as directories.
e	Print as decimal short words.
i	Print as inodes.
o	Print as octal short words.
x	Print as hexadecimal short words.

Mnemonics

The following mnemonics are used for inode examination and refer to the current working inode:

a#	Data block numbers (0-12)
at	Access time
gid	Group ID number
ln	Link count
maj	Major device number
md	Mode
min	Minor device number
mt	Modification time
sz	Filesize
uid	User ID number

Examples

386i	Prints inumber 386 in an inode format. This now becomes the current working inode.
ln=4	Changes the link count for the working inode to 4.
ln+1	Increments the link count by one.
fc	Prints, in ASCII, block zero of the file associated with the working inode.

512B.p0x

Prints superblock of filesystem in hexadecimal.

2i.a0b.p3d

Prints first three entries in the root directory.

2i.a0b.d7=3

Changes the inumber for the seventh directory slot in the root directory to 3.

/etc/fsname [*options*] /dev/device

fsname

Print or change the name of a filesystem (XENIX filesystems only).
Default is to print the name of the filesystem.

Options

-p   Select "pack" name field instead of the filesystem name
        field.

-s *name*
        Change specified field in the superblock.

fsphoto [*options*] schedule [*drive*]

fsphoto

Perform periodic semi-automated system backups. **fsphoto** interprets *schedule*, and the database describing which filesystems are to
be backed up when, and at what dump level for each filesystem to
be backed up that day, runs **fsave** to interact with the operator and
backup the filesystem without error. **fsphoto** can be executed only
by superusers and is invoked most easily from the **sysadmsh**.

Options

drive   Magtape or floppy to use; default is specified in *sched-
         ule*.

-i   Ignore any pending partial backups.

/etc/fsstat special_file

fsstat

Report status of the filesystem on *special_file*. During startup, **fsstat**
determines if the filesystem needs checking before it is mounted.
fsstat succeeds if the filesystem is unmounted and appears okay.

/etc/fstyp *device*

fstyp

Determine filesystem identifier. **fstyp** runs the programs in
/etc/fscmd.d/TYPE in alphabetical order, passing *device* as an argument; if any program succeeds, its filesystem type identifier is
printed, and **fstyp** exits immediately. If no program succeeds, **fstyp**
prints:

```
Unknown_fstyp
```

to indicate failure.

/etc/ftpd [*options*]

ftpd

TCP/IP command—DARPA Internet File Transfer Protocol server.
The server uses the TCP protocol and listens at the port specified
in the **ftp** service specification. **ftpd** is started by **inetd**, and must
have an entry in **inetd**'s configuration file, /etc/inetd.conf.

$\rightarrow$

**System Admin.
Commands**

ftpd ←	**Options**
	
	-d Write debugging information to the syslog.
	
	-l Log each FTP session in the syslog.
	
	-T *maxtimeout*
	         Set maximum timeout period. Default limit is two hours.
	
	-t*timeout*
	         Set timeout period to *timeout* seconds.
	
	-u*mask*
	         Set file creation mask to *mask.*
	
	-v Debugging information is written to the standard output.

fuser	**/etc/fuser** [*options*] *files* | *filesystems* Identify processes that are using a file or filesystem. **fuser** outputs the process IDs of the processes that are using the *files* or local *filesystems.* Each process ID is followed by a letter code: **c** if process is using file as current directory, **p** if parent of current directory, and **r** if root directory. Any user with permission to read **/dev/kmem** and **/dev/mem** can use **fuser**, but only the superuser can terminate another user's process. **fuser** does not work on remote (NFS) files. If more than one group of files is specified, the options may be respecified for each additional group of files. A lone dash (–) cancels the options currently in force, and the new set of options applies to the next group of files. **Options** -k SIGKILL signal sent to each process. -u User login name, in parentheses, also follows process ID.
fwtmp	**/usr/lib/acct/fwtmp** [*option*] Convert binary records of the type found in **wtmp** to formatted ASCII records. **fwtmp** reads from the standard input and writes to the standard output. **Option** -ic Input is in ASCII form, and output is to be written in binary form.
gated	**gated** [*options*] TCP/IP command—gateway routing daemon. **gated** handles multiple routing protocols and replaces **routed** and any routing daemons

that speak the HELLO, EGP, or BGP routing protocols. **gated** currently handles the RIP, BGP, EGP, and HELLO routing protocols, and can be configured to perform all or any combination of the four.

Options

-c   Parse configuration file for syntax errors, then exit **gated**, leaving a dump file in **/usr/tmp/gated_dump**.

-f<*config_file*>
     Use alternate configuration file, *config_file*. Default is **/etc/gated.conf**.

-n   Do not modify kernel's routing table.

-t<*trace_options*>
     Trace flags to be enabled on startup. If no flags specified, **ier** is assumed, and the **-t** option must be followed by another switch to avoid the *trace_file* name from being parsed as flags. The trace flags are:

A	All
B	BGP
C	**icmp**
e	External
H	Hello
i	Internal
J	Job
k	Kernel
m	Mark
P	Protocol
p	EGP
R	RIP
r	Route
t	Nostamp
u	Update

getid *arguments*

TCP/IP command—retrieve system MIB variables from an SNMP entity. **getid** is an SNMP application that retrieves the variables **sysDescr.0**, **sysObjectID.0**, and **sysUpTime.0** from an SNMP entity. The primary purpose of this application is to illustrate the use of the SNMP library routines.

Arguments

entity_addr
     SNMP entity's address

community_string
     Community string needed for access to the SNMP entity

getmany	**getmany** *arguments*
	TCP/IP command—retrieve classes of variables from an SNMP entity.
	Arguments
	entity_addr
	Address of SNMP entity
	community_string
	Community string for access to SNMP entity
	variable_class_name
	Variable class name(s), expressed as an object identifier in either dot notation or as the MIB-variable from the MIB document.
getnext	**getnext** *arguments*
	TCP/IP command—retrieve variables from an SNMP entity using a **GET-NEXT** request.
	Arguments
	entity_add
	Address of SNMP entity
	community_string
	Community string for access to the SNMP entity
	variable_name
	Variable name(s) expressed as either dot notation or the variable name as it appears in the MIB document
getone	**getone** *arguments*
	TCP/IP command—retrieve variables from an SNMP entity using a **GET** request.
	Arguments
	entity_add
	Address of SNMP entity
	community_string
	Community string for access to the SNMP entity
	variable_name
	Variable name(s) expressed as either dot notation or the variable name as it appears in the MIB document
getroute	**getroute** *arguments*
	TCP/IP command—extract routing information from an SNMP entity by traversing the **ipRouteDest**, **ipRouteIfIndex**, **ipRouteMetric1**, **ipRouteNextHop**, **ipRouteType**, and **ipRouteProto** variable classes for each route found.

  entity_add

    Address of SNMP entity

  community_string

    Community string for access to the SNMP entity

/etc/gettable [*option*] *host* [*outfile*]

TCP/IP command—get NIC format host tables from *host*. The tables, if retrieved, are placed in the file *outfile* or, by default, **hosts.txt**. **gettable** operates by opening a TCP connection to the port indicated in the service specification for *host*. **gettable** is best used in conjunction with the **htable** program, which converts the NIC standard file format to that used by the network library lookup routines.

Option

 -v Get just the version number instead of the complete host table.

---

goodpw [*options*]

Check passwords for non-obviousness. **goodpw** reads a proposed password from the standard input and applies a variety of checks intended to spot poor password choices.

Options

 -a Use American spelling (default).

 -b Use British spelling.

 -d *file* Read *file* (which should be in same format as /etc/default/goodpw) and apply various checks specified.

 -M*expr*

    Password must match *expr*, a boolean combination of regular expressions. If first character of *expr* is a slash (/), and a regular file by that name exists, the contents of that file are used as the expression.

 -m Stop list terminates with an empty line, one line is written to the standard output indicating the acceptance or rejection of the password, and entire procedure is repeated using a new password and stop list read from standard input.

 -R*expr* Password must not match *expr*.

→

goodpw ←	-r *reason* Specify message to be issued in case proposed password matches one in the stop list. Default *reason* is "same as previous password." -s No reason issued for rejection.
grpck	**grpck** [*file*] Verify all entries in the group file. This verification includes a check of the number of fields, group name, group ID, and whether all login names appear in the password file. Default group file is **/etc/group**.
haltsys	**/etc/haltsys** [*option*] Close out filesystems and shut down the system. It takes effect immediately, so it should only be run in single-user mode. **Option** -d System will remain down and not give the option to reboot.

htable	**/etc/htable** [*options*] *file*
	TCP/IP command—convert NIC standard format host tables. **htable** is used to convert host *files* in the format specified in Internet RFC 810 to the format used by the network library routines. Three files are created as a result of running **htable: hosts, networks,** and **gateways**. The **hosts** file is used by the **gethostbyname** routines in mapping host names to addresses if the nameserver, **named** is not used. The **networks** file is used by the **getnetent** routines in mapping network names to numbers. The **gateways** file is used by the routing daemon in identifying "passive" Internet gateways.
	Options
	-c *connected-nets*
	  If the **gateways** file is to be used, specify list of networks to which the host is directly connected. The networks may be given by name or in Internet standard dot notation.
	-l *local-nets*
	  If this option is given with a list of networks (see -c), the networks are treated as local, and information about hosts on local networks is taken only from the **localhosts** file.

hwconfig	**/etc/hwconfig** [*options*] ... Return configuration information contained in */usr/adm/hwconfig/* or in file specified on command line with -f*filename* option. Using

combinations of the remaining options, the user can view as much information as needed from the configuraton file. The display format is as follows:

```
magic_char  device_name  base+finish  vec  dma  rest
```

where:

magic_char
> is the character **%**.

device_name
> is the name of the device driver.

base+finish
> are the starting and finishing addresses of the driver working space.

vec is the interrupt vector number in decimal.

dma is the DMA channel number.

rest is a possibly empty list of *parameter=value* pairs. **hwconfig** returns 0 for success, 1 for conflicts detected, 2 for invalid arguments. It is runnable only by root.

Options

-c Check for device conflicts.

-f*filename*
> Use *file* as input file instead of default **/usr/adm/hwconfig**.

-h Use long format of device configuration content, with headers.

-l Use long format of device configuration content.

-n Always print out device name.

param Show all values of *param* throughout configuration file. Current valid system parameters are: **name, base, offset, vec, dma, unit, type, nports, hds, cyls, secs, drvr.**

param=val
> Show only information from line where *param* equals the value *val*.

-q Check quietly for device conflicts; display nothing. When used with -c, display conflicts only.

-n, -l, and -h are in increasing overriding power. That is, if -n and -l are both specified, -l will be used.

/etc/conf/bin/idaddld [*options*]

Add or remove line disciplines from kernel configuration files. With no options, **idaddld** enters an interactive mode, from which the user can add, delete, or view the current configuration. It is the responsibility of the calling program to ensure that the kernel is relinked to effect the desired changes.

→

idaddld ←	**Options**
	-a *prefix routine1 ... routine8*
	Add a line discipline to configuration files. *prefix* is a tag used to identify the line discipline for future inquiries or removal. *routine1* through *routine8* define the list of line discipline routines. There must be eight routines with the keyword **nulldev** used as a placeholder. The order of the routines is critical and must be as follows: open, close, read, write, ioctl, rxint, txint, modemint.
	-d*prefix*
	Remove line discipline whose identifier matches *prefix*.
	-c*prefix*
	Scan line discipline switch table for an entry that matches *prefix*. Report result in exit status.
idbuild	**/etc/conf/bin/idbuild** [*option*]
	Build a new UNIX system kernel. **idbuild** uses the current system configuration in **/etc/conf**, and calls the following commands:
	idconfig Build system kernel configuration files.
	idmkunix Process configuration files and link-edit a new UNIX system image.
	idmkenv Back up current **/unix** and replace it with the new kernel, and rebuild the kernel environment.
	idvidi Read the video driver configuration.
	Option
	-p Do not delete temporary files created during the build.
idcheck	**/etc/conf/bin/idcheck** [*options*]
	Return selected information about system configuration.
	Options
	-a Check whether IOA region bounded by *lower* and *upper* (specified by **-l** and **-u** options) conflicts with another DSP. The exit code is based on first conflicting device found.
	-c Return 1 if CMA region bounded by *lower* and *upper* (specified by **-l** and **-u** options) conflicts with another DSP.
	-d *dma-channel*
	Return 1 if dma channel specified is being used.
	-i *dir* Directory in which the ID files **sdevice** and **mdevice** reside. Default is **/etc/conf/cf.d**.

-l *address*
> Lower bound of address range specified in hex.

-p *device-name*
> Check for existence of four different components of the DSP. The exit code is the addition of the return codes from the four checks.

-r   Report device name of any conflicting device on **stdout**.

-u *address*
> Upper bound of address range specified in hex.

-v *vector*
> Return value of the type field in the **mdevice** file for the device that is already using the vector.

/etc/conf/bin/idconfig

Build the system kernel configuration files. **idconfig** is invoked by **idbuild** when new UNIX system kernel is being built.

/etc/conf/bin/idinstall [*options*]

Add, delete, update, or get device driver configuration data. **idinstall** is called by a Driver Software Package (DSP) Install script or Remove script. When components are installed or updated, they are moved or appended to files in the **/etc/conf** directory, then deleted from the current directory.

Options

-a   Add DSP components.

-c   Mfsys component: filesystem type config (Master) data

-d   Delete DSP components.

-e   Disable free disk space check.

-g   Get DSP components (print to stdout, except Master).

-h   Device shutdown (sd) component

-i   Inittab component

-k   Keep files on add or update (do not remove from current directory).

-l   Sfsys component: filesystem type local (System) data

-m   Master component

-n   Node (special file) component

-o   Driver.o component

-p   Space.c component

-r   Device Initialization (rc) component

-s   System component

-t   Stubs.c component.

-u   Update DSP components

idinstall	**Examples**
←	In the simplest case of installing a new DSP, the command syntax used by the DSP's installation script should be:

   idinstall -a *dev_name*

In this case, the command will require and install a Driver.o, Master and System entry, and optionally install the Space.c, Stubs,c, Node, Init, Rc, Shutdown, Mfsys, and Sfsys components if those modules are present in the current directory.

---

idleout

idleout [*minutes* | *hours:minutes*]

Log out users whose terminal remains idle longer than a specified period of time. Minutes are assumed; if a colon appears in the number, hours are assumed. **idleout** uses a default file, **/etc/default/idleout**, to indicate the interval a user's terminal may remain idle before being logged out.

You can run **idleout** either from the command line, or each time the system is rebooted, by adding the program name in **/etc/rc2.d/S88USRDEFINE**.

---

idmkenv

/etc/conf/bin/idmkenv

Back up current UNIX, replace it with the new kernel, and rebuild the kernel environment. **idmkenv** is invoked by **idbuild** after new UNIX system kernel has been configured and linked.

---

idmkinit

/etc/conf/bin/idmkinit [*options*]

Read files containing inittab specifications and construct a new **inittab** file in **/etc/conf/cf.d**.

Options

   -e *directory*
      Find the Init modules in *directory*, rather than in **/etc/conf/init.d**.

   -i *directory*
      Find the ID file **init.base** in *directory* rather than in **/etc/conf/init.d**.

   -o *directory*
      Create **inittab** in *directory* rather than in **/etc/conf/cf.d**.

---

idmknod

/etc/conf/bin/idmknod [*options*]

Remove nodes and read specifications of nodes. **idmknod** removes the nodes for non-required devices from **/dev**, and reads the specifications of nodes given in the files contained in **/etc/conf/node.d** and installs these nodes in **/dev**. **idmknod** is run automatically when **idbuild** installs a newly built kernel as **/unix**.

Options

-e *directory*
> Find the Node modules in *directory* rather than in /etc/conf/node.d.

-i *directory*
> Find the *mdevice* file in *directory* rather than in /etc/conf/cf.d.

-o *directory*
> Install nodes in *directory* rather than /dev.

-s   Suppress removing nodes; just add new nodes.

/etc/conf/bin/idmkunix

When a new UNIX system kernel is being built, **idmkunix** is invoked by **idbuild** to process the configuration files and link the necessary modules to create the new kernel.

/etc/conf/bin/idscsi

When a new UNIX system kernel is being built, **idscsi** is invoked by **idbuild** to read the SCSI driver configurations.

/etc/conf/bin/idspace [*options*]

Investigate free space in the root (/), /usr, and /tmp filesystems to determine whether sufficient disk blocks and inodes exist in each of potentially three filesystems.

Options

-i *inodes*
> Override the default test for 100 inodes in all of the **idspace** checks.

-r *blocks*
> Override the default test for /unix size = 400 blocks when checking the root filesystem; /usr and /tmp filesystems are not tested unless explicitly specified.

-t *blocks*
> Override the default test for 400 blocks when checking the tmp filesystem; root and /usr filesystems are not tested unless explicitly specified.

/etc/conf/bin/idtune [*options*] *name value*

Attempt to set value of a tuneable parameter. The tuneable parameter to be changed is indicated by *name*. The desired value for the tuneable parameter is *value*. In order for the change in parameter to become effective, the UNIX system kernel must be rebuilt and the system rebooted.

→

idtune ←	**Options**
	-f The change will always be made and no messages will ever be given (force option).
	-m If there is an existing value that is greater than the desired value, no change will be made and no message given (minimum option).

---

idvidi

/etc/conf/bin/idvidi

When a new UNIX system kernel is being built, **idvidi** is invoked by **idbuild** to read the video driver.

---

ifconfig

/etc/ifconfig [*arguments*] *interface address_family* [*address* [*dest_address*]] [*parameters*]
ifconfig *interface* [*protocol_family*]

TCP/IP command—assign an address to a network interface and/or configure network interface parameters. **ifconfig** must be used at boot time to define the network address of each interface present on a machine. It may also be used at a later time to redefine an interface's address or other operating parameters. Used without arguments, **ifconfig** displays the current configuration for a network interface.

Arguments

interface
String of the form *name unit*, for example "en0".

address_family
Since an interface may receive transmissions in differing protocols, each of which may require separate naming schemes, it is necessary to specify the *address_family*, which may change the interpretation of the remaining parameters. Currently, only the Internet address family is supported. Thus, the only valid value for the *address_family* is **inet**.

[*address* [[*dest_address*]]]
For the DARPA-Internet family, either a hostname present in the hostname database, **hosts**, or a DARPA Internet address expressed in the Internet standard dot notation.

[*protocol_family*]
Report only the details specific to *protocol_family*.

[*parameters*]
The following parameters may be set with **ifconfig**:

arp/-arp
Enable/disable use of the Address Resolution Protocol in mapping between network-level addresses and link-level addresses (default).

broadcast

> (inet only) Specify address to use to represent broadcasts to the network. Default is the address with a host part of all 1's.

debug/-debug

> Enable/disable driver-dependent debugging code.

dest_address

> Specify the address of the correspondent on the other end of a point to point link.

down   Mark an interface "down."

metric *n*

> Set routing metric of the interface to *n*. Default is 0.

netmask *mask*

> (inet only) Specify how much of the address to reserve for subdividing networks into subnetworks. *mask* can be specified as a single hexadecimal number with a leading 0x, a dot notation Internet address, or with a pseudo-network name listed in the network table **networks**.

onepacket/-onepacket

> Enable/disable **one-packet** mode of operation. **onepacket** must be followed by two numeric parameters, giving the small packet size and threshold, respectively.

up   Mark an interface "up."

trailers/-trailers

> Request/disable use of a "trailer" link-level encapsulation when sending.

---

infocmp [*options*]

Compare or print out terminfo descriptions. **infocmp** can be used to compare a binary *terminfo* entry with other terminfo entries, to rewrite a *terminfo* description to take advantage of the **use=** terminfo field, or to print out a *terminfo* description from the binary file (**term**) in a variety of formats. In all cases, the Boolean fields will be printed first, followed by the numeric fields, followed by the string fields.

infocmp ←	*Options*
	−1 Print out fields one to a line.

	−A *directory*
	    Override location of compiled *terminfo* database—set
	    TERMINFO for the first *termname*.

	−B *directory*
	    Override location of compiled *terminfo* database—set
	    TERMINFO for *termnames* other than the first.

	−C Use the *termcap* names to produce a source listing for each terminal named.
	−c Produce a list of each capability common between the two entries. Capabilities not set are ignored.
	−d Produce a list of each capability that is different.
	−I Use the *terminfo* names to produce source listing for each terminal named.
	−L Use the long C variable name listed in *term.h* to pro- duce a source listing for each terminal named.

	−n Produce a list of each capability that is in neither entry.
	    If no *termnames* are given, the environment variable
	    TERM will be used for both of the *termnames*.

	−r When using −C, put out all capabilities in *termcap* form.
	−s Sort the fields within each type according to the argu- ment below:

Options

−1   Print out fields one to a line.

−A *directory*
    Override location of compiled *terminfo* database—set TERMINFO for the first *termname*.

−B *directory*
    Override location of compiled *terminfo* database—set TERMINFO for *termnames* other than the first.

−C   Use the *termcap* names to produce a source listing for each terminal named.

−c   Produce a list of each capability common between the two entries. Capabilities not set are ignored.

−d   Produce a list of each capability that is different.

−I   Use the *terminfo* names to produce source listing for each terminal named.

−L   Use the long C variable name listed in *term.h* to produce a source listing for each terminal named.

−n   Produce a list of each capability that is in neither entry. If no *termnames* are given, the environment variable TERM will be used for both of the *termnames*.

−r   When using −C, put out all capabilities in *termcap* form.

−s   Sort the fields within each type according to the argument below:

    c   Sort by the *termcap* name.
    d   Leave fields in the order that they are stored in the *terminfo* database.
    i   Sort by *terminfo* name.
    l   Sort by the long C variable name.

    If no −s option is given, the fields printed out will be sorted alphabetically by the *terminfo* name within each type (except for −C or −L options).

−u   Produce a *terminfo* source description of the first terminal *termname* that is relative to the sum of the descriptions given by the entries for the other terminals' *termnames*.

−V   Print out the version of the program in use on standard error, and exit.

−v   Print out tracing information on standard error as the program runs.

−w *width*
    Change output to *width* characters.

---

inetd

/etc/inetd [*option*] [*configuration_file*]

TCP/IP command—Internet services daemon. **inetd** listens on multiple ports for incoming connection requests. When it receives one, it spawns the appropriate server. When started, **inetd** reads its configuration information from either *configuration_file*, or the default configuration file, **/etc/inetd.conf**. It then issues a call to **get-servbyname**, creates a socket for each server, and binds each socket to the port for that server. It does a **listen** on all connection-based sockets, and waits, using **select** for a connection or datagram.

When a connection request is received on a listening socket, **inetd** does an **accept**, creating a new socket. It then forks, dups, and execs the appropriate server. The invoked server has I/O to **stdin**, **stdout**, and **stderr** done to the new socket, connecting the server to the client process.

When there is data waiting on a datagram socket, **inetd** forks, dups, and execs the appropriate server, passing it any server program arguments. A datagram server has I/O to **stdin**, **stdout**, and **stderr** done to the original socket. If the datagram socket is marked as "wait," the invoked server must process the message before **inetd** considers the socket available for new connections. If the socket is marked "nowait," **inetd** continues to process incoming messages on that port.

The following servers may be started by **inetd**: **fingerd**, **ftpd**, **rexecd**, **rlogind**, **rshd**, **talkd**, **telnetd**, and **tftpd**. Do not arrange for **inetd** to start **named**, **routed**, **rwhod**, **sendmail**, **listen**, or any NFS server.

inetd rereads its configuration file when it receives a hangup signal, SIGHUP. Services may be added, deleted, or modified when the configuration file is reread.

Option

-d   Turn on socket-level debugging and print debugging information to **stdout**.

/tcb/lib/initcond [init | getty] [*args*...]

Special security actions for **init** and **getty**. To save space in **init** and **getty**, which are memory-resident, the space-intensive security actions are done in **initcond** as a subprocess of these programs.

Arguments

init   One of two actions may occur: if no argument is given, **sulogin** should prompt for and verify a single-user password if required by the System Default database. If two other arguments are supplied, they are the terminal device name and the user name, respectively, of the session that just terminated.

getty   If one additional argument is provided, it is the terminal to be invalidated before a login.

/bin/sh /etc/initscript *id rstate action process*

Shell script used by **init** to execute inittab commands. **initscript** sets the PATH variable, sets the HZ (Hertz value) variable, checks

→

initscript ←	for an **/etc/TIMEZONE** file (that sets and exports the TZ variable) and executes it, sets the **umask**, and runs the fourth argument *process*, the process field from **/etc/inittab**.

install	**install** [*options*] *file* [*directories*] Used primarily in makefiles to update files. **install** tries to locate an old version of *file* by searching user-supplied *directories* (or default directories such as **/bin** or **/etc**). *file* is then copied to the directory, overwriting the older version. Normally, if no older *file* exists, **install** does nothing.

Options

- **-c** *dir*   Conditional copy; if *file* already exists in *dir*, do nothing; otherwise, copy *file* to *dir*.
- **-f** *dir*   Forced copy; copy *file* to *dir*, whether or not *file* is already there.
- **-g** *group*   Set group ID of new file to *group* (privileged users only).
- **-i**   When searching for *file*, ignore default directories but search specified *directories*. **-c** and **-f** are invalid with **-i**.
- **-m** *mode*   Set permissions of new file to *mode*.
- **-n** *dir*   Place *file* in *dir* if it's not in any of the default directories.
- **-o**   Save old version of *file* in **OLD***file* instead of overwriting it.
- **-s**   Suppress all messages except error messages.
- **-u** *user*   Set owner of new file to *user*.

installf	**installf** [*options*]
	
	Add a file to the software installation database. The three synopses of **installf** are as follows:
	
	    installf [**-c** *class*] *pkginst pathname* [*ftype* [[*major minor*] [*mode owner group*]]]
	    installf [**-c** *class*] *pkginst* -
	    installf -**f** [**-c** *class*] *pkginst*
	
	When the second synopsis is used, the pathname descriptions will be read from standard input. After all files have been appropriately created and/or modified, **installf** should be invoked with the third synopsis to indicate that installation is final.

Options

- **-c** *class*
                Class to which installed objects should be associated. Default class id **none**.

-f	Indicates installation is complete. This option is used with the final invocation of **installf**.	**installf**
ftype	One-character field that indicates the file type. Possible file types include: b Block special device c Character special device d Directory e File to be edited upon installation or removal f Standard executable or data file l Linked file p Named pipe s Symbolic link v Volatile file—one whose contents are expected to change x Exclusive directory	
group	Group to which file belongs	
major	Major device number	
minor	Minor device number	
mode	Octal mode of the file	
owner	Owner of the file	
pathname	Pathname being created or modified	
pkginst	Name of package instance with which pathname should be associated	

installpkg

installpkg

Install an AT&T-style UNIX system software package. **installpkg** prompts you to insert the floppy disk that the installation package resides on; everything else is automatic. You have to be root to install certain packages successfully.

/tcb/bin/integrity [*options*]

integrity

Examine system files against the authentication (File Control) database. If owner, group, or permissions are different, an error message is output. Only root can run this utility.

Options

-e	Explain why discretionary checks fail and exactly what the discrepancy is.
-m	Report files in the File Control database that are missing from the filesystem (default is to not report them).
-v	List all files under consideration, even those that match.

| **ipcrm** | **ipcrm** [*options*] |

Remove a message queue, semaphore set, or shared memory identifier as specified by the *options*. Use **ipcs** first to list items to remove.

Options

-m *shmid*	Remove shared memory identifier *shmid*.
-M *shmkey*	Remove *shmid* created with key *shmkey*.
-q *msqid*	Remove message queue identifier *msqid*.
-Q *msgkey*	Remove *msqid* created with key *msgkey*.
-s *semid*	Remove semaphore identifier *semid*.
-S *semkey*	Remove *semid* created with key *semkey*.

---

ipcs   **ipcs** [*options*]

Print data about active interprocess communication facilities.

Options

-m	Report on active shared memory segments.
-q	Report on active message queues.
-s	Report on active semaphores.

With the -m, -q, or -s options, only the specified interprocess facility is reported on. Otherwise information about all three is printed.

-a	Use all of the print options (short for -bcopt).
-b	Report maximum allowed number of message bytes, segment sizes, and number of semaphores.
-c	Report the creator's login name and group.
-C*file*	Read status from *file* instead of from **/dev/kmem**.
-N*list*	Use the argument for the named *list* instead of **/stand/unix**.
-o	Report outstanding usage.
-p	Report process numbers.
-t	Report time information.
-X	Print information about XENIX interprocess communication, in addition to the standard interprocess communication status.

---

kbmode   **/etc/kbmode** *command* [*file*]

Set keyboard mode or test keyboard support. **kbmode** can be used to determine if your system keyboard suports AT mode. If it does, this utility can change the keyboard mode between AT mode and PC/XT-compatibility mode. If *file* is specified, it should be a tty device of one of the multiscreens of the keyboard's group. Valid *commands* are:

test	Determine if keyboard supports AT mode.	**kbmode**
at	Set keyboard to AT mode.	
xt	Set keyboard to PC/XT compatibility mode.	

---

kill [*options*] *IDs*

kill

Terminate one or more process *IDs*. You must own the process or be a privileged user. This command is similar to the **kill** command that is built into the Bourne, Korn, and C shells. A minus sign before an *ID* specifies a process group ID. (The built-in version doesn't allow process group IDs, but it does allow job IDs.)

Options

| -l | List the signal names. (Used by itself.) |
| - *signal* | The signal number (from **ps -f**) or name (from **kill** -l). With a signal number of 9, the kill is absolute. |

/etc/killall [*signal*]

killall

Used by **/etc/shutdown** to kill all active processes not directly related to the shutdown procedure. **killall** terminates all processes with open files so that the mounted filesystems will be unbusied and can be unmounted. It sends *signal* to all processes it is going to kill. If no *signal* is specified, a default of 9 is used.

/etc/labelit *special* [*fsname volume* [*option*]]

labelit

Provide labels for filesystems. With optional arguments omitted, **labelit** prints current label values. The *special* name should be the physical disk section. The *fsname* argument represents the mounted name of the filesystem. *volume* may be used to equate an internal name to a volume name applied externally to the disk pack, diskette, or tape.

Option

| -n | Provides for initial labeling only. This destroys previous contents. |

---

last [*options*]

last

Indicate last logins of users and teletypes. **last** checks the **wtmp** file, which records all logins and logouts, for information about users, tty lines or any group of users and lines. Options specify a user name and/or tty. With no options, **last** displays a record of all logins and logouts, in reverse chronological order.

$\rightarrow$

last
←
	Options
	
	-h No header.
	
	-n *limit*
	        Limit report to *n* lines.
	
	-t *tty* Specifies tty.
	
	-w *wtmpfile*
	        Use *wtmpfile* instead of **/etc/wtmp**. This file must have
	        same format as **/etc/wtmp**.
	
	name User name.

lckclnt	**lckclnt** [*nclienthandles*] NFS/NIS command—create lock manager client handles. Lock manager client programs obtain a client handle for the duration of an RPC operation. *nclienthandles* is the number of client handles allocated. If additional client handles are required, more **lckclnt** processes may be started.
ldsocket	**ldsocket** [*options*] TCP/IP command—load socket configuration. **ldsocket** initializes the "System V STREAMS TCP/IP" Berkeley networking compatibility interface, an alternate stream head supporting the **socket** system call family. **ldsocket** loads the kernel with associations between the protocol family, type, and number triplets passed to the **socket** system call, and the STREAMS devices supporting those protocols. **ldsocket** reads the file **/etc/sockcf** to obtain configuration information and must be run before the Berkeley networking interface can be used. **Options** -c *file* Use *file* instead of **/etc/sockcf**. -v Verbose—a message is written to **stderr** for each protocol loaded.
link	**/etc/link** *file1 file2* Link files and directories. **link** creates a filename that points to another file. **link** can be run only by the superuser. Similar to **ln**, but with no error checking.
link_unix	**/etc/conf/cf.d/link_unix** Used to build a new UNIX system kernel after installing a device driver. **link_unix** builds **/etc/conf/cf.d/unix** using the current system configuration in **/etc/conf**.

MMDF command. MMDF channel program for handling mail lists. **list** functions as a feed-through between **deliver** and **submit**. It is called by **deliver** and is not meant to be invoked directly by users.

To use **list** to process a list, make three entries in the alias file(s). To set up a list called `ora`, and have it processed by the **list** channel, put the following entries in the alias file:

```
ora:        ora-outbound@list-processor
ora-outbound:   :include: /usr/mmdf/lists/ora-file
ora-request:    maintainer
```

In the first line, `ora` is sent through the list processor, readdressed to `ora-outbound`. The second line is what actually references the mailing list file for `ora`. The third line is optional. It is used to set up the standard maintenance address and is also used by **list** as the return address for mail submitted to the list.

---

lmail *user* . . .

lmail

TCP/IP command—interprets incoming mail received from **sendmail** and delivers it to the specified *user* on the local machine. **lmail** locks the user's mailbox using the **mail** locking mechanism.

/etc/lockd [*options*]

lockd

NFS/NIS command. Network lock daemon—processes lock requests that are either sent locally by the kernel or remotely by another lock daemon. **lockd** forwards lock requests for remote data to the server site's lock daemon through the RPC/XDR package. It then requests the status monitor daemon, **statd**, for monitor service. The reply to the lock request will not be sent to the kernel until the status daemon and the server site's lock daemon have replied.

Options

  -d *debuglevel*

      Set debugging level (number). A level of 2 will report significant events. A level of 4 will report internal state and all lock request traffic in verbose form.

  -g *graceperiod*

      Use *graceperiod* (seconds) as the grace period duration instead of the default value of 45 seconds.

  -h *hashsize*

      Use *hashsize* number of hash buckets internally instead of the default value of 29.

$\rightarrow$

-l *k2utimeout*
> Use *k2utimeout* (seconds) as the interval instead of the default value (two seconds) to retransmit kernel lock manager requests. This is the timeout value used for local lock requests.

-t *timeout*
> Use *timeout* (seconds) as the interval instead of the default value (five seconds) to retransmit a lock request to the remote server.

login [-r *remotehost remotename localname*] . . .

Log in to the system. **login** asks for a username (*name* can be supplied on the command line), and password (if appropriate).

The -r form of the command is used for remote logins across a network. *remotehost* is the name of the remote host from which the login is being attempted; *remotename* is the user's name on the remote host; and *localname* is the user's name on the local host. This form of **login** is intended for use by network software rather than users.

If successful, **login** updates accounting files, notifies users if they have mail, and executes startup shell files. **login** checks /etc/default/login for the following definitions, of the form **DEFINE=***value*:

ALTSHELL
> If **ALTSHELL** is set to **YES**, or if it is not present in /etc/default/login, the **SHELL** environment variable is set to whatever shell is specified in the user's /etc/passwd entry. If If **ALTSHELL** is set to **NO**, then the **SHELL** environment variable is set only if the shell is defined it the /usr/lib/mkuser directory.

CONSOLE
> **CONSOLE=***device* means that root can only log in on the device listed.

ALLOWHUSH
> Enable (if **ALLOWHUSH=YES**) or disable (if **ALLOWHUSH=NO**) the hushlogin feature on a system-wide basis. If **ALLOWHUSH=YES**, **login** checks for a .hushlogin file in the user's home directory. If the file exists, the **HUSHLOGIN** variable is set to **TRUE** and a quiet login takes place. If the file does not exist, or **ALLOWHUSH=NO**, **HUSHLOGIN** is set to **FALSE** and the normal login messages appear.

IDLEWEEKS
> If a password has expired beyond **IDLEWEEKS**, the user is not allowed to log in.

OVERRIDE
> Allow root to log in on the console even if the Protected Password database entry for root is corrupted.

PASSREQ	If **PASSREQ=YES**, a password is required. **PASSREQ=NO** allows users to have accounts without passwords.	lockd
SUPATH	If user's UID is 0 (superuser), the **PATH** variable is set to **SUPATH**, if **SUPATH** is specified in /etc/default/login.	
ULIMIT	Maximum allowable file size, specified in even numbers. Default is one gigabyte.	
UMASK	Default file creation mask.	

/usr/bin/logger [*options*] [*message* ...]   logger

TCP/IP command—add entries to the system log. A message can be given on the command line, in which case it is logged immediately, or a file is read and each line is logged. If no *message* or file is specified, standard input is logged.

Options

-f *file*   Log the specified file.

-i   Log process id of the logger process with each line.

-p *pri*   Enter message with the specified priority *pri*. Default is "user.notice".

-t *tag*   Mark every line in the log with the specifed *tag*.

/usr/lib/lpadmin [*options*]   lpadmin

Configure the **lp** print service to describe printers and devices. **lpadmin** is used to add and change printers, to remove printers from the service, to set or change the system default destination, to define alerts for print wheels, and to define printers for remote printing services.

Options

For ease of discussion, the *printer* argument to **lpadmin** will be referred to in discussions below as "the printer."

-A *alert–type* [-W *integer*]

-A *alert–type* [-W *integer1*] [-Q *integer2*]

-A is used to send the alert type *alert-type* to the administrator. It will do this when a printer fault is first detected, and periodically thereafter until the printer fault is cleared by the administrator. -A will also, when used with -S *print-wheel*, send the *alert-type* to the administrator as soon as the *print-wheel* needs to be mounted. If -W is not given, or integer is zero (**once**, the default), only one message will be sent per fault, or per need to mount a print wheel. If -Q is also given, the alert will be made when *integer* print requests that need the print wheel are waiting. The alert types are:

mail	Send alert message via **mail** to the administrator who issues this command.
write	Write the message to the terminal on which the administrator is logged in.
quiet	Do not send messages for the current condition.
none	Do not send messages until this command is given again with a different *alert-type*; remove any existing alert definition.

shell-command
Run *shell-command* each time the alert needs to be sent.

list	Display the type of alert for the printer fault on the standard output.

-F *fault-recovery*
Restore the **lp** print service after a printer fault, according to the following *fault-recovery* values:
continue
Continue printing on the top of the page where printing stopped.
beginning
Start printing the request again from the beginning.

wait	Disable printing on the printer and wait for the administrator or a user to enable printing again.

-c *class*
Insert the printer into the specified *class*.

-D *comment*
Save *comment* for display whenever a user asks for a full description of the printer.

-d [*dest*]
Make *dest*, an existing destination, the new system default destination. No other options are allowed with **-d**.

-e *printer*
Copy an existing *printer*'s interface program to be the new interface program for the printer.

-f allow:*form-list*
-f deny:*form-list*
Allow or deny the forms in *form-list* to be printed on the printer.

-h	Indicate that the device associated with the printer is hardwired.

-i *interface*
Establish a new interface program (*interface* is the pathname) for the printer.

-I *content–type–list*

    Assign the printer to handle print requests with content of a type listed in *content-type-list.*

-l   Device associated with the printer is a login terminal.

-M -f *form–name* [**-a** [**-o** *filebreak*]]

    Mount the form *form-name* on the printer. With the **-a** option, an alignment pattern is printed, preceded by the same initialization of the physical printer that precedes a normal print request, with one exception: no banner page is printed. With the **-o** *filebreak* option, a formfeed is inserted between each copy of the alignment pattern.

    A form is unmounted by mounting a new form in its place using the **-f** option. The **-f none** option can be used to specify no form. By default, a new printer has no form mounted.

-M -S *print–wheel*

    Mount the print wheel *print-wheel* on the printer. A print wheel is unmounted by mounting a new print wheel in its place, or by using the **-S** option.

-m *model*

    Select a model interface program provided with the **lp** print service for a given printer.

-o *printing–option*

    Each **-o** option listed below is the default given to an interface program if the option is not taken from a pre-printed form description or is not explicitly given by the user submitting a request. The options are:

        length = *scaled-decimal-number*
        width = *scaled-decimal-number*
        cpi = *scaled-decimal-number*
        lpi = *scaled-decimal-number*
        stty = *stty-option-list*

    scaled-decimal-number refers to a non-negative number used to indicate a unit of size. *stty-option-list* is not checked for allowed values, but is passed directly to the **stty** program by the standard interface program.

-o *nobanner*

    Allow users to submit a print request that asks that no banner page be printed.

-o *banner*

    Force a banner page to be printed with every print request, even when a user asks for no banner page. This is the default.

-R *machine–list*

    Set up remote machines in *machine-list* to share print services.

lpadmin
←
	-r *class*
	      Remove a given printer from the specified *class*.
	-S *list* Allow the aliases for character sets or print wheels named in *list* to be used with a given printer.
	-S *print–wheel*
	      See –**A** *alert-type* and –**M** –**S** *print-wheel* options.
	-T *printer–type*
	      Assign the given *printer-type*—a representation of a physical printer of type *printer-type*.
	-u allow:*user–list*
	-u deny:*user–list*
	      Allow or deny the users in *user-list* access to a given printer.
	-U *dial–info*
	      Assign the dialing information *dial-info* to the printer.
	-v *device*
	      Associate a new device with a given printer. *device* is the pathname of a file writable by **lp**. The same *device* can be associated with more than one printer.
	-x *dest*
	      Remove the destination *dest* from the **lp** print service. No other options are allowed with –**x**.

lpd	**/usr/lib/lpd** [*options*]
	
	TCP/IP command—line printer daemon. **lpd** is usually invoked at boot time from the **rc2** file. It makes a single pass through the *printcap* file to find out about the existing printers and prints any files left after a crash. It then accepts requests to print files in a queue, transfer files to a spooling area, display a queue's status, or remove jobs from a queue. In each case, it forks a child process for each request and continues to listen for subsequent requests.
	
	The file *lock* in each spool directory prevents multiple daemons from becoming active simultaneously. After the daemon has set the lock, it scans the directory for files beginning wth **cf**. Lines in each **cf** file specify files to be printed or non-printing actions to be performed. Each line begins with a key character to specify what to do with the remainder of the line. Key characters are:
	  C Classification—string to be used for the classification line on the burst page.
	  f Formatted file—name of a file to print that is already for-matting.
	  H Hostname—name of machine where **lp** was invoked.
	  J Jobname—string to be used for the jobname on the burst page.
	  L Literal—this line contains identification information from the password file and causes the banner page to be printed.

M	Mail—send mail to the specified user when the current print job completes.
P	Person—login name of person who invoked **lp**.
r	Request ID. This is used by the **cancel** command.
T	Title—string to be used as the title for **pr**.
U	Unlink—name of file to remove upon completion of printing.

Options

-l	Log valid requests received from the network.
port #	Specify Internet port number. Default is obtained with **getservbyname**.

Files

/etc/printcap
> Printer description file

/usr/spool/* Spool directories

/usr/spool/*/minfree
> Minimum free space to leave

/dev/lp* Line-printer devices

/etc/hosts.equiv
> Machine names allowed printer access

/etc/hosts.lpd
> Machine names allowed printer access, but not under same administrative control

---

/usr/lib/lpfilter -f *filtername* [*options*]

Administer filters, specified by -f *filtername*, to be used with the print service. The functions of this command are also accessible through the **sysadmsh** Printers–>Auxillary–>Filter selection.

Options

The argument **all** can be used instead of a *filtername* with any of these options:

-C *pathname*
> Add or change a filter.

-i
> Reset an original LP print service filter to its factory setting.

-x
> Delete a filter.

-l
> List a filter description.

/usr/lib/lpforms -f *formname* [*options*]

Administer forms used with the print service. The functions of **lpforms** are also accessible throught the **sysadmsh**'s Printers–>Auxiliary–>Forms selection.

→

lpforms	Options
←	**-A** *alert–type*

              Define the type of alerting method to be used. The values are **list, quiet, none, mail, write**, and ´**command**´.

   -   Add or change a form and supply information from standard output.

-F *pathname*
           Add or change a form as specified by the information in *pathname*.

   -l   List the attributes of a form. This option cannot be used with any other option.

-Q *number*
           Define the threshold in number of requests waiting (that is, used to restart the alert). Must be used with **-A** option.

-u allow:*user–list*
           Allow users to request a form. This option can be used with the **-F** or **-** option.

-u deny:*user–list*
           Deny users access to a form. This option can be used with the **-F** or **-** option.

-W *minutes*
           Define the number of minutes between alerts. Must be used with **-A** option.

   -x   Delete a form. This option cannot be used with any other option.

---

lpmove

/usr/lib/lpmove *arguments*

Move print requests that were queued by **lp** between LP destinations.

Arguments

   requests dest
           Move named *requests* to the LP destination *dest*.

   dest1 dest2
           Move all requests for destination *dest1* to destination *dest2*; **lp** will then reject any new requests for *dest1*.

---

lpsched

/usr/lib/lpsched [*options*]

Start the print service. Requests that were printing at the time a printer was shut down will be reprinted from the beginning.

Options

   -a *integer*
           Specify number of alert structures you want to allocate. By default, 40 empty alert structures are allocated, in addition to one for each printer or form on the system.

-p *integer*

Specify number of print status structures you want to allocate. By default, 25 empty printer status structures are allocated, in addition to one for each printer on the system.

-q *integer*

Specify number of request structures you want to allocate.

-s *integer*

Specify number of slow filters per printer that can be run simultaneously.

/usr/lib/sysadm/lpsh

Menu-driven **lp** print service administration utility. **lpsh** is the screen interface invoked by the **sysadmsh**. It performs all of the **lp** print service functions that require system administrator authorization. For more details, see the section on **sysadmsh**.

/usr/lib/lpshut

Shut down the print service. All printers that are printing at the time **lpshut** is invoked will stop printing.

---

lpusers /usr/lib/lpusers [*options*]

Set printing queue priorities.

Options

-d *priority–level*

Set system-wide priority default to *priority-level*, where *priority-level* is a value of 0 to 39, with 0 being the highest priority.

-l   List default priority level and priority limits assigned to users.

-q *priority–level*

With -u *user-list*, set default highest *priority-level* (0-39) that users can request when submitting a print request. Without -u *user-list*, set default highest priority level for all users not explicitly covered by -u *user-list*.

-u *user–list*

Remove users from any explicit priority level and return them to default priority level.

/etc/conf/cf.d/majorsinuse

Display the list of major device numbers currently specified in the **mdevice** file.

makedbm	**makedbm** [*options*] *infile outfile*

Make NIS **dbm** file. **makedbm** takes *infile* and converts it to a pair of files in **ndbm** format, namely *outfile*.**pag** *and outfile*.**dir**. Each line of the input file is converted to a single **dbm** record. All characters up to the first TAB or SPACE form the key, and the rest of the line is the data. If line ends with '', the data for that record is continued on to the next line. It is left for the NIS clients to interpret #; **makedbm** does not itself treat it as a comment character. *infile* can be -, in which case the standard input is read.

makedbm generates a special entry with the key **yp_***last_modified*, which is the date of infile (or the current time, if infile is -).

Options

-b   Interdomain. Propagate a map to all servers using the interdomain name server **named**.

-d yp_*domain_name*
      Create a special entry with the key **yp_***domain_name*.

-i yp_*input_file*
      Create a special entry with the key **yp_***input_file*.

-l   Convert keys of the given map to lowercase.

-m yp_*master_name*
      Create a special entry with the key **yp_***master_name*. If no master hostname is specified, **yp_***master_name* will be set to the local hostname.

-o yp_*output_file*
      Create a special entry with the key **yp_***output_name*.

-s   Secure map. Accept connections from secure NIS networks only.

-u dbm*filename*
      Undo a **dbm** file—print out a **dbm** file, one entry per line, with a single space separating keys from values.

Example

It is easy to write shell scripts to convert standard files such as **/etc/passwd** to the key value form used by **makedbm**. For example, the **awk** program:

```
BEGIN { FS =":";OFS = "\t";}
{ print $1, $0}
```

takes the **/etc/passwd** file and converts it to a form that can be read by **makdbm** to make the NIS file **passwd.byname**. That is, the key is a username and the value is the remaining line in the **/etc/passwd** file.

makekey	/usr/lib/makekey

Generate an encryption key. **makekey** improves the usefulness of encryption schemes by increasing the amount of time required to

search the key space. It reads 10 bytes from its standard input, and
writes 13 bytes on its standard output. The first eight input bytes
(the input key) can be arbitrary ASCII characters. The last two input
bytes (the salt) are best chosen from the set of digits, dot (.), slash
(/), and upper- and lowercase letters. The salt characters are
repeated as the first two characters of the output. The remaining 11
output characters are chosen from the same set as the salt and con-
stitute the output key.

makekey

---

map2ascii
/etc/yp/map2ascii/passwd.nam
/etc/yp/map2ascii/group.nam
/etc/yp/map2ascii/hosts.nam
/etc/yp/map2ascii/netwks.nam
/etc/yp/map2ascii/proto.no
/etc/yp/map2ascii/rpc.no
/etc/yp/map2ascii/srvcs.nam
/etc/yp/map2ascii/ethers.adr
/etc/yp/map2ascii/ethers.nam
/etc/yp/map2ascii/group.gif
/etc/yp/map2ascii/hosts.adr
/etc/yp/map2ascii/mail.alias
/etc/yp/map2ascii/netgroup
/etc/yp/map2ascii/netgrp.hst
/etc/yp/map2ascii/netgrp.usr
/etc/yp/map2ascii/netwks.adr
/etc/yp/map2ascii/passwd.uid
/etc/yp/map2ascii/proto.nam
/etc/yp/map2ascii/ypserver

map2ascii

NIS database conversion routines. **map2ascii** routines are shell
scripts used by **ypxfr** to convert NIS databases (maps) into their
ASCII counterparts. The names of the files in the directory
/etc/yp/map2ascii correspond to shortened UNIX System V NIS map
names. After transferring an NIS map, **ypxfr** checks for the existence of a file in the /etc/yp/map2ascii directory with the same
name as the map. If it exists, **ypxfr** forks a shell to run the script.

Scripts

passwd.nam
> Combines the contents of the **passwd.nam** map and
> /etc/group.local (if it exists) to make the **/etc/passwd**
> file.

group.nam
> Combines the contents of the **group.nam** map and
> /etc/group.local (if it exists) to make the **/etc/group** file.

hosts.nam
> Copies the contents of the **hosts.name** map to
> /etc/hosts.

map2ascii
←
	netwks.nam
	    Copies the contents of the **netwks.nam** map to /etc/net-works.
	proto.no
	    Copies the contents of the **proto.no** map to /etc/proto-cols.
	rpc.no Copies the contents of the **rpc.no** map to /etc/rpc.
	srvcs.nam
	    Copies the contents of the **srvcs.nam** map to /etc/ser-vices.
	
	The rest of the **map2ascii** scripts exist merely to force the corresponding NIS map to be updated during system initialization time.

mconnect	**mconnect** [*options*]
	
	TCP/IP command—connect to SMTP mail server socket. **mconnect** opens a connection to the mail server on a given host so that the mail server can be tested independently of all other mail software. If no host is given, the connection is made to the local host. Exit by typing the **quit** command.
	
	Options
	
	-h *hostname*
	    Specify destination host *hostname* instead of default host (localhost).
	-p *port*
	    Specify port number *port* instead of default SMTP port (number 25).
	-r "Raw" mode—disable the default line buffering and input handling.

menumerge	**menumerge** *menulist addlist* Merge **sysadmmenu** files. **menumerge** is used to customize the extensible menus in **sysadmsh** and would usually be run from an installation script, merging the entries from the file *addlist*, present on the installation media, into the *menulist* file chosen from the following list:

menulist file	*Extensible menu area*
/usr/lib/sysadmn/.menu-execute	System–>Execute
/usr/lib/sysadmn/.menu-hardware	System–>Hardware
/usr/lib/sysadmn/.menu-kernel	System–>Configure–>Kernel
/usr/lib/sysadmn/.menu-network	System–>Configure–>Network
/usr/lib/sysadmn/.menu-other	System–>Configure–>Other

The *addlist* file must be in the same **sysadmmenu** format as the *menulist* file.

Create the device file(s) associated with a peripheral device and put the drivers into the kernel. Based on the arguments supplied, **mkdev** calls a script found in the directory **/usr/lib/mkdev**. With no arguments, **mkdev** prints a usage message.

Arguments

aio	Add support for asynchronous disk I/O to the kernel.
bitpad	Configure supported bitpad devices.
cdrom	Add CD-ROM support to the kernel.
dos	Initialize necessary devices and configure system to support mounted DOS filesystems.
dda	Add direct device access support for SCO VP/ix to the kernel.
eccd	Configure corollary ECC daemon.
fd	Create bootable, root, and filesystem floppy disks.
fs	Perform the system maintenance tasks required to add a new filesystem to the system after the device is configured using **mkdev hd**.

graphics
Configure graphics adapters for use with applications that can take advantage of them.

hd	Create device files for use with a peripheral hard disk.

high–sierra
Configure a mountable filesystem found on a CD-ROM drive.

ida	Configure intellegent drive array.
layers	Add support for serial terminals with AT&T windowing capabilities to the kernel.
lp	Add or modify a printer configuration.
mmdf	Interactively alter MMDF configuration.
mouse	Initialize necessary devices and configure the system to use any supported mouse.

parallel
Allow configuration of multiple parallel ports.

ptty	Add pseudo-ttys to the system.
serial	Create device files for use with serial cards.
shl	Initialize necessary devices and configure kernel parameters associated with the number of shell layers sessions available on the system.

streams
Configure the kernel for streams support.

tape	Configure tape driver in preparation for linking a new kernel that includes tape support.
vpixld	Add line discipline for SCO VP/ix to the system.

System Admin. Commands

mkfs	**/etc/mkfs** [*options*]

Construct a filesystem by writing on the special file *filesys* according to *options*. **mkfs** is actually a frontend that invokes the appropriate version of **mkfs** according to a filesystem type specified by the -f option.

Syntax

/etc/mkfs [-y|-n] [-f *fstype*] *filsys blocks* [:*inodes*]
[*gap blocks/cylinder*] [*filesystem–specific options*]

/etc/mkfs [-y|-n] *filsys proto* [*gap blocks/cylinder*]
[*filesystem–specific options*]

XENIX filesystem options: [-s *blocks*[:*inodes*]]
UNIX filesystem options: [-b *blocksize*]
AFS filesystem options: [-E][-C *clustersize*]

Options

  blocks Size of filesystem interpreted as a decimal number; number of physical (512K) disk blocks the filesystem will occupy, if *proto* (see below) not given as an argument.

  -C *clustersize*
      Cluster size for the filesystem. This only applies to AFS (Acer Fast Filesystem) and EADF (Extended Acer Fast Filesystem).

  -f   Filesystem type, one of: AFS (Acer Fast Filesystem), S51K (UNIX), XENIX, or DOS.

  :*inodes* Number of inodes for filesystem.

  gap blocks/cylinder
      Rotational gap and number of blocks/cylinder.

  -n   Terminate without question if target contains an existing filesystem.

  proto Prototype file that **mkfs** takes directions from, if *blocks* (see above) not given as an argument.

  -s   XENIX filesystem option—command-line override of the size and number of inodes in the *proto* file.

  -y   Overwrite existing data without operator confirmation. |
| **mkhosts** | **mkhosts**

TCP/IP command. Make node name commands. **mkhosts** makes the simplified forms of the **rcmd** and **rlogin** commands. For each node listed in **/etc/hosts**, *mkhosts* creates a link to **/usr/bin/rcmd** in **/usr/hosts**. Each link's name is the same as the node's official name in **/etc/hosts**. |

mmdf

Route mail locally and over any supported network.

/usr/mmdf/table/tools/mmdfalias

MMDF command—convert XENIX-style aliases file to MMDF format. After installing MMDF with **custom**, restore **/usr/lib/mail/aliases** from backup tape. Place the following line in the file to indicate where the list aliases end and the mapping aliases begin:

```
#  user-to-machine mapping
```

Log in as *mmdf* and run the **/usr/mmdf/table/tools/mmdfalias** conversion script from the **/usr/mmdf/table** directory. You now have two MMDF files, **alias.list** and **alias.user**, in the current directory. After creating these files, you must rebuild the MMDF hashed database. While logged in as *mmdf*, run **dbmbuild** from **/usr /mmdf/table**.

/usr/mmdf/table/tools/mnlist

MMDF command—convert a XENIX-style Micnet routing file to MMDF format. After installing MMDF with **custom**, restore **/usr/lib/mail/top** from backup media. Log in as *mmdf* and run the conversion script **/usr/mmdf/table/tools/mnlist** from the **/usr /mmdf/table** directory, producing a Micnet channel file, **micnet.chn**, in the current directory. After creating these files, you must rebuild the MMDF hashed dabase. While logged in as *mmdf*, run **dbmbuild** from **/usr/mmdf/table**.

/usr/bin/mnt [*options*] [*directory*]

Mount selected filesystems. The superuser can define how and when a filesystem mount is permitted via the **/etc/default/filesys** file.

Options

- `-a`   Use when system has autobooted.
- `-n`   Mount filesystems defined as **fstyp** "NFS" with **rcmount** set to **yes** in the **/etc/default/filesys** file. Filesystems of this type should have **bdev** defined as follows:

    bdev=*hostname:pathname*

- `-r`   File to be mounted read-only.
- `-t`   Display contents of **/etc/default/filesys**.
- `-u`   Force **mnt** to behave like **umnt**; unmount filesystems.

/etc/default/filesys

The following options can be defined in the */etc/default/filesys* entry for a filesystem:

bdev=/dev/device
> Name of block *device* associated with filesystem.

cdev=/dev/device
> Name of character *device* associated with filesystem.

mountdir=/directory
> Directory filesystem to be mounted on.

desc=name
> String describing filesystem.

passwd=string
> Optional password prompted for at mount request time.

fsck=yes, no, dirty, prompt
> If **yes/no**, tells whether or not to run **fsck**. If **dirty**, **fsck** is run only if filesystem requires cleaning. If **prompt**, user is prompted for a choice. If no entry is given, default value is **dirty**.

fsckflags=flags
> Any flags to be passed to **fsck**.

rcfsck=yes, no, dirty, prompt
> Similar to **fsck** entry, but only applies when **-r** flag is passed.

maxcleans=n
> Number of times to repeat cleaning of a **dirty** filesystem before giving up. Default is 4.

mount=yes, no, prompt
> If **yes** or **no**, users are allowed or disallowed to mount the filesystem, respectively. If **prompt**, the user specifies whether filesystem should be mounted.

remount=yes, no, prompt
> If **yes**, filesystem is mounted by **/etc/rc2** when system comes up as multiuser. If **no**, the filesystem is never mounted by **/etc/rc2**. With **prompt**, a query is displayed at boot time to mount the filesystem.

mountflags=flags
> Any flags to be passed to **mount**.

prep=yes, no, prompt
> Whether any **prepcmd** entry should always be executed, never executed, or executed as specified by user.

prepcmd=command
> An arbitrary shell command to be invoked immediately following password check and prior to running **fsck**.

init=yes, no, prompt
> Whether an **initcmd** entry should always be executed, never be executed, or executed as specified by user.

initcmd=*command*
> Optional, arbitrary shell command to be invoked immediately following a successful mount.

fstyp=*type*
> Defines filesystem type. Available types include NFS, S51K, XENIX, and DOS.

nfsopts=*opts*
> Defines NFS options for NFS filesystems.

/etc/mount [*options*] *special–device directory*

Mount a file structure. **mount** announces to the system that a removable file structure is present on *special-device*. The file structure is mounted on *directory*, which must already exist and should be empty; it then becomes the name of the root of the newly mounted file structure. If **mount** is invoked with no arguments, it displays the name of each mounted device, the directory on which it is mounted, whether the file structure is read-only, and the date it was mounted. Only the superuser can use the **mount** command.

Options

-f *fstyp*
> Mount filesystem of type *fstyp*.

-r   Mount file read-only.

-v   Display mount information verbosely.

/etc/mountd [*options*]

NFS mount request server. **mountd** reads the file **/etc/xtab**, described in **exports**, to determine which filesystems are available for mounting by which machines. It also provides information as to what filesystems are mounted by which clients.

/etc/mountall [*option*]

Mount multiple filesystems. **mountall** is used to mount filesystems according to **/etc/default/filesys**.

Option

-a   Write output messages to the **/etc/bootlog** file, and mail them later to the system administrator. **mount** is called with -a when the system autoboots.

/etc/mvdir *dirname newdirname*

Move a directory, *dirname*, to a new directory, *newdirname*. If there is already a directory or file with the same name as *newdirname*, **mvdir** fails. Neither name may be a subset of the other.

named	# named [*options*]
	
	TCP/IP command—Internet domain name server. **named** is used by resolver libraries to provide access to the Internet distributed naming database. With no arguments, **named** reads **/etc/named.boot** for any initial data and listens for queries on a privileged port. See RFC 1034 and RFC 1035 for more details.
	
	Options
	
	-d *debuglevel*
	   Print debugging information. *debuglevel* is a number indicating the level of messages printed.
	
	-p *port#*
	   Use *port#* as the port number. Default is standard port number as listed in **/etc/services**.
	
	[-b] *bootfile*
	   This is optional and allows you to specify a file with a leading dash—any additional argument is taken as the name of the boot file.

ncheck	# /etc/ncheck [*options*] [*filesystem*] Generate names from inode numbers. A single *filesystem* may be specified rather than the default list of mounted filesystems. **Options** -a Allow printing of names . and .., which are ordinarily suppressed. -i *numbers* Limit report to those files whose inode numbers follow. -s Limit report to special files and files with setuid mode.
netconfig	# netconfig [*options*] [*chain*] [*element*] TCP/IP command—configure networking products. **netconfig** installs the device drivers, configures the kernel, and modifies the startup files to support the newly installed device. **netconfig** views the layers of the TCP/IP architecture as links in a chain. Adding a chain enables the functions of the chain components with a single command. Removing a chain disables the functions of the chain components. **netconfig** can be used either interactively or from the command line. Interactively, **netconfig** gives the user a list of the currently configured chains as part of the main menu. **Menu options** The **netconfig** menu has the following options: **Add a Chain** Enable (configure) specified chain. **Remove a Chain** Disable specified chain.

Reconfigure an Element
Reconfigure part of a chain.

Quit   Exit **netconfig**.

Command-line options

When using **netconfig** from the command line, the following options are available:

-a *chain*   Add specified *chain*.

-C -a|r *chain*
            Check specifed *chain*.

-c *chain element*
            Reconfigure an *element* in a *chain*.

-d   Use defaults for all prompts. Vendor-specific configuration scripts should supply the defaults.

-e *chain*   Output list of elements in given *chain*.

-L *chain*   Output list of *chain*'s elements and their descriptions.

-l   Relink and install kernel. Suppress link kernel prompt.

-m *chain* | -m
            Provide menu of allowable next-level down chain elements. If specified *chain* is a null word (""), provide list of top-level products.

-n   Do not link kernel even if changes were made that require relinking.

-r *chain*   Remove specified *chain*.

-s   Print list of currently installed chains and exit.

-t   Print only terse chain names.

-v   Print **netconfig** version number and exit.

---

netstat [*options*] [*interval*] [*system*] [*corefile*]

TCP/IP command—show network status. If an *interval* is specified, **netstat** will continuously display the information regarding packet traffic on the configured network interfaces, pausing *interval* seconds before refreshing the screen. The defaults for *system* and *corefile* are **/unix** and **/dev/kmem**, respectively.

Options

-A   Show the address of any protocol control blocks associated with sockets. Used for debugging.

-a   Show the state of all sockets.

-f*address_family*
            Limit statistics or address control block displays to *address_family*. The only *address_family* currently supported is **inet**.

-I *interface*
            Show interface state for *interface* only.

$\rightarrow$

netstat
←
	-i Show the state of interfaces that have been auto-config-
	        ured.
	-m Show network memory usage.
	-n Show network addresses as numbers.
	-p *protocol_name*
	        Limit statistics and control block displays to *proto-
	        col_name.*
	-r Show routing tables.
	-s Show per-protocol statistics.

---

netutil

/etc/netutil [*arguments*]

TCP/IP command—administer the Micnet network, a link through serial lines of two or more systems. **netutil** allows the user to create and maintain a network of UNIX machines. It is used to send mail between systems with **mail**, transfer files between systems with **rpc**, and execute commands from a remote system with **remote**. **netutil** is used to create and distribute the data files needed to implement the network.

Arguments

   option The *option* argument may be any one of:
       install   Interactively create data files needed to run
                 the network.
       restore   Copy data files from floppy disk back to a
                 system.
       save   Save data files on floppy or hard disks.
       start   Start the network.
       stop   Stop the network.
       If **netutil** is invoked without an *option*, it displays a
       menu of options. Decimal digit options 1 to 5 corre-
       spond to those menu options.
   -e   Log errors.
   -x   Log transmission.

---

nfs

/etc/nfs
/etc/nfs start
/etc/nfs stop

NFS start/stop script. NFS will start automatically at system startup time if **/etc/nfs** is linked to **/etc/rc2.d/S**name. Similarly, NFS will stop automatically at system shutdown time if **/etc/nfs** is linked to **/etc/rc0.d/K**name. **/etc/nfs** must be customized for a particular installation before it can be used. The following items may need to be edited:

   domain name
          The YPDOMAIN variable must be set to the name of
          your NFS domain.

PATH	The supplied path may require modification if commands run by /etc/nfs are in other directories.
PROCS	The **PROCS** variable contains a space-separated list of names of processes to kill when executing the **stop** function. If additional daemons are used, their names should be added to this list.
daemons	The standard NFS daemons are started at this point. Any additional daemons or other commands may be included in this section. Any standard daemons that are not desired may be removed or commented out. By default, **pcnfsd**, **ypserv**, and **yppasswdd** are disabled.

---

nfsclnt [*nclienthandles*]

Create NFS client handles. NFS client programs obtain a client handle for the duration of an RPC operation. *nclienthandles* is the number of client handles allocated. If additional client handles are required, more **nfsclnt** processes may be started. The number of client handles available to NFS client programs is the sum of the number of client handles allocated by each **nfsclnt** program.

/usr/etc/nfsd [*nservers*]

Daemon that starts the NFS server daemons that handle client filesystem requests. *nservers* is the number of filesystem request daemons to start.

---

nfsstat [*options*]

NFS/NIS command—display statistical information about the NFS and RPC interfaces to the kernel. It can also be used to reinitialize this information. If no options are given the default is:

    nfsstat -cnrs

That is, display everything, but reinitialize nothing.

Options

- **-c** Display client information. Only the client-side NFS and RPC information will be printed. Can be combined with the **-n** and **-r** options to print client NFS or client RPC information only.
- **-n** Display NFS information. NFS information for both the client and server side will be printed. Can be combined with the **-c** and **-s** options to print client or server NFS information only.
- **-r** Display RPC information.
- **-s** Display server information.

nfsstat ←	-z Zero (reinitialize) statistics. This option can be combined with any of the above options to zero particular sets of statistics after printing them. The user must have write permission on **/dev/kmem** for this option to work.

nictable	**/usr/mmdf/table/nictable** [*options*]
	
	Process NIC database into channel/domain tables. **nictable** is the tool responsible for taking the **hosts.txt** table supplied by the SRI Network Information Center and creating domain and channel tables.
	
	Options
	   -C Generate a channel table on the standard output.
	   -D Create a domain table. This option should be combined with the -d option, which identifies the domain table to be built.
	   -d *domain*
	       Output hosts in *domain* only, unless combined with the -T option, in which case all entries will be output *except* for those in *domain*.
	   -s *service*
	       Output only hosts listed as supporting *service*.
	   -T Create a *top* or *rootdomain* table. No trailing domain spec is removed from the LHS entry.
	   -t *transport*
	       Output only hosts listed as supporting the *transport* protocol specified.

nlsadmin	**nlsadmin** [*options*]
	
	NFS/NIS command—administer network listener process(es) on a machine. **nsladmin** can establish a listener process for a given network, configure its specific attributes, and start and kill the listener process for that network. It can also report on the listener processes on a machine, either individually or collectively. Invoked with no options, **nsladmin** gives a brief usage message.
	
	In the following options, *net_spec* represents a particular listener process, specifically the relative pathname of the entry under **/dev** for a given network. *service_code* is the code for the service, *cmd* is the command to be invoked in response to that code, and *comment* is a brief description of the service for use in reports.
	
	Options
	   -d *service_code net_spec*
	       Disable service indicated by *service_code* for the specified network.

-e *service_code net_spec*

    Enable service indicated by *service_code* for the specified network.

-i *net_spec*

    Initialize or change a listener process for the network specified by *net_spec*.

-k *net_spec*

    Kill listener process for indicated *net_spec*.

-l *addr net_spec*

    Change or set address on which listener listens.

[-m] -a *service_code* [-p *modules*][-w *id*] -c *cmd* -y*comment net_spec*

    Add new service to the list of services available through the indicated listener. -m specifies the entry will be marked as an administrative entry. -m with -a indicates that special handling internally is required for those servers added with the -m set. With -p, *modules* will be interpreted as a list of STREAMS modules for the listener to push before starting the service being added. With -w, *id* is interpreted as the user name from /etc/passwd that the listener should look up.

-q *net_spec*

    Query status of *net_spec* for the specified network and reflect the result of that query in the exit code.

-r *service_code net_spec*

    Remove entry for *service_code* from that listener's list of services.

-s *net_spec*

    Start listener process for indicated network.

-t *addr net_spec*

    Change or set address on which listener listens for requests for terminal service.

-v *net_spec*

    Print verbose report on servers associated with *net_spec*, giving the service code, status, command, and comment for each.

-x

    Report status of all listener processes installed on machine.

-z *service_code net_spec*

    Print a report on the server associated with *net_spec* that has service code *service_code*, giving the service code, status, command, and comment.

/etc/nmountall

NFS/NIS command—mount multiple filesystems. **nmountall** is used to mount NFS filesystems according to entries in **/etc/fstab**. This command may be executed only by the superuser.

numountall	**/etc/numountall**
	NFS/NIS command—unmount multiple filesystems. **numountall** causes all NFS mounted filesystems to be unmounted. Processes which hold open files or have current directories on these filesystems are killed by being sent a series of signals: SIGHUP; one second later SIGTERM; and one second later SIGKILL. This command may be executed only by the superuser.
nslookup	**nslookup** [*–option . . .*] [*host–to–find*	*–* [*server*]]
	TCP/IP command—query Internet domain name servers. **nslookup** has two modes: interactive and non-interactive. Interactive mode allows the user to query name servers for information about various hosts and domains or to print a list of hosts in a domain. It is entered when either no arguments are given (default name server will be used), or when the first argument is a hyphen and the second argument is the hostname or Internet address of a name server. Non-interactive mode is used to print just the name and requested information for a host or domain. It is used when the name of the host to be looked up is given as the first argument. The optional second argument specifies a name server.

Interactive commands

    exit   Exit the **nslookup**.

    finger [*name*] [>|>>*filename*]
        Connect with finger server on current host, optionally creating or appending to *filename*.

    help   ? prints a brief summary of commands.

    host [*server*]
        Look up information for **host** using the current default server or using *server* if specified.

    ls **-**[**ahd**] *domain* [>|>>*filename*]
        List information available for *domain*, optionally creating or appending to *filename*. The **-a** option lists aliases of hosts in the domain. **-h** lists CPU and operating system information for the domain. **-d** lists all contents of a zone transfer.

    lserver *domain*
        Change the default server to *domain*. Use the initial server to look up information about *domain*.

    root   Change default server to the server for the root of the domain name space.

    server *domain*
        Change the default server to *domain*. Use the current default server to look up information about *domain*.

    view *filename*
        Sort and list output of previous **ls** command(s) with **more**.

Change state information affecting the lookups. Valid keywords are:

all Print the current values of the frequently-used options to **set**.

class=*name*

  Set query class to one of IN (Internet), CHAOS, HESIOD or ANY. Default is IN.

domain=*name*

  Change default domain name to *name*.

[no]debug

  Turn debugging mode on or off.

[no]d2 Turn exhaustive debugging mode on or off.

[no]defname

  Append default domain name to every lookup.

[no]ignore

  Ignore truncate error.

[no]recurse

  Tell name server to query or not query other servers if it does not have the information.

[no]search

  With *defname*, search for each name in parent domains of current domain.

[no]vc Always use a virtual circuit when sending requests to the server.

port=*port#*

  Connect to name server using *port#*.

querytype=*value*

  See **type=***value*.

retry=*number*

  Set number of retries to *number*.

root=*host*

  Change name of root server to *host*.

srchlist=*domain*

  Set search list to domain.

timeout=*number*

  Change time-out interval for waiting for a reply to *number* seconds.

type=*value*

  Change type of information returned from a query to one of:

A	Host's Internet address
CNAME	Canonical name for an alias
HINFO	Host CPU and operating system type
MD	Mail destination
MX	Mail exchanger
MG	Mail group member
MINFO	Mailbox or mail-list information
MR	Mail rename domain name
NS	Nameserver for the named zone

*System Admin.
Commands*

ntpdate	**ntpdate** [*options*] *host* ...

TCP/IP command—set the date and time via NTP. **ntpdate** polls the Network Time Protocol server(s) on the host(s) given as arguments to determine the correct time. It must be run as root on the local host. **ntpdate** can be inserted in the **/etc/rc.local** startup script to set the time of day at boot time and/or can be run from time-to-time via **cron**. **ntpdate** will decline to set the date if an NTP server daemon is running on the same host.

Options

   -a *key#*
       All packets should be authenticated using key number *key#*.

   -b   Step the time.

   -d   Determine what **ntpdate** would do, without actually doing it. Information useful for general debugging is also printed.

   -e *authdelay#*
       Specify authentication processing delay, *authdelay#*, in seconds.

   -k *keyfile*
       Read keys from *keyfile* instead of default **/etc/ntp.keys**.

   -o   Force **ntpdate** to poll as an NTP version 1 implementation.

   -p *samples*
       Set number of *samples* acquired from each server to between 1 and 8 inclusive. Default is 4.

   -s   Log actions via **syslog** rather than to standard output.

   -t *timeout*
       Time **ntpdate** will spend waiting for a response, rounded to a multiple of 0.2 seconds. Default is 1 second. |
| **ntpq** | **ntpq** [*options*] [*host*] [...]

TCP/IP command—Standard Network Time Protocol query program. **ntpq** queries NTP servers that implement the recommended mode 6 control-message format about current state and requests changes in that state. The program may be run either interactively or with command-line arguments.

Options

   Options other than **-i** or **-n** will cause the specified query to be sent to the indicated host immediately. Otherwise, **ntpq** will attempt to read interactive format commands from the standard input. |

-c *command*

> *command* is interpreted as an interactive format command and is added to the list of commands to be executed on the specified host(s). Multiple **-c** options may be given.

-i
> Force **ntpq** to operate in interactive mode. Prompts will be written to the standard output and commands read from the standard input.

-n
> Output all host addresses in dotted-quad numeric format, rather than converting to the canonical hostnames.

-p
> Print a list of the peers known to the server as well as a summary of their state.

Interactive format commands

Interactive format commands consist of a keyword followed by zero to four arguments. The output of a command is normally sent to standard output, but may optionally be sent to a file. A number of interactive format commands are executed entirely within the **ntpq** program itself and do not result in NTP mode 6 requests being sent to a server. Following are these format commands:

? [*command_keyword*]

> A **?** by itself will print a list of all the command keywords known to this incarnation of **ntpq**. A **?** followed by a command keyword will print function and usage information about the command.

addvars *variable_name*[*=value*][, ...]

rmvars <*variable_name*> [, ...]

clearvars The data carried by NTP mode 6 messages consists of a list of items of the form:

$$<variable\_name>=<value>$$

> **addvars** allows variables and their optional values to be added to the list, **rmvars** removes individual variables from the list, and **clearvars** removes all variables from the list.

authenticate yes|no

> Normally, requests are not authenticated unless they are write requests. **authenticate yes** causes **ntpq** to send authentication with all requests it makes.

cooked Causes output from query commands to be "cooked." Variables which are recognized by the server will have their values reformatted for human consumption. Variables which **ntpq** thinks should have a decodeable value, but didn't, are marked with a trailing **?**.

debug *more| less| off*

> Turn internal query program debugging on and off.

→

*System Admin.
Commands*

delay *milliseconds*
> Specify a time interval to be added to timestamps included in requests which require authentication.

host *hostname*
> Set the host to which future queries will be sent. *hostname* may be either a hostname or a numeric address.

hostnames yes|no
> If **yes** is specified, hostnames are printed in information displays. If **no** is given, numeric addresses are printed instead. Default is **yes** unless modified using the command line –**n** option.

keyid #
> Allow specification of a key number to be used to authenticate configuration requests.

ntpversion 1|2
> Set the NTP version number that **ntpq** claims in packets. Defaults to 2 since mode 6 control messages (and modes, for that matter) didn't exist in NTP version 1. There appear to be no servers left which demand version 1.

passwd
> Prompt for password to be typed in that will be used to authenticate configuration requests. Password will not be echoed.

poll [#] [verbose]
> Poll the current server in client mode. The first argument is the number of times to poll (default is 1). The second argument may be given to obtain a more detailed output of the results. This command is currently just wishful thinking.

raw
> All output from query commands is printed as it was received from the remote server.

timeout *milliseconds*
> Specify a timeout period for responses to server queries. The default is about 5000 milliseconds.

quit
> Exit **ntpq**.

Control message commands

Control message commands result in one or more NTP mode 6 messages being sent to the server and cause the data returned to be printed in some format. Most commands send a single message and expect a single response. Current exceptions are the **peers**, **mreadlist** and **mreadvar** commands, which will iterate over a range of associations.

associations
> Obtain and print a list of association identifiers and peer statuses for in-spec peers of the server being queried.

clockvar [*assocID*][<*variable_name*>[=<*value*>[, ...]

> Requests that a list of the server's clock variables be sent.

cv [*assocID*][<*variable_name*>[=<*value*>[, ...]

> Easy-to-type short form of **clockvar** command.

lassociations

> Obtain and print a list of association identifiers and peer statuses for all associations for which the server is maintaining state.

lpassociations

> Print data for all associations, including out-of-spec client associations, from the internally cached list of associations.

lpeers Like **peers**, except a summary of all associations for which the server is maintaining state is printed.

mreadvar *assocID* *assocID* [<*variable_name*>[=<*value*>[, ...]

> Like **readvar**, except query is done for each of a range of (nonzero) association IDs.

mrv *assocID* *assocID* [<*variable_name*>[=<*value*>[, ...]

> Easy-to-type short form of **mreadvar**.

mreadlist *assocID* *assocID*

> Like **readlist**, except the query is done for each of a range of (nonzero) association IDs.

mrl *assocID* *assocID*

> Easy-to-type short form of **mreadlist** command.

opeers An old form of the peers command, with the reference ID replaced by the local interface address.

passociations

> Print association data concerning in-spec peers from the internally cached list of associations.

peers Obtain a list of in-spec peers of the server, along with a summary of each peer's state.

pstatus *assocID*

> Send a read status request to the server for the given association.

readvar [*assocID*][<*variable_name*>[=<*value*>[, ...]

> Request that values of the specified variables be returned by the server by sending a read-variables request. If the association ID is omitted or is given as zero, the variables are system variables; otherwise they are peer variables, and the values returned will be those of the corresponding peer.

readlist [*assocID*]

> Request that values of the variables in the internal variable list be returned by the server. If the association ID is omitted or is 0 the variables are assumed to be system variables. Otherwise they are treated as peer variables.

→

ntpq ←	**rl** [*assocID*]
	Easy-to-type short form of **readlist**.
	rv [*assocID*][<*variable_name*>[=<*value*>[, ...]
	Easy-to-type short form for **readvar**.
	writelist [*assocID*]
	Like **readlist**, except the internal list variables are written instead of read.
	writevar [*assocID*][<*variable_name*6>[=<*value*>[, ...]
	Like **readvar**, except the specified variables are written instead of read.

passmgmt	**passmgmt** *arguments* [*options*] *name*

NFS/NIS command—update information in the password files. **passmgmt** works with **/etc/passwd.local**. The login name of the user, *name*, must be unique.

Arguments

-a   Add an entry for user *name* to the login password files. This command does not create any directory for the new user, and there is no password until **passwd** or **yppasswd** is executed to set the password. Options (listed below) may be used with this argument.

-d   Lock the account for user *name* from the login password files. This does not remove any files owned by the user on the system; they must be removed manually.

-f   Unlock the account for user *name* from the login password files. This will not remove any files owned by the user on the system; they must be removed manually.

-m   Modify the entry for user *name* in the login password files. All the fields in the **/etc/passwd.local** entry can be modified by this command. Only fields entered on the command line will be modified. Options (listed below) may be used with this argument.

-n   Alter the status for networked user *name* from a networked account to a local account.

-r   Retire the account for user *name* from the login password files. This will not remove any files owned by the user on the system; they must be removed manually.

Options

The following options may be used with the -a and -m arguments of **passmgmt**.

-c *comment*
    Short description of the login, limited to a maximum of 128 characters. Default is an empty field.

-g *gid*   GID of the *name* argument. This number must range from 0 to the maximum value for the system. Default is 1.

-h *homedir*

Home directory of *name* argument, limited to a maximum of 256 characters. Default is **/usr/name**.

-l *logname*

Change *name* argument to *logname*. Used with **-m** option only.

-o Allow a UID to be non-unique. Used with the **-u** option only.

-s *shell*

Login shell for *name* argument. *shell* should be the full pathname of the program that will be executed when the user logs in. Maximum length of *shell* is 256 characters. The default is for this field to be empty and to be interpreted as **/bin/sh**.

-u *uid* UID of *name* argument. This number must range from 0 to the maximum value for the system. It defaults to the next available UID greater than 100. Without the **-o** option, it enforces the uniqueness of a UID.

Diagnostics

passmgmt exits with one of the following values:

0	SUCCESS
1	Permission denied
2	Invalid command syntax
3	Invalid argument provided to option
4	UID in use
5	Inconsistent password files
6	Unexpected failure. Password files unchanged.
7	Unexpected failure. Password files missing.
8	Password files busy; try again later.
9	*name* argument either does not exist (if **-m** or **-d** is specified), already exists (if **-a** is specified), or *logname* already exists (if **-m -l** is specified).

pax [*arguments*] [*options*]

Portable archive exchange. **pax** reads and writes archive files that conform to the "Archive/Interchange File Format" specified in *IEEE Std. 1003.1-1988*. **pax** will also support traditional **cpio** and System V **tar** interfaces if invoked with the name **cpio** or **tar** respectively.

Operands

The following operands are available:

directory

Destination directory pathname for copies when both **-r** and **-w** options are specified.

pathname

File whose contents are used instead of files named on the standard input.

System Admin.
Commands

→

pattern

> A *pattern* is given in the standard shell pattern-matching notation. The default, if no pattern is specified, is *, which selects all files.

Command-line arguments

Combinations of the -r and -w command-line arguments specify whether **pax** will read, write, or list the contents of the specified archive, or move the specified files to another directory. The command-line arguments are:

-w   Write files and directories specified by *pathname* operands to the standard output, together with the pathname and status information prescribed by the archive format used.

-r   Read an archive file from standard input. Only files with names matching any of the *pattern* operands are selected for extraction.

-rw   Read files and directories named in *pathname* operands and copy them to the destination *directory*.

Options

-a   Files specified by *pathname* are appended to the specified archive.

-b *blocking*

> Block the output at *blocking* bytes per write to the archive file.

-d   Do not create intermediate directories not explicitly listed in the archive. This option is ignored unless -r option is specified.

-f *archive*

> Pathname of input or output archive

-i   Interactively rename files.

-L   Follow symbolic links.

-l   Link files rather than copy, when possible.

-m   Do not retain file-modification times.

-o   Restore file ownership as specified in the archive.

-p   Preserve access time of input files after they have been copied.

-s *replstr*

> Filenames are modified according to substitution using the syntax of **ed**:

>   -s /old/new

-t *device*

> *device* is an implementation-defined identifier that names the input or output archive device.

-u   Copy each file only if it is newer than a pre-existing file with the same name.

-v   List filenames as they are encountered.

-x *format*

        Output archive format

-y   Interactively prompt for disposition of each file.

/etc/pcnfsd [*options*]

NFS/NIS command—NFS authentication and print request server. **pcnfsd** is an RPC server that supports ONC clients on PC systems. It is started from **/etc/nfs**. **pcnfsd** reads the configuration file **/etc/pcnfsd.conf**, if present, then services RPC requests directed to program number 150001. This release of the **pcnfsd** daemon supports both version 1 and version 2 of the **pcnfsd** protocol. Requests serviced by **pcnfsd** fall into three categories: authentication, printing, and other. Only the authentication and printing services have administrative significance.

Authentication

When **pcnfsd** receives a PCNFSD_AUTH or PCNFSD2_AUTH request, it will log in the user by validating the username and password and returning the corresponding uid, gids, home directory, and umask. At this time, **pcnfsd** will also append a record to the *wtmp* database. If you do not want to record PC logins in this way, add the line:

    wtmp off

to the **/etc/pcnfsd.conf** file.

Printing

pcnfsd supports a printing model based on the use of NFS to transfer the actual print data from the client to the server. The client system issues a PCNFSD_PR_INIT or PCNFSD2_PR_INIT request, and the server returns the path to a spool directory that the client may use and that is exported by NFS. **pcnfsd** creates a subdirectory for each of its clients: the parent directory is normally **/usr/spool/pcnfs** and the subdirectory is the hostname of the client system. If you want to use a different parent directory, add the line:

    spooldir *path*

to the **/etc/pcnfsd.conf** file. Once a client has mounted the spool directory and has transferred print data to a file in this directory, it will issue a PCNFSD_PR_START or PCNFSD_PR_START request. **pcnfsd** constructs a command based on the printing services of the server operating system and executes the command using the identity of the PC user. Every print request includes the name of the printer to be used. **pcnfsd** interprets a printer as either a destination serviced by the system print

→

pcnfsd ←	spooler, or as a virtual printer. Virtual printers are defined by the following line in the **/etc/pcnfsd.conf** file: *printer name alias-for command* where *name* is the name of the printer you want to define, *alias-for* is the name of a real printer that corresponds to this printer, and *command* is a command that will be executed whenever a file is printed on *name*.

---

pipe

/etc/pipe [*options*]

List or define pipe filesystem. Only one pipe filesystem may be designated at a time.

Options

- -d   Disable pipes (there is no pipe filesystem). Existing pipes are not affected.
- -l   List name of pipe filesystem (*/dev/xxx*). **If there is no pipe filesystem, nothing is output.**
- -s *path_name*
     Designate pipe filesystem to be that on which *path_name* resides.

---

pkgadd

/usr/bin/pkgadd [*options*]

Transfer a software package to the system. When executed without options, **pkgadd** uses **/usr/spool/pkg** (the default).

Options

- -a *admin*
     Define an installation administration file, *admin*, to be used in place of the default administration file.
- -d *device*
     Install or copy a package from *device*. *device* can be a full pathname to a directory or the identifiers for tape, floppy disk, or removable disk. It can also be the device alias.
- -n   Installation occurs in non-interactive mode (default is interactive). Installation will halt if any interaction is needed to complete it.
- *pkginst*   Package instance or list of instances to be installed. The token **all** may be used to refer to all packages available on the source medium. The form *pkginst.** can be used to indicate all instances of a package.

-r *response*

> Identify a file or directory *response* (must be full path-name) that contains output from a previous **pkgask** session.

-s *spool*

> Read the package into the directory *spool* instead of installing it.

/usr/bin/pkgask [*options*]

Store answers to a request script.

Options

-d *device*

> Run request script for a package on *device*. *device* can be a full pathname to a directory or the identifiers for tape, floppy disk, or removable disk. Default *device* is the installation spool directory.

-r *response*

> Create file or directory *response* to contain responses to interactions with the package.

pkginst Package instance or list of instances for which request scripts will be created. The token **all** may be used to refer to all packages available on the source medium. *pkginst.** can be used to indicate all instances of a package.

/usr/bin/pkgchk [*options*]

Check accuracy of installation. Discrepancies are reported on standard error along with a detailed explanation of the problem.

Options

-a

> Audit file attributes only; do not check file contents. Default is to check both.

-c

> Audit file contents only; do not check file attributes. Default is to check both.

-d *device*

> Device on which a spooled package resides. *device* can be a directory pathname or identifiers for tape, floppy disk, or removable disk.

-e *envfile*

> Use **pkginfo** file *envfile* to resolve parameters noted in the specified **pkgmap** file.

-f

> Correct file attributes if possible. When invoked with this option, **pkgchk** creates directories, named pipes, links, and special devices, if they do not already exist.

-i *file* Read list of pathnames from *file* and compare against the installation software database or indicated *pkgmap* file.

→

pkgchk ←	-l	List information on the selected files that make up a package. Not compatible with -a, -c, -f, -q, and -v options.
	-m *pkgmap*	Request that package be checked against the indicated *pkgmap* file.
	-n	Do not check volatile or editable files. This should be used for most post-installation checking.
	-p *pathname*	Check accuracy only of pathname(s) listed.
	-q	Quiet mode; do not give messages about missing files.
	-v	Verbose mode. Files are listed as processed.
	-x	Search exclusive directories only, looking for existing files that are not in the installation software database or the indicated *pkgmap* file. If used with -f option, hidden files are removed and no other checking is done.
	pkginst	Package instance or instances to be checked. The format *pkginst*.* can be used to check all instances of a package.

---

pkginfo

pkginfo [*options*]

Display software package information. For packages installed using **custom**, no information will be displayed. For packages displayed using **installpkg**, only the package name and abbreviation will be displayed. Without options, **pkginfo** lists the primary category, package instance, and name of all completely and partially installed packages.

Options

- -a *arch*
  Specify architecture of the package as *arch*.

- -c *category*
  Select packages to be displayed based on the category *category*.

- -d *device*
  Define a device on which the software resides. *device* can be a full pathname to a directory, or the identifiers for tape, floppy disk, or removable disk.

- -i Present information only for fully installed packages.

- -l Long format, which includes all available information about designated packages.

- -p Present information only for partially installed packages.

- -q Use from a program to check whether or not a package has been installed; this option does not list any information.

-v *version*

> Version of the package is specified as *version*. All compatible versions can be requested by preceding the version name with a tilde (~).

-x

> Extract listing of package information, containing package abbreviation, package name, and, if available, package architecture and package version.

pkginst Designate package by its instance. An instance can be the package abbreviation or a specific instance. The form *inst.** can be used to request all instances of a package.

pkgmk [*options*]

Produce an installable package to be used as input to the **pkgadd** command. The package contents will be in directory structure format. **pkgmk** uses the package *prototype* file as input and creates a *pkgmap* file. The contents for each entry in the *prototype* file are copied to the appropriate output location. Information concerning the contents is computed and stored in the *pkgmap* file, along with attribute information specified in the *prototype* file.

Options

-a *arch*

> Override architecture information provided in the *pkginfor* file with *arch*.

-b *basedir*

> Prepend indicated *basedir* to locate relocatable objects on source machine.

-d *device*

> Create package on *device*. *device* can be a full pathname to a directory, or the identifiers for tape, floppy disk, or removable disk. Default device is the installation spool directory.

-f *prototype*

> Use file *prototype* as input to the command. Default name for this file is either *Prototype* or *prototype*.

-l *limit*

> Maximum size, in 512-byte blocks, of the output device as *limit* packages.

-o

> Overwrite the same instance; package instance will be overwritten if it already exists.

-p *pstamp*

> Override production stamp definition in *pkginfo* file with *pstamp*.

-q

> Use from a program to check whether or not a package has been installed. This option does not list any information.

→

pkgmk ←	**-r** *rootpath* 　　Ignore destination paths in the *prototype* file. Instead, use indicated *rootpath* with the source pathname appended to locate objects on the source machine. *variable=value* 　　Place indicated variable in the packaging environment. **-v** *version* 　　Override version information provided in the *pkginfo* file with *version*. *pkginst* Specify package by its instance. **pkgmk** will automatically create a new instance if the version and/or architecture is different.
pkgparam	**pkgparam** [*options*] Display package parameter values. If no parameters are specified on the command line, values for all parameters associated with the package are shown. **Syntax** 　　pkgparam [-v] [-d *device*] *pkginst* [*param* [...]] 　　pkgparam -f *file* [-v][*param* [...]] **Options** 　　**-d** *device* 　　　　*device* on which a *pkginst* is stored. It can be a full pathname to a directory, or the identifiers for tape, floppy disk, or removable disk. Default *device* is installation spool directory. 　　**-f** *file*　Request that **pkgparam** read *file* for parameter values. 　　**-v**　　Verbose mode; display name of parameter and its value. 　　*param*　Specific parameter whose value should be displayed. 　　*pkginst* Specific package instance for which parameter values should be displayed. The format *pkginst.** can be used to indicate all instances of a package.
pkgproto	**pkgproto** [*options*] Generate a prototype file. **pkgproto** scans the indicated paths and generates a *prototype* file that may be used as input to the **pkgmk** command. By default, **pkgproto** creates symbolic link entries for any symbolic link encountered (**ftype=s**). **Options** 　　**-c** *class* 　　　　Map class of all paths to *class*. 　　**-i**　　Ignore symbolic links and record the paths as **ftype=f** (file), versus **fytpe=s** (symbolic link—the default).

pkgrm [*options*]

Remove a package from the system. A check is made to determine if any other packages depend on the one being removed. The action taken if a dependency does exist is defined in the *admin* file (see below). The default state for **pkgrm** is interactive mode.

Options

-a *admin*

> Define an installation administration file, *admin*, to be used in place of the default administration file.

-n

> Non-interactive mode. If there is a need for interaction, the command will exit.

-s *spool*

> Remove specified package(s) from the directory *spool*.

pkginst Package to be removed. The format *pkginst.** can be used to remove all instances of a package.

pkgtrans [*options*] *device1 device2* [*pkginst* ...]

Translate an installable package from one format to another. *device1* is source device, *device2* is target device.

Options

-i

> Copy only *pkginfo* and *pkgmap* files.

-n

> Create new instance if any instance of this package already exists.

-o

> Overwrite the same instance on the destination device; package instance will be overwritten if it already exists.

-s

> Write package to *device2* as a datastream rather than as a filesystem. Default is to write a filesystem format on devices that support both formats.

pkginst Package instance(s) on *device1* to be translated. The token **all** may be used to indicate all packages. *pkginst.** can be used to indicate all instances of a package.

Examples

The following example translates all packages on the floppy drive **/dev/diskette** and places the translations on **/tmp**:

```
pkgtrans /dev/diskette /tmp all
```

The next example translates packages *pkg1* and *pkg2* on **/tmp** and places their translations on the cartridge tape output device:

```
pkgtrans /tmp ctape1 pkg1 pkg2
```

portmap	**/etc/portmap** [*options*]
	
	NFS/NIS command—DARPA port to RPC program number mapper. (**portmap** is a server that converts DARPA protocol port numbers into RPC program numbers. It must be running in order to make RPC calls.) When an RPC server is started, it will tell **portmap** what port number it is listening to and what RPC program numbers it is prepared to serve. When a client wishes to make an RPC call to a given program number, it will first contact **portmap** on the server machine to determine the port number where RPC packets should be sent.
	
	Options
	   -d Run **portmap** in debugging mode.
	   -v Display **portmap** information verbosely.

ppp	**/usr/lib/ppp/ppp** TCP/IP command—login shell for the Point-to-Point Protocol. **ppp** provides a method for transmitting datagrams over serial point-to-point links. It passes the name of its controlling tty to **pppd** through shared memory, then waits for the PPP datagram traffic on this link to stop, either through a timeout or an active close of the link. When the tty is released, **pppd** will kill the **ppp** process and break the IP connection to the remote host.

prfdc	**/etc/prfdc** *file* [*options*]
	
	Perform data collection function of the system profiler by copying the current value of all the text address counters to a file where the data can be analyzed.
	
	Options
	  period Store counters in *file* every *period* minutes.
	  off_hour
	          Turn **prfdc** off at *off_hour*.

prfld	**/etc/prfld** [*option*]
	
	Initialize the recording mechanism in the system.
	
	Option
	  system_namelist
	          Generate a table containing the starting address of each system subroutine as extracted from *system_namelist*.

prfpr	**/etc/prfpr** *file* [*options*] Format data of system profiler collected by **prfdc** or **prfsnap**.

Options

> cutoff Text address is printed if the percent activity for that range is greater than *cutoff*.

> system_namelist
>> Each text address is converted to the nearest text symbol as found in *system_namelist*.

/etc/prfsnap *file*

Perform data collection function of the system profiler by copying the current value of all the text address counters to a file where the data can be analyzed. **prfsnap** collects data at the time of invocation only, appending the counter values to *file*.

/etc/prfstat *on | off*

Enable (**on**) or disable (**off**) the sampling mechanism in the system. Profiler overhead is less than one percent, as calculated for 500 text addresses. **prfstat** will also reveal the number of text addresses being measured.

/usr/lib/cron/.proto
/usr/lib/cron/.proto.queue

Prototype job file for **at**, **cron**, and **batch**. Job files are constructed as shell scripts. If the job is submitted in queue *queue*, **at** uses the file **/usr/lib/cron/.proto.queue** as the prototype file, if it exists; otherwise **at** uses the file **/usr/lib/cron/.proto**.

Example

> The standard .proto file supplied is:

```
#ident "@(#)adm:.proto 1.2"
cd $d
ulimit $1
umaks $m
$<
```

> which causes commands to: change the current directory in the job to the current directory at the time **at** was run; change the file size limit in the job to the file size limit at the time **at** was run; and to change the umask in the job to the umask at the time **at** was run, to be inserted before the commands in the job.

---

prwarn [*options*] [*users*]

Issue a warning about password expiration. By default, warnings will be issued at six hour intervals if password is due to expire within seven days. If no *users* are specified, logged-in user is assumed.

→

prwarn
←
	Options
	    -d *days*
	        Days left until password expiration.
	    -t *hh*[*mm*]
	        Interval in hours and minutes since last warning of password expiration.

ps	**ps** [*options*]
	
	Report on active processes. In options, *list* arguments should either be separated by commas or put in double quotes. In comparing the amount of output produced, note that -e > -d > -a and -l > -f.
	
	Options
	
	    -a List all processes except group leaders and processes not associated with a terminal.
	    -d List all processes except session leaders.
	    -e List all processes.
	    -f Produce a full listing.
	    -g*list* List data only for specified *list* of group leader ID numbers (i.e., processes with same ID and group ID).
	    -l Produce a long listing.
	    -n*list* Use the alternate *list* of names (default is **/unix**).
	    -p*list* List data only for process IDs in *list*.
	    -t*list* List data only for terminals in *list* (e.g., **tty1**).
	    -u*list* List data only for usernames in *list*.

pwck	**pwck** [*file*] Check password file *file*. Checks include: validation of the number of fields, login name, user ID, group ID, and whether the login directory and optional program name exist. The default password file is **/etc/passwd**.
pwconv	**pwconv** Install and update the shadow password file. **pwconv** creates and updates **/etc/shadow** with information from the Protected Password database and **/etc/passwd**. The command populates **/etc/shadow** with the user's login name, password, and password aging information. Following is the format of an entry in **/etc/passwd**: *username:passwd,aging:uid:gid:comment:homedir:shell*
pwunconv	**pwunconv** Remove the shadow password file. Password and password aging information held in **/etc/shadow** are written back to **/etc/passwd**

and to the Protected Password database, then **/etc/shadow** is removed.

pwunconv

---

quot [*options*] ... [*filesystem*]

quot

Summarize filesystem ownership by printing the number of blocks in the *filesystem* currently owned by each user. Blocks are reported in 512-byte blocks. If no *filesystem* is named, filesystems given in **/etc/mnttab** are examined.

Options

- **-c**   Display three columns giving filesize in blocks, number of files of that size, and cumulative total of blocks in files of that size or smaller.
- **-f**   Display a count of the number of files, as well as space owned by each user.
- **-n**   Process standard input. This option makes it possible to produce a list of all files and their owners, with the following command:

    ncheck *filesystem* **| sort +0n | quot -n** *filesystem*

/etc/rarpd [*options*]

rarpd

TCP/IP Reverse Address Resolution Protocol daemon. **rarpd** starts a daemon that responds to RARP requests. For the request to be answered, a machine's name-to-IP-address entry must exist in the */etc/hosts* file or must be available from the domain name server, and its name-to-Ethernet-address entry must exist in the **/etc/ethers** file. **rarpd** forks a copy of itself, and requires *root* privileges.

Options

- **-a**   Invoke daemon on all configured interfaces, excluding: interfaces marked down, interfaces on which **arp** has been disabled, the loopback interface, point-to-point interfaces, and interfaces not supporting broadcast packets.
- **-d**   Print debug information to standard output.
- **if** [*hostname*]
        Interface parameter string of the form "name unit"; for example: **wde0**. *hostname* is the interface's corresponding hostname. **if** *hostname* should be the same as the arguments passed to **ifconfig**.

/etc/rc0

rc0

Run commands to stop the operating system. One system state requires this procedure: state 0 (the system halt state). Whenever a change to this state occurs, the **/etc/rc0** procedure is run. The recommended sequence for **/etc/rc0** is:

→

rc0 ←	1. Stop system services and daemons. 2. Terminate processes. 3. Kill processes. 4. Unmount all filesystems (except root).

rc2	**/etc/rc2** Run commands for multiuser environment. **/etc/rc2** is executed via an entry in **/etc/inittab**, and is responsible for those initializations that bring the system to a ready-to-use state, traditionally state2, called the multiuser state. **/etc/rc2** is intended for execution by **init** and must never by executed directly by a user. **/etc/rc2** performs the following functions in the following order: 1. Run the script **/etc/conf/bin/idmkenv**, which sets up the new kernel environment, calls **idmkinit** to rebuild the **/etc/inittab** file, and links files to the **/etc/idrc.d** and **/etc/idsd.d** directories to be run by **/etc/rc2**. 2. Run the system setup scripts in the directory **/etc/rc2.d**. 3. Run the system setup scripts in the directory **/etc/rc.d**, which exists for XENIX compatibility. 4. Run the system setup scripts in the directory **/etc/idrc.d**, which contains scripts from the driver packages linked from **/etc/conf/rc.d**. 5. Run the scripts in **/etc/idsd.d**, which contains shutdown scripts linked from **/etc/conf/sd.d**. 6. Runs the script **/etc/rc**, which exists for XENIX compatibility. It is an empty file, but you can add initialization commands to the file.

rcmd	**rcmd** *node* [*options*] [*command*]
	
	TCP/IP command—remote shell command execution. **rcmd** sends *command* to *node* for execution. It passes the resulting remote command its own standard input and outputs the remote command's standard output and standard error. *command* can consist of more than one parameter. A second, simplified form of the command is available if the system administrator previously ran **mkhosts**:
	
	    /usr/hosts/node [*options*] [*command*]
	
	Options
	
	    −1 *user*
	        The command is to belong to *user* on *node*.
	
	    −n Prevent remote command from blocking on input by making its standard input be **/dev/null** instead of **rcmd**'s standard input.

Examples

The following command runs **who** on a node called "central," putting the output in a file on the local machine:

```
rcmd central who > /tmp/c.who
```

---

rdate

TCP/IP command—notify the time server that date has changed. If the local time server is a master, it will notify all of the slaves that the time has been changed. If the local time server is a slave, it will request that the master update the time.

/etc/reboot [*options*]

Close out filesystems, shut down the system, then reboot the system. Because this command immediately stops all processes, it should be run only in single-user mode.

/tcb/bin/reduce [*options*]

Perform audit data analysis and reduction. The format of the reduced data varies with the type of event being processed. Each record will include the process ID of the process being audited, the date and time of the event, the type of audit event, an indication of success or failure for the event, and, if applicable, the object names that were accessed.

Options

-s *session*
>   Specified boot session during which reduction is performed.

-p *selection_file*
>   Audit selection file on which reduction to be performed.

/etc/relax *level*

Change system security defaults to one of several predefined *levels* located in **/tcb/lib/relax**.

/usr/lib/layersys/relogin [*options*]

Rename login entry to show current layer. **relogin** changes the terminal *line* field of a user's *utmp* entry to the name of the windowing terminal layer attached to standard input.

$\rightarrow$

relogin ←	**Options** *line* *utmp* entry to change. -s Suppress error messages.
removef	**removef** *pkginst path1* [*path2*] **removef -f** *pkginst* Checks if a filename can be removed. Output from **removef** is the list of input pathnames that may be removed safely (no other packages have a dependency on them). **Option** -f After all files have been processed, **removef** should be invoked with -f to indicate that the removal phase is complete.
removepkg	**removepkg** [*software_package*] Remove installed package. **removepkg** will search the list of previously installed packages and remove the first name matched by *software_package*. With no argument, **removepkg** will query the user, via a menu, as to which package to remove. **removepkg** does not work on packages installed with **custom**.

restore	**restore** [*options*]
	
	Incremental filesystem backup restore. **restore** acts as a front end to **cpio** and thus reads **cpio**-format tapes or floppies. It should only be used to restore backups made with the AT&T **backup** utility, not **xbackup**.
	
	Options
	
	-c Complete restore. All files on the tape are restored.
	
	-d *device*
	     device is the raw device to be used. It defaults to /dev/rdsk/f0q15d (the 1.2M floppy).
	
	-i Get the index file off the medium. This only works when the archive was created using **backup**. The output is a list of all the files on the medium. No files are actually restored.
	
	-o Overwrite existing files. If file being restored already exists, it will not be restored unless this option is specified.
	
	pattern
	     When doing restore, one or more *patterns* can be specified to match against the files on the tape. When a match is found, the file is restored.

-t Use tape device. This option must be used with the **-d** option when restoring from tape.	**restore**

/etc/rexd

NFS/NIS command—RPC-based remote execution server. For noninteractive programs, the standard file descriptors are connected directly to TCP connections. Interactive programs involve pseudo-terminals, in a fashion that is similar to the login sessions provided by **rlogin**. This daemon may use NFS to mount filesystems specified in the remote execution request.

/etc/rexecd [*options*]

TCP/IP command—server for the **rexec** routine, providing remote execution facilities with authentication based on usernames and passwords. **rexecd** is started by **inetd** and must have an entry in inetd's configuration file, /etc/inetd.conf. When **rexecd** receives a service request, the following protocol is initiated:

1. The server reads characters from the socket up to a null byte. The resultant string is interpreted as an ASCII number, base 10.

2. If the number received in step 1 is non-zero, it is interpreted as the port number of a secondary stream to be used for the stderr. A second connection is then created to the specified port on the client's machine.

3. A null-terminated username of at most 16 characters is retrieved on the initial socket.

4. A null-terminated, unencrypted password of at most 16 characters is retrieved on the initial socket.

5. A null-terminated command to be passed to a shell is retrieved on the initial socket. The length of the command is limited by the upper bound on the size of the system's argument list.

6. **rexecd** then validates the user as is done at login time and, if the authentication was successful, changes to the user's home directory and establishes the user and group protections of the user.

7. A null byte is returned on the connection associated with the stderr and the command line is passed to the normal login shell of the user. The shell inherits the network connections established by **rexecd**.

Diagnostics

`username too long`
         Name is longer than 16 characters.

→

rexecd
←
	`password too long`
	     Password is longer than 16 characters.
	`command too long`
	     Command passed exceeds the size of the argument list.
	`Login incorrect`
	     No password file entry for the username exists.
	`Password incorrect`
	     Wrong password was supplied.
	`No remote directory`
	     chdir to home directory failed.
	`Try again` **fork** by server failed.
	`<shellname>: . . .`
	     fork by server failed. User's login shell could not be started.

---

ripquery

ripquery [*options*] *gateway*

TCP/IP command—query RIP gateways—request all routes known by a RIP *gateway* by sending a RIP request or POLL command. The routing information in any routing packets returned is displayed numerically and symbolically. **ripquery** is intended to be used as a tool for debugging gateways, not for network management.

Options

-**n**   Display network and host numbers numerically only.

-**p**   Use RIP POLL to request information from the routing table. This is the default, but is an undocumented extension supported only by some versions of **routed** and later versions of **gated**.

-**r**   Use RIP REQUEST to request information from the gateway's routing table. Unlike RIP POLL, all gateways should support the RIP REQUEST.

-**v**   Display version information about **ripquery** before querying the gateways.

-**w** *time*
    Time in seconds to wait for the initial response from a gateway. Default is five seconds.

---

rlogind

/etc/rlogind

TCP/IP command—server for the **rlogin** program, providing a remote login facility with authentication based on privileged port numbers from trusted hosts. **rlogind** is invoked by **inetd** when a remote login connection is established and executes the following protocol:

• The server checks the client's source port. If the port is not in the range 0-1023, the server aborts the connection.

• The server checks the client's source address and requests the corresponding hostname. If the hostname cannot be determined, the dot-notation representation of the host address is used.	**rlogind**

The login process propagates the client terminal's baud rate and terminal type, as found in the environment variable, TERM.

/etc/rlpconf	**rlpconf**

TCP/IP command—configure remote line printers. **rlpconf** edits the remote line printer description file **/etc/printcap** and creates the spooling directory for the remote line printers. The spooling directory is always located in **/ust/spool/lpd** and bears the name of the printer. **rlpconf** is used interactively.

rmail *user*...	**rmail**

TCP/IP command—handle remote mail received via **uucp**, collapsing From lines in the form generated by **mail** into a single line of the form return-path!sender and passing the processed mail onto **sendmail**. **rmail** is explicitly designed for use with **uucp** and **sendmail**.

/tcb/bin/rmuser *users* **/tcb/lib/auth_scripts/rmgroup** **/tcb/lib/auth_scripts/rmpasswd**	**rmuser**

Remove user accounts from the system. A user account consists of a line in **/etc/passwd**, entries in **/etc/group** and a Protected Password database file. **rmuser** removes all three entities from the system. If no *users* are specified, then **rmuser** will read standard input for account names, one per line. **rmuser** uses **ale** and two underlying shell scripts, **rmpasswd** and **rmgroup** to do the actual removal.

/etc/route [*options*] *add* | *delete*	**route**

TCP/IP command—manually manipulate the routing tables normally maintained by **routed**. **route** accepts two commands: **add**, to add a route, and **delete**, to delete a route. All commands have the following syntax:

   /etc/route *command destination gateway* [*metric*]

where *destination* is a host or network for which the route is to, *gateway* is the gateway to which packets should be addressed, and *metric* is an optional count indicating the number of hops to the *destination*. If no *metric* is specified, **route** assumes a value of 0. Only the superuser may modify the routing tables.

→

route
←
	Options
	
	  -f Flush the routing tables of all gateway entries.
	
	  -n Prevents attempts to print host and network names symbolically when reporting actions.

routed	**/etc/routed** [*options*] [*logfile*]
	
	TCP/IP command—network routing daemon. **routed** is invoked by the superuser at boot time to manage the Internet Routing Tables. The routing daemon uses a variant of the Xerox NS Routing Information Protocol in maintaining up-to-date kernel routing-table entries. When **routed** is started, it uses the SIOCGIFCONF ioctl to find those directly connected interfaces configured into the system and marked up. **routed** transmits a REQUEST packet on each interface and enters a loop, listening for REQUEST and RESPONSE packets from other hosts. When a REQUESTP packet is received, **routed** formulates a reply based on the information maintained in its internal tables. The generated RESPONSE packet contains a list of known routes. Any RESPONSE packets received are used to update the Routing Tables as appropriate.
	
	When an update is applied, **routed** records the change in its internal tables, updates the kernal Routing Table, and generates a RESPONSE packet reflecting these changes to all directly-connected hosts and networks.
	
	Options
	
	  -d Stop **routed** going into background and releasing itself from the controlling terminal, so that interrupts from the keyboard will kill the process.
	
	  -g Offer a route to the default destination.
	
	  -q Opposite of -s option
	
	  -s Force **routed** to supply routing information, whether it is acting as an internetwork router or not.
	
	  -t Increment the tracing level. Successive levels are:
	        routed -t Trace actions only.
	        routed -t -t Trace actions and packets.
	        routed -t -t -t
	                Trace actions and history of packets and contents after change.
	        routed -t -t -t -t
	                Trace actions, packets, and contents.

rpcgen	**rpcgen** *infile* **rpcgen** [*options*] [*infile*] NFS/NIS command—RPC protocol compiler. The input to **rpcgen** is a language similar to C, known as the RPC Language (Remote Procedure Call Language). In the first syntax above, **rpcgen** takes an input file and generates four output files. If *infile* is named *proto*.x,

then **rpcgen** will generate: a header file in *proto*.h, XDR routines in *proto_xdr*.c, server-side stubs in *proto_*svc.c, and client-side stubs in *prot_clnt*.c. The second syntax example of **rpcgen** uses the options listed below.

Options

-c   Compile into XDR routines.

-h   Compile into C data-definitions (a header file).

-l   Compile into client-side stubs.

-m   Compile into server-side stubs, but do not produce a *main()* routine.

-o *outfile*
> Specify the name of the output file. If none is specified, standard output is used (-c, -h, -l, and -s modes only).

-s *transport*
> Compile into server-side stubs, using the given transport.

---

rpcinfo [*options*] [*host*] [*program*] [*version*]

NFS/NIS command—report RPC information. *program* can be either a name or a number. If a *version* is specified, **rpcinfo** attempts to call that version of the specified *program*. Otherwise, it attempts to find all the registered version numbers for the specified *program* by calling version 0, and it attempts to call each registered version.

Options

-b *program version*
> Make an RPC broadcast to procedure 0 of the specified *program* and *version*, using UDP, and report all hosts that respond.

-n **portnum**
> Use **portnum** as the port number for the -t and -u options, instead of the port number given by the port-mapper.

-p [*host*]
> Probe the portmapper on host and print a list of all registered RPC programs. If *host* is not specified, it defaults to the value returned by hostname.

-u *host program* [*version*]
> Make an RPC call to procedure 0 of *program* on the specified *host* using UDP and report whether a response was received.

-t *host program* [*version*]
> Make an RPC call to procedure 0 of *program* on the specified *host* using TCP and report whether a response was received.

rpcinfo
←
	Examples
	
	To show all of the RPC services registered on the local machine use:
	
	`$ rpcinfo -p`
	
	To show all of the RPC services registered on the machine named klaxon use:
	
	`$ rpcinfo -p klaxon`
	
	To show all machines on the local net that are running the Network Information Service (NIS) use:
	
	`$ rpcinfo -b ypserv` *version* `| uniq`
	
	Where *version* is the current NIS version obtained from the results of the -p switch above.

rshd	**/etc/rshd** TCP/IP command—remote shell server for programs such as **rcmd** and **rcp**, which need to execute a noninteractive shell on remote machines. **rshd** is started by **inetd**, and must have an entry in **inetd**'s configuration file, **/etc/inetd.conf**.
runacct	**/usr/lib/acct/runacct** [*mmdd* [*state*]] Run daily accounting. **runacct** is the main daily accounting shell procedure and is normally initiated by **cron**. It processes connect, fee, disk, and process accounting files. *mmdd* specifies the month and day for which **runacct** will rerun the accounting and is necessary if **runacct** is being restarted. **runacct** breaks its processing into separate restartable *states*. Following are the *states*, and the order in which they are executed: SETUP Move active accounting files into working files. WTMPFIX <blockquote>Verify integrity of **wtmp** file; correct data changes if necessary.</blockquote>CONNECT1 <blockquote>Produce connect session records in **ctmp.h** format.</blockquote>CONNECT2 <blockquote>Convert **ctmp.h** records to **tacct.h** format.</blockquote>PROCESS <blockquote>Convert process accounting records to **tacct.h** format.</blockquote>MERGE <blockquote>Merge connect and process accounting records.</blockquote>FEES Convert output of **chargefee** into **tacct.h** format and merge with connect and process accounting records.

DISK Merge disk accounting records with connect, process, and fee accounting records.	**runacct**

MERGETACCT
>Merge daily total accounting records in **daytacct** with the summary total accounting records in **/usr/adm/acct/sum/tacct**.

CMS   Produce command summaries.

USEREXIT
>Any installation-dependent accounting programs may be included here.

CLEANUP
>Clean up temporary files and exit.

/etc/ruserd

ruserd

Network user name server. **ruserd** returns a list of users on the network. This daemon is usually invoked by **inetd**.

/etc/rwhod

rwhod

TCP/IP command—system status server that maintains the database used by the **rwho** and **ruptime** programs. Its operation is predicated on the ability to broadcast messages on a network. As a producer of information, **rwhod** periodically queries the state of the system and constructs status messages which are broadcast on a network. As a consumer of information, it listens for other **rwhod** servers' status messages, validates them, then records them in a collection of files located in the directory **/usr/spool/rwho**. Messages received by the **rwhod** server are discarded unless they originated at an **rwhod** server's port. Status messages are generated approximately once every five minutes.

/usr/lib/sa/sa1 [*options*]

sa1

Part of the system activity report package. **sa1**, a variant of **sadc**, is a shell script used to collect and store data in the binary file **/usr/adm/sa/sa**dd, where dd is the current day.

Options

n Number of times to sample system data. Default is once.

t Interval of seconds between samples.

/usr/lib/sa/sa2 [*options*]

sa2

Part of the system activity report package. **sa2**, a variant of **sar**, is a shell script used to write a daily report in file **/usr/adm/sa/sar**dd, where dd is the current day.

$\rightarrow$

sa2 ←	**Options** *sa2* uses the same options as **sar** except for the following: *t*, *n*, -o *file*, and -f *file*.

sadc	**/usr/lib/sa/sadc** [*options*]
	
	sadc, the data collector of the system activity report package, samples system data and writes in binary format to *ofile*, or to standard output. If both **t** and **n** are omitted, a special record is output. This facility is used at boot time when booting to a multiuser state to mark the time at which the counters restart from zero.
	
	Options
	  n Number of times to sample system data
	  ofile Binary file written to by **sadc**
	  t Interval of seconds between samples

sag	**sag** [*options*]
	
	System activity graph. **sag** graphically displays the system activity data stored in a binary data file by a previous **sar** run. **sag** invokes **sar** and finds the desired data by string-matching the data column header. The following options are passed through to **sar**:
	
	Options
	  -e *time*
	     Select data up to *time*. Default is 18:00.
	  -f *file* Use *file* as data souce for **sar**. Default is the current daily data file **/usr/adm/sa/sadd**.
	  -i *sec* Select data at intervals as close as possible to *sec* seconds.
	  -s *time*
	     Select data later than *time* in the form *bb*[:*mm*]. Default is 08:00.
	  -T *term*
	     Produce output suitable for terminal *term*. Default is **$TERM**.
	  -x *spec*
	
	     x-axis specification with *spec* in the form: "*name* [*op name*]…[*lo bi*]," where *name* is either a string that will match a column header in the **sar** report, with an optional device name in square brackets, or an integer value.
	  -y *spec*
	
	     y-axis specification with *spec* in the same form as above.

sar [*options*]

System activity report package.

Options

-A	Report all data. Equivalent to **-udqbwcayvmprSDC**.
-a	Report use of file-access system routines.
-b	Report buffer activity.
-C	Report Remote File Sharing buffer-caching overhead.
-c	Report system calls.
-D	Report Remote File Sharing activity. **-Du** is assumed when only **-D** is specified.
-d	Report activity for each block device.

-e *time*
> End time of report in the form *hh*[:*mm*[:*ss*]].

-f *file* Extract data from a previously recorded *file*, either one specified by -f or, by default, the standard system activity daily data file **/usr/adm/sa/sa***dd* for the current day *dd*.

-i *sec* Select records at *sec*-second intervals. Otherwise, all intervals found in the date file are reported.

-m	Report message and semaphore activities.
-n	Report name-cache statistics.

-o *file* Save samples in *file* in binary format.

-p	Report paging activities.
-q	Report average queue length while occupied and percent of time occupied.
-r	Report unused memory pages and disk blocks.
-S	Report server- and request-queue status.

-s *time*
> Start time of report in the form *hh*[:*mm*[:*ss*]].

-u	Report CPU utilization (the default).
-v	Report status of process, inode, file tables.
-w	Report system swapping and switching activity.
-y	Report TTY device activity.

t [*n*] Sample cumulative activity counters in the operating system at *n* intervals of *t* seconds, where *t* should be 5 or greater. Default value of *n* is 1.

schedule

Database for automated system backups. **schedule** is used in conjunction with **fsphoto** to partially automate system-wide backups. For each filesystem to be backed up, a cyclical schedule of **xbackup** or **cpio** levels is specified. This cyclical schedule is a list of backup levels to perform and a pointer to the last-used element of that list. The pointer is advanced to the next element of the list on a regular basis, starting at the beginning each time it falls off the

→

schedule
←
	end. It is advanced only on success. Several keywords in the **schedule** file are recognized:
	
	[0-9] *size savetime importance marker*
	    Description of each backup level, as described in **fsave**. All four fields must be specified. A *size* means to use the first size listed in the appropriate **media** *sizes* list.
	
	media *drive* **k** *size* [*size* ...] [*format*]
	    Device *drive* is a floppy disk or tape drive capable of handling volumes with any of the listed *sizes* (in kilobytes). If specified, *format* is the command used to format the described floppies.
	
	media *drive* **d** *density size* [*size* ...] [*format*]
	    Device *drive* is a *density* BPI magtape drive capable of handling tapes of any of the indicated *sizes* (in feet). If specified, *format* is the command used to format the described floppies.
	
	site *sitename*
	    sitename is passed to **fsave** as a description to place on each tape label.

script	**script** [*option*] [*file*] TCP/IP command—make typescript of a terminal session. The typescript is written to *file*. If no *file* is given, the typescript is saved in the file *typescript*. The script ends when the forked shell exits. *Option* -a *file* Append typescript to *file* instead of *typescript*.
sd	**sd** *command* [*argument*] **tcb/files/no_luid/sdd** Start a no-LUID (login user identifier) daemon. **sd** is only necessary if the kernel is configured to enforce LUID restrictions. Daemons are normally started from **/etc/rc2.d** and set their LUID using the **su** command. Daemons like **cron** that must run specifically without an LUID should be run via **sdd**. **sdd** is itself a daemon process, started from **inittab**. **sd** sends requests to **sdd** for other daemon processes to be started.
sendmail	**/usr/lib/sendmail** [*flags*] [*address* ...] **sendmail** is a mail router. It accepts mail from a user's mail program, interprets the mail address, rewrites the address into the proper form for the delivery program, and routes the mail to the correct delivery program. *Syntax* **/usr/lib/sendmail** [*flags*] [address ...]

- -b*x* Set operation mode to *x*. Operation modes are:
  - a   Run in ARPAnet mode.
  - d   Run as a daemon.
  - i   Initialize the alias database.
  - m   Deliver mail (default).
  - p   Print the mail queue.
  - s   Speak SMTP on input side.
  - t   Run in test mode.
  - v   Merely verify addresses, do not collect or deliver.
  - z   Freeze the configuration file.
- -C*file* Use configuration file *file*.
- -d*level* Set debugging level.
- -F *name*

    Set full name of user to *name*.
- -f *addr*

    Sender's machine address is *addr*.
- -h *cnt* Set hop count (number of times message has been pro-
    cessed by **sendmail** to *cnt*.
- -n   Do not alias or forward.
- -o*x value*

    Set option *x* to value *value*. Options are described
    below.
- -q*time* Try to process queued-up mail.
- -r *addr*

    Obsolete form of -f.
- -t   Read head for To:, Cc:, and Bcc: lines, and send to
    everyone on those lists.
- -v   Verbose.

Configuration options

The following options can be set with the -o flag on the command line, or the O line in the configuration file:

A*file* Use alternate alias file.

B*c*   Set blank substitution character to *c*.

c   On mailers that are considered "expensive" to connect
      to, don't initiate immediate connection.

d*x*   Set the delivery mode to *x*. Delivery modes are **i** for
      interactive (synchronous) delivery, **b** for background
      (asynchronous) delivery, and **q** for queue only—i.e.,
      actual delivery is done the next time the queue is run.

D   Try to automatically rebuild the alias database if neces-
      sary.

e*x*   Set error processing to mode *x*. Valid modes are **m** to
      mail back the error message, **w** to write back the error
      message, **p** to print the errors on the terminal (default),
      q to throw away error messages, and **e** to do special
      processing for the BerkNet.

sendmail	F*mode*	Mode to use when creating temporary files.
←	f	Save UNIX-style From: lines at the front of messages.
	g*n*	Default group id to use when calling mailers.
	H*file*	SMTP help file
	i	Do not take dots on a line by themselves as a message terminator.
	I	Use Domain Name Server, **named**.
	L*n*	Log level
	M*xvalue*	
		Set macro *x* to *value*.
	m	Send to "me" (the sender) also if I am in an alias expansion.
	o	If set, this message may have old-style headers. If not set, this message is guaranteed to have new-style headers (i.e., commas instead of spaces between addresses).
	Q*queuedir*	
		Select the directory in which to queue messages.
	r*timeout*	
		The timeout on reads; if none is set, **sendmail** will wait forever for a mailer.
	S*file*	Save statistics in the named file.
	s	Always instantiate the queue file, even under circumstances where it is not strictly necessary.
	T*time*	Set the timeout on undelivered messages in the queue to the specified time.
	t*stz, dtz*	
		Set name of the time zone.
	u*N*	Set default user ID for mailers.
	w	Allow wildcard MX records.

---

setany

setany *arguments*

TCP/IP command—retrieve and set variables in an SNMP entity. **setany** does a GET request to get the current values of the variables to be set, then performs a SET request on the variables.

Arguments

entity_addr
> Entity name or address in Internet dot-notation

community_name
> Community name for access to the SNMP entity

[*"variable_name"* –<i/o/d/a/c/g/t/s/n> *value*] . . .
> Triplet for each variable to be set, consisting of:
> * Variable name in dot-notation
> * Letter preceded by a dash to indicate if the variable's value is being given as an integer (i), octet string (o), object identifier (d), IP address

(a), counter (c), gauge (g), time-tick (t), string (s), or null (n).

• The value

For example:

```
setany 128.169.1.1 suranet0 "ifAdminStatus.2" -i 3
```

sets the administrative status of interface 2 to 3.

---

setclock [*time*]

Set the system real-time (time-of-day) clock to the given *time*. If *time* is not given, the current contents of the battery-powered clock are displayed. *time* must be a combination of digits with the form:

MMddhhmmyy

where *MM* is the month, *dd* is the day, *hh* is the hour, *mm* is the minute, and *yy* is the last two digits of the year. If *yy* is not given, it is taken from the current system time.

Example

The command:

```
setclock 0826150385
```

sets the time-of-day clock to 15:03 on August 26, 1985.

/etc/setmnt

Create **etc/mnttab** table, which is needed for both the **mount** and **umount** commands. **setmnt** reads the standard input and creates a mnttab entry for each line. Input lines have the format:

filesys node

where *filesys* is the name of the filesystem's *special file* (for example, **hd0**) and *node* is the root name of that filesystem. Thus *filesys* and *node* become the first two strings in the **mnttab** entry.

---

settime [*options*] *name*

Change the access and modification dates of files. There are two methods available to specify the new date(s):

Options

mmddhhmm [*yy*]

Change the access and modification dates to *mmddhhmm*[*yy*]. The first *mm* is the month number; *dd* is the day number in the month; *hh* is the hour number; the second *mm* is the minute number; *yy* is the last two digits of the year (optional).

$\rightarrow$

settime ←	-f *fname* 　　　　Change access and modification dates to that of file 　　　　*fname*.
sfmt	**/etc/sfmt** [*device_name*] Perform special formatting. **sfmt** performs low-level formatting, initializes non-standard disk parameters, and performs initial processing of manufacturer-supplied defect lists of the disk *device_name*. **sfmt** must be issued from the Boot: prompt, and should be used only if the type=E banner appears during power-up.
sg	**sg** [*options*] Set groups—allow users to run shells and commands with a different group ID and a modified supplemental group list. *Options* 　　**sg** reads its options from left to right and performs them as they are read. The **-g**, **-a**, **-r**, and **-s** options are cumulative, but they only take effect when a command is executed by the **-c** option. A *grouplist* is a comma- or whitespace-separated list of group names and group IDs. 　　**-a** *grouplist* 　　　　Add groups to supplemental group list. 　　**-c** *command* 　　　　Pass *command* to user's login shell for execution with the specified supplemental group and/or group ID modifications. Giving the empty string "" as the argument to **-c** causes the user's shell to be run. 　　**-e**　Display supplemental group access list of current process. This is the default. 　　**-g** *group* 　　　　Set real and effective group ID to *group* for subsequent commands to be executed by **sg**. 　　**-r** *grouplist* 　　　　Remove groups from supplemental group list. 　　**-s** *grouplist* 　　　　Set supplemental group list to grouplist. 　　**-t**　Display user's login group plus any groups the user is a member of in **/etc/group**. 　　**-v**　Display new supplemental group access list before each command or shell is run. With **-a** or **-s**, **-v** warns if group to be added is already in supplemental group access list or if group cannot be added because supplemental group access list is full.

Examples

Assuming the user is listed as a member of groups *author* and *editor*, with group IDs of 100 and 200, respectively, here's how to execute a shell with both groups added to the current supplemental group access list:

    sg -a author, editor -c ""

This can also be achieved with:

    sg -a "100 200"

/etc/shutdown [*options*]

Terminate all processing. A broadcast message notifies all users to log off the system. **/etc/init** is called to perform the actual shutdown. Only superusers can execute the **shutdown** command. Broadcast messages, default or defined, are displayed at regular intervals during the grace period; the closer the shutdown time, the more frequent the message.

Options

-f *file* Pathname (*file*) for a file containing a message to be sent to all terminals, warning of the imminent shutdown.

-f Send a message enclosed in double quotes (*"mesg"* to all terminals, warning of the imminent shutdown.

-g[*hh:*]*mm*
Specify number of hours and minutes before shutdown; default is one minute, maximum is 72 hours.

-i[0156sS]
Specify the init level to bring the system to (see **init** for definitions of system levels); default is level 0.

su Let the user go single-user without completely shutting down the system. This option is identical to **-i1**, and is present for backwards compatibility with XENIX.

-y Run command silently. If this option is not specified, **shutdown** will prompt for confirmation to shut down the system.

/etc/sink *host megs*

TCP sink test. **sink** writes *megs* megabytes of data to the discard port on *host*. It is used only for network debugging.

---

slattach [*options*] *tty_name source_address destination_address* [*baud_rate*]

TCP/IP command—attach serial lines as network interfaces. **slattach** assigns the tty line *tty_name* to a network interface, and defines the

→

network *source_address* and *destination_address* values. *baud_rate* is used to set the speed of the connection (default is 9600). To detach a SLIP interface, kill the **slattach** process, then use the following command to remove this Point-to-Point route from the Routing Table:

> **route delete** *destination_address gateway_address*

Only the superuser may attach or detach a network interface.

Options

{+ | -}c   Turn TCP/IP header compression mode on or off. Default is off.

{+ | -}e   Turn automatic detection and use of TCP/IP header compression on or off. Default is off.

{+ | -}i   Turn suppression of ICMP packets on or off. Default is off.

{+ | -}m *mtu*
     Set maximum transmission unit of network interface to *mtu*. Default *mtu* value is 296.

{+ | -}v   Print or do not print various messages about network interface as it is being brought up. Default is to not print messages.

---

slink

slink [*options*] [*func* [*arg1 arg2* ...]]

TCP/IP command—streams linker. Input to **slink** is in the form of a script specifying the STREAMS operations to be performed. Input is normally taken from the file **/etc/strcf**. The configuration file contains a list of functions, each of which is composed of a list of commands. Each command is a call to one of the functions defined in the configuration file or to one of a set of built-in functions, described below.

slink processing consists of parsing the input file, then calling the user-defined function **boot**, which is normally used to set up the standard configuration at boot time. A function to be called instead of **boot** may be specified on the command line.

Options

-c *file*   Use *file* instead of **/etc/strcf**.

-f   Do not fork (i.e. **slink** will remain in foreground).

-v   Verbose—log each operation to standard error.

Built-in functions

dlattach *fd unit*
     Send a DL_ATTACH_REQ message down the stream referenced by *fd* specifying unit *unit*.

initqp *path qname lowat hiwat* ...
     Send an INITQPARAMS ioctl to the driver corresponding to pathname *path*. *qname* specifies the queue for which

the low and high water marks will be set, and must be one of:

hd	Stream head
rq	Read queue
wq	Write queue
muxrq	Multiplexor read queue
muxwq	Multiplexor write queue

link *fd1 fd2*

Link the stream referenced by *fd2* beneath the stream referenced by *fd1*. Returns link identifier associated with the link.

open *path*

Open device specified by pathname *path*. Returns a file descriptor referencing the open stream.

push *fd module*

Push module *module* onto stream referenced by *fd*.

return *val*

Set return value for current function to *val*.

sifname *fd link name*

Send an SIOCSIFNAME ioctl down the stream referenced by *fd* for the link associated with link identifier *link* specifying the name *name*.

strcat *str1 str2*

Concatenate strings *str1* and *str2* and return the resulting string.

unitsel *fd unit*

Send an IF_UNITSEL ioctl down the stream referenced by *fd* specifying unit *unit*.

/etc/slot [*options*]

Read microchannel configuration registers. **slot** displays the contents of the configuration POS registers on a microchannel architecture machine and names the adapter cards currently configured in each slot. For each of the eight adapter slots, **slot** shows the slot number, the unique adapter id (four digits in hexadecimal from registers 0x100 and 0x101), the contents of the remaining six POS registers (two hexadecimal digits each), followed by the adapter card name. The **slot** options select a particular id, a particular slot, or select an alternative names file.

Options

-a *adid*

Show only information for those slots in which an adapter of that id is configured. *adid* should be specified in hexadecimal.

$\rightarrow$

slot ←	-f *adnamesfile* Redirect text displayed by /etc/slot to read from an alternative names file, *adnamesfile*, rather than from /etc/default/slot. -s *slot* Show only information for that *slot*.
smmck	**smmck** [*options*] Single-user mode tcb check script. See **tcbck** for more details on using **smmck**.
snmp	**/etc/snmp stop	start** TCP/IP command—Script to start or stop the SNMP software. For information on automotive *snmp*, see the *rco* and *rc2* commands. SNMP will start automatically at system startup time if **/etc/snmp** is linked to */etc/rc2.d/Sname*snmp (*name* is installed as 73 by default). SNMP will stop automatically at system shutdown time if **/etc/snmp** is linked to */etc/rc0.d/Kname*snmp.

snmpstat	**snmpstat** [*options*] [*host*] [*session*]
	
	TCP/IP command—show network status using SNMP. **snmpstat** symbolically displays the contents of various network-related data structures. *host* and *session* allow substitutes for the defaults **localhost** and **public**. *session* refers to the SNMP session or community in which to make the specified requests.
	
	Options
	
	    -a Show address translation table.
	    -i Show status of active interfaces.
	    -n Display addressses and port numbers numerically instead of symbolically.
	    -r Show routing table.
	    -S Show SNMP status.
	    -s Show variables comprising the *system* group of the MIB.
	    -t Show complete transport endpoint table.

statd	**/etc/statd** [*option*] NFS/NIS command—network status monitor. **statd** interacts with **lockd** to provide the crash and recovery functions for the locking services on NFS. **statd** preserves crash/recovery state in the directory **/etc/sm**. The **record** file records the hostname of all currently monitored systems; **recover** records the hostnames of systems that have not yet been notified of the **statd**'s failure; and **state** records the **statd**'s current version number.

-d *debuglevel*

Activate internal reporting capabilities. A *debuglevel* level of 2 reports significant events; 4 will report internal state and all status monitor request traffic.

---

strace [*arguments*]

Print STREAMS trace messages. Without arguments, **strace** writes all STREAMS event trace messages from all drivers and modules to its standard output. If arguments are provided, they must be in triplets of the form *mid, sid, level*, where *mid* is a STREAMS module id number, *sid* is a sub-id number, and *level* is a tracing priority level. The token *all* may be used for any member to indicate no restriction for that attribute. The format of each trace message output is:

seq time ticks level flags mid sid text

Where:

seq	Trace sequence number
time	Time of message in hh:mm:ss
ticks	Time of message in machine ticks since boot
level	Tracing priority level
flags	E Message is also in the error log.
	F Fatal error
	N Mail was sent to the system administrator.
mid	Module-id number of source
sid	Sub-id number of source
text	Formatted text of the trace message

Examples

Output all trace messages from the module or driver whose module id is 41:

    strace 41 all all

Output those trace messages from driver/module id 41 with sub-ids 0, 1, or 2:

    strace 41 0 1 41 1 1 41 2 0

---

strclean [*options*]

Clean up the STREAMS error-logger directory on a regular basis. By default, all files with names matching **error.*** in **/usr/adm/streams** that have not been modified in the last three days are removed.

→

strclean ←	**Options** -d *logdir* Specify directory other than **/usr/adm/streams**. -a *age* Maximum age, in days, for a log file.

strerr	**strerr**
	
	STREAMS error logger daemon. **strerr** receives error-log messages from the STREAMS log driver and appends them to a log file. The error log files produced reside in the directory **/usr/adm/streams** and are named **error.mm-dd**, where *mm* is the month and *dd* is the day of the message contained in each log file. The format of an error log message is:
	
	   seq time ticks flags mid sid text
	
	Where:
	
	  seq Error sequence number
	  time Time of message in hh:mm:ss
	  ticks Time of message in machine ticks since boot
	  flags T Message was also sent to a tracing process.
	          F Fatal error
	          N Mail was sent to the system administrator.
	  mid Module-id number of source.
	  sid Sub-id number of source.
	  text Formatted text of the error message.

submit	**/usr/mmdf/bin/submit** MMDF mail queue manager. All mail enters into MMDF through **submit**, which allows flexibility in batching multiple submissions, response and error handling, and address source specification. **submit** can be called directly from a user's terminal, but is better accessed through a program such as **mail**.
sulogin	**sulogin** Access single-user mode. **sulogin** is automatically invoked by **init** when the system is first started. It prompts the user to type the root password to enter system maintenance mode (single-user mode), or to type CTRL-d for normal startup (multiuser mode). **sulogin** should never be directly invoked by the user.
swap	**/etc/swap** [*options*] Swap administrative interface. **swap** provides a method of adding, deleting, and monitoring the system swap areas used by the memory manager.

-a *swapdev swaplow swaplen*

Add the specified swap area. *swapdev* is the name of
the block special device. *swaplow* is the offset in
512-byte blocks into the device where the swap area
should begin. *swaplen* is the length of the swap area in
512-byte blocks. This option can only be used by the
superuser.

-d *swapdev swaplow*

Delete the specified swap area. *swapdev* is the name of
the block special device. *swaplow* is the offset in
512-byte blocks into the device where the swap area
should begin. This option can only be used by the
superuser.

-1   List the status of all the swap areas.

---

swconfig [*options*]   swconfig

Produce a list of software modifications to the system. **swconfig**
displays modifications to the system software since its initialization,
telling the user what sets have been installed or removed from the
system, as well as what release and what parts of the packages
were installed at that time.

Options

-a   List all information contained in **/usr/lib/custom/history**,
        but sorted by date. Groups products installed at the
        same time, but displays entries in reverse chronological
        order.

-p   Display package information in addition to default
        information. A list of all packages in a set is stored and
        their installed status tracked by the sequence of infor-
        mation in **/usr/lib/custom/history**.

---

sync   sync

Update the super block. **sync** executes the **sync** system primitive. If
the system is to be stopped, **sync** must be called to ensure filesystem integrity. Note that **shutdown** automatically calls **sync** before
shutting down the system.

---

sysadmsh   sysadmsh

Menu-driven system administration utility. For details on using
sysadmsh, see Section 16, The *sysadmsh* Shell.

*System Admin.
Commands*

sysdef   */etc/sysdef* [*system_namelist* [*conf*]]

Output values of tuneable parameters. The output is generated by analyzing the named operating system file *system_namelist* and extracting the configuration information from the name list itself.

---

syslogd   */etc/syslogd* [*options*]

TCP/IP command—log system messages into a set of files described by the configuration file **/etc/syslog.conf**. Each message is one line. A message can contain a priority code, marked by a number in angle braces at the beginning of the line. Priorities are defined in **<sys/syslog.h>**. **syslogd** reads from an Internet domain socket specified in **/etc/services**. To bring **syslog** down, send it a terminate signal.

Options

   -d   Turn on debugging.

   -f*configfile*
          Specify alternate configuration file.

   -m*markinterval*
          Select number of minutes between mark messages.

---

talkd   */etc/talkd* [*option*]

TCP/IP command—remote user communication server. **talkd** notifies a user that somebody else wants to initiate a conversation. A **talkd** client initiates a rendezvous by sending a CTL_MSG of type LOOK_UP to the server. This causes the server to search its invitation tables for an existing invitation for the client. If the lookup fails, the caller sends an ANNOUNCE message causing the server to broadcast an announcement on the callee's login ports requesting contact. When the callee responds, the local server responds with the rendezvous address, and a stream connection is established through which the conversation takes place.

Option

   -d   Write debugging information to the syslog.

---

tapecntl   **tapecntl** [*options*]

AT&T tape control for QIC-24/QIC-02 tape device. **tapecntl** sends optioned commands to the tape device driver subdevice **/dev/rmt/c0s0** for all commands (except position, which will use subdevice **/dev/rmt/c0s0n** using the **ioctl** command). **/dev/rmt/c0s0** provides a rewind on close capability, while **/dev/rmt/c0s0n** allows for closing of the device without rewind. Error messages are written to standard error.

- -e   Erase tape. This activates the erase bar while moving the tape from end to end, erasing all data tracks in a single pass over the tape.
- -p[*n*]   Position tape to end-of-file mark *n*, an integer argument.
- -r   Reset tape device, initializing the tape controller registers and positioning tape at beginning of tape mark.
- -t   Retension tape. This moves the tape from end to end, repacking it with proper tension across its length.
- -w   Rewind tape, moving it to beginning of tape mark.

---

tapedump [*options*] *tape_device output_file*

Dump magnetic tape *tape_device* to output file *output_file*. Default *output_file* is standard output.

Options

- -a   Convert from EBCDIC input to ASCII output.
- -b *num*[**bkw**]

  Set both input and output block size. *num* is number of blocks. **b**, **k**, or **w** indicates block size: 1024-, 512-, or 2-byte, respectively.
- -e   Convert from ASCII input to EBCDIC output.
- -h   Display tape output in hexadecimal format.
- -n *num*

  Specify dump of *num* blocks.
- -o   Display tape output in octal format.
- -s *num*

  Skip *num* input records before starting dump.
- -t*num*   Specify which tape file to begin dump from. *num* is tape file sequence number.

Examples

The following command reads a tape starting at block 400 and outputs the results in hexadecimal format into a user-specified file called **/tmp/hex.dump**:

```
tapedump -b400 -h /dev/rct0 /tmp/hexdump
```

The next command reads an EBCDIC tape and converts the standard output to ASCII:

```
tapedump -a /dev/rct0
```

---

tcbck

Trusted computing base checker. **tcbck** checks the files in the trusted computing base for files that were caught in the process of being updated when the system went down and for files that have

$\rightarrow$

tcbck

←

been removed. **tcbck** is invoked by **smmk** during system maintenance mode, and by **authckrc** when the system enters multiuser mode. **tcbck**, **smmk**, and **authckrc** can only be run as root. The check proceeds as follows:

1. **smmck** runs **tcbck** to clean up any database files that were left in an interim state while being updated.

2. **tcbck** then checks that key system files are present, and that they are not of zero length.

3. If critical database files have been removed or corrupted, then the system enters maintenance mode automatically, without asking for the root password. If no critical database files were lost, the system prompts for maintenance mode or normal operation.

3. **tcbck** then removes the files **/etc/auth/system/pw_id_map** and **/etc/auth/system/gr_id_map**, because the modification times of these files are compared with those of **/etc/passwd** and **/etc/group** and problems can occur when the system clock is reset.

4. **tcbck** then tries to rebuild the map files using **cps**. If this fails, then either the File Control database is missing, or the File Control database entry for **/** is missing, or there are syntax errors in **/etc/passwd** or **/etc/group**.

5. After the system goes to init level 2, **authckrc** reinvokes **tcbck** to confirm that the files reported missing previously have been restored.

6. **authckrc** then runs **passwdupd** to check that all users in **/etc/passwd** have Protected Password database entries. **authckrc** is then run to check the subsystem databases for errors. Finally, **ttysupd** is run to check that all ttys in **/etc/inittab** have entries in the Terminal Control database.

tcp

/etc/tcp start|stop

Start or stop TCP. TCP will start automatically at system startup time if **/etc/tcp** is linked to **/etc/rc2.d/S***name*. Similarly, TCP will stop automatically at system shutdown time if **/etc/tcp** is linked to **/etc/rc0.d/K***name*. **/etc/tcp** must be customized for a particular installation before it can be used. This is normally done by the **netconfig** utility. The following items must be edited:

Domain name
> Set environment variable DOMAIN to the name of your domain.

Interface configuration
> Set the Internet address (and any other desired options) for each of your interfaces with **ifconfig** commands.

The following items may need to be edited:

PATH Modify the supplied path if commands run by **/etc/tcp** are in other directories.

PROCS The **PROCS** variable contains a space-separated list of names of processes to kill when executing the **stop** function. If additional daemons are used, their names can be added to this list.

daemons

The standard internetworking daemons are started at this point. Any additional daemons or other commands may be included in this section. Any of the standard daemons that are not desired may be removed or commented out.

---

telnetd [*options*]

TCP/IP command—DARPA TELNET protocol server. **telnetd** is invoked by the Internet server for requests to connect to the TELNET port as indicated by the **/etc/services** file. **telnetd** allocates a pseudo-terminal device for a client, thereby creating a login process which has the slave side of the pseudo-terminal serving as **stdin**, **stdout**, and **stderr**. **telnetd** will manipulate the master side of the pseudo-terminal by implementing the TELNET protocol and by passing characters between the remote client and the login process.

Options

-**debug** [*port*]

Start **telnetd** manually instead of through **inetd**. *port* may be specified as an alternate TCP port number on which to run **telnetd**.

-**h** Do not print a login banner.

-**D** *modifier*(s)

Debugging mode. This allows **telnet** to print out debugging information to the connection, enabling the user to see what **telnet** is doing. Several modifiers are available for the debugging mode:

exercise	Has not been implemented yet.
netdata	Display data stream received by **telnetd**.
options	Print information about the negotiaiton of the TELNET options.
ptydata	Display data written to the pty.
report	Print **options** information, as well as some additional information about what processing is going on.

/tcb/lib/auth_scripts/termupd

Script called by **ttyupd** to create Terminal Control database entries for terminals present in the **/etc/inittab** file, but not present in the Terminal Control database. **termupd** generates a list of the

$\rightarrow$

termupd ←	terminals in **/etc/inittab** and substitutes the name of the real terminal for any alias. Next, it makes a list of the terminals in the Terminal Control database. Finally the Terminal Control database is copied to the lockfile, and any terminals appearing in the first list, but not the second, are added to the end of the lockfile.

tftp	**tftp** [*host* [*port*]]
	
	TCP/IP command—user interface to the DARPA TFTP (Trivial File Transfer Protocol) protocol, which allows users to transfer files to and from a remote machine. The remote *host* may be specified, in which case **tftp** uses *host* as the default host for future transfers.
	
	Commands
	
	    Once **tftp** is running, it issues the prompt:
	
	        `tftp>`
	
	    and recognizes the following commands:
	? [*command–name* ...]
	        Print help information.
	ascii Shorthand for mode ascii
	binary Shorthand for mode binary
	connect *hostname* [*port*]
	        Set the *hostname*, and optionally **port**, for transfers.
	get *filename*
	get *remotename localname*
	get *filename1 filename2 filename3* ... *filenameN*
	        Get a file or set of files from the specified remote sources.
	mode *transfer–mode*
	        Set the mode for transfers. *transfer-mode* may be one of ascii or binary. The default is ascii.
	put *filename*
	put *localfile remotefile*
	put *filename1 filename2* ... *filenameN remote–directory*
	        Transfer file or a set of files to the specified remote file or directory.
	quit Exit **tftp**.
	rexmt *retransmission–timeout*
	        Set the per-packet retransmission timeout, in seconds.
	status Show current status.
	timeout *total–transmission–timeout*
	        Set the total transmission timeout, in seconds.
	trace Toggle packet tracing.
	verbose
	        Toggle verbose mode.

/etc/tftpd [option] [homedir]

TCP/IP command—DARPA Trivial File Transfer Protocol server. **tftpd** is normally started by **inetd** and operates at the port indicated in the **tftp** Internet service description in the **/etc/inetd.conf** file. By default, the entry for **tftpd** in **etc/inetd.conf** is commented out; the comment character must be deleted to make **tfptd** operational. Before responding to a request, the server attempts to change its current directory to *homedir*; the default value is **tftpboot**.

Option

-s   Secure option. The directory change must succeed, and the daemon also changes its root directory to *homedir*.

/etc/timed [options]

TCP/IP command—timeserver daemon. **timed** is normally invoked at boot time from the STREAMS TCP/IP startup script. It synchronizes the hosts's time with the time of other machines in a local area network running **timed**. It is based on a master-slave scheme. When started on a machine, **timed** asks the master for the network time and sets the host's clock to that time. After that, it accepts synchronization messages periodically sent by the master and calls **adjtime** to perform the needed corrections on the host's clock.

Options

-i *network*
        Add *network* to list of networks to ignore. All other networks are used.

-M   If machine running the master crashes, the slaves will elect a new master from among slaves running with the -M flag. A **timed** running without the -M flag will remain a slave.

-n *network*
        Add *network* to list of valid networks. All other networks are ignored.

-t   Trace messages that are received in the file **/usr/adm/timed.log**.

timedc [command [argument ...]]

TCP/IP command—control operation of **timed**. With no arguments, **timedc** will prompt for commands from the standard input. With arguments, **timedc** interprets the first argument as a command and the remaining arguments as parameters to the command. Standard input may be redirected, causing **timed** to read commands from a file. Recognized commands are:

? [command ...]

timedc
←
	help [*command* ...]
	    Print short description of each command specified in the argument list. If no arguments are given, print list of recognized commands.
	clockdiff *host* ...
	    Compute differences between clock of host machine and clocks of machines given as arguments.
	trace [on | off]
	    Enable/disable tracing of incoming messages to **timed** in the file **/usr/adm/timed.log**.
	quit Exit from **timedc**.

timex	**timex** [*options*] *command*
	
	Time a command; report process data and system activity. The given *command* is executed, and the elapsed time, user time, and system time spent in execution are reported in seconds. The output of **timex** is written on standard error.
	
	Options
	  -p List process accounting records for *command* and all its children. This option works only if the process accounting software is installed. Suboptions **f**, **h**, **k**, **m**, **r**, and **t**, modify the data items reported. The suboptions are as follows:
	    -f Print the **fork/exec** flag and system exit status columns in the output.
	    -h Instead of mean memory size, show the fraction of total available CPU time consumed by the process during its execution.
	    -k Instead of memory size, show total kcore-minutes.
	    -m Show mean core size (the default).
	    -r Show CPU factor (user-time/(system-time + user-time).
	    -t Show separate system and user CPU times. The number of blocks read or written and the number of characters transferred are always reported.
	  -o Report total number of blocks read or written and total characters transferred by *command* and all its children. This option works only if the process accounting software is installed.
	  -s Report total system activity (not just that due to *command*) that occurred during the execution interval of *command*.

tplot	**tplot** [*options*] Graphics filters. **tplot** reads plotting instructions from the standard input and produces, on the standard output, plotting instructions

suitable for a particular *terminal*. If no *terminal* is specified, the environment parameter for **$TERM** is used.

Options

-T*terminal*

Terminal specified. Known *terminals* are:

300	DASI 300.
300S	DASI 300s.
450	DASI 450.
4014	Tektronix 4014.
ver	VERSATEC D1200A.

-e*raster*

Send a previously scan-converted file *raster* to the plotter.

trap_rece

TCP/IP command—receive traps from a remote SNMP trap generating entity. **trap_rece** binds to the SNMP trap port to listen for the traps, and thus must be run as root. It prints, to standard output, messages corresponding to the traps it has received. The primary purpose of **trap_rece** is to demonstrate how traps are parsed using the SNMP library.

trpt [*options*] [*system* [*core*]]

TCP/IP command—transliterate protocol trace. **trpt** interrogates the buffer of TCP trace records created when a socket is marked for debugging and prints a readable description of these records. When no options are supplied, **trpt** prints all the trace records found in the system grouped according to TCP connection protocol control block (PCB). If debugging is being performed on a system or core file other than the default, the last two arguments may be used to supplant the defaults.

Options

-a   In addition to the normal output, print values of the source and destination addresses for each packet recorded.

-f   Follow trace as it occurs, waiting a short time for additional records each time the end of the log is reached.

-j   Just give a list of the protocol control block addresses for which there are trace records.

-p *hex–address*

Show only trace records associated with the protocol control block, of address *hex-address*.

→

trpt ←	-s In addition to the normal output, print a detailed description of the packet sequencing information. -t In addition to the normal output, print values for all timers at each point in the trace.
ttyupd	**/tcb/bin/ttyupd** Update the Terminal Control database. **ttyupd** attempts to create Terminal Control database entries for terminals present in the **/etc/inittab** file but not present in the Terminal Control database. **ttyupd** calls **ale**, passing the Terminal Control database and the script **termupd** as parameters.
uadmin	**/etc/uadmin** *command function* Provide control for basic administrative functions. *command* and *function* are converted to integers and passed to the **uadmin** system call. **uadmin** is tightly coupled to the system administration procedures and is not intended for general use. It may only be invoked by the superuser.
umount	**/etc/umount** *special–device/directory* Unmount a filesystem. **umount** announces to the system that the removable file structure previously mounted on device *special-device* is to be removed. **umount** also works by specifying the directory. Any pending I/O for the filesystem is completed, and the file structure is flagged as clean.
umountall	**/etc/umountall** [*option*] Unmount multiple filesystems. **umountall** unmounts all mounted filesystems except the root filesystem. **Option** -k Send a SIGKILL signal, via **fuser**, to processes that have files open.
unlink	**/etc/unlink** *file* Unlink files and directories. It is strongly recommended that the **rm** and **rmdir** commands be used instead of **unlink**. **unlink** can be run only by the superuser.
unretire	**/tcb/bin/unretire** [*options*] *users* Change the user type of an account. By default, **unretire** expects the accounts specified on the command line to be currently retired, and sets their type back to general, or pseudo, if the account has an owner. **unretire** can also be used to retire users by specifying a

usertype of retired. If no users are specified on the command line, **unretire** will read standard input for account names.	**unretire**

Option

  -t *usertype*

/usr/lib/uucp/uuchat *ttyname speed chat–script*	**uuchat**

UUCP command—dial a modem. **dial -h** (hang up) is executed by **getty** when it is respawned on a line shared between dial-in and dial-out. If there is no **dial** program, **getty** uses **uuchat**, passing it the & chat-script from **/usr/lib/uucp/Dialers**. See also **dial**.

/usr/lib/uucp/uucheck [*options*]	**uucheck**

UUCP command—check the UUCP directories and permissions files. **uucheck** can only be used by the superuser or *uucp*.

Options

  -v   Give detailed explanation of how the UUCP programs will interpret the **Permissions** file.

  -x *debug_level*
        Used for debugging. *debug_option* is a single digit in the range 1-9; the higher the value, the greater the detail.

/usr/lib/uucp/uucico [*options*] *system_name*	**uucico**

UUCP command—file transport program.

Options

  -d *spool_directory*
        Specify the *spool* directory; default is **/usr/spool/uucp**.

  -i *interface*
        Define interface used with **uucico**. This interface only affects the slave mode. Known interfaces are: UNIX (default), TLI (basic Transport Layer Interface), and TLIS (Transport Layer Interface with Streams modules, read/write).

  -r *role_number*
        Role numbers for the **-r** are the digit 1 for master mode or 0 for slave mode (default). This option should be specified as the digit 1 for master mode when **uucico** is started by a program or **cron**.

  -s *sitename*
        Make a call to the specified site, even if there is no work for site *sitename* in the spool directory. Call only when times in the **Systems** file permit it.

→

uucico
←
	-S *system_name*
	    Specify *system_name*, overriding the call schedule given in the **Systems** file.
	-x *debug_level*
	    Used for debugging. *debug_level* is a single digit in the range 1-9; the higher the value, the greater the detail.

uuclean	**/usr/lib/uucp/uuclean** [*options*]
	
	UUCP command—spool directory clean-up. **uuclean** scans the spool directories for old files and takes appropriate action. **uuclean** is typically started by the shell **uudemon.clean**, which should be started by **cron**. **uuclean** can only be executed by the superuser or **uucp**.
	
	Options
	
	-C*time* Remove any C. files greater than or equal to *time* days old, reporting appropriate information to the requestor. Default is 7 days.
	
	-D*time*
	    Remove any D. files greater than or equal to *time* days old. Default is 7 days.
	
	-m*string*
	    Include this line in the warning message generated by the -**W** option. The default line is See your local administrator to locate the problem.
	
	-o*time* Delete other files whose age is more than *time* days. Default is 2 days.
	
	-s*system*
	    Execute for *system* spool directory only.
	
	-W*time*
	    Any C. files equal to *time* days old will cause a mail message to be sent to the requestor warning about the delay in contacting the remote system.
	
	-X*time*
	    Remove any X. files greater than or equal to *time* days old. Default is 2 days.
	
	-x*debut_level*
	    The -**x** debug level is a single digit between 0 and 90; higher numbers give more detailed debugging information.

uudemon	uudemon uudemon.admin uudemon.clean uudemon.hour uudemon.poll uudemon.poll2

UUCP administrative scripts. UUCP communications and file maintenance can be automated with the use of the shell scripts described below.

Scripts

uudemon.admin

>Runs the **uustat** command with **-p** and **-q** options. **-q** reports on the status of work files (C.), data files (D.), and execute files (X.) that are queued. **-p** prints process information for networking processes listed in the lock files. It sends resulting status information to the UUCP administrative login (*uucp* via **mail**.

uudemon.clean

>Takes log files for individual machines from the /usr/spool/.Log directory, merges them, and places them in the /usr/spool/.Old directory with other old log information. It also removes work files (C.) seven days old or older, data files (D.) seven days or older, and execute files (X.) two days old or older from the spool files. **uudemon.clean** mails a summary of the status information gathered during the current day to the UUCP administrative login (*uucp*).

uudemon.hour

>Calls the **uusched** program to search the spool directories for work files (C.) that have not been processed and schedule these files for transfer to a remote machine. **uudemon.hour** then calls the **uuxqt** daemon to search the spool directories for execute files (X.) that were transferred to your computer and were not processed at the time they were transferred.

uudemon.poll

>Uses the *Poll* file for polling remote computers. **uudemon.poll** does not actually perform the poll, it merely sets up a polling file in the /usr /spool/-uucp/nodename directory, where *nodename* is replaced by the name of the machine. **uudemon.poll** is scheduled to run twice an hour just before **uudemon.hour** so that the work files will be there when **uudemon.hour** is called.

uudemon.poll2

>**uudemon.poll2** is an alternative to **uudemon.poll** that uses a different scheme and different poll files; it permits more control of scheduling. In order to use **uudemon.poll2**, you must remove the call to **uusched** from **uudemon.hour**, and run **uudemon.poll2** in place of **uudemon.poll** from **cron**.

uuinstall	**/etc/uuinstall** [*option*]

UUCP command—administer UUCP control files. **uuinstall** allows users to change the contents of these files without using a text editor. It can only be executed by the superuser.

Option

-r   Do not allow any files to be modified. |
| **uulist** | **/usr/mmdf/table/tools/uulist** [*options*]

UUCP command—convert a UUCP routing file to MMDF format. After installing MMDF with **custom**, restore **/usr/lib/uucp/Systems** from backup media. Login in as root and run the conversion script **/usr/mmdf/table/tools/uulist** from the **/usr/mmdf/table** directory. You now have UUCP domain and channel files, **uucp.dom** and **uucp.chn**, in the current directory. Make the files owned by *mmdf*. After creating these files, you must rebuild the MMDF hashed database. |
| **uusched** | **/usr/lib/uucp/uusched** [*options*]

UUCP command—scheduler for the UUCP file transport system. **uusched** is usually started by the daemon **uudemon.hour**.

Options

-u *debug_level*
    Passed as -x *debug_level* to uucico.
-x *debug_level*
    Output debugging messages. *debug_level* is a number between 0 and 9; higher numbers give more detailed information. |
| **uustat** | **uustat** [*options*]

UUCP command—provide information about **uucp** requests. This command can also be used to cancel **uucp** requests. Options -a, -j, -k, -m, -p, -q, and -r cannot be used with each other.

Options

-a   Report all queued jobs.
-k*n*   Kill job request *n*; you must own it.
-m   Report accessibility of other systems.
-p   Execute a **ps -flp** on active processes.
-q   Report the jobs queued for all systems.
-r*n*   Renew job *n* by issuing a **touch** on its associated files. |

`-s`*system* Report the status of jobs for *system*.	**uustat**
`-u`*user* Report the status of jobs for *user*.	

/usr/lib/uucp/uutry [*options*]

uutry

UUCP command—try to contact remote system with debugging on. **uutry** is a shell script that invokes **uucico** to call a remote site. If connection is successful, **uutry** stores the debugging output in the file **/tmp/system**, where *system* is the name of the remote system.

Options

`-x` *debug_level*

> Set *debug_level* to a number between 0 and 9; higher numbers give more detailed information. Default debug level is 5.

`-r`   Override retry time in **/usr/spool/uucp/.status**.

---

uux [*options*] [[*sys*]!*command*]

uux

UUCP command—gather files from various systems and execute *command* on the specified machine *sys*. **uux** also recognizes the **uucp** options `-c`, `-C`, `-g`, `-r`, `-s`, and `-x`.

Options

`-`   Same as `-p` (pass standard input to *command*).

`-a`*user* Notify *user* upon completion (see `-z`).

`-b`   Print the standard input when the exit status indicates an error.

`-j`   Print the **uux** job number.

`-n`   Do not send mail if *command* fails.

`-p`   Pass the standard input to *command*.

`-z`   Notify invoking user upon successful completion.

/usr/lib/uucp/uuxqt [*options*]

uuxqt

UUCP command—execute remote command requests. **uuxqt** searches the spool directories looking for X. files. For each X. file, **uuxqt** checks to see if all the required data files are available and accessible, and file commands are permitted for the requesting system. There are two environment variables that are set before the **uuxqt** command is executed:

3UU_MACHINE   Machine that sent the job (the previous one).

UU_USER   User that sent the job.

Options

`-s` *system*

> Execute for *system* spool directory only.

→

uuxqt ←	**-x** *debug_level* Set debugging level to a number between 0 and 9; higher numbers give more detailed debugging information.
vectorsinuse	**/etc/conf/cf.d/vectorsinuse** Display the list of vectors currently specified in the **sdevice** file. You must be in **etc/conf/cf.d** to execute **vectorsinuse**.

volcopy	**/etc/volcopy** [*options*] *fsname srcdevice volname1 destdevice volname2*
	
	Make literal copy of UNIX filesystem. *fsname* represents the mounted name. *srcdevice* and *volname1* are the device and volume from which the copy of the filesystem is being extracted. *destdevice* and *volname2* are the target device and volume.
	
	Options
	   -a Invoke a verification sequence requiring a positive operator response instead of the standard 10-second delay before the copy is made.
	   -s Invoke the DEL if wrong verification sequence (default).

w	**w** [*options*] [*users*]
	
	Print summaries of system usage, currently logged-in users, and what they are doing. **w** is essentially a combination of **uptime**, **who**, and **ps -a**. Display output for one user by specifying *user*.
	
	Options
	   -h Suppress headings and **uptime** information.
	   -l Display in long format (the default).
	   -q Quick format with limited information.
	   -n*namelist*
	        Use alternate *namelist* instead of **/unix**.
	   -s*swapdev*
	        Use *swapdev* in place of **dev/swap**. Useful when examining core files.
	   -t Only print header (equivalent to **uptime**).
	   -u *utmpfile*
	        Use *utmpfile* instead of **/etc/utmp**.

wall	**/etc/wall** [*options*] Write to all users. **wall** reads a message from the standard input until an end-of-file. It then sends this message to all users currently logged in, preceded by Broadcast Message from . . . .

who [*options*] [*file*]
who am i

Display information about the current status of the system. With no options, list the names of users currently logged in to the system. An optional system *file* (default is **/var/adm/utmp**) can be supplied to give additional information.

Options

-A	Display UNIX accounting information.
-a	Use all options.
-b	Report information about the last reboot.
-d	Report expired processes.
-f	Suppress pseudo-ttys except for remote logins.
-H	Print headings.
-l	Report inactive terminal lines.
-n*x*	Display *x* users per line (works only with **-q**).
-p	Report previously spawned processes.
-q	"Quick." Display only the usernames and total number of users.
-r	Report the run level.
-s	List the name, line, and time fields (the default behavior).
-t	Report the last change of the system clock (via **date**).
-T	Report whether terminals are writable (+), not writable (−), or unknown (?).
-u	Report terminal usage (idle time). A dot (.) means less than one minute idle; **old** means more than 24 hours idle.
am i	Print the username of the invoking user.

Example

This sample output was produced at 8 a.m. on April 17:

```
who -uH
NAME    LINE    TIME        IDLE   PID   COMMENTS
Earvin  ttyp3   Apr 16 08:14 16:25  2240
Larry   ttyp0   Apr 17 07:33  .     15182
```

Since Earvin has been idle since yesterday afternoon (16 hours), it appears that Earvin isn't at work yet. He simply left himself logged in. Larry's terminal is currently in use.

/usr/lib/layersys/wtinit [*options*] *file*

Object downloader for the 5620 DMD terminal. **wtinit** downloads the named *file* for execution in the AT&T TELETYPE 5620 DMD terminal connected to its standard output. *file* must be a DMD object file.

→

System Administration Commands

System Admin. Commands

wtinit ←	*Options*
	-d Print sizes to the text, data, and bss portions of the downloaded file on standard error.
	-p Print downloading protocol statistics and a trace on standard error.
wtmpfix	**/usr/lib/acct/wtmpfix** [*files*]
	Correct *wtmp* files by examining either the standard input (indicated by a dash) or *files* in *wtmp* format, correcting the time/date stamps to make the entries consistent, and writing to the standard output. In addition, **wtmpfix** will check the validity of the "name" field to ensure that it consists solely of alphanumeric characters or spaces. If it encounters a name that is considered invalid, it will change the login name to INVALID and write a diagnostic to the standard error.
xntpd	**xntpd** [*options*]
	TCP/IP command—Network Time Protocol daemon. **xntpd** maintains a UNIX system's time-of-day in agreement with Internet standard time servers. **xntpd** is a complete implementation of the Network Time Protocol (NTP) version 2 standard as defined by RFC 1119; it also retains compatibility with version 1 servers as defined by RFC 1059. Ordinarily, **xntpd** reads its configuration from a file at startup time. The default configuration file is **/etc/ntp.conf**, though this may be overridden from the command line.

Options

    -a   Run in authenticate mode.

    -b   Listen for broadcast NTP and sync to this if available.

    -c *conffile*
        Specify alternate configuration file.

    -e *authdelay*
        Specify the time (in seconds) it takes to compute the NTP encryption field on this computer.

    -f *driftfile*
        Specify the location of the drift file.

    -k *keyfile*
        Specify the location of the file containing NTP authentication keys.

    -r *broaddelay*
        Specify the default round trip delay (in seconds) to be used when synchronizing to broadcasts.

    -t *trustedkey*
        Add a key number to the trusted key list.

authdelay *seconds*

> Amount of time it takes to encrypt an NTP authentication field on the local computer. The value is usually computed using the **authspeed** program included with the distribution.

authenticate yes|no

> Whether local server should operate in authenticate mode. **yes** means only peers which include an authentication field encrypted with one of our trusted keys (see below) will be considered as candidates for synchronizing to. Default is **no**.

broadcast *host_address* [*key#*] [*version#*] [**minpoll**]

> The broadcast statement requests your local daemon to transmit broadcast NTP to the specified address.

broadcastclient yes|no

> Whether local server should listen for, and attempt to synchronize to, broadcast NTP. The default is no.

broadcastdelay *seconds*

> Default round trip delay to the host whose broadcasts are being synchronized to. Value is specified in seconds and is typically a number between 0.007 and 0.015 seconds. Default is 0.008 seconds.

controlkey #

> Certain changes can be made to the **xntpd** server via mode 6 control messages. The **controlkey** statement specifies an encryption-key number to be used for authenticating such messages.

driftfile *filename#*

> Name of the file used to record the drift (frequency error) value **xntpd** has computed.

keys *filename*

> Specify the name of a file containing the encryption keys to be used by **xntpd**.

maxskew *seconds*

> Set the system maximum skew parameter to the number of seconds given. The default value is 0.010 seconds.

monitor yes|no

> Whether the **xntpd** traffic-monitoring function should be enabled. Default is **no**.

peer *host_address* [*key#*] [*version#*] [**minpoll**]

> Specify that the given host is to be polled in symmetric active mode—the host is requested to provide time which you might synchronize to and, in addition, indicates that you are willing to have the remote host synchronize to your time if need be.

→

precision#
> Precision of local timekeeping. The value is an integer which is approximately the base 2 logarithm of the local timekeeping precision in seconds. Default value is –6.

restrict *address* [**mask** *numeric_mask*] [*flag*] [. . .]
> General-purpose address-and-mask based restriction list. The list is sorted by *address* and *mask*, and is searched in this order for matches, with the last match found defining the restriction *flags* associated with the incoming packets. Flags can be classed into two categories: those which restrict time service, and those which restrict informational queries and attempts to do runtime reconfiguration of the server. One or more of the following flags may be specified:

> **ignore** — Ignore all packets from hosts which match this entry.

> **lowpriotrap** — Declare traps set by matching hosts to be low priority.

> **nomodify** — Ignore all NTP mode 6 and 7 packets that attempt to modify the state of the server.

> **noquery** — Ignore all NTP mode 6 and 7 packets from the source.

> **nopeer** — Provide stateless time service to polling hosts, but do not allocate peer memory resources to these hosts, even if they otherwise might be considered useful as future synchronization partners.

> **noserve** — Ignore NTP packets whose mode is other than 6 or 7.

> **notrap** — Decline to provide mode 6 control-message trap service to matching hosts.

> **notrust** — Treat these hosts normally in other respects, but never use them as synchronization sources.

> **ntpport** — This is actually a match algorithm modifier rather than a restriction flag. It causes the restriction entry to be matched only if the source port in the packet is the standard NTP UDP port (123).

resolver */path/xntpres*
> Indicate to the daemon the full path to the **xntpres** program.

select *algorithm_number*
> Select use of one of five selection-weight algorithms. Default is algorithm number 1, which is the algorithm specified in RFC 1119. Algorithm numbers 2 through 5 select alternative, experimental selection-weighting algorithms,

trap *host_address* [port *port_number*] [interface *interface_address*]

> Configure a trap receiver at the given host address and port number, sending messages with the specified local interface address.

requestkey #

> Allows the specification of a 32-bit unsigned integer key number to be used for authenticating requests for runtime reconfiguration to be performed using **xntpdc**.

server *host_address* [*key#*] [*version#*] [**minpoll**]

> Specifies that the given host is to be polled in client mode—the host is requested to provide time which you might synchronize with, but that you are unwilling to have the remote host synchronize to your own time.

trustedkey # [# ...]

> Allows the specification of the encryption key numbers which are trusted for the purposes of determining peers suitable for time sychonization, when authentication is enabled. The arguments are 32 bit unsigned integers.

Authentication-key file format

The NTP standard specifies an extension allowing verification of the authenticity of received NTP packets, and to provide an indication of authenticity in outgoing packets. This is implemented in **xntpd** using the DES encryption algorithm. The specification allows any one of a possible four billion keys, numbered with 32-bit unsigned integers, to be used to authenticate an association. The keys are standard 56-bit DES keys. The key file uses the same comment conventions as the configuration file. Key entries use a fixed format of the form:

> *keyno type key*

where *keyno* is a positive integer, *type* is a single character which defines the format the key is given in, and *key* is the key itself. The three key *types* are:

S   64-bit hexadecimal number in the format specified in the DES document

N   64-bit hexadecimal number in the format specified in the NTP standard

A   1-to-8 character ASCII string

/etc/ypbind [*options*]

NFS/NIS command—NIS binder process. **ypbind** is a daemon process typically activated at system startup time from **/etc/nfs**. Its function is to remember information that lets client processes on a single node communicate with some **ypserv** process. The information **ypbind** remembers is called a *binding*—the association of a domain name with the Internet address of the NIS server and the port on that host at which the *ypserv* process is listening for service

→

System Admin.
Commands

ypbind
←
	requests. This information is cached in the directory **/etc/yp/binding** using a filename of *domainname.version*.
	
	Options
	
	   -s Secure. When specified, only NIS servers bound to a reserved port are used. This allows for a slight increase in security in completely controlled environments, where there are no computers operated by untrusted individuals.
	
	  ypset May be used to change the binding. This option is very dangerous and should only be used for debugging the network from a remote machine.
	
	  -ypsetme
	           ypset requests may be issued from this machine only. Security is based on IP address checking, which can be defeated on networks where untrusted individuals may inject packets. This option is not recommended.

ypcat	**ypcat** [*options*] *mname*
	
	NFS/NIS command—print values in an NIS database specified by *mname*, which may be either a mapname or a map nickname.
	
	Options
	
	  -d Specify domain other than default domain.
	
	  -k Display keys for maps in which values are null or key is not part of value.
	
	  -t Inhibit translation of *mname* to mapname.
	
	  -x Display map nickname table listing the nicknames (*mnames*) known, and mapname associated with each nickname.

ypinit	**ypinit** [*options*]
	
	NFS/NIS command—build and install an NIS database on an NIS server. **ypinit** can be used to set up a master or a slave server or slave copier. Only root can run **ypinit**.
	
	Options
	
	  -c *master_name*
	           Set up a slave copier database. *master_name* should be the hostname of an NIS server, either the master server for all the maps or a server on which the database is up-to-date and stable.
	
	  -m Indicates that the local host is to be the NIS server.
	
	  -s *master_name*
	           Set up a slave server database. *master_name* should be the hostname of an NIS server, either the master server for all the maps or a server on which the database is up-to-date and stable.

/etc/yp/ypmake [*map*]

NFS/NIS command—rebuild NIS databases. If **make** is on the system, it builds the NIS database using the file *makefile* in the directory /etc/yp. If **make** is not on the system, **ypmake** will create the database unconditionally. With no arguments, **ypmake** creates **dbm** databases for any NIS maps that are out-of-date and then executes **yppush** to notify the slave databases that there has been a change. If you supply a *map* on the command line, **ypmake** will update that map only.

There are three special variables used by **ypmake**: DIR, which gives the directory of the source files; NOPUSH, which, when non-null, inhibits doing a **yppush** of the new database files; and DOM, used to construct a domain other than the master's default domain.

/etc/yp/YP_MAP_X_LATE

NFS/NIS command—translation table to handle long NIS map names. **ypmapxlate** was written to avoid a (now-obsolete) restriction on System V filenames. An NIS map named *X*, under domain *Y*, exists as the two files named *X.pag* and *X.dir*, both under the directory path, */etc/yp/Y/*. *YP_MAP_X_LATE* contains a complete listing of active NIS maps, as well as NIS aliases for NIS maps. **ypinit** consults *YP_MAP_X_LATE* when NIS is initialized and creates the maps listed in it. *YP_MAP_X_LATE* contains entries of the form:

    long_map_name   short_map_name

When the NIS server receives a packet containing a logical (long) map name, *YP_MAP_X_LATE* is used to determine the physical (short) map name. Conversely, when the server transmits a packet containing a physical map name, that name is looked up in *YP_MAP_X_LATE* to find the corresponding logical map name.

ypmatch [*options*] *key . . . mname*

NFS/NIS command—print value of one or more *keys* from an NIS map specified by *mname*. *mname* may be either a mapname or map nickname.

Options

-d   Specify domain other than default domain.

-k   Before printing value of a key, print key itself, followed by a colon (:).

-t   Inhibit translation of nickname to mapname.

-x   Display map nickname table listing the nicknames (*mnames*) known, and mapname associated with each nickname.

yppassmgmt	**yppassmgmt** *arguments* [*options*] *name*

NFS/NIS command—update information in the network password file. This command works with **/etc/passwd.yp**. The login name of the user, *name*, must be unique.

Arguments

-a   Add an entry for user *name* to the network password files. This command does not create any directory for the new user, and there is no password until **yppasswd** is executed to set the password. Options (listed below) may be used with this argument.

-m   Modify the entry for user *name* in the network password files. All the fields in the **/etc/passwd.local** entry (except the password field) can be modified by this command. Only fields entered on the command line will be modified. Options (listed below) may be used with this argument.

-d   Lock the account for user *name* from the network password files. This does not remove any files owned by the user on the system; they must be removed manually.

-f   Unlock the account for user *name* from the network password files. This will not remove any files owned by the user on the system; they must be removed manually.

-n   Alter the status for local user *name* from the local user to a networked user.

-r   Retire the account for user *name* from the network password file. This will not remove any files owned by the user on the system; they must be removed manually.

Options

The following options may be used with the -a and -m arguments of **passmgmt**.

-c *comment*
     Short description of the login, limited to a maximum of 128 characters. Default is an empty field.

-g *gid*   GID of the *name* argument. This number must range from 0 to the maximum value for the system. Default is 1.

-h *homedir*
     Home directory of *name* argument, limited to a maximum of 256 characters. Default is */usr/name*.

-l *logname*
     Change *name* argument to *logname*. Used with -m argument only.

-o   Allows a UID to be non-unique. This option is used only with the -u option.

-s *shell*

Login shell for *name* argument. It should be the full pathname of the program that will be executed when the user logs in. Maximum length of *shell* is 256 characters. The default is for this field to be empty and to be interpreted as **/bin/sh**.

-u *uid* UID of *name* argument. This number must range from 0 to the maximum value for the system. It defaults to the next available UID greater than 100. Without the -o option, it enforces the uniqueness of a UID.

Diagnostics

passmgmt exits with one of the following values:

0	SUCCESS
1	Permission denied
2	Invalid command syntax
3	Invalid argument provided to option
4	UID in use
5	Inconsistent password files
6	Unexpected failure. Password files unchanged.
7	Unexpected failure. Password files missing.
8	Password files busy. Try again later.
9	*name* argument does not exist (if -m or -d is specified), already exists (if -a is specified), or *logname* already exists (if -m -l is specified).

yppasswd [*name*]

NFS/NIS command—change login password in network information service. **yppasswd** prompts for the old password, then for the new one. New passwords must be at least four characters long if a combination of upper- and lowercase characters are used, six characters long if monocase.

/etc/yppasswdd *file* [*option*]

NFS/NIS command—server for modifying the NIS password file. **yppasswdd** handles password change requests from **yppasswd**. It changes a password entry in *file* only if the password represented by **yppasswd** matches the encrypted password of that entry. This server is not run by default. To enable remote password updating for NIS, an entry for **yppasswdd** in the **/etc/nfs** file of the host serving as master for the NIS *passwd* file.

→

yppasswdd
←
	Option
	    -m *arg1 arg2 . . .*
	           After *file* is modified, perform a **make** in the directory
	           /etc/yp. Any arguments following the flag will be pas-
	           sed to **make**.
	
	Example
	    If the NIS password file is stored as **/etc/yp/passwd**, then to
	    have password changes propagated immediately, the server
	    should be invoked as:
	
	    `/etc/yppasswdd /var/yp/passwd -m passwd DIR=/var/yp`

yppoll	**yppoll** [*options*] *mapname*
	
	NFS/NIS command—determine version of NIS map at NIS server.
	yppoll asks a **ypserv** process for the order number and the host-
	name of the master NIS server for the named map. If the server is a
	v.1 NIS protocol server, **yppoll** uses the older protocol to communi-
	cate with it. In this case, it also uses the older diagnostic messages
	in case of failure.
	
	Options
	    -h *host* Ask the **ypserv** process at *host* about the map
	                    parameters. If *host* is not specified, the NIS server
	                    for the local host is used—the default host is the
	                    one returned by **ypwhich**.
	    -d *domain* Use *domain* instead of the default domain.

yppush	**yppush** [*options*] *mapname*
	
	NFS/NIS command—force propagation of changed NIS map.
	yppush copies a new version of a NIS map, *mapname*, from the
	master NIS server to the slave NIS servers. It first constructs a list of
	NIS server hosts by reading the NIS map **ypservers** within the -d
	option's *domain* argument. Keys within this map are the ASCII
	names of the machines on which the NIS servers run. A "transfer
	map" request is sent to the NIS server at each host, along with the
	information needed by the transfer agent to call back the **yppush**.
	When the attempt has completed and the transfer agent has sent
	yppush a status message, the results may be printed to **stdout**.
	
	Options
	    -d *domain*
	           Specify a *domain*.
	    -v Verbose—print message when each server is called and
	           for each response.

/etc/ypserv [option]

NFS/NIS command—NIS server process. **ypserv** is a daemon process typically activated at system startup time from **/etc/nfs**. It runs only on NIS server machines with a complete NIS database. Its primary function is to look up information in its local database of NIS maps. The operations performed by **ypserv** are defined for the implementor by the NIS protocol specification, and for the programmer by the header file **<rpcvc/yp_prot.h>**. Communication to and from **ypserv** is by means of RPC calls.

Options

-d
> NIS service should go to the DNS for more host information.

-localonly
> Indicates **ypserv** should not respond to outside requests.

ypset [options] server

NFS/NIS command—point **ypbind** at a particular server. **ypset** tells **ypbind** to get NIS services for the specified *domain* from the **ypserv** process running on *server*. *server* indicates the NIS server to bind to and can be specified as a name or an IP address.

Options

-d *domain*
> Use *domain* instead of the default domain.

-h *host*
> Set **ypbind**'s binding on *host*, instead of locally. *host* can be specified as a name or an IP address.

-V1
> Bind *server* for the (old) v.1 NIS protocol.

-V2
> Bind *server* for the (current) v.2 NIS protocol.

ypshad2pwd *inpasswd_file inshadow_file outpasswd_file*

NFS/NIS command—install and update the **etc/passwd.yp** file. **ypshad2pwd** takes the user's login name, password, user id, group id, comment, home directory, and shell information from *outpasswd_file*. The *passwd* field is taken from *inshadow_file*, if it exists, otherwise it is taken from *inpasswd_file*. *outpasswd_file* is expected to be **/etc/passwd.yp**, for use in creating the NIS password map on an NIS master server. Typical usage is:

```
ypshad2pwd /etc/passwd etc/shadow etc/passwd.yp
```

Following is the format of an entry in **/etc/passwd.yp**:

```
username:passwd:uid:gui:command:homedir:shell
```

ypwhich

ypwhich [*options*] [*hostname*]

NFS/NIS command—return hostname of NIS server or map master. If invoked without arguments, **ypwhich** cites the NIS server for the local machine. If *hostname* is specified, that machine is queried to find out which NIS master it is using.

Options

-d *domain*
> Use *domain* instead of the default domain.

-m *mname*
> Find master NIS server for a map. No *hostname* can be specified with -m. *mname* can be a mapname or a nickname for a map.

-t *mapname*
> Inhibit nickname translation.

-V1
> Indicate which server is serving v.2 NIS protocol client processes.

-V2
> Indicate which server is serving v.2 NIS protocol client processes.

-x
> Display map nickname table.

---

ypxfr

ypxfr [*options*] *mapname*

NFS/NIS command—transfer an NIS map in the default domain for the local host to the local host by making use of normal NIS services. **ypxfr** creates a temporary map in the directory **/etc/yp/***domain* (where *domain* is the default domain for the local host), fills it by enumerating the map's entries, and fetches the map parameters and loads them. If run interactively, **ypxfr** writes its output to the terminal. However, if it is invoked without a controlling terminal, and if the log file **/usr/admin/nislog** exists, it will append all its output to that file.

Options

-b
> Preserve the resolver flag in the map during the transfer.

-C *tid prog ipadd port*
> This option is only for use by **ypserv**. When **ypserv** invokes **ypxfr**, it specifies that **ypxfr** should call back a **yppush** process at the host with IP address *ipaddr*, registered as program number *prog*, listening on port *port*, and waiting for a response to transaction *tid*.

-c
> Do not send a "Clear current map" request to the local **ypserv** process.

-d *domain*
> Specify a domain other than the default domain.

-f
> Force the transfer to occur even if the version at the master is older than the local version.

-h *host*
>
> Get the map from *host*, regardless of what the map says the master is. If host is not specified, **ypxfr** asks the NIS service for the name of the master, and tries to get the map from there. *host* may be a name or an internet address in the form a.b.c.d.

-S
>
> Only use NIS servers running as root and using a reserved port.

-s *domain*
>
> Specify a source *domain* from which to transfer a map that should be the same across domains (such as the *services.byname* map).

ypxfrd

NFS/NIS command—transfer NIS maps. For systems that use this daemon, map transfers will be 10 to 10,000 times faster, depending on the map. To use this daemon, **ypxfrd** should be run on an NIS server.

Index

A

access time, updating, 125
Accessories icon, 5
accounting, calculate disk consumption for accounting records, 388
command summary from per-process accounting records, 386
connect-time accounting, 387-388
gather user disk block data, 388
generate accounting total records, 388
generating per process accounting records, 388
merge or add total accounting files, 388
running daily, 500
search and print process accounting file(s), 386
shell procedures for, 389
turn on accounting, 388
accounts, user, 379, 382
acctcms, 386
acctcom, 386
acctcon1, 387
acctcon2, 388
acctdisk, 388
acctdusg, 388
acctmerg, 388
accton, 388
acctprc1, 388
acctprc2, 388
acctsh, 389
adb, 282
addition operator, 158
addresses, checking validity of, 401
IP, 360
addressing, in sed, 255
admin, 284
AIO, printing statistics, 390
setting up memory locking permissions, 390
aioinfo, 390
aiolkinit, 390
ale, 390
alias, 162, 198
ap, 391
applications, running; from SCO shell, 213
ar, 285

archive files, converting to common formats, 295
disassembling, 308
archives, file, 285
portable archive exchange, 479
arguments, evaluating as expressions, 52
arithmetic, converting numbers from one base to another, 22
arithmetic expressions, Korn shell, 158
arithmetic operators, C shell, 193
arrays, Korn shell, 158
as, 286
ASCII, converting binary records to, 430
asktime, 391
asroot, 391
assemblers, Microsoft 8086/286/386, 327
assembly programs, debuggers, 343
assembly source files, translating into object files, 286
assign, 391
assign value operator, 193
assignment operators, 159
C shell, 193
at, 20
administration utility, 392
job file, 489
atcronsh, 392
atdialer, 21, 372
AT&T compiler, 333
audit data, analyzing, 493
audit records, producing for subsystem events, 420
audit subsystem, 392
daemon, 392
utility, 393
auditcmd, 392
auditd, 392
auditing, enabling and disabling, 402
auditsh, 393
authck, 393
authckrc, 393
authentication database, checking internal consistency of, 393
examining system files against, 445
making system files consistent with, 409, 424

---

mscreen, 85
multiple files, in vi, 233
multiple filesystems, mounting, 465, 471
    unmounting, 472, 524
multiplication operator, 158
multiscreens utility, 85
multiuser environment, running
    commands for, 492
mv, 85
mvdir, 465

N

name, searching Internet directory
    for, 138
name list, printing for object files,
    331
name service, 362
named, 466
naming conventions, files; in SCO
    shell, 213
nawk, 86
ncheck, 466
netconfig, 363, 466
netstat, 467
netutil, 468
network, configuring, 440
    listener processes; administering,
    470
network lock daemon, 449
network status, showing, 467
Network Time Protocol query program, 474
networking, commands; table of
    commonly used, 354
    overview, 357-374
networks, configuring, 466
    local; listing users logged in on,
    103
    password file; updating, 538
    routing daemon, 498
    status monitor, 512
    status; showing with SNMP, 512
newform, 86
newgrp, 170
news, 86
nfs, 468
NFS, administering, 365

authentication and print request
    server, 481
client handles; creating, 469
commands, 15, 358
daemons, 365
locking services, 512
mount request server, 465
overview, 365-366
server daemons, 469
setting up a server, 365
starting, 366, 468
stopping, 366, 468
nfsclnt, 469
nfsd, 365, 469
nfsstat, 469
NIC databases, processing into channel/domain tables, 470
NIC host tables, converting, 434
    getting, 433
nice, 87, 201
nictable, 470
NIS, 366-367
    administering, 367
    binder process, 535
    changing login password, 539
    databases; building, 367;
        building and installing, 536;
        conversion routines, 459;
        installing, 367;
        printing values in, 536;
        rebuilding, 537
    domains, 366;
        displaying name of, 420
    maps, 366-367;
        forcing propagation of, 540;
        printing key values, 537;
        transferring, 542-543;
        translation table for long names,
        537
    overview, 366
    password file; modifying, 539
    returning hostname of map master,
        542
    returning hostname of server, 542
    server process, 541
    servers, 366;
        adding, 367;
        setting up, 367
    starting, 367
    translation table for long map
        names, 537
    user accounts, 367

timeserver daemon, 521
timex, 522
timing a command, 522
topological sorts, 128, 347
touch, 125
tplot, 522
tput, 125
tr, 126
trace messages, printing, 513
transferring, file; with ftp, 59
translate, 126
translating, characters, 126;
    in sed, 263
    files, 126
    packages, 487
transliterate protocol trace, 523
trap, 176
trap_rece, 523
traps, receiving, 523
Trivial File Transfer Protocol
    (TFTP), server, 521
trpt, 523
true, 127
trusted computing base, checking,
    517
tset, 127
tsort, 128, 347
tty, 128
tty lines, attaching as network inter-
    faces, 509
ttyupd, 524
tunable parameters, 439, 516
type, 177
typescript, of terminal session, 504
typeset, 177

U

uadmin, 524
ulimit, 178
umask, 128, 179, 203
umnt, 128
umount, 83, 129, 524
umountall, 524
unalias, 179, 204
uname, 129
unary minus operator, 158
uncompress, 129
uncompressing files, 129
unget, 347
unhash, 204

uniq, 129
units, 130
    convert numbers between, 130
UNIX, reaching from vi editor, 234
UNIX 80286, emulating, 69
unlink, 524
unlinking, directories, 524
    files, 524
unmounting, filesystems, 128-129,
    507, 524;
        multiple, 524
unpack, 130
unretire, 524
unset, 179, 204
until, 179
updating files, 444
uptime, 130
usemouse, 130
user commands, alphabetical listing
    of, 19-140
users, access single-user mode, 514
    accounts, 379, 382
    changing passwords, 89
    changing user type of an account,
        402, 524
    creating passwords, 89
    displaying logged-in, 137, 531
    displaying data about, 58
    generating account profiles for, 391
    information server, remote, 423
    interactive conversations, 139
    listing users logged-in on local net-
        works, 103
    logging out idle, 438
    logins, 379, 382
    on remote machines, listing, 102
    passwords, 379, 382
    printing number logged in, 130,
        136, 530
    removing accounts, 497
    searching for, 138
    super; (see superuser)
    talking to another, 114
    writing to all, over a network, 103
    writing to, 530
utilities, running; from SCO shell, 214
uuchat, 525
uucheck, 525
uucico, 372, 525
uuclean, 526
uucp, 132
UUCP, 368-373

X

Y

About the Author

Ellie Cutler has worked at O'Reilly & Associates since 1990 as a web developer, writer, and indexer. She was an editor with ORA's pilot online project, the Global Network Navigator, and now runs the O'Reilly web site. Prior to landing at ORA, she worked as a musician, teacher, dog groomer, warehouse manager, tractor-trailer driver, technical writer, and at the *Burlington Free Press* (Vermont's largest newspaper!).

A professional musician, Ellie received her Bachelor of Music degree in voice and violin from Utah State University in 1974, and has performed under conductors including Ozawa, Bernstein, Rostropovich, and Robert Shaw at Symphony Hall, Carnegie Hall, Tanglewood, and Lincoln Center.

She lives in Woodstock, NH with assorted partners: human, canine, and feline.

Colophon

Our look is the result of reader comments, our own experimentation, and feedback from distribution channels. Distinctive covers complement our distinctive approach to technical topics, breathing personality and life into potentially dry subjects.

The animal featured on the cover of *SCO UNIX in a Nutshell* is a grizzly bear. The grizzly inhabits the colder regions of the Northern Hemisphere. In North America it is found in Canada and the northwestern U.S. Though not as big as some of the brown bears, a full grown grizzly can weigh up to 700 pounds and is the most aggressive of the bear family. Although they are omnivores, grizzlies will eat meat whenever possible. Also, though heavy, thickset animals with a lumbering gait, grizzlies are capable of moving at 25 mph over short distances.

Grizzlies are solitary except during mating or when females are rearing cubs. However, they seem to communicate using "bear-trees." There are certain trees that bears will tear a piece of bark off of whenever they pass. It is not known what this signifies, but the bear tree does serve as some kind of signal.

Edie Freedman designed the cover of this book, using a 19th-century engraving from the Dover Pictorial Archive. The cover layout was produced with Quark XPress 3.32 using the ITC Garamond font. The inside layout was designed by Nancy Priest and implemented in troff by Lenny Muellner. The text and heading fonts are ITC Garamond Light and Garamond Book. The illustrations that appear in the book were created in Macromedia Freehand 5.0 by Chris Reilley. Whenever possible, our books use RepKover™, a durable and flexible lay-flat binding. If the page count exceeds RepKover's limit, perfect binding is used.

More Titles from O'Reilly

Unix Basics

Learning the UNIX Operating System, 4th Edition

By Jerry Peek,
Grace Todino & John Strang
4th Edition December 1997
106 pages, ISBN 1-56592-390-1

If you are new to UNIX, this concise introduction will tell you just what you need to get started and no more. The new fourth edition covers the Linux operating system and is an ideal primer for someone just starting with UNIX or Linux, as well as for Mac and PC users who encounter a UNIX system on the Internet. This classic book, still the most effective introduction to UNIX in print, now includes a quick-reference card.

Learning GNU Emacs, 2nd Edition

By Debra Cameron,
Bill Rosenblatt & Eric Raymond
2nd Edition September 1996
560 pages, ISBN 1-56592-152-6

Learning GNU Emacs is an introduction to Version 19.30 of the GNU Emacs editor, one of the most widely used and powerful editors available under UNIX. It provides a solid introduction to basic editing, a look at several important "editing modes" (special Emacs features for editing specific types of documents, including email, Usenet News, and the World Wide Web), and a brief introduction to customization and Emacs LISP programming. The book is aimed at new Emacs users, whether or not they are programmers. Includes quick-reference card.

Learning the bash Shell, 2nd Edition

By Cameron Newham &
Bill Rosenblatt
2nd Edition January 1998
336 pages, ISBN 1-56592-347-2

This second edition covers all of the features of *bash* Version 2.0, while still applying to *bash* Version 1.x. It includes one-dimensional arrays, parameter expansion, more pattern-matching operations, new commands, security improvements, additions to ReadLine, improved configuration and installation, and an additional programming aid, the *bash* shell debugger.

Learning the Korn Shell

By Bill Rosenblatt
1st Edition June 1993
360 pages, ISBN 1-56592-054-6

This Nutshell Handbook is a thorough introduction to the Korn shell, both as a user interface and as a programming language. The Korn shell is a program that interprets UNIX commands. It has many features that aren't found in other shells, including command history. This book provides a clear and concise explanation of the Korn shell's features. It explains *ksh* string operations, co-processes, signals and signal handling, and command-line interpretation. The book also includes real-life programming examples and a Korn shell debugger called *kshdb*, the only known implementation of a shell debugger anywhere.

Using csh and tcsh

By Paul DuBois
1st Edition August 1995
242 pages, ISBN 1-56592-132-1

Using csh and tcsh describes from the beginning how to use these shells interactively to get your work done faster with less typing. You'll learn how to make your prompt tell you where you are (no more pwd); use what you've typed before (history); type long command lines with few keystrokes (command and filename completion); remind yourself of filenames when in the middle of typing a command; and edit a botched command without retyping it.

Learning the vi Editor, 5th Edition

By Linda Lamb
5th Edition October 1990
192 pages, ISBN 0-937175-67-6

This book is a complete guide to text editing with *vi*, the editor available on nearly every UNIX system. Early chapters cover the basics; later chapters explain more advanced editing tools, such as *ex* commands and global search and replacement.

O'REILLY™

Unix Basics

sed & awk, 2nd Edition

By Dale Dougherty & Arnold Robbins
2nd Edition March 1997
432 pages, ISBN 1-56592-225-5

sed & awk describes two text manipulation programs that are mainstays of the
UNIX programmer's toolbox. This new
edition covers the *sed* and *awk* programs as they are now mandated by the
POSIX standard and includes discussion of the GNU versions
of these programs.

SCO UNIX in a Nutshell

By Ellie Cutler &
the staff of O'Reilly & Associates
1st Edition February 1994
590 pages, ISBN 1-56592-037-6

The desktop reference to SCO UNIX
and Open Desktop®, this version of
UNIX in a Nutshell shows you what's
under the hood of your SCO system. It
isn't a scaled-down quick reference of
common commands, but a complete
reference containing all user, programming, administration,
and networking commands.

UNIX in a Nutshell: System V Edition

By Daniel Gilly &
the staff of O'Reilly & Associates
2nd Edition June 1992
444 pages, ISBN 1-56592-001-5

You may have seen UNIX quick-reference
guides, but you've never seen anything
like *UNIX in a Nutshell*. Not a scaled-
down quick reference of common commands, *UNIX in a Nutshell* is a complete
reference containing all commands and
options, along with generous descriptions and examples that
put the commands in context. For all but the thorniest UNIX
problems, this one reference should be all the documentation
you need. Covers System V, Releases 3 and 4, and Solaris 2.0.

What You Need to Know: When You Can't Find Your UNIX System Administrator

By Linda Mui
1st Edition April 1995
156 pages, ISBN 1-56592-104-6

This book is written for UNIX users,
who are often cast adrift in a confusing
environment. It provides the background and practical solutions you need
to solve problems you're likely to
encounter—problems with logging in, printing, sharing files,
running programs, managing space resources, etc. It also
describes the kind of info to gather when you're asking for a
diagnosis from a busy sys admin. And, it gives you a list of
site-specific information that you should know, as well as a
place to write it down.

Volume 3M: X Window System User's Guide, Motif Edition, 2nd Edition

By Valerie Quercia & Tim O'Reilly
2nd Edition January 1993
956 pages, ISBN 1-56592-015-5

The *X Window System User's Guide,
Motif Edition* orients the new user to
window system concepts and provides detailed tutorials for many
client programs, including the
xtermterminal emulator and the twm,
uwm, and mwmwindow managers. Later chapters explain
how to customize the X environment. Revised for Motif 1.2
and X11 Release 5.

UNIX Tools

Programming with GNU Software

By Mike Loukides & Andy Oram
1st Edition December 1996
260 pages, ISBN 1-56592-112-7

This book and CD combination is a complete package for programmers who are new to UNIX or who would like to make better use of the system. The tools come from Cygnus Support, Inc., and Cyclic Software, companies that provide support for free software. Contents include GNU Emacs, *gcc*, C and C++ libraries, *gdb*, RCS, and *make*. The book provides an introduction to all these tools for a C programmer.

Applying RCS and SCCS

By Don Bolinger & Tan Bronson
1st Edition September 1995
528 pages, ISBN 1-56592-117-8

Applying RCS and SCCS is a thorough introduction to these two systems, viewed as tools for project management. This book takes the reader from basic source control of a single file, through working with multiple releases of a software project, to coordinating multiple developers. It also presents TCCS, a representative "front-end" that addresses problems RCS and SCCS can't handle alone, such as managing groups of files, developing for multiple platforms, and linking public and private development areas.

lex & yacc, 2nd Edition

By John Levine, Tony Mason & Doug Brown
2nd Edition October 1992
366 pages, ISBN 1-56592-000-7

This book shows programmers how to use two UNIX utilities, lex and yacc, in program development. The second edition contains completely revised tutorial sections for novice users and reference sections for advanced users. This edition is twice the size of the first, has an expanded index, and covers Bison and Flex.

Managing Projects with make, 2nd Edition

By Andrew Oram & Steve Talbott
2nd Edition October 1991
152 pages, ISBN 0-937175-90-0

make is one of UNIX's greatest contributions to software development, and this book is the clearest description of *make* ever written. It describes all the basic features of *make* and provides guidelines on meeting the needs of large, modern projects. Also contains a description of free products that contain major enhancements to *make*.

Software Portability with imake, 2nd Edition

By Paul DuBois
2nd Edition September 1996
410 pages, ISBN 1-56592-226-3

This Nutshell Handbook®—the only book available on *imake*—is ideal for X and UNIX programmers who want their software to be portable. The second edition covers the current version of the X Window System (X11R6.1), using *imake* for non-UNIX systems such as Windows NT, and some of the quirks about using *imake* under OpenWindows/ Solaris.

Porting UNIX Software

By Greg Lehey
1st Edition November 1995
538 pages, ISBN 1-56592-126-7

This book deals with the whole life cycle of porting, from setting up a source tree on your system to correcting platform differences and even testing the executable after it's built. It exhaustively discusses the differences between versions of UNIX and the areas where porters tend to have problems.

UNIX Tools

Exploring Expect

By Don Libes
1st Edition December 1994
602 pages, ISBN 1-56592-090-2

Written by the author of Expect, this is the first book to explain how this part of the UNIX toolbox can be used to automate Telnet, FTP, passwd, rlogin, and hundreds of other interactive applications. Based on Tcl (Tool Command Language), Expect lets you automate interactive applications that have previously been extremely difficult to handle with any scripting language.

Writing GNU Emacs Extensions

By Bob Glickstein
1st Edition April 1997
236 pages, ISBN 1-56592-261-1

This book introduces Emacs Lisp and tells you how to make the editor do whatever you want, whether it's altering the way text scrolls or inventing a whole new "major mode." Topics progress from simple to complex, from lists, symbols, and keyboard commands to syntax tables, macro templates, and error recovery.

UNIX Power Tools, 2nd Edition

By Jerry Peek,
Tim O'Reilly & Mike Loukides
2nd Edition August 1997
1120 pages, Includes CD-ROM
ISBN 1-56592-260-3

Loaded with even more practical advice about almost every aspect of UNIX, this new second edition of *UNIX Power Tools* addresses the technology that UNIX users face today. You'll find increased coverage of POSIX utilities, including GNU versions, greater *bash* and *tcsh* shell coverage, more emphasis on Perl, and a CD-ROM that contains the best freeware available.

Tcl/Tk Tools

By Mark Harrison
1st Edition September 1997
678 pages, Includes CD-ROM
ISBN 1-56592-218-2

One of the greatest strengths of Tcl/Tk is the range of extensions written for it. This book clearly documents the most popular and robust extensions—by the people who created them— and contains information on configuration, debugging, and other important tasks. The CD-ROM includes Tcl/Tk, the extensions, and other tools documented in the text both in source form and as binaries for Solaris and Linux.

System Administration

Essential System Administration

By Æleen Frisch
2nd Edition September 1995
788 pages, ISBN 1-56592-127-5

Thoroughly revised and updated for all major versions of UNIX, this second edition of *Essential System Administration* provides a compact, manageable introduction to the tasks faced by everyone responsible for a UNIX system. Whether you use a stand-alone UNIX system, routinely provide administrative support for a larger shared system, or just want an understanding of basic administrative functions, this book is for you. Offers expanded sections on networking, electronic mail, security, and kernel configuration.

System Performance Tuning

By Mike Loukides
1st Edition November 1990
336 pages, ISBN 0-937175-60-9

System Performance Tuning answers the fundamental question: How can I get my UNIX-based computer to do more work without buying more hardware? Some performance problems do require you to buy a bigger or faster computer, but many can be solved simply by making better use of the resources you already have.

Using & Managing UUCP

By Ed Ravin, Tim O'Reilly,
Dale Dougherty & Grace Todino
1st Edition September 1996
424 pages, ISBN 1-56592-153-4

Using & Managing UUCP describes, in one volume, this popular communications and file transfer program. UUCP is very attractive to computer users with limited resources, a small machine, and a dial-up connection. This book covers Taylor UUCP, the latest versions of HoneyDanBer UUCP, and the specific implementation details of UUCP versions shipped by major UNIX vendors.

termcap & terminfo

By John Strang,
Linda Mui & Tim O'Reilly
3rd Edition April 1988
270 pages, ISBN 0-937175-22-6

For UNIX system administrators and programmers. This handbook provides information on writing and debugging terminal descriptions, as well as terminal initialization, for the two UNIX terminal databases.

Managing NFS and NIS

By Hal Stern
1st Edition June 1991
436 pages, ISBN 0-937175-75-7

Managing NFS and NIS is for system administrators who need to set up or manage a network filesystem installation. NFS (Network Filesystem) is probably running at any site that has two or more UNIX systems. NIS (Network Information System) is a distributed database used to manage a network of computers. The only practical book devoted entirely to these subjects, this guide is a "must-have" for anyone interested in UNIX networking.

Volume 8: X Window System Administrator's Guide

By Linda Mui & Eric Pearce
1st Edition October 1992
372 pages, ISBN 0-937175-83-8

This book focuses on issues of system administration for X and X-based networks—not just for UNIX system administrators, but for anyone faced with the job of administering X (including those running X on stand-alone workstations).

How to stay in touch with O'Reilly

1. Visit Our Award-Winning Site

http://www.oreilly.com/

★ "Top 100 Sites on the Web" —*PC Magazine*
★ "Top 5% Web sites" —*Point Communications*
★ "3-Star site" —*The McKinley Group*

Our web site contains a library of comprehensive product information (including book excerpts and tables of contents), downloadable software, background articles, interviews with technology leaders, links to relevant sites, book cover art, and more. File us in your Bookmarks or Hotlist!

2. Join Our Email Mailing Lists

New Product Releases
To receive automatic email with brief descriptions of all new O'Reilly products as they are released, send email to:
listproc@online.oreilly.com
Put the following information in the first line of your message (*not* in the Subject field):
subscribe oreilly-news

O'Reilly Events
If you'd also like us to send information about trade show events, special promotions, and other O'Reilly events, send email to:
listproc@online.oreilly.com
Put the following information in the first line of your message (*not* in the Subject field):
subscribe oreilly-events

3. Get Examples from Our Books via FTP

There are two ways to access an archive of example files from our books:

Regular FTP
- ftp to:
  ftp.oreilly.com
  (login: anonymous
  password: your email address)
- Point your web browser to:
  ftp://ftp.oreilly.com/

FTPMAIL
- Send an email message to:
  ftpmail@online.oreilly.com
  (Write "help" in the message body)

4. Contact Us via Email

order@oreilly.com
To place a book or software order online. Good for North American and international customers.

subscriptions@oreilly.com
To place an order for any of our newsletters or periodicals.

books@oreilly.com
General questions about any of our books.

software@oreilly.com
For general questions and product information about our software. Check out O'Reilly Software Online at http://software.oreilly.com/ for software and technical support information. Registered O'Reilly software users send your questions to:
website-support@oreilly.com

cs@oreilly.com
For answers to problems regarding your order or our products.

booktech@oreilly.com
For book content technical questions or corrections.

proposals@oreilly.com
To submit new book or software proposals to our editors and product managers.

international@oreilly.com
For information about our international distributors or translation queries. For a list of our distributors outside of North America check out:
http://www.oreilly.com/www/order/country.html

O'Reilly & Associates, Inc.
101 Morris Street, Sebastopol, CA 95472 USA
TEL   707-829-0515 or 800-998-9938
       (6am to 5pm PST)
FAX   707-829-0104

O'REILLY™

International Distributors

UK, EUROPE, MIDDLE EAST AND NORTHERN AFRICA (except France, Germany, Switzerland, & Austria)

INQUIRIES
International Thomson Publishing Europe
Berkshire House
168-173 High Holborn
London WC1V 7AA, UK
Telephone: 44-171-497-1422
Fax: 44-171-497-1426
Email: itpint@itps.co.uk

ORDERS
International Thomson Publishing Services, Ltd.
Cheriton House, North Way
Andover, Hampshire SP10 5BE,
United Kingdom
Telephone: 44-264-342-832 (UK)
Telephone: 44-264-342-806 (outside UK)
Fax: 44-264-364418 (UK)
Fax: 44-264-342761 (outside UK)
UK & Eire orders: itpuk@itps.co.uk
International orders: itpint@itps.co.uk

FRANCE
Editions Eyrolles
61 bd Saint-Germain
75240 Paris Cedex 05
France
Fax: 33-01-44-41-11-44

FRENCH LANGUAGE BOOKS
All countries except Canada
Telephone: 33-01-44-41-46-16
Email: geodif@eyrolles.com

ENGLISH LANGUAGE BOOKS
Telephone: 33-01-44-41-11-87
Email: distribution@eyrolles.com

GERMANY, SWITZERLAND, AND AUSTRIA

INQUIRIES
O'Reilly Verlag
Balthasarstr. 81
D-50670 Köln
Germany
Telephone: 49-221-97-31-60-0
Fax: 49-221-97-31-60-8
Email: anfragen@oreilly.de

ORDERS
International Thomson Publishing
Königswinterer Straße 418
53227 Bonn, Germany
Telephone: 49-228-97024 0
Fax: 49-228-441342
Email: order@oreilly.de

JAPAN
O'Reilly Japan, Inc.
Kiyoshige Building 2F
12-Banchi, Sanei-cho
Shinjuku-ku
Tokyo 160 Japan
Tel: 81-3-3356-5227
Fax: 81-3-3356-5261
Email: kenji@oreilly.com

INDIA
Computer Bookshop (India) PVT. Ltd.
190 Dr. D.N. Road, Fort
Bombay 400 001 India
Tel: 91-22-207-0989
Fax: 91-22-262-3551
Email: cbsbom@giasbm01.vsnl.net.in

HONG KONG
City Discount Subscription Service Ltd.
Unit D, 3rd Floor, Yan's Tower
27 Wong Chuk Hang Road
Aberdeen, Hong Kong
Telephone: 852-2580-3539
Fax: 852-2580-6463
Email: citydis@ppn.com.hk

KOREA
Hanbit Publishing, Inc.
Sonyoung Bldg. 202
Yeksam-dong 736-36
Kangnam-ku
Seoul, Korea
Telephone: 822-554-9610
Fax: 822-556-0363
Email: hant93@chollian.dacom.co.kr

TAIWAN
ImageArt Publishing, Inc.
4/fl. No. 65 Shinyi Road Sec. 4
Taipei, Taiwan, R.O.C.
Telephone: 886-2708-5770
Fax: 886-2705-6690
Email: marie@ms1.hinet.net

SINGAPORE, MALAYSIA, AND THAILAND
Longman Singapore
25 First Lok Yan Road
Singapore 2262
Telephone: 65-268-2666
Fax: 65-268-7023
Email: daniel@longman.com.sg

PHILIPPINES
Mutual Books, Inc.
429-D Shaw Boulevard
Mandaluyong City, Metro
Manila, Philippines
Telephone: 632-725-7538
Fax: 632-721-3056
Email: mbikikog@mnl.sequel.net

CHINA
Ron's DataCom Co., Ltd.
79 Dongwu Avenue
Dongxihu District
Wuhan 430040
China
Telephone: 86-27-83892568
Fax: 86-27-83222108
Email: hongfeng@public.wh.hb.cn

AUSTRALIA
WoodsLane Pty. Ltd.
7/5 Vuko Place, Warriewood NSW 2102
P.O. Box 935,
Mona Vale NSW 2103
Australia
Telephone: 61-2-9970-5111
Fax: 61-2-9970-5002
Email: info@woodslane.com.au

ALL OTHER ASIA COUNTRIES
O'Reilly & Associates, Inc.
101 Morris Street
Sebastopol, CA 95472 USA
Telephone: 707-829-0515
Fax: 707-829-0104
Email: order@oreilly.com

THE AMERICAS
McGraw-Hill Interamericana Editores,
S.A. de C.V.
Cedro No. 512
Col. Atlampa 06450
Mexico, D.F.
Telephone: 52-5-541-3155
Fax: 52-5-541-4913
Email: mcgraw-hill@infosel.net.mx

SOUTHERN AFRICA
International Thomson Publishing Southern Africa
Building 18, Constantia Park
138 Sixteenth Road
P.O. Box 2459
Halfway House, 1685 South Africa
Tel: 27-11-805-4819
Fax: 27-11-805-3648